ONE HUNDRED YEARS OF
CAL BOXING

1916-2016

EDITED BY PAUL REIN & LISA REIN

Copyright ©2016 by Paul Rein and Lisa Rein

All rights reserved. No part of this book may be used or reproduced in any manner whatsoever without written permission of the author.

Published 2016.

Printed in the United States of America.

ISBN: 978-1-63385-532-8

Published by

Word Association Publishers
205 Fifth Avenue
Tarentum, Pennsylvania 15084

www.wordassociation.com
1.800.827.7903

DEDICATION

This book is dedicated to Ed Nemir, a legendary coach for 37 years, beloved by all who knew him, and an inspiration to many who followed; and to Jim Riksheim, who, with little support from the Cal Administration, kept boxing alive for his 30 years of coaching (1982-2012), and remains a key team supporter.

ACKNOWLEDGMENTS:

In addition to major thanks to my daughter and co-editor of this Book, Lisa Rein, thank you to Phil Nemir and Chris Morales, both former Intercollegiate Boxing Champions and the Alumni organizers of the May 7, 2016, "100 Years of Cal Boxing" Celebration, and of past Reunions, including 2004 and 2011; Mike Huff, Cal Boxing coach and major alumni Reunions supporter; Herb Davis, Brian Kahn, Ken Bigham, Dick Carter, Dale Jeong, Todd Gaylord, Paul O'Neil, Ron Dell'Immagine, Floyd Salas, Dave Keegan, and Jon Zaul, all past and present Cal Fighters and Boxing Coaches and major contributors of materials for this book; and some of my closest friends and long time supporters of Cal Boxing: Deborah Abbley, John and Julie Kolar, Jim and Mina Jenner, Claire Otalda (Salas); and my brother and office manager, Steve Rein, who has kept me in business and alive for the past 30 years! Some of the other WCBA coaches, past and present, who have helped to keep intercollegiate boxing alive and well: the late Jimmy Olivas of Nevada; Nevada coaches Pat Schellin, Mike Martino, Pat "Paddy" Jefferson, Dan Holmes, and 30+ year UNR Alumni Coordinator, Mike Schellin; Santa Clara University Head Coach Pierre Moynier, and Coach Candy Lopez of San Jose State University. Also thanks to our publishers Tom Costello and Jason Price of Word Association Publishers. Thanks also to Jonathan Wafer, great grandson of Walter Gordon, who shared family photographs and information about his legendary grandfather. Special Thanks to Nevada alumni boxers and UNR team supporters Tony Scheullor, and Riley Beckett, and the late John McSweeny, for great fights with me 50 years ago and continuing to support the sport and the Western Conference.

CONTENTS

Dedication iii

Acknowledgments v

Introduction 1

Cal Boxing Legends, Linked through the years: Walter Gordon, Donald Lawton,
    Ed Nemir and Sam Gold 2

Stanford's 1916 Racial Discrimination Against Cal Great Walter Gordon, Exposed
    by Donald Lawton; Cal Boxing Teams Later Stand Against Racism 2

"Beating up Stanford" by Donald Lawton (Recalling Cal 1916) 4

The Cal Boxers' 1952 Reunion Linked Walter Gordon, Donald Lawton, Sam Gold
    and Ed Nemir (Handwritten key to page 6 photo at page 8) 5

1952 "Boxer and Wrestlers Reunion" 1953 Cal Monthly article by Irving H "Brick" Marcus 9

Walter Gordon 11

Ed Nemir (Coach 1933-1969) 14

Sam Gold 34

History of College Boxing and 1960's Threat to Ban Boxing 37

"NCBA Boxing: A Safe Approach" (1984) 41

"The History of Collegiate Boxing" 2015 article by Chrisopher Mendez 42

1963 Pro Boxing Deaths and Distinguishing Collegiate Boxing Safety 44

1964 "Intercollegiate Boxing Given Reprieve" (by 10-1 Nevada Student Vote)
    by Penny Howe for the Daily Cal 52

"Colleges Still in Boxing" - Ring Magazine [March 1965] by Paul Rein 52

"College Boxing's Last Round" by Martin Kane 53

"College Boxers to Continue After Coach Nemir's Death" by Frank McDermott 55

"Cal Boxing's Transition After Coach Ed Nemir," By Dick Carter 56

Boxing Enthusiast Jack London - briefly a Cal student 62

1910-1915: The Beginnings of the Cal Boxing Team; "The Polyducean Club" 63

1919-1949 (Mostly from "Blue and Gold" Yearbooks) 65

1920s	66
1930s	73
1940s	78
1950s: "Butch" and "Kayo" Hallinan, sons of Vincent Hallinan, and George Pelonis	86
Kayo Clippings (from 1996 article by Edvina Beitiks)	87
1950s-1952 (including Pax Beale, Ken Hansen and Myron Hansen)	88-90
1956-57 Teams	93
Herb Davis Stories	95
Sports Illustrated Article re: NCAA Boxing (April 20, 1959)	113
Bob Ettinger and son (1957)	115
1958-1959 Teams	116
Cal Boxing in the 1960s: Introduction	119
1960 NCAA Champions	122
1960 CCBC Champions	123
1960-1961 Teams (Clippings, Photos, Articles)	124
"Tom Gioseffi: A Boxing Legend" (Fighting Against Tommy Gioseffi) "First Fight" by Paul Rein	127
Tom Gioseffi (1963-1965) and Cal Athletic Hall of Fame	130
1961 (Fall) Intramural Championships	133-134
1962 Teams Photos	136
1963 Team Photos and Clippings	137-150
1963 "Gioseffi Takes 147 Pound Title; Voted Loop's Outstanding Boxer"	151
1964 - "Boxing Against Stanford: 'Alice In Wonderland'" by Paul Rein	152
1964 - "Remember Me?" by Paul Rein	154
1964-1965 Teams (Clippings, photos, scoring cards)	155-183
1965 - "I Was A Cal Boxer" by Paul Rein	184
1965 - CCBC Champions From Cal	185
1965 - Cal CCBC Championship Team Photo	187

1965 - "Blow by Blow Knockdown Picture" with Tom Gioseffi 188

Reunion of 1960-1965 Cal Boxers (1989 189

December 1965 Intramural Championships 190

1966-1969 Teams 191

"Life Lessons from Cal Boxing" by Dale Jeong 194

1970s - Introduction 200

"Cal Boxing 1968-1975" by Brian Kahn 201

1970 - 1972 - Articles and Photos 209

1972 - "My Heavyweight Battle" (1972) by Paul Rein (1965 graduate) 215

1972 - Alumni v Varsity Exhibition; "A Giroday v Gioseffi Punch Out" 218

1974 - Cal Boxing Schedule 219

1976 Clippings from Coach Ken Bigham 220

1976 Cal v Navy Program Lineup 221

1976 East v West College Boxing Tournament 222

1976 "Diehard Boxing Fans Should Remember All Star Card" by Don McGrath 225-226

1976 "Kahn Connects" article about Coach Brian Kahn 228

1977 "LA Road Trip" by Paul O'Neil 229

1979 Team 230

1980s - Introduction 231

1980 to 1981 Cal Boxing Newsletters and Articles 232

1982 Cal Invitational and Programs, Articles and Newsletters 236

1983 Photos, Programs and Newsletters 244

1983 "A 'Thunderous' Finale: Boxers Claim Western Title" 249

1984 "Challenge to Attain Excellence" 250

1984 Cal Boxing Newsletters 251

1984 "Just Gutting It Out Offers Satisfaction" by Francis Kane 254

1984 Flyer, "1984 National Collegiate Boxing Championships" 256

1984 "Golden Bear Profiles" (From 1984 Nationals Program) 257

1984 "Cal's Morales, Heffernon Win Titles" by Dave LeVecchio 258

1984 "Kindling the Killer Instinct" by Avram Gimbel 259

1984 "Hometown Hero Tackles Tornado" by David Darlington 261

1985-1987 Program Articles, Photos and Newsletters 263

1988 Newsletter, including induction of Ed Nemir into UC Athletic Hall of Fame 267

1988 "Plannings For Reunions:1988" 268

1988 Sam Moreno (Former Coach) at the 1988 "Reunion"; Jim Riksheim and Sean Mockler 269

1989 Boxing Newsletters, including "1989 WCBA Championship Tournament" 271

1989 Varsity v Alumni Boxing Meet Announcements 273

1989 Varsity v Alumni Autographed Programs, Participants, Photo, Newsletter 277

1989 Western Collegiate Boxing Association Championship Programs 281

1990 Coaches Jim Riksheim and Sean Mockler with Boxer Rogelio Sandoval 283

1991 "Cal Boxing" by Floyd Salas (Asst Coach 1977-1991) 286

1992 Alumni v Varsity Exhibition Bouts and Program 289

1992 - 1993 Boxing Newsletters 292

1996 Two Boxing Students in headgear 295

1997 Boxer Tom Clayton, "Champion in the Ring" 296

1998-1999 Newsletters 297

2000s Todd Gaylord with National Championship Belt and Trophy 299

2000-2002 Boxing Newsletters and Materials 300

2002 "Cal's Oldest Sports Club More Competitive Than Ever" by Ian M Fein 302

2004 "Wearing the Belt Proudly" By Barry Kelly 305

2005 Program, NCBA Western Regional Championships 307

2005 Nine Fighters from the 2005 Cal Boxing Team 308

2007 Season: "Lord of the Ring" (Todd Gaylord) by Nima Wedlake 309

2007 Todd Gaylord in protective headgear 311

2009 Cal Team Photo with Coach Jim Riksheim 312

2010 "March Madness: College Boxers Seek Tournament Glory of Their Own"
    by Ryan Maquiñana (Featuring Dave Rosenfield and Lauren Pettis) 313

"2011 Cal Boxing Team" by Ryan Macquiñana 321

2010 Photos of Cal Boxers Dave Rosenfield and Phil Bremner 323

2011 "Cal Boxing Alums Share Much More than War Stories at 95th Reunion"
    By Ryan Maquiñana 326

2012 - "March Madness Begins for College Boxers" by Ryan Maquiñana 331

2012 "Cal's Ramos Best Middleweight in West" by Ryan Maquiñana.. 333

2012 Photo of Jose Jiminez with Coach Jim Riksheim 333

2013 - UC Boxing Team Photo 334

2013 - "NCBA Western Regional Championships" Semi-Finals Program 335

2014 - UC Boxing Club Photo 336

2015 "UC Berkeley Invitational" 337

Photos of Nessa Nemir, with father Phil (holding bag) and Cousin Don Nemir 338

2015 Photo of Coaches Dave Keegan and Jon Zaul and Fighters Claire Glowniak
    and Gerald Santos 339

2015 Flyer for "California Boxing Fight Night" 340

2015 Western Regional Championships and 2015 Cal Boxing Club Photo 341

2015 "Cal Boxing Club Receives Recognition" 342

2015-2016 "September 2015 Reno, Nevada, Tournament with Nevada and Army" 343

2015 Cal Boxing Team 344

2015 Cal Boxing Team Photo by Juan Reyes 345

2015 Cal Boxing Team 346

2016 Cal Boxing Team 348

2016 "UC Berkeley Boxing Club Celebrates 100 Year Anniversary with 6 wins"
    by Alex Quintana for The Daily Cal 349

Women Fighters Remember Cal Boxing... 352

Conclusion 357

Photos of 2015 Coaches Jon Zaul and David Keegan 358

Photos from 2004 Reunion 359

Floyd Salas and Lisa Rein 362

Cal Boxers by Team "Year," (Using Spring Dates) 363

Cal Coaches and Assistant Coaches (Alphabetically) 388

Coaches from University of Nevada, Reno (UNR) 390

Referees and Judges 390

Cal Boxers Alphabetically, 1916-2016 391

Women Boxers by Name 417

Introduction

In the last section of this book we'll give as complete a listing as we can for all boxers of record for California for 1916-2016, alphabetically and with team rosters for each year.

But first we'll start with a story about four former fighters who reunited at a 1952 Boxer's Reunion: Ed Nemir, the legendary Cal coach from 1933-1969; Sam Gold, who boxed at Cal, undefeated from 1924-1927, and later became an Oakland lawyer for 64 years; Walter Gordon, an African American All American Football player and Heavyweight Boxing Champion who was <u>kept out</u> of a 1916 Boxing tournament at Stanford because of race prejudice, but went on to become a Berkeley Policeman, Boalt Hall-graduated lawyer, Director of the California Department of Corrections and Governor of the Virgin Islands; and the excellent published story by Donald Larson, a 1916 teammate of Walter Gordon, who was substituted for the far superior fighter, Gordon, in the 1916 Stanford tournament and later wrote vividly of his resulting fight with a Stanford Heavyweight 50 pounds heavier than himself, not learning till 36 years later why he had fought that day instead of Gordon!

After a brief reference to a boxing club, the Polydeucean Club, which preceeded the Intercollegiate boxing which started in 1916, we'll introduce you to notable Cal boxers, and memorable first person accounts of bout experiences.

These tales and stories (such as a first round knock out in a fight by Gordon's friend Jimmy Doolittle, who as a World War II general led a squadron of fighter bombers on the famous 1942 "30 Seconds over Tokyo" raid) intermixed with team photos, news clippings, fight descriptions and names of Cal Boxing team members going back over the last 100 years, will help us celebrate "100 Years of Cal Boxing" in the year 2016.

The hundredth year represents the longest continuous intercollegiate boxing program in the United States. Other colleges adopted boxing programs after World War I, as boxing had been taught to military recruits after America's entry into World War I in 1917. The University of Nevada started its boxing program in 1928. But Cal's 100 years is the longest continuing intercollegiate boxing program in the country..

[Note that, throughout this book, you will sometimes see CCBC (California Collegiate Boxing Conference) and WCBC (Western Collegiate Boxing Conference) used interchangeably, as the CCBC changed its name to the WCBC when it expanded to host national competitions, as part of the NCBA formed in the 1970s, and include 30 to 40 schools competing in the Modern era.]

Cal Boxing Legends Linked Through the Years: Walter Gordon, Donald Lawton, Ed Nemir and Sam Gold

Stanford's 1916 Racial Discrimination Against Cal Great Walter Gordon Exposed By Donald Lawton

In 1916 Cal boxer Donald Lawton boxed as Cal's heavyweight in the featured match at Stanford. Lawton, at 170 lbs., fought against Stanford's 225 lb. heavyweight champ in place of Cal heavyweight champion and 220 lb. All-American football player, Walter Gordon. Lawton managed to finally win - at the end of five rounds, the last two as tie breakers - against the much larger and more experienced Stanford fighter. The Cal boxer, Donald Lawton, never learned, however, until he talked to Walter Gordon 36 years later (at a 1952 Cal boxers' reunion) "why I had been the one to go down to fight at Stanford and not him." Walter Gordon, one of the few African-American students at Cal, had been excluded from the contest on a racial basis after famous Stanford President Ray Lyman Wilbur had telephoned famous Cal President Benjamin Ide Wheeler and threatened to cancel the tournament if Cal brought a black fighter to compete on the Stanford campus.

Donald Lawton wrote a great story about the 1916 Cal v. Stanford boxing match, and the racial exclusion of Walter Gordon. This story was published in 1995 in the Cal Monthly magazine.

An article about the 1952 Cal "Boxers and Wrestlers Reunion," published in the Cal Monthly in April 1953, and included here, described how the 1923 boxing team had taken on a similar issue of racial discrimination by "one" of its opposing universities (presumably Stanford). The boxers of the 1923 Cal team supported the "unquestioned right of any California student, regardless of race, color, or creed, to represent the University in the boxing ring against any opposing school. Even five decades ago, this was not an unquestioned right. Not because of prejudice within the University but because of the bias of other colleges. One university, for example, was then pursuing the policy of defaulting any bout in which a colored boxer represented the opposing school. The school's boxers were willing to meet any white opponents, but in any scheduled bout in which the opposing school had a colored representative, it would simply not enter a man at that weight and would concede that particular fight."

"In 1923, however, when that school indicated it would default the scheduled bout in the lightweight division to Negro Errol Jones, who was the California representative, the University boxing squad voted unanimously to cancel the entire match and to refuse to meet the school again in the boxing ring until the color line was completely withdrawn. Considerable newspaper publicity and the adamant position of the boxing squad, backed by the Senior Class of 1923 in an open meeting, finally resulted in the school's backing down from its position; and the question has never again been raised."

Another Cal boxing team's stand against racism occurred in Reno, Nevada in the Spring of 1959, according to a story told by Cal boxing alumnus Al Adams at the March, 2004, Cal Boxers

Reunion. The 1959 team had reserved rooms at a prominent Reno hotel-casino, but were told that Bill Holliman, the only African-American team member, was not welcome. Two team members who later became well known criminal defense lawyers, Patrick ("Butch") Hallinan and Terrence ("KO") Hallinan, took direct action by making phone calls to the Governor of Nevada; to Goodwin Knight, Governor of California, and to Earl Warren, Chief Justice of the United States Supreme Court, and within an hour the hotel retreated from its racist policy, with apologies. (The Hallinans were the sons of legendary San Francisco trial attorney Vincent Hallinan; "KO" later was elected to several terms as San Francisco's District Attorney during the 1990s.)

Recalling Cal 1916

Beating up Stanford

BY DONALD LAWTON x19

I decided to go out for boxing in my junior year at Berkeley, and though I weighed just 170 pounds, became one the two heavyweights on the Cal team. The other was Walter Gordon '18, a great all-around athlete and the team's star, a 220-pound black man who was so good he almost turned professional.

Those were the fledgling days of intercollegiate boxing. When the Cal team was invited to go down to Stanford for a boxing tournament on April 20, 1916, it was to be the first ever meet between the two schools.

On the day of the tryouts, I didn't even show up at the gym, so sure was I that Walt Gordon would be the heavyweight representative. Besides, I didn't want to get pounded just to find out what we all already knew. So I just dropped by later to see how the tryouts had gone. Little did I know what was about to happen.

When Coach Frank Kleeberger '08 saw me, he told me to get my boxing trunks on quickly; there would be a match. I thought that was a bit crazy, but I went a couple of rounds with Walt Gordon. Walt hit me so hard in the jaw that he knocked me against the wall, and the wooden dumbbells fell down on top of me. Kleeberger said, "That's fine, Lawton; you're all right. Let's have one more round." I shuddered, but went ahead. And at the end of it, Kleeberger walked over and said to me, "Lawton, you go to Stanford!" I couldn't believe it. It made no sense at all.

(What I didn't know was that on the morning of the tryouts, Ray Lyman Wilbur, the president of Stanford, had telephoned Benjamin Ide Wheeler, the president of Cal, to say that no black man would be allowed to compete on the Stanford campus. And that if Cal sent its black boxer, the tournament would be canceled.)

Coach Kleeberger decided I needed some work on developing my right guard. So he called me back to the gym the next day for some sparring practice with him. After I repeatedly failed to keep my right guard up, Kleeberger warned, "If you don't keep it up this next time, I'm gonna hit you. This fellow you're fighting down at Stanford is no amateur. He's a real all-American." So we took our stance, then he let go and hit me on the chin. I fell flat on the gym floor on the back of my head, and I saw all the stars in the heavens above.

Next day, after the knockdown, I wasn't exactly filled with confidence at the prospect of stepping into the arena with the man who was then the amateur heavyweight champion of southern California. And whatever apprehensions I had on my way down to Stanford were magnified when I saw my opponent, a man named Tom Carey. He looked like Smokey the Bear, only about eight feet tall.

But as good fortune would have it, just before that match I received some free advice from the man who had set up the fight, a professional boxing coach. He said, "Don, if you're gonna get clobbered anyway, open your gloves up, bury your head in both gloves, and bring your elbows into your stomach. Just hold on tight and let him use you for a punching bag. Then, when he gets really tired, let him have it."

The match between our two teams at the Stanford gymnasium was all tied up at 11:30 that night when we finally came to the last fight, the heavyweight division between Tom Carey at 225 pounds and me at 170. From his lightning attack during round one, Carey looked like a sure winner. But I followed my game plan, staying protected. In the second round Carey hit me square in the nose with his first hard blow, breaking my nose. I had blood all down the front of me like stuck pig. I was a mess. They shoved cotton up my nose and said to go back in. For the third and last round, I thought: Well, by durned, my nose is busted now, it can't get any worse. So I let go with everything I had. Carey was basically a three-rounder, so big and heavy that he got tired easily after that. But I was still jumping around.

PUNCHING BEARS: Two members of Cal's 1925 boxing squad square off.

An extra round was ordered. As the sports section of the newspapers wrote, "Lawton did nothing but jab Carey on the nose so fast they could not be tallied. In spite of this it was decided to give the boys a four-minute rest and go for a fifth round. This time the judges awarded the decision to Lawton."

Walt Gordon, the man who should have fought that day, went on to become Cal's Alumnus of the Year for 1955 and governor of the Virgin Islands. It wasn't until we met again at a Cal boxers' reunion at the Palace Hotel in 1952, 36 years later, that he told me why I had been the one to go down to fight at Stanford, and not him. ☻

Donald Lawton was born on August 2, 1894, the youngest of six children, all but one of whom went to Cal.

We invite alumni to send anecdotes about their Cal experiences to "Recalling Cal," California Monthly, Alumni House, Berkeley 94720-7520. Contributors will be paid $100 upon publication.

The Cal Boxers' 1952 Reunion Linked Walter Gordon, Donald Lawton, Sam Gold and Ed Nemir

Donald Lawton's story about the 1916 Cal v. Stanford boxing match was illustrated with a photograph of "Punching Bears: two members of CAL's 1925 Boxing Squad Square Off." The boxer on the left is the late Sam Gold, undefeated in 20 fights.

Two members of 1925 Cal Boxing Team (Sam Gold on left)

Sam Gold boxed undefeated for four years at Cal from 1924-1927, then went on to Boalt Hall Law School, became a lawyer in 1931, and practiced law in Sacramento and Oakland for the next 64 years! He not only attended the 1952 Reunion - and is pictured in a Reunion photo - but 52 years later was the most popular Cal boxer at the March, 2004 Reunion held in Berkeley.

Also attending the 1952 Reunion, besides Walter Gordon and Donald Lawton, was Ed Nemir, a Cal boxing (and wrestling) star from 1929-1932, a silver medalist in wrestling at the 1932 Olympics, and the Cal boxing coach (except for two brief interludes) continually from 1933 to 1969. He also attended Boalt Hall and received his law degree in 1933. In 1988, he was inducted into the Cal Athletic Hall of Fame.

"Top Row: Unknown, Unknown, Walter Gordon, Unknown, Donald Lawton, Sam Gold, Unknown Bottom Row: Sol Silverman, Unknown, Ed Nemir"

In this 1952 Cal Boxing reunion photo, Ed Nemir is sitting to the far right of the couch, leaning away from a punch thrown by Abe Rubin (Cal Boxing 1921-1923).

To Abe Rubin's left is Sam Gold, and next to him, directly behind Ed Nemir, is Donald Lawton. Sam Gold and Ed Nemir were two men who later had important roles as friends and mentors. (Another prominent alumni, Sol Silverman, is seated on the far left. His story about Walter Gordon is recounted below.) (Handwritten list, "Reunion of Ex-California Boxers" follows this article.)

Walter Gordon, Sam Gold, and Ed Nemir set a Cal tradition of championship college boxing, attending Boalt Hall, and becoming lawyers. Paul Rein was one of those who followed this tradition by boxing from 1963-1965 on the Cal boxing team, attending Boalt Hall Law School from 1965-1968, and practicing as a trial lawyer since 1969. Other prominent trial lawyers were Terrance (KO) Hallinan, Patrick "Butch" Hallinan, Bruce Simon, Chris Morales, Claude Wyle, George Choulos, and Judges Lew Lercara, Frank Roesch, and Bill McAdam. At the 2004 Cal Boxing Reunion, when we interviewed about 50 ex-boxers on videotape, at least one-third of them were lawyers!

Walter Gordon, won honors as a police officer, Boalt Hall graduate, lawyer, Governor of the Virgin Islands, and federal judge. Ed Nemir was one of the most beloved faculty members at Cal, teaching boxing classes and coaching the Intercollegiate team from 1933 until his death at ringside during a 1969 Cal v. Nevada match at Reno. Sam Gold remained a Cal Boxing Fan and supporter until his passing in late May, 2005, one week before his 99th birthday on June 2nd, still fit at his 175 lb. fighting weight and still working out at the gym! Far from the stereotypes of "punch-drunk" boxers, these men lived lives as admirable role models for others.

**Sol Silverman, team captain in 1923, supported Cal Boxing
for more than 50 years after he graduated in 1923.**

An April, 1953 Cal Monthly article, "Boxers and Wrestlers Reunion" noted that "Many of the University's boxers and wrestlers went on to achieve honors in the outside world. These include Jimmy Doolittle (Class of 1917, now a general in the U.S. Air Force and World War II hero); Walter Gordon, now Chairman of the California Adult Authority; ... and Irving Stone, Class of '23, now a famous author." General Doolittle led the American squadron which dropped the famous "Bombs over Tokyo" during World War II. Irving Stone wrote numerous best selling historical biographies, including "Lust for Life" (about artist Vincent van Gogh), "The Agony and the Ecstasy" (Michelangelo), "Clarence Darrow for the Defense"; and "Sailor on Horseback" (about Jack London, a native son of Oakland, and, briefly, a Cal Student).

1952

REUNION OF EX-CALIFORNIA BOXERS

STANDING: THIRD FROM LEFT, WALTER GORDON PLAYED ON VARSITY FOOTBALL TEAM. BECAME FIRST BLACK POLICEMAN ON CITY OF BERKELEY'S POLICE FORCE. MEMBER OF STATE BAR OF CALIFORNIA. APPOINTED GOVERNOR OF THE VIRGIN ISLANDS.

FOURTH FROM LEFT: FORREST THEISS BOXING TEAM 1922, 1923. BECAME PROMINENT STOCK BROKER IN THE CITY OF OAKLAND.

SIXTH FROM LEFT: SAMUEL L. GOLD BOXING TEAM 1925, 1926 AND 1927. TEAM CAPTAIN 1927. REMAINED UNDEFEATED DURING ENTIRE BOXING CAREER. NOW ATTORNEY IN THE CITY OF OAKLAND.

SEATED: AT LEFT: SOLLY SILVERMAN ON BOXING TEAM 1922, 1923, AND 1924. BECAME PROMINENT ATTORNEY IN SAN FRANCISCO AND ADVISER TO STATE ATHLETIC COMMISSION.

THIRD FROM LEFT: ED NEMIR ON BOXING TEAM IN 1929 AND LATER BECAME THE COACH OF THE BOXING TEAM

MIDDLE POSING: ABE RUBIN ON BOXING TEAM 1921, 1922 AND 1923. BECAME FOUNDER OF GLOBE METALS CO. OAKLAND AND PROMINENT IN CIVIC AFFAIRS.

Boxers and Wrestlers Reunion

By Irving H. "Brick" Marcus '28

THE MEN who in the past learned to dish it out as boxers and wrestlers for the University are currently determined to dish it out once again. But while they first used jabs and hooks and wrist locks, what they expect to dish out now is support for the University's boxers and wrestlers in the form of interest, enthusiasm and scholarships.

The first fruit of their determination was the establishment last Fall of a permanent organization called "U.C. Boxers and Wrestlers Reunion" whose aims, apart from conducting an annual get-together, are to focus attention on University boxing and wrestling, and to establish scholarships for participants of worth and need.

Already, purely as a personal contribution, two former members of the boxing team have sent the University a check to be used for this purpose. Scholarship funds of greater substance will be one of the major goals of the new graduate group.

The birth of this group, believed to be the first university boxing and wrestling graduate organization in the nation, was indirectly due to the death last year of a former University heavyweight boxer, Milton Aftergut.

Aftergut, a San Franciscan who represented the University as a boxer from 1919 to 1922, had long been interested in creating a graduate organization of former University boxers, and had discussed the matter from time to time with teammates in the Bay area.

However, business and family interests always seemed to keep the talk from turning into action; and at Aftergut's death in July, 1952, no real step forward had been taken.

The knowledge that one of their group had already been lost, led two other former school boxers, Errol Jones (class of 1924) and Sol Silverman, captain of the boxing team of 1923, to take immediate action.

The result of their efforts was a luncheon reunion, held at San Francisco's Palace Hotel the day before the last Big Game.

Conceived mainly as a social gathering to permit teammates of thirty years ago to meet for the first time as a group and to re-hash their University experiences, the meeting generated such enthusiasm among the 65 participants that a suggestion to establish a permanent organization was voted in almost before it was voiced.

ENJOYING REUNION PROGRAM are, left to right, Don Thomson, George H. Bereton, John Bussy, Sidney Garfield, James Allen, Dr. Shirley Baron, Ray Bowers, Walter Gleason and George Long. A scholarship was established at the meeting.

If the opinions expressed at that initial gathering are any criteria, University boxers and wrestlers, past and present, have an extraordinarily high regard for their sports. Boxing and wrestling have value, they feel, because they are tests between individuals, they involve fierce but not brutish physical contact, and they breed physical confidence.

The former boxers and wrestlers believe that these two sports should be expanded to include a multiple number of their present undergraduate devotees; and that they should be given "major" status rather than be considered a "minor" sport.

These targets, however, are beyond the present scope of the group's plans. Their main efforts will be focused on making their organization as inclusive as possible of all who represented the school in the squared circle, and of using the organization for the overall good of the University.

The sponsoring group of the first

AT THE HEAD TABLE, left to right: John F. Moran, Luther Nichols, Irving Alhswede, Kenneth Hanson, Earl Jones, Walter Gordon, Sol Silverman, Stanley Jones, Eddie Nemir, James "Crip" Toomey, Webster Clark, Lester Hink and Don Lawton.

Left to right: Earle Steel, John Connolly, George Reed, Al Monaco, John O'Donnell, Stan Thompson, C. Morse and Len Brown.

reunion was composed mainly of members of California's "Wonder Teams" of 1920-1923—not the gridiron squads whose achievements are now part of the sports folk lore of the University, but the boxing teams of the same period, which did not lose a single intercollegiate match during the first four years of the 1920's.

These boxers brought many honors to the University, and the cups and plaques earned by their prowess would fill considerable shelf space. One of the greatest honors they brought, however, is not marked by silver cup or embossed plaque or pendant medal.

It is marked instead by the unquestioned right of any California student, regardless of race, color or creed, to represent the University in the boxing ring against any opposing school.

Three decades ago, this was not an unquestioned right. Not because of prejudice within the University, but because of the bias of other colleges.

One University, for example, was then pursuing the policy of defaulting any bout in which a colored boxer represented the opposing school. The schools boxers were willing to meet any white opponents, but in any scheduled bout in which the opposing school had a colored representative, it would simply not enter a man at that weight and would concede that particular fight.

In 1923, however, when the school indicated it would default the scheduled bout in the lightweight division to negro Errol Jones, who was the California representative, the University boxing squad voted unanimously to cancel the entire match and to refuse to meet the school again in the boxing ring until the color line was completely withdrawn.

Considerable newspaper publicity, and the adamant position of the boxing squad, backed by the senior class of 1923 in an open meeting, finally resulted in the school's backing down from its position; and the question has never again been raised.

From honors in school, many of the University's boxers and wrestlers went on to achieve honors in the outside world. These include Jimmy Doolittle (class of 1917), now a general in the U.S. air force and a World War II hero; Walter Gordon, now chairman of the California Adult Authority; James "Crip" Toomey, also a former football star; now Athletic Director of the University's campus at Davis; Irving Stone '23, now a famous author; and numerous noted medical men and recognized legal authorities.

Inevitably, during the many years in which boxing and wrestling have been part of the University's sports curricula, a number of wrestlers and boxers representing the Blue and Gold have in their heyday possessed the skill to succeed in their sport at the professional level. The writer has seen clippings of news stories, by sports editors considered authorities in the profession, in which certain California boxers have been judged capable of going far in the professional field.

Yet not a single University boxer has ever gone into the sport as a professional.

Considering the fact that monetary returns for success in professional boxing and wrestling can come fast and in surprising sums, this indicates that, in the minds of the school's boxers and wrestlers, the sport is engaged in for sport's sake alone, and is subordinate to the main job of getting an education.

It is in the hope of extending what they believe to be the proved benefits of collegiate boxing and wrestling that these former California athletes last Fall joined together in their new association.

They hope and expect to do active work in encouraging boxing and wrestling at the University—and they are thoroughly sold on the idea that the extension of these two sports will work to the greater glory of California.

Officers of the U.C. Boxers and Wrestlers Reunion are:

Honorary Chairmen: Stan Jones, former California boxing coach; Eddie Nemir, present boxing coach at Berkeley; and Crip Toomey, ex-boxer, ex-football player, and now athletic director at the University's Davis campus. *Chairman:* Sol Silverman. *Co-chairmen:* Errol Jones and Jimmy Cline.

It was estimated by the organization's chairman that between 700 and 800 former boxers and wrestlers are eligible for membership. By the time the budding group holds its first formal meeting in San Francisco the day before the next Big Game, it is Silverman's hope that a large number of former University representatives in boxing and wrestling will have joined the fold.

All interested can obtain particulars by writing to Sol Silverman at Mills Tower, San Francisco 4.

Walter Gordon

Walter Gordon - the African-American man Stanford barred from competing in their 1916 boxing tournament even though he was the Cal heavyweight champion - boxed for Cal from 1916 to 1917 and later went on to achieve many professional honors. Born in Atlanta, Georgia on October 10, 1894, his father, a Pullman porter, moved the family to Riverside, California, 10 years later. Walter graduated from Riverside's Polytechnic High School and then entered the University of California, Berkeley, in 1914. He was an excellent student and active in campus affairs. He co-founded and was a charter member of the Alpha Phi Alpha fraternity, and eventually became California State Champion in both boxing and wrestling.

Playing on the first of Coach Andy Smith's legendary football teams, Gordon was selected by Walter Camp as an All-American in 1918, his senior year. He was Cal's first All-American. As a football player, Gordon drew attention as a powerful lead blocker on offense and a "devastating" tackler on defense.

He went on to become Cal's assistant football coach and chief scout, staying with the Cal football program for 24 years, including the "Wonder Team" years in the 1920s. He was described by Sol Silverman as a "dynamo on the campus." Meanwhile he was hired by Berkeley Chief of Police August Vollmer as Berkeley's first "Negro" police officer.

In 1920 Walter Gordon married Elizabeth Fisher. He enrolled at Boalt Hall Law School in 1921, and in 1923 graduated Boalt Hall and began practicing law in an office "above the Wells Fargo building at the corner of University Ave. and San Pablo Ave. in West Berkeley." He was President of the Alameda County NAACP from 1923 to 1933, and practiced law for ten years. He was a member of the Oakland YMCA Board and vice-president of the Lawyers Guild of San Francisco.

In 1943, his longtime friend (and Boalt classmate) California Governor Earl Warren appointed him to the Board of Prison Terms. He was later named Chairman of the new California Adult Authority. In 1955 President Dwight Eisenhower appointed him Governor of the Virgin Islands where he served for three years. He was later named United States District Judge for the Virgin Islands, and served as a federal judge until his retirement in 1969, when he returned to Berkeley. He died in 1976 at the age of 81.

Undeterred by Stanford's 1916 racial discrimination, Walter Gordon lived a life of excellence, high achievement, and public service. In 1955 he was named Cal's Alumnus of the Year. Enclosed is a family portrait taken in Walter Gordon's later years. At the far left is his son, Walter Gordon, Jr., whose grandson, Jonathan Wafer, supplied some of the details recounted here of his great-grandfather's life.

As an aside, a story Walter told about another famous Cal boxer was recounted by former Cal boxer, Sol Silverman. Silverman, interviewed in the late 1970s, had fought on the Cal team from 1920 to 1923. He was the Cal Boxing Team captain. According to Silverman, Walter Gordon had told Silverman a story about *another* legend in California boxing, Jimmy Doolittle, later a general during World War II who became famous for leading the "Bombs over Tokyo" raid on Japan early in the war (April 1942). Jimmy Doolittle at Cal was a "great boxer, a welterweight, at 145 lbs. He fought a Stanford fighter, Eric Pedley, who was actually a 158 lb. middleweight. When asked if he would fight this middleweight, Doolittle said, 'Sure, I'll take him on!' The two fighters met in the center of the ring, shook hands, then Pedley looks down contemptuously on Doolittle before each returned briefly to his corner. Walter Gordon was in Doolittle's corner and he told me that when Doolittle came back he vengefully said, 'Wait till you see what I do to that guy!' (a haughty polo player). So in the first round he came out fast and hit Pedley on the chin and down he went. Pedley was down not for seconds but for minutes. He laid him out cold, that's all! Doolittle was a great boxer with a fighting heart."

Sol Silverman recounted that, when he started in 1920, "I remember the first time I boxed, they had the band there! Really. Boxing was a big thing. It was right after the war, and athletics were a big thing in those days. It was a matter of a man having muscle and might. Physical fitness was a big thing on campus in those days..."

Walter Gordon and Family

From Boxing writer Ryan Macquinana's 2010 article about Walter Gordon:

He was the first African American to receive honors as an All American Football player, and served later as an Assistant Coach while Cal beat Ohio State in the Rose Bowl and Cal won the National Championship in 1920. In 1975, he was inducted into the College Football Hall of Fame.

Off the field, he graduated Boalt Hall to become a lawyer in 1923, a close friend of Boalt classmate and later U.S. Chief Justice Earl Warren; founded his university's chapter of Alpha Phi Alpha (the first Greek letter fraternity established by African-Americans); served as President of the Alameda County NAACP from 1923-1933; and was appointed Governor of the U.S. Virgin Islands by President Eisenhower in 1955. In 1958, he resigned as governor, but stayed in the Virgin Islands for 10 more years after being appointed as a Federal Judge.

Ed Nemir - Coach 1933-1969
(By Paul Rein, '65)

Ed Nemir was one of the most beloved persons in the Cal Boxing program for over 40 years, starting as a Cal boxer in 1926 and serving as the Cal boxing coach from 1933 through 1969 (with an interruption from 1942 to 1946 to serve in the United States Navy, rising to the rank of Lieutenant Commander, and taking a one year sabbatical in 1958-1959). Ed was my boxing coach from 1961 to 1965. As a lawyer, and as a friend, mentor, and role model, Ed Nemir had a profound impact on my life. His fatherly advice and practical counsel helped get me out of several difficult personal jams while I was a student, and he influenced me toward going to law school and becoming a civil rights attorney.

Edgar Nemir was born in Waco, Texas, on July 23, 1910. When he enrolled at Cal Berkeley in 1926, he entered the intramural programs in both boxing and wrestling; he was outstanding in both sports, and won intercollegiate championships in both boxing and wrestling. In 1930 he won the Pacific Coast Conference Boxing Championship, as well as the Pacific Coast Conference Wrestling Championship, while serving as the Cal Wrestling Team captain. He finally had to choose between boxing and wrestling when it came to trying out for the 1932 United States Olympic Team. He chose wrestling and won the United States Olympic Team tryouts in his 134 lb. weight division. He represented the United States in the 1932 Olympic Games (in Los Angeles), and won an <u>Olympic silver medal</u>, losing in the finals on a close split decision.

Academically, Ed achieved Phi Betta Kappa honors in 1929, his <u>junior</u> year at Cal. He graduated in 1930 with an A.B. degree and went on to law school at Boalt Hall, graduating in 1933, while also serving as the Cal freshman wrestling coach from 1930 to 1933. But after being sworn in as a lawyer, he was hired as the Cal Intercollegiate Boxing Team coach starting in 1933.

Why did Ed Nemir, a lawyer, become a boxing coach? He graduated Boalt Hall in 1933 in the midst of the depression. Jobs were scarce for lawyers, so he accepted the coaching job at Cal, and remained an instructor and coach at Cal for the next 36 years.

Ed Nemir, 1968

In an interview, he said he loved teaching boxing and coaching teams because he felt he was "contributing something to the individual because I see him gain poise, confidence, and watch him grow mentally and physically."

In May of 1942 Ed Nemir married Erna Roth. Their son, Phil, was born 1947, boxed under his father's coaching in the late 1960s and later served as the Cal boxing coach during the 1976-1977 season. Ed's daughter, Marie, was born in 1950. Ed's granddaughter and Phil's daughter, Nessa Nemir, was born in 1977. Nessa is a beautiful fashion model, as well as a skillful amateur boxer. For the last several years, she regularly works out (and spars) with the men of the Cal boxing team, and is admired for her skill and courage. Her grandpa would have been proud!

Ed Nemir appears in the top row left in a photograph of the 1947 Cal Boxing Team which follows this article. (Warren Simmons, developer of Pier 39 in San Francisco, is in the second row, second from the right.)

My personal memories of Ed Nemir are limited to the period of 1961 through 1968 while I was first an undergraduate, then a law student at Cal Berkeley. In September, 1961, I enrolled for .5 credits in a "Beginning Boxing" course, with Ed Nemir as my instructor. He encouraged me, as a 17 year old freshman, to enter the intramural boxing tournament as a 156 lb. light middleweight, and later to try out for the Varsity Intercollegiate Boxing Team. In May, 1962, I was invited to join the members of the team for a team dinner at Ed's house in Walnut Creek, and met his wife, Erna, and his son, Phil, then about 14 years old.

Although shorter than most of his teammates when be boxed, and of most of the men that he instructed, Ed Nemir was a deep-chested, fire plug of a man, still in terrific physical shape in his 50s. He was reputed, in what was then recent memory, to have administered a thrashing to several of the 1950s Cal boxing team's larger fighters when they had gotten out of line and were "too big for their britches." When I was his pupil during the 60s he would demonstrate a left jab with "pop" power that could set you back on your heels during routine drills.

He was a highly respected member of the U.C. athletic department, and was reputed to have single handedly kept the boxing program alive at Cal during periods when it was threatened by members of the administration - either for economic reasons or as the result of anti-boxing sentiment stemming from certain unfortunate deaths to boxers in the amateurs or pros. Ed always focused on safety, and deplored the use by certain teams of "ringers" - fighters who had substantial previous experience by the time they got to college and were no longer 'beginners." These included veterans who had boxed competitively for several years in the armed services and then boxed college, where they faced younger boxers with far less experience. Ed's focus on safety caused him to join with several other prominent West Coast coaches to break away from the NCAA in 1959 and form the

"CCBC" (California Collegiate Boxing Conference). These West Coast coaches were concerned with the recruitment of experienced Golden Gloves and Armed Services boxers by certain of the other NCAA teams. They strove to avoid mismatches and carefully scheduled bouts so that they would be as competitive as possible. As later noted,

> In 1959 Ed Nemir was the prime mover in the formation of the California Collegiate Boxing Conference, dedicated to the promotion of safer rules for the conduct of boxing competition. Basic to their new program was the rule that any individual who had boxed before coming to college was automatically barred from collegiate competition. This eliminated the recruiting problem and assured that contestants would learn their boxing skills in college.

This change proved prescient in 1960 when Charlie Mohr, a boxer from the University of Wisconsin who was the previous year's NCAA middleweight champion and winner of the "Outstanding Boxer" award in the 1959 NCAA National tournament, *died* after losing a decision in the 1960 National Championship middleweight bout against a fighter from San Jose State. Ed Nemir's policy of banning "ringers" from competing against much less experienced fighters is one reason why the Cal boxing program has always had such an excellent safety record.

Despite his competitiveness, Ed always looked to avoid unnecessarily embarrassing fighters on other teams. I still remember an "exhibition" bout against a team from U.C. Santa Barbara, at Santa Barbara, in 1963. (Coach Nemir hoped to interest that school into entering the CCBC competition.) Although I fought that year at 156 lb., I was matched at 165 lb. in a post-season exhibition against a relatively inexperienced fighter. (However, I learned that the fighter was in excellent physical shape and had represented Greece in the 1960 Olympic games - as a swimmer.) The coach told me before the bout in no uncertain terms, "If you knock this guy out, you're off the team!" It was rough going into a fight against an opponent who was green but in excellent shape, while I was under instructions to effectively "pull" my punches and avoid at all costs knocking the other fighter out! (I was lucky I didn't get knocked out myself!)

(Speaking of "defense," I didn't have much, at least during my first two years boxing. Coach Nemir would scowl in disgust when I'd get into a fight and forget everything that he'd taught me, flailing away in the heat of the moment. It wasn't until my junior year that I finally learned that great moral maxim, "It is better to give than to receive!" The coach disapproved of my tactic of blocking punches with my face in the hope that the other fighter's knuckles would get *really* sore.)

While the coach approved of and encouraged the way that my superstar teammate Tom Gioseffi and I would work with our team's younger fighters, he was often frustrated by my not following his directions during a fight. In my junior year, he seemed genuinely disappointed when we went to Reno, Nevada, for the 1964 CCBC Championship Tournament and found that the Reno newspaper's write-up about the upcoming bouts featured a large picture of me on the front sports page! (I fought as a light-heavyweight, out of my weight division, against Nevada's Joe Curry at 172 lbs., and lost a split decision.)

Ed Nemir always urged his students to focus on the *primary* reason that we were in school, which was to get excellent grades and go on to graduation and success in the real world. During the years I was at Cal, the boxing team always had one of the highest grade point averages of any Cal sports team at Cal, second only to the Crew Team. When we had a major "Cal Boxing" alumni reunion in Berkeley in March, 2004, at least one third of the ex-boxers in attendance were lawyers or judges, and many of the others had succeeded in various professions including engineering, medicine, dentistry, and teaching. Ed Nemir was an important reason for this tradition of scholastic excellence.

On February 1, 1969, Ed Nemir, still apparently in robust physical condition, suffered a heart attack and died at ringside, in the Reno "mile high" altitude, shortly after he had coached his son, Phil, to a victory against the University of Nevada. Many of his friends have commented, "What a way to go, doing what he loved to do!"

At the time of Ed's passing, the University's obituary contained the following paragraph:

"Edgar Nemir was one of the most admired and respected men in the Department of Physical Education by his students in boxing and wrestling, by his colleagues in the department, and by other campus luminaries in academic and administrative positions. His thoughtful consideration for the welfare and protection of his students, his unselfishness in working for the continued betterment of the department, and the esteem with which he was held by fellow coaches and teachers in the combative fields indicate that here was a man deserving of the highest recognition in the teaching profession."

A colleague further remarked on the "exceptionally high respect and regard extended him by students, fellow coaches and faculty. More than any other coach, his impact on the students and athletes has been recognized as developing a real attitude of sportsmanship... He has been a real friend to hundreds of students, one of the reasons why he is held in such high esteem."

At the 2004 Cal Boxers Reunion, in video taped interviews, many former Cal students and boxers, who had gone on to personal and professional success, commented on the important role Ed Nemir had played in their lives. He remains vivid in the memories of many as a beloved friend and role model.

**1947 Cal Boxing Team, Coach Ed Nemir at Top Left
Warren Simmons, second row, second from Right**

Letter from Ed Nemir to Ed Farris, March 31, 1965

UNIVERSITY OF CALIFORNIA, BERKELEY

BERKELEY · DAVIS · IRVINE · LOS ANGELES · RIVERSIDE · SAN DIEGO · SAN FRANCISCO  SANTA BARBARA · SANTA CRUZ

DEPARTMENT OF PHYSICAL EDUCATION
DIVISION FOR MEN

HARMON GYMNASIUM
BERKELEY, CALIFORNIA

March 31, 1965

Dear Ed:

First, I want to let you know that it was great to get your call. And naturally to hear that you had been promoted! I never did understand how such a lousy bowler could get so much work done! You do have my sincerest congratulations.

Second, the enclosed ducats give you the privilege of joining the society for the promotion, encouragement, and retention of intercollegiate boxing, together with a very remote possibility that you may win a prize. Which, if you do, I will be glad to open the same and drink to your long life! [Cost you one buck!]

We wound up a very good season the other day. Had Cal boxers in the finals of every weight, except heavy, and won 6 out of the at home, I guess. In addition we won all of our dual meets by big scores, both here and in the enemy camps, so we couldn't be accused of home town decisions. All in all it was a good season. But it's nice to have it over with.

I trust that things are going along OK for you at school. You had the right idea — if the guy couldn't see it your way, let him go somewhere else. And the sooner the better. It's not your job to remake him, or shape him up. Life's too short. You have too much at stake and are building too good a program to have a loose nut in the machinery.

Glad to hear things are good at home also. That's the way it should be. Same here. Everyone seems to keep busy all the time. Only trouble is we'll probably lose Phil for the summer and I'll have to do all the garden work! Take care, Ed, and love to your gang from ours —

Ed

Approx 1956

'Amateur' turns in pro job

"Make sure you make it a good story." These were the words of Boxing club V.P. Sammy Moreno when he heard that the Daily Californian was going to do a feature on boxing coach Ed Nemir.

The esteem with which Moreno holds his coach is matched by all who know him. Cal's coaching roster is filled with men who are admired and respected for their work on and off the playing fields, arenas and gyms, and Nemir rates among the best.

We asked him what was the best thing that had happened to him in his long years as a coach. His answer was typical of the way he thinks, "Each year good things come up. I like to see a green man suddenly make good in a match. But it's the friendship of these kids which means the most to me. I hate to see them graduate but I know that each year there'll be new boys and new friendships."

And then again we asked him why he liked to teach and coach boxing. His reply, "Why I like boxing? . . . In teaching boxing and conducting teams I feel that I am contributing something to the individual because I see him gain poise, confidence, and I watch him grow mentally and physically."

Nemir has had a long association with the University. He enrolled as a student in 1926 and received his degree in 1930, then graduated from Boalt hall in 1933.

He stepped out of Boalt into a depression. Jobs were scarce, especially for young lawyers, so when he was offered a coaching job at Cal he took it and has remained here ever since.

One notable break in his studying while a student came in 1932, the year of the Olympic games. One of the men competing for the red, white and blue was Nemir. For a boy who had learned boxing and wrestling in an intramural class, and as beginner yet, he had come a long way.

It was somewhat of a surprise to learn that the boxing coach went to the Olympics as a wrestler, where he competed in the 134 lb. class. He went to the finals, but lost on a split decision.

His coach in those days was the late Henry Stone.

Those 1932 Olympics were a very trying period in his life. "I felt worried and anxious about every bout I had, and I didn't usually sleep all night before a match."

Still reminiscing he said, "The 1937 team was about the most outstanding team I coached. They won almost all their bouts by knockouts. George Pelonis was the best boy I ever had as far as boxing and cleverness go."

Nemir got his start in boxing and wrestling when he went out for intramural sports on the beginner's level. The intramural program which helped him then is helping him now in his interschool teams. The bulk of the boxing team, as well as the wrestling, trampoline and other teams, get the bulk of their men from the University's physical education program.

Therefore he urges students, even though they have had no experience, to sign up in a P. E. class. Even if a person doesn't compete for a school term, the sport he engages in will improve him mentally and physically. And this is what Nemir believes in and wants.

ED NEMIR

1956

COLLEGE BOXING

Boxing in college is quite different from the boxing you see on TV. It is a game of long range, skillful, quick hitting. The mauling and wrestling that occurs in professional fights is missing. College boxing is one of the safest of all athletic activities. Everything that can be done to protect the competitors is provided. Headgear must be worn, the gloves are bigger, the mat they box on is thicker, the referees are instructed to stop the fights at the slightest sign that one of the boys can no longer defend himself.

Boxing is a sport that will help you develop self-confidence because you know that you can take care of yourself if anyone ever tries to start trouble. It teaches you to move quickly, to see things rapidly, and to take advantage of any opening of your opponent by hitting instantly to his weak spots. You learn to develop reflex actions which means that when your eyes see your opponent start a blow you will move your hands into blocking positions without thinking about it, you will do it automatically. Or if your eye sees him leave his jaw open, you will hit for it without taking too much time.

If you c an box, you will never be a bully. A bully is someone who goes around picking on little fellows just so he can feel like a big shot. If you can box you dont have to do that, because you know what you can do. You dont go around looking for fights, but if someone picks on you you dont run away. And if you ever have to get in a fight, you dont cry when you get hurt. You just grit your teeth and hit back a little harder. And if you ever get in a fair fight and the other fellow beats you, you dont get mad about it. You shake his hand and tell him it was a good fight, and maybe next time you can beat him.

Most of the boxers at the University of California didnt have any boxing before they came to school, but learned in the beginning classes. This year's team only had three men back from last year. The rest of them were all boxing against other schools for the first time. They did real well and next year our team should be better than ever. But win or lose, our boys are all swell fellows and its a real pleasure to be their coach.

--Edgar Nemir

1956

Ed Nemir, Cal Boxing Coach, Dies

Ed Nemir, a man dedicated to pure collegiate boxing, will be buried in Walnut Creek this morning. Funeral services will be held at 11 a.m. at Oak Park Hills Chapel, 3111 North Main, Walnut Creek.

Nemir died of a heart attack Saturday night at ringside in Reno, Nevada.

Only shortly before he collapsed, Nemir had thrilled to a unanimous decision won by his son Phil in a 139-pound division fight.

"It's always great to box in Reno. There's a lot of enthusiasm for college boxing there and there's always a large turnout," Nemir had said last week before leaving.

A crowd of 3,000 attended the dual meet between California and Nevada. It filed out silently after Nemir collapsed and couldn't be revived. Four bouts remained on the card.

One of the prime movers in organizing the California Collegiate Boxing Conference in 1959, Nemir fought for the sport's existence on purely a novice basis.

Disturbed by the trend in intercollegiate boxing towards vigorous recruiting of Golden Glove boxers, he broke away from the Pacific Coast Boxing Conference.

In setting up the new conference, he was instrumental in having a novice rule passed — No students can compete in intercollegiate boxing who after a 16th birthday engange in competitive bouts other than under the auspices of a school.

The result was a student program, producing boxers from instruction classes and intramurals.

Nemir said he always looked for enthusiasm first and then to the skills of the sport.

Nemir was a fierce competitor himself.

A Berkeley High School graduate, he enrolled at Cal and took up wrestling and boxing. Before graduation in 1930, he won the Pacific Coast 129-pound boxing title.

Also an outstanding student, Nemir went on to the University Law School. While in Law School, he became serious in wrestling and won the silver medal in the 134-pound class of the 1932 Olympic Games.

He graduated from Law School in 1933 and that same year became the California boxing coach.

In the 36 years as Cal boxing coach, his teams won 120 dual meets and lost 61.

The four schools with surviving boxing programs — Cal, Stanford, Chico State and Nevada — will surely miss the man responsible for the sport's existence on a college level.

Edgar Nemir: California Boxing Legend

Edgar Nemir dedicated his life to the University, his sport and his students. In a very small way, California Boxing hopes to acknowledge and honor a great man this weekend.

During his nearly 40 year association with boxing at the University of California, Edgar Nemir dedicated himself to his students, his school and his sport. This weekend California Boxing salutes Edgar Nemir for his loyalty and his commitment to his programs.

Saturday evening California Boxing officially dedicates its new training facility to the legendary Nemir. The room which formerly housed boxing, and more recently the University's Martial Arts program, is located in the northeast corner of Harmon Gymnasium.

It is difficult to imagine how college boxing in general, and Cal Boxing in particular, could have survived the past three decades had it not been for Nemir. His association with boxing here at the University began in the late '20s as an undergraduate. Nemir's competitive *Boxing* career culminated in his capture of the 129 pound title in the Pacific Coast Conference Championships in 1929.

Nemir entered the University's Boalt Law School in 1930 turning his attention to a slightly different interest: Wrestling. He capped his wrestling career by winning a Silver Medal at the 1932 Olympic Games in Los Angeles. Nemir graduated with distinction from Boalt Law School in 1933. After graduating, young Edgar chose a career in "the ring" over one "on the bar."

Nemir assumed the head coaching responsibilities at Cal and continued in that role (with the exception of military duty during World War II) until his death in 1968. As a coach and teacher, Nemir had few peers. He compiled a 120-61 dual meet won-lost record during his tenure as Instructor/Coach at Cal. Nemir's effect on his sport and his influence on students is what really set Edgar Nemir apart from his contemporaries.

During the 1950s, when collegiate boxing was at the crest of its popularity, Coach Nemir became concerned that the intense recruiting of highly skilled and experienced boxers could create wide variances in ability between competitors. Because of Nemir's philosophical concerns and his commitment to safety in college boxing, California broke away from the Pacific Coast Boxing Conference of the NCAA. Cal became a charter member of the California Collegiate Boxing Conference (CCBC) in 1959. The CCBC's values of education and safety are the underlying principles of today's NCBA.

Nemir served as President of the CCBC for four years and was selected by his peers as President of the National Boxing Coaches Association. In addition to being a respected part of the boxing community, Nemir was the perfect ambassador for the sport on the Berkeley campus. He was admired and respected by colleagues both within and outside of the Physical Education Department. Nemir was first an educator influencing the lives of his students; and second, a scientific teacher of boxing skills.

Nemir described the values he hoped his students would acquire from college boxing: "...a sound knowledge of the game, bodily agility and ease of movement, coordination of the body with eye, quicker reflexes, a training of the mind to make instantaneous decisions, a satisfaction for your competitive urges and a self-confidence which has been gained through proof that you were able to stand up to others in rough situations and acquit yourself creditably."

Nemir died on February 1, 1968 of a heart attack suffered at ringside, moments after his son, Phil, had won a decision in a dual bout with Reno. He was 58. Phil has since continued the Nemir legacy at Cal.

Ed Nemir—Competitor, Coach, Champion

Ed Nemir, a landmark in the rolls of California collegiate boxing for thirty-six years, has fought the final bout. Nemir died of a heart attack during the season while at ringside in a match between Cal and Nevada.

Nemir was a fiery competitor in whatever he undertook. As a result, he broke away from the Pacific Coast Boxing Conference and fought vigorously as one of the prime movers in organizing the California Collegiate Boxing Conference in 1959. He was instrumental in having a novice rule passed—no students can compete in intercollegiate boxing who after a sixteenth birthday engages in competitive bouts other than under the auspices of a school.

In his thirty-six years of coaching, he compiled a record of 120 wins and 61 losses in dual meets. Perhaps the greatest tribute that can be made to such a man as Ed Nemir is the living monument of the four schools that still possess boxing programs in the country. He fought long and hard to keep boxing programs at Cal, Stanford, Chico State and Nevada. They will truly miss this champion who is responsible for the sport's existence at the college and university level.

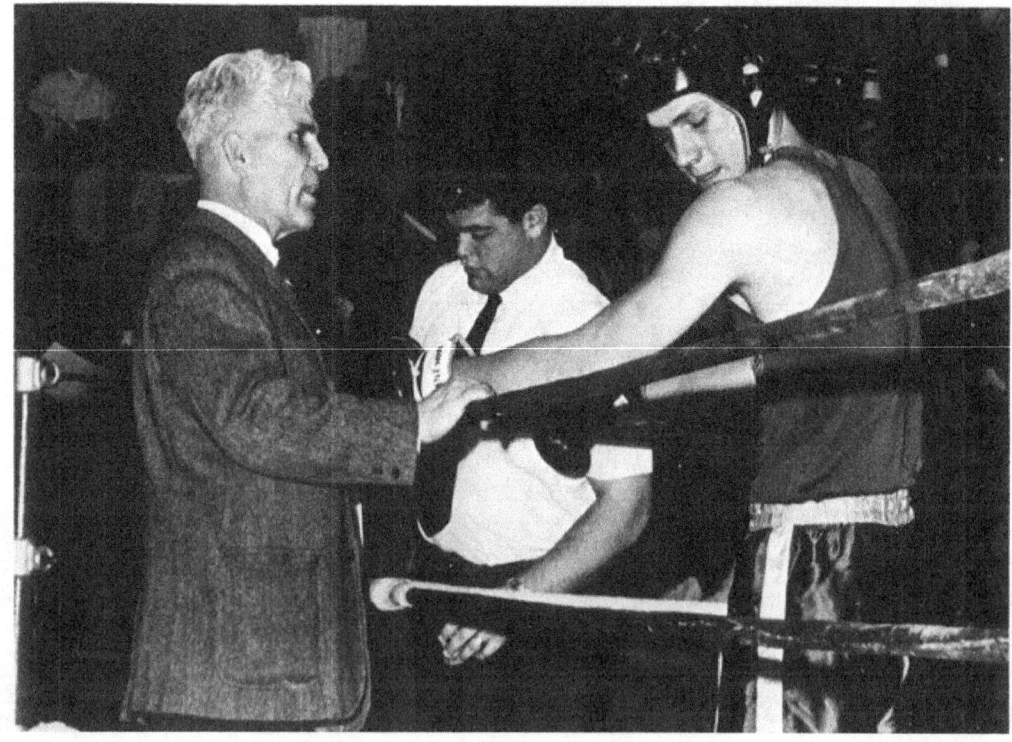

1969

EDGAR NEMIR

Edgar Nemir was one of the most admired and respected men in the Department of Physical Education by his students in boxing and wrestling, by his colleagues in the Department, and by other campus luminaries in academic and administrative positions. His thoughtful consideration for the welfare and protection of his students, his unselfishness in working for the continued betterment of the department, and the esteem with which he was held by fellow coaches and teachers in the combatives field indicate that here was a man deserving of the highest recognition in the teaching profession.

Mr. Nemir received the highest recognition in the country from fellow boxing coaches - having been selected to serve as President of the National Boxing Coaches Association and also as President of the California Collegiate Boxing Conference. His sound judgment concerning boxing as a collegiate sport was manifested by that recognition.

He carried the idea of amateurism in combatives through his career as a participant and into the coaching field. Eddie was first an educator who influenced the lives of his students; and second, he was a scientific teacher in the field of combatives. He has left an influencing mark on the lives of his students and especially the members of his boxing squad.

He began his duties as boxing coach in 1933 and has carried them out with increasing effectiveness. In attending intercollegiate boxing contests one would be impressed by the fact that after most bouts, the opponent (whether he lost or won) usually went over to the California corner and paid his respects to Mr. Nemir. Not any other coach was honored in this manner; and should be direct evidence that his influence was considerably more than local in its scope.

Mr. Nemir has given long and faithful service to the Department and to the University, beginning with his appointment as Freshman Wrestling Coach in 1930. In 1933 he was appointed Assistant in Physical Education (Specialist in Boxing) and Boxing Coach in which position he served until the War Years as Assistant Supervisor. Returning from War Leave in 1946, when he again received advancement and continued until his death as Boxing Coach and instructor of boxing.

In summary we would like to quote from an excerpt of a letter written by a colleague:

"From the very beginning years that I have been a colleague of Mr. Nemir, I have been aware of the exceptionally high respect and regard extended him by students, fellow coaches, and faculty. More than any other coach, his impact on the students and athletes has been recognized as developing a real attitude of sportsmanship...

As an informal counsellor to undergraduate students from a variety of majors, Mr. Nemir has given unstintingly of his time. He has been a real friend to hundreds of students, and this is one of the reasons why he is held in such high esteem...

During the period of the year in our department, as in others, there have been periods of trouble and uncertainty. Chairmen have died; other emergencies have intruded; differences in philosophy and policy have been debated in department meetings. Mr. Nemir has been tolerant of the opinions of others, but at the same time has been willing to argue for his own carefully considered analysis of a situation. He has been a steadying influence during periods of stress."

Mr. Nemir demonstrated the qualities which have made him such a valuable member of the staff, including his extreme conscientiousness as a teacher.

In 1959 Mr. Nemir was the prime mover in the formation of the California Collegiate Boxing Conference, which was dedicated to the promotion of safer rules for the conduct of boxing competition. Basic to their new program was the rule that any individual who had boxed before coming to college was automatically barred from collegiate competition. This eliminated the recruiting problem and assured that contestants would learn their boxing skills in college. During 1961 the State of Nevada joined this conference. Mr. Nemir was the first President of the California Collegiate Boxing Conference, 1958-60; 60-61; 61-62.

Born: Waco, Texas
Date: July 23, 1910
Married: Erna Louise Roth in May, 1942.
    Two children - Philip and Marie Louise Nemir

A. Professional Preparation
    1. 1930 - A. B. degree, University of California, Berkeley, California
        a. Elected to Phi Beta Kappa during his Junior year.
        b. Member of Boxing Team - won letters.
        c. Member of Wresting Team - won letters.
           Captain of the Team - 1930.
        d. Freshman Wrestling Coach - 1930-1933.

A. Professional Preparation (continued)
1.
    e. Won United States Olympic Wrestling Team Try-outs
    f. Won second place (Silver Medal) on Olympic Wrestling Team in the 134-lb. division in 1932. Olympic Games held in Los Angles, California that year.
2. 1933 - LLB degree, University of California, Berkeley (Boalt Hall).
    a. Third highest in the State in Law Examination in passing the Bar Examination.
3. 1947-51 Graduate study in Education - General Secondary Teaching Credential.

4. Elected to the following:
    a. 1929 - Phi Beta Kappa (during his Junior year).
    b. 1933 - Phi Alpha Delta
    c. 1935 - Sigma Alpha
    d. 1949 - Phi Delta Kappa
    e. 1949 - Theta Xi
    f. Big "C" Society:
        Ed Nemir, as stated previously, was a member of both the wrestling and boxing teams during his undergraduate days. At that time, both sports were minor sports, but after his winning second place on the Olympic Wrestling Team in 1932 he was elected to become a member of the Big "C" Society.

B. Position's Held:
1. 1930-33 - Freshman Wrestling Coach, University of California, Berkeley.
2. 1933-37 - Assistant in Physical Education, University of California.
3. 1937-43 - Junior Supervisor of Physical Education
4. War Leave - April, 1942 to January, 1945. United States Navy, Lt. Commander, rank on leaving service.
5. Military Service 1942-1961 - United States Navy - On War Leave April 1942 to January, 1946: Athletic and Physical Education Programs at Corpus Christi, Texas and Del Monte, California. Overseas duty in the Pacific Area. Entered as Lieutenant (j.g.) now Lt. Commander.

    Member of Navy Volunteer Unit in Welfare and Recreation from its inception in 1949.

    Additional work through annual correspondence courses in such areas of study as "Education and Welfare," "Personnel Administration," and "National Resources."

B. Positions Held (continued)
   6. Advanced to Full Supervisor - July 1, 1962.

C. Departmental Responsibilities and Other University Services
   1. Yearly:
      a. Faculty Sponsor, University of California Boxing Club - since 1946.
      b. Boxing Team Coach
      c. Exhibitions and addresses to schools; service clubs on boxing; etc.
      d. Organizing and conducting an intramural boxing tournament in the Fall Semester. At this tournament the MILTON T. CUNHA AWARD was given to the outstanding boxer of the tournament in the memory of this former boxer who was killed during the war while in action in the Pacific Area.
   2. Teaching:
      a. Activities taught: boxing and wrestling
      b. Professional course for Physical Education Majors - P.E. 308 - The Theory and Teaching of Boxing and Wrestling.
      c. Coaching Intercollegiate Boxing Team 1933-1957 and 1958-until his death.
      d. Faculty sponsor of California Boxing Club. Club composed of students who are both Varsity and non-Varsity boxers who are interested in the development and encouragement of the sport of boxing in the University and community. (See further explanation under Public Service.)
   3. Adviser of undergraduate students in College of Letters and Science
   4. Committee Service - Chairman, Henry A. Stone Memorial Fund Association.
   5. Served on Departmental Committees during the years.

C. Evidence of Professional Growth:
   1. Attendance at Annual Meetings of National Collegiate Athletic Association, Division of Boxing 1952-53; 54-55; 55-56; 59-61.
   2. 1956 - Olympic Committee for Boxing
   3. Societies and Associations:
      a. National Boxing Coaches Association, President also 1961-62
      b. State Bar Association of California
      c. United States Naval Reserve (Retired)
      d. California Boxers and Wrestlers Alumni Association - Director.
   4. Sabbatical Leave - Fall, 1958

D. Public Service
   1. Olympic Committee 1956
   2. Television show in cooperation with the Olympic Club.
   3. President, University Campus Credit Union - 1958-1961.
   4. Exhibitions
      a. School Assemblies, Dad's Clubs, etc.
   5. As Faculty Sponsor of the California Boxing Club, and as a member of the Board of Directors of the California Alumni of Boxers and Wrestlers, Mr. Nemir served as coordinator between the two groups in answering the many requests for boxing instructors and assistance which were received from various Boys' Clubs in the Bay Area and other organizations.

E. Honors:
   1. 1929 - Phi Beta Kappa (Junior Year).
   2. 1932-33 - Phi Alpha Delta Legal Fraternity.
   3. 1949 - Phi Delta Kappa

F. Sports Awards:
   1. 1929 - Boxing, University of California, second place, Pacific Coast Conference.
   2. 1930 - Boxing, University of California, first place, Pacific Coast Conference.
   3. 1929, 1930 - Wrestling University of California, first place, Pacific Coast Conference, Captain in 1930.
   4. 1932 - Represented United States in Olympic Games, won second place in 134-lb. class on Olympic Wrestling Team.

Ed Nemir passed away on Saturday, February 1, 1969, while in attendance at the California-Nevada meet between his boxing Bears and the Wolfpack of the University of Nevada. His son, Philip, had just won a convincing decision over his opponent. He died at the ringside of a heart attack.

Funeral: Oak Park Hills Chapel   Wednesday, 11:00 a.m.
         3111 N. Main Street
         Walnut Creek
Burial: Oakmont Memorial Park, Lafayette, California

IN MEMORIUM

In reflection, as our American flag flies at half-mast on our University of California flagstff in your memory, Ed Nemir, we salute you as the Dean of American Collegiate Boxing Coaches; as our friend and colleague through the years; for being the man of honor and integrity that you were; for your forthrightness in dealing with all with whom you came in contact; your friendship and affection for those with whom and for whom you served; you touched our lives in a wonderful manner and we are deeply grateful that we called you "friend" - we shall ever remember, Ed Nemir

1965

The Ol' Perfesser
Nemir and Boxing Still Going Strong

By BILL ROWEN

Ed Nemir graduated from Boalt Hall law school during the early 1930's, having been a Phi Beta Kappa during his undergraduate days at Cal. Unfortunately, the Great Depression was not particularly impressed with his qualifications.

"If you wanted to become a lawyer in those days, you had to pay an established lawyer $25 a month for the privilege, in addition to sharing the rent payments for his office," Nemir recalls.

At the same time, however, Cal was looking for a boxing coach. Nemir, who had been a great boxer and wrestler for the Bears, gratefully accepted the job. He passed his bar examinations, anyway, but ever since that distant day in the 30's, his law license has hung on the wall in the Harmon Gym boxing office.

"I've never regretted the decision to become a boxing coach," Nemir says flatly. "It's been tremendously enjoyable. I certainly can't complain."

OLYMPIC STAR

In a way, Nemir grew up with boxing. He entered Cal as "a small kid, about 120 pounds," never having competed in any sport in high school.

When Nemir was a freshman, phys. ed. was a required course, and Nemir decided to take boxing.

Later, he also took up wrestling, but he never went out for a team until his junior year. You can find the results in the record books: Nemir went on to become an NCAA champion in his weight division, and, while attending law school, won a silver medal in the 1932 Olympics. He still remains the only Cal wrestler ever to go to the Olympics.

"I never did grow very much," Nemir states, "but boxing and wrestling are great as far as giving confidence to the little man."

Now that Brutus Hamilton is about to retire, Nemir becomes the dean of Cal's coaches, and the coming CCBC (California Collegiate Boxing Conference) tournament to be held this weekend in Harmon Gym serves as a fitting tribute to the man and his love for college boxing.

This is the first time Cal has hosted the tourney, since the CCBC was only born in 1961, after almost every school in the country dropped boxing, leaving Cal, Stanford, Chico State, and Nevada alone in the college ring.

It is really ironic that these were the four schools to survive. Cal bolted from the old Pacific Coast Boxing Conference in the mid-50's when it became clear that opposing schools were bringing in "ringers" with as many as 150 amateur fights to their credit.

When a Wisconsin boxer died in the ring in 1957, the schools who had abused the sport were the first targets for the "anti-boxing crowd."

ED NEMIR
Gave up law for "violence"

1924-1927

Sam Gold

Sam Gold was born June 2, 1906 in Las Vegas, New Mexico. His parents were from near Kiev, Russia. His father escaped from Russia in order to avoid conscription into the Russian army. His favorite "Gemini" characteristic, he believed, was to "have fun." His family moved to Oakland in 1912. He had two sisters and two brothers. His older brother, Hymie Gold, became a famous local fighter during the 1920s, although he fought under the name "Oakland Jimmy Duffy," and eventually founded "Duffy's Boxing Gym," an Oakland landmark during the 1930s and 1940s.

When Sam was ten years old, he sold soda water and peanuts at the West Oakland Club at 24th and Harrison Streets in Oakland, and saw future heavyweight champion Jack Dempsey fight there twice against Willie Meehan. "To me Jack Dempsey was the greatest." Dempsey became a friend of Sam's brother, "Jimmy Duffy," and would visit Jimmy when he came to Oakland. Jimmy Duffy later opened "Duffy's" bar in Oakland in the early 1970s, on 11th Street between Broadway and Franklin.

Sam fought on the Cal Boxing Team for four years, 1924 to 1927, winning all of his 20 fights and being elected Cal's team captain. In a 2004 Cal Boxers Reunion videotaped interview, he told of his "favorite" fight, one against UCLA. At the opening bell, the UCLA fighter charged across the ring and swung a left hook at Sam, but missed, leaving himself open for a perfect right cross on the chin, going down for a 10 second knockout. Sam thought "that might be a record." The other fighter, displaying his sportsmanship, came to Sam's dressing room after the fight, remarking, "I wanted to *meet* you, as I never had a chance to meet you in the ring!"

Like Walter Gordon, Sam Gold also had a close connection to Earl Warren. Many years before Governor Warren was appointed to be Chief Justice of the United States Supreme Court, he was Attorney General of California during the 1930s. In 1930 Sam Gold graduated Boalt Hall in a class of 50 law students, and became a lawyer. Several years later, during the mid-depression years, Sam was hired by Earl Warren to be a Deputy Attorney General. Sam's most vivid memory of Earl Warren was playing racquet ball against him in Sacramento.

Sam Gold practiced law in Oakland for many years, finally retiring around 1998. "I figured 64 years as a lawyer was enough!" He continued to work out regularly in local gyms, and attributed his health and longevity to his exercise regime. "I'm still at my 175 lb. fighting weight." Paul Rein met him when they were both punching on heavy bags at the Oakland Athletic Club around 1985. Rein told him he had boxed at Cal "way back in 1965." "1965?" he countered. "I was captain of the Cal Boxing Team in 1925!" When interviewed in 2003, he was still working out several times a week - at the age of 97! In 2004, he was the most popular ex-fighter at a Cal Boxing Alumni Dinner.

Sam Gold at 89

Paul Rein, Sam Gold, Bill Harrison, Cal grads 1965, 1927, 1960

History of College Boxing and 1960's Threat to Ban Boxing

According to former Cal Boxer and boxing Coach Phil Nemir, who wrote a comprehensive paper in 1970, recorded boxing competition began on college campuses around 1880, with an intramural program carried out at Harvard. World War I "provided a strange new impetus for the sport as many college men received boxing instruction as part of their physical conditioning program while in the Armed Forces, then returned to college and the development of intercollegiate competition."

One of the earliest verified matches was Cal v. Stanford in 1916, the bout so well described by Donald Lawton. By 1943, over 100 colleges were participating nationally in Intercollegiate Boxing. In 1932 and 1936, the first two NCAA tournaments were held, followed by annual tournaments till 1960.

In supporting the positive effect intercollegiate boxing had on participating students, in the 1960's, Ed Nemir wrote that boxing advanced positive values, including: "a sound knowledge of the game, bodily agility and ease of all movement, coordination of the body with the eye, quick reflexes, a training of the mind to make instantaneous decisions, a satisfaction for your competitive urges, and a self-confidence which has been gained through proof that you were able to stand up to others in rough situations and acquaint yourself creditably."

Opponents of boxing during the 1950's caused the number of collegiate programs to decline. The death of Charles Mohr, the defending National Champion at 165 lbs, during the 1960 NCAA tournament, caused a cancellation of the NCAA program.

After Charles Mohr's death in 1960, the only survivors of College Boxing were in the West, thanks to Jimmy Olivas of Nevada (Reno), Ed Nemir of Cal, Ray Lunny of Stanford, and Willie Simmons of Chico State. (Each of these four coaches had, at one time, or another, one of their own sons boxing on their schools' teams.) Safety Rules were adopted.

The surviving west coast teams formed the Calif. Collegiate Boxing Conference, in 1959, and "opposed the recruiting practices and eligibility requirements allowed under NCAA rules."

Those founding the CCBC in 1959 adopted rules focused on avoiding mismatches with novices fighting boxers already experienced before entering college. They adopted the rule that "boys who box in other than interscholastic competition after reaching the age of 16 years are not eligible to compete in college."

CCBA rules required, since 1959, safety equipment including large gloves (12 oz and 14 oz for fighters over 147 lbs), form fitting mouth pieces and protective headgear, all mandatory. Other safety features were a thick boxing mat on the floor, preseason physicals for team members, doctor's medical examination before and after each fight, doctors in attendance of all meets, and competent and trained safety conscious coaches and instructors. Further safeguards include competent and trained referees, matching of fights a fairly as possible, and stopping of fights whenever a fighter appears unable to properly defend himself.

Threats to end college boxing let to formation of the College Rules, including:

- 12 weight devisions to diminish mismatches due to size and strength advantages
- Boxers wear mandatory headgear, mouthpiece and supporter ("cup")
- Boxers use 12 and 14 ounce gloves
- Bouts consist of three 2 minute rounds with one-minute rest period between rounds
- Referees administer standing eight counts if a fighter is stunned or unable to effectively defend himself
- Boxers of roughly equal caliber are matched according to skill, strength, conditioning, and number of competitive bouts."

A 1983 program spelled out the safety reasons for the Collegiate Rules: "The decline of College Boxing in the 1960's was mainly due to an overemphasis on recruiting and providing scholarships for experienced boxers in order to build winning teams. This emphasis on winning often produced dangerous mismatches in boxing contests. As a result, the NCBA adopted a rule to protect the student competition in college boxing."

"Recruiting and scholarships are illegal in the NCBA (National Collegiate Boxing Association), because it is felt that highly skilled, experienced boxers have other, more serious, avenues through which they can pursue their boxing. This eliminated experienced boxers through recruitment and scholarship restrictions, and the sixteen year old rule, forces schools to develop their instructional and intramural programs, because the emphasis is on teaching fundamentals to novices."

"To ensure safe participation of boxers having roughly equal ability and strength, the NCBA eligibility rule states: Any student, in or out of college, who, after his sixteenth birthday, participates in a boxing contest other than one sponsored by his college or university, shall be rendered ineligible to compete in collegiate boxing. This rule tends to equalize competition and reduce injuries resulting from mismatches. By reducing the variation of skill among and between competitors, the rule insures that young men of different abilities do not face each other."

Phil Nemir's 1970 paper offered that, statistically, boxing is also a lot safer than many other sports, including baseball and football, with a 1951 study in the Journal of the American Medical Association concluding: It seems that the moral and physical benefits derived from boxing far outweigh the dangers inherent in it or any of the other competitive sports.

In professional championship fights, in 1962, Benny "Kid" Paret, was killed in a fight by Emile Griffith, and in March 1963, just a few days after California Governor Pat Brown had committed himself to preserving College Boxing while seeking to end professional boxing, boxer Davey Moore was killed in a fight with Sugar Ramos.

Chico State and Nevada Reno had popular fan support for their teams. A 1964 University of Nevada faculty and student poll on whether to continue intercollegiate boxing resulted in numbers more than 10 to 1 favoring retention of boxing 885 to 87.

"At Cal, the boxing program struggled after the February 1969 ringside heart attack death of Cal Coach Ed Nemir, who had led the program for more than 35 years. The Cal Physical Education department discontinued boxing classes and dropped boxing as an intramural sport. Only passionate efforts by alumni and students kept the Intercollegiate program alive."

As of 1970, there were only 3 schools left with intercollegiate Boxing: Cal, Chico State, and University of Nevada, Reno. (Stanford dropped its Intercollegiate program in 1969.)

Although a 1968 article lamented, "College Boxing's Last Round," and the University administration did little to help the Cal Boxing Program, forcing it to become a "club sport," privately financed since 1970, the Collegiate sport rebounded due to the dedicated efforts of Phil Nemir, Ron Dell'Immagine, Dick Carter, Mike Huff, Brian Kahn, and others during the 1970s, keeping the program alive while schools in the rest of the country joined in the Intercollegiate competition. Soon, there were more than 30 schools, including the military service academies, which form the National Collegiate Boxing Conference, which continues to this day. The "NCBC" was formed in 1976. Today there are approximately 80 schools which participate in NCBA boxing.

In the 21st century, these rules still theoretically exist. However, the Nationals now include competitors from the Armed Services academies: the Air Force Academy, West Point and Annapolis. For example, each year, approximately 4,000 men at the Air Force Academy take boxing instruction, and fierce competition between 10 "wings" result in champions in each weight division. Thus a student at Cal who may have had three or four fights may face a service competitor who has had 15 or 20 bouts experience.

The article, "Cal Boxing's Transition After Coach Ed Nemir," by former Cal Boxer (1969) and coach (1971-72), Dick Carter, eloquently describes the difficult but successfull fight to save Cal Boxing after the February, 1969 death of coach Ed Nemir. Coach Nemir's popularity and influence, as the "Dean" of all Cal Sports Coaches, had helped keep boxing alive at Cal. Within two months of Ed Nemir's death, the Cal Physical Education Department had moved to discontinue boxing, and stopped funding, took away the "boxing room" and made it difficult for team members to find anywhere to train.

Fortunately, Cal Boxing survived till the mid-eighties, when "slim Jim" Riksheim took over as coach, and dedicated himself to coaching and training young boxers, both in the ring and in their personal development -- a coaching tradition since the reign of Ed Nemir. Jim Riksheim and his assistants, including Sean Mockler, Floyd Salas and Tom Pedamonte, kept Cal Boxing alive and competitive for the next 30 years. Jim Riksheim was only recently succeeded by Dave Keegan (since 2011), a dedicated leader and teacher who had demonstrated unusual courage while fighting at Cal, and subsequently becoming assistant coach and accepting increased responsibility. Co-coach with Dave Keegan was Jon Zaul, from 2012-2015. Jon has taken over as Coach of the team for Fall 2015 to Spring 2016, despite continuing his "day job" as an outstanding San Francisco lawyer. He boxed for Cal from 2002-2005.

According to Leo Gaspardone (who boxed at Cal in the 1950's and spoke at the 2011 Cal Boxing Reunion), university administrators had also tried to shut down boxing in the 1950's but efforts by Cal's coach Ed Nemir, Nevada's Jimmy Olivas, Stanford's Ray Lunny, and Chico State's Willie Simons, were successful in keeping boxing alive. These coaches formed the California Collegiate Boxing Conference (CCBC) in 1959 and were able to continue the intercollegiate sport after the NCAA dropped boxing after a death occurred in the 1960 NCAA middleweight championship bout. Gaspardone, who attributed his boxing experiences as influencing his decision to become a school teacher, was one of many successful professional men who spoke at the 2004 and 2011 reunions and attributed Cal Boxing as being one of the most positive influences in their lives.

The following page, from the 1984 NCBA (National Collegiate Boxing Association) Championships Program (held at Cal Berkeley in 1984) spells out the major safety precautions used to maximize safety during collegiate boxing competition:

[From 1984 Nationals Program]

NCBA Boxing: A Safe Approach

Since its inception in 1976, the National Collegiate Boxing Association has served a unique role for the sport at the college level. In addition to helping organize regional and national competitions and monitoring eligibility standards, the Association has actively intervened to see that collegiate boxing adheres to the NCBA's philosophy of safety and education. This has been accomplished through rules and guidelines which insure a healthy, positive experience for student-athletes.

In an effort to equalize the competitive experience and prevent mismatches, the NCBA enforces the "sixteen-year old rule," which states that any student who participates in a contest outside of college after his sixteenth birthday is rendered ineligible to compete in college boxing. This has helped reduce the injury potential caused by variances in skill, strength or experience. The primary goal of college boxing thus becomes teaching boxing fundamentals to novices.

In addition, the following rules and safety features are part of the NCBA's commitment to safety and education.

- Boxers use twelve and fourteen ounce thumbless gloves.
- Bouts consist of three two minute rounds, reducing the effects of fatigue.
- Boxers wear mandatory headgear.
- Twelve weight divisions diminish mismatches due to differences in size and strength.
- Boxers are matched with opponents of comparable skill and experience.
- Referees administer standing eight counts if a boxer is stunned, and stop a fight immediately if a boxer is mismatched.

With these provisions, the NCBA fulfills its commitment as an organization dedicated to promoting college boxing as a healthy learning experience for students across the country.

NCBA SCHOOLS BY REGION

NORTH-EAST
Central Connecticut State
Dickenson College
Lock Haven State
Penn-State University
St. Francis College
Shippensburg State
Springfield College
Syracuse University
Westfield State
West Point
University of Toronto

SOUTH-EAST
*Lehigh
*Naval Academy
Temple University
Trenton State
University of Delaware
University of Pennsylvania
University of Virginia
Villanova University
Virginia Military Institute
West Chester State

MID-WEST
Air Force Academy
The Citadel
Ohio University
University of Miami at Ohio
University of Notre Dame
University of Cincinnati
University of South Carolina
**University of Wisconsin
Xavier University

WEST
**Chico State
**Sacramento State
University of California, Berkeley
**University of California, Santa Cruz
**University of Nevada, Las Vegas
University of Nevada, Reno
University of Santa Clara

*Swing schools for North-East and South-East Regionals.
**Inactive in 1983-84.

The History of Collegiate Boxing
By Christopher Mendez

Collegiate boxing is a byproduct of World War I. During the war, Professor Raycraft was the Chief Administrator for Army Training camp activities where boxing was a means of conditioning new soldiers and used for recreational purposes on the camps. Upon returning to civilian life, collegiate faculty members and students teturned with a passion for the sport and in 1921 the Eastern Collegiate Boxing Association (ECBA) was established with teams such as Penn State, Westchester University and University of Pennsylvania leading from the front. Other schools quickly followed such as Virginia, North Carolina, and Florida in the South, Wisconsin and Colorado in the Midwest, and Washington State, Idaho State, NV Reno and California Berkeley in the West. College boxing soon became a NCAA sponsored activity with over 200 schools participating.

College boxing was once followed as closely as its professional counterparts. The famed example goes back to March 29th, 1940 at Madison Square Garden, where Joe Louis defended his heavyweight crown against Johnny Paycheck in front of a crowd of 11,620. On that same night in Madison, Wisconsin, over 15,000 spectators tuned in to watch the pugilists of Washington State face off against the University of Wisconsin, proving that collegiate boxing viewership operated on an even, if not greater, level as the professional ranks. The sport enjoyed a firm following until 1960 when Charlie Mohr of the legendary University of Wisconsin squad died in the hospital after suffering a KO loss. Though studies have suggested his death may have been caused by unrelated pre-boxing conditions, a ban was put on nonetheless.

Sixteen years later, boxing reemerged onto the college landscape, but not sanctioned under the traditionally recognized NCAA. Instead it operates under the sport specific banner of the National College Boxing Association (NCBA). The NCBA was formed in 1976 and is a group member of USA Boxing whose goal is to provide a safe, positive experience for student athletes. Currently there are over 80 colleges and universities participating in collegiate boxing nationwide. In order to be eligible to participate in an NCBA member school, a collegiate boxer must be a full-time student or graduate student at an accredited institution. All collegiate boxers are certified amateur boxers that follow strict and rules through USA Boxing.

Finally, we are proud to share a few key facts about local collegiate teams and their contributions and dominance of collegiate boxing in the West: First, the University of California Berkeley Boxing Club is celebrating 100 years of competition this year. It is the longest continuous program in the Country. Next, it was Jimmy Olivas from the University of Reno Nevada along with Al McChesney and Dean Plemmons from Westchester that helped spearhead the development and creation of the NCBA. Finally, the West has captured 24 of 38 National Championships in the history of the NCBA between the Air Force Academy led by legendary Coach Eddie Weichers, University of Nevada Las Vegas led by Coach Skipper Kelp and the University of Nevada Reno led by Mike Martino.

Thank you for supporting the NCBA and collegiate boxing!
Christopher Mendez
NC BA West Chair
[From 2015 Western Regionals Program]

1963

Chico Enterprise-Record, Saturday, March 23, 1963
1963 Pro Boxing Deaths and Distinguishing Collegiate Boxing Safety

'Chances Are Poor'
Ex-Champ Davey Moore Remains in Deep Coma

By JOOSEPH A. ST. AMANT

LOS ANGELES (UPI) — Former featherweight champion Davey Moore, knocked out only twice in his professional boxing career, hovered near death in a deep coma today as the result of brain injuries in a bruising bout with Sugar Ramos.

The 29-year-old Moore, who had held the 126-pound title for almost four years and appeared invincible to some, lost his title—and as it turned out endangered his life—Thursday night when Ramos, 21-year-old Cuban refugee, scored a 10th round kayo.

Moore, a veteran of 64 bouts, was draped on the ropes as the fight ended at Dodger Baseball Stadium. He went to his dressing room under his own power, talked lucidly about "a bad night" to sports writers and then collapsed 40 minutes later. Unconscious, he was taken to White Memorial Hospital where Dr. Philip Vogel, after a preliminary examination, said: "His chances are poor."

Still unconscious, Moore lasted the night and an 11 a.m. medical bulletin Friday said this was an encouraging sign.

Another bulletin—issued at 4 p.m. Friday—said, however, his condition worsened and his chances of survival were "poorer."

Moore suffered "massive bruises" on the brain from the beating he took, the hospital said, and surgery was not feasible because of the wide area of damage.

A medical bulletin issued at 8 p.m., said a team of three neurological specialists had examined Moore. They succeeded in keeping his temperature stationary by cooling methods, including ice packing.

Moore's pulse has "elevated, and the blood pressure decreased slightly," the bulletin stated. There was no mention of possible surgery, indicating Moore's condition remained so critical an operation was not planned.

Moore's wife, Geraldine, mother of their five young children, was at his bedside Friday morning but then she too was admitted as a patient for treatment of shock and fatigue. Mrs. Moore did not witness the fight but came here from her Columbus, Ohio, home to be with her husband.

Moore's collapse was the signal for California Gov. Edmund G. Brown and several legislators to reiterate a proposal to outlaw boxing.

In addition to Ramos, two other new champions were crowned Thursday night. Another Cuban exile, Luis Rodriguez, scored a 15-round unanimous decision over Emile Griffith to win the welterweight crown. Roberto Cruz of the Philippines kayoed Battling Torres of Mexico in the first round to take the vacant junior welterweight title.

New Attack on Sport
Brown Wants Boxing Issue Put Before Voters in '64

SACRAMENTO (UPI)—If Gov. Edmund G. Brown has his way, Californians will vote in 1964 on whether to abolish boxing in the state.

The governor, an outspoken foe of the sport, Friday opened a new attack on boxing because of the Los Angeles fight that left dethroned featherweight champion Davey Moore near death.

He said the Moore bout saw a championship fighter in prime condition with only one technical knockout on his record, who had been carefully examined before the fight.

"During the fight he did not appear to be badly hurt," the governor said. "All the regulations were fully complied with."

He suggested that this proved that the powers of the state Athletic Commission were not enough.

"I can only conclude once again that there is only one way to prevent deaths and severe injuries in the ring and that is to abolish the so-called sport completely," the governor said.

Brown said he intended to ask for the immediate introduction of a bill which would ask the voters to outlaw boxing in the 1964 election. At the same time, he called for an "emergency committee" to survey the safeguards that now exist and recommend new ones.

Butts Talked With Bryant About Rules

By AL KUETTNER

ATLANTA (UPI)—The president of the University of Alabama says Alabama coach Paul (Bear) Bryant talked about possible rules infractions with Wallace Butts before the 1962 Alabama-Georgia football game but learned no secrets from the former Georgia athletic director.

Butts warned Bryant that the Crimson Tide, defending national champions, had several defensive "techniques" that might result in penalties, Frank Rose said in a confidential letter to Dr. O. C. Aderhold, University of Georgia president.

Rose said in the letter, written two weeks ago and made public Friday, that the Alabama defense was changed and Bryant was ― for call-

New Grants to Be ―
By UCLA, California

BERKELEY (UPI)

1963

Letter from Paul Rein to Governor Edmund "Pat" Brown

The Hon. Edmund G. Brown
Executive Mansion,
Sacramento, California

Dear Governor Brown:
   While I strongly support your efforts to stamp out the corruption which pollutes professional boxing, I was disturbed by your recent public statements which condemned "boxing" in general, without differentiating between professional prize-fighting and the amateur sport. While pro boxing may be a shady business well deserving of your strong opposition, amateur boxing is a sport in which I participate and which I believe to be a builder of health, character, and good sportsmanship. As I love the sport and want very much to see it survive and flourish in the future, I write to you with the ardent hope that you will publicly clarify your opposition and differentiate between the pro boxing, which you oppose, and amateur boxing, an entirely different entity. Confusing the two in the public mind might serve to weaken opposition to professional boxing by those who know and support amateur boxing, and may serve to weaking amateur boxing as people may misinterpret criticism intended for pro boxing as also applying to amateur boxing, and unjust and mistaken inference.
   I am a boxer on the boxing team at the University of California, Berkeley. Our school is one of the four schools which still have boxing as an intercollegiate sport in this country (although many schools have it at the intramural level) and I see grave danger that misdirected criticism may keep other schools who have shown an interest from joining our league or, worse still, cause pressure-wary administrators at one of the surviving schools to drop the sport, spelling total doom for collegiate boxing. I write in the hope that, should they not already be clear to you, I might bring to your attention some of the major differences between my sport and the professional business.
   In proboxing the sole intent is to please the crowd and thereby make bigger gate receipts. Little attention is given to the boxers safety or to developing skills. For this reason boxing on the pro level is brutal game fought to the point where one man is so badly damaged that he can no longer continue. Fights are 10 to 15 rounds, headgear are not used, few safety precautions are taken.
   In amateur boxing, particularly the collegiate sport with which I am well acquainted, the psychology is one which puts development of skills and safety to the boys boxing as of the first concern. Rounds are not 10 or 15 of 3 minutes duration but 3 two minute rounds. Each boxer is protected by heavily insulated headgear which protect the ears, eyes, and protect against cuts or excessive shock, and also wear protective cups to protect against accidental low blows. Boxing is done with 14oz. gloves, as opposed to the 6 and 8 oz. gloves used by the professionals. Doctors are at ringside for all bouts, and a bout will not be allowed to continue if either fight shows any sighn of not being able to continue adequately defending himself. Judging is

1963

not on the basis of damage done or blood spilled, as in pro boxing, but on the basis of skill shown and points scored. Injuries are very rare and serious injuries nearly nonexistant; certainly medical records will show that amateur boxing, especially on the collegiate level, is far safer than such sports as football, rugby, or even baseball and basketball. Collegiate boxing coaches insist that their boys be in the peak of physical condition before they will permit them to box, and the coaches see to it also that no mismatched fights are allowed to take place.

It has been my experience that boxing as a sport not only serves to develop self-confidence and channel competitive spirit, but also to build good sportsmanship. Collegiate boxing is to me one of the cleanest and purest of sports: two men stand in a ring alone and oppose each other with all eyes upon them; there is no question of dependence on others, no opportunity nor desire to cheat or break the rules: each man concentrates on pursuing his sport with all the skill and heart he can muster I have participated in several other sports besides boxing and in no other have I seen such good sportsmanship and friendly fellings among opponents, such a lack of bitterness or ill-will. Boxers who have gone three rugged rounds with each other, win, lose or draw, emerge from the ring with only the highest feeling of respect for their opponents. The boys I have known in boxing emerge from competition healthier individuals, both physically and in their relations with their fellow men.

Governor, I hope that, should you have any doubts or questions on this subject, you will check for yourself. I am sure that you will come to the conclusion that amateur boxing is a safe, clean sport, worthy not only of acceptance but of encouragement. If curious to see a typical collegiate bout for yourself you might be interested in attending Cal's last home meet of the season, this Saturday, March 2, at 8p.m. in Harmon Gymnasium at U. C.

Collegiate boxing is a sport sorely hurt by unfavorable criticism launched against pro boxing, and is in danger of dying out. Statements condemning "boxing" in general may serve to damage the hope for amateur boxing, in the future, and to discourage other universities from entering the sport on the collegiate level. It would be greatly appreciated by myself and by others who enjoy participation in or watching collegiate and other amateur boxing if you would publicly clarify your oppostition to "boxing" by limiting your condemnation to professional prizefighting.

Thank you for your time,

Paul L. Rein.

Letter from Governor Edmund G. "Pat" Brown, promising to limit his comments to criticizing professional, not amateur boxing.

EDMUND G. BROWN
GOVERNOR

State of California
GOVERNOR'S OFFICE
SACRAMENTO

March 6, 1963

Mr. Paul L. Rein
19 Hillside Court
Berkeley 4, California

Dear Mr. Rein:

Thank you for calling my attention to the distinction between amateur and professional boxing. I have tried to be careful to qualify my statements by making it clear that I am talking only about professional prize fights. In this case, I am sorry I slipped and I will make sure to draw the line in the future.

Sincerely

EDMUND G. BROWN, Governor

1963

San Francisco Chronicle, March 27, 1963

The Daily Californian, March 28, 1963

The Bear Backer
College Boxing Not Affected By Hassle

By Lowell Hickey, Assistant Sports Editor

With all the current talk about abolishing professional boxing, another sport which is only slightly related to it—college boxing—has received a boost.

Governor Pat Brown said that while he is in favor of abolishing boxing on the professional level, he thinks "college boxing is a good sport and should be continued."

"This is the first time that college boxing has been specifically excepted from the plans to abolish boxing," said Cal coach Ed Nemir. "Before it has always been 'abolish boxing' with no exceptions. I look at this as a good sign for college boxing."

The trouble is that too many people don't, or won't, distinguish between professional and college boxing. When Benny "Kid" Paret was killed last year pressure was put on the colleges to drop boxing and Santa Clara succumbed.

But Athletic Director Pete Newell said that so far he has felt no pressure put on him to drop boxing since the recent death of Davey Moore. "This is a credit to Eddie (Nemir)," said Newell. "People who follow college boxing realize it is so well regulated that it hardly resembles pro boxing."

ED NEMIR

"When a team is beaten by 60 points in a basketball game," said the ex-Cal cage coach, "you can't tell who won and who lost when the boys come out of the shower room. But when a boy is beaten decisively in a boxing match anyone with eyes can tell who won and who lost."

A stress on winning NCAA boxing championships is exactly what killed the sport in all colleges and universities in the United States except four (Cal, Stanford, Nevada and Chico State). Colleges were recruiting Golden Gloves and other amateur boxers who had had as many as 75 bouts.

But the schools in Cal's conference always kept the sport at the novice level. What it amounts to is that the intramural champs of one school compete with the intramural champs of another. For example, nine of the Bears' ten letter winners this year are first year men.

In this kind of situation the chances of someone getting seriously hurt are no greater than in any contact sport. And the benefits which the participants receive far outweigh any of the drawbacks.

The sport teaches confidence and a care for the body which few other sports can match. In most sports if an athlete is out of shape the worst that can happen is that he causes his team to lose. But if a boxer goes into the ring out of shape it's only he that pays for it—the hard way.

Newell communicated with Santa Clara about returning to boxing, but this week he received a negative reply. He also mentioned the possibility to USF, but they are not considering it either.

"Right now it's hard to build college boxing," said Newell, "because whenever you mention boxing there's an emotional climate involved."

"It would be nice to have a fifth team," said Nemir, "but we don't really need one. We already have nine meets scheduled for next year—six collegiate dual meets, one Navy tournament and the conference tournament at the end of

1964

Article from Daily Californian, Thursday, April 9, 1964

Nevada Vote Could End Intercollegiate

By LOWELL HICKEY

College boxing, a sport that has been hanging on by a limb since 1958, may have that limb cut off next Thursday.

On that day a referendum to outlaw boxing at the University of Nevada will be presented for a student vote.

Nevada is one of four schools still offering an intercollegiate boxing program. The others are California, Stanford and Chico State. All four are in the California College Boxing Conference.

One more school dropping boxing would probably mean the end of the sport on an intercollegiate level. As Cal coach Ed Nemir said yesterday, "If they go, we'll go."

Nevada's Board of Intercollegiate Athletics, comprised of four faculty members and one student, voted 3-2 to recommend the removal of the sport at Nevada. They said they would leave the final decision up to the students since they helped pay for the athletic program.

So come next Thursday, April 16, one week from today, the students at the University of Nevada will be holding the fate of college boxing in their hands.

This whole thing caught Nemir by complete surprise. "Everything looked rosy at a recent CCBC meeting," he said. "Stanford scheduled a full slate for next year and everything seemed fine."

College boxing has been declining since Wisconsin's Charlie Moore was killed in a bout with a San Jose State boxer in 1958. The NCAA discontinued to recognize the sport in 1960.

Cal Poly and Santa Clara were in the CCBC in 1962, but they discontinued the sport as a result of protests when Benny "Kid" Paret was killed in a professional championship fight with Emile Griffiths.

PAUL REIN
The end of his sport

1964

Article from Daily Californian, Thursday, April 16, 1964

Intercollegiate Boxing Given Reprieve

By PENNY HOWE

College boxing was given a stay of execution yesterday when students at the University of Nevada voted overwhelmingly — 885-87 — to keep boxing a recognized intercollegiate sport on the University of Nevada campus.

Last week Nevada's Board of Intercollegiate Athletics, comprised of four faculty members and one student, voted 3-2 to eliminate the sport at Nevada. However, the board agreed to leave the decision to the students.

The University of Nevada paper, The Sagebrush, has been crusading to save boxing on the Nevada campus. Yesterday's vote was all-important as only four schools in the country still have intercollegiate boxing. They are: University of California, Stanford, Chico State, and of course, Nevada, all members of the California Collegiate Boxing Conference.

Cal's boxing coach, Ed Nemir, commented when he heard of the referendum last week. "If they go, we'll go."

The Nevada Board of Regents still has to make the final decision on the question, but the board had agreed to go along with the student decision if the voting turnout approached 50 per cent.

The student turnout was around 40-45 per cent and a spokesman for the Sagebrush said, "The board will undoubtedly abide by the student decision."

College boxing has been declining since 1958 when Wisconsin's Charlie Moore was killed in a bout with a San Jose State boxer. The NCAA discontinued to recognize the sport in 1960.

Although the decision to put the issue to a vote on the Nevada campus came as a surprise to Coach Nemir, it should not have really been much of a shock. He has been fighting the death of college boxing for years.

Most of the people who oppose college boxing associate it with boxing on the professional level. The similarity between the two is very slight.

So the students of the University of Nevada have the distinction of saving college boxing, for the time being, anyway, single-handedly.

Nemir was unavailable for comment on the voting outcome.

"Colleges Still In Boxing" - Ring Magazine, March 1965

COLLEGES STILL IN BOXING

California Boxing Conference flourishes despite NCAA abandonment of the sport

By PAUL L. REIN

BERKELEY, CAL.—There is a belief around the country that there no longer is intercollegiate boxing. The general understanding is that the varsities dropped the sport after 1960. However, the fact remains that there is a compact and interesting intercollegiate league out here on the West Coast.

While it is true that many schools discontinued boxing after an unfortunate freak death in the 1960 NCAA tournament, the California Collegiate Boxing Conference has continued a full intercollegiate and tournament schedule.

The Conference which includes the University of California at Berkeley, the University of Nevada, Stanford University, and Chico State College, will continue its schedule into 1965 with home and away matches and a championship tournament March 19 and 20 in Berkeley.

The matches are fought with one man from each team at each of the Olympic weight divisions, and are exhibitions of exciting and skillful boxing which do credit to the sport. The participants find the sport enjoyable, healthful, and stimulating, and are well-trained by coaches who have been instructing men and boys in boxing for an *average* of over twenty years each.

For example, our own coach, Ed Nemir, was a boxing champ here at Cal over thirty years ago and has coached ever since. He also wrestled and won a silver medal in the 1932 Olympics. Like the other coaches whose schools have maintained boxing, he is dedicated to the sport, and chose to coach boxing instead of opening a law practice after passing the California bar.

At a time when boxing has been subjected to many harsh words, even a critic like Governor Brown of California has praised college boxing, calling it a "good sport" which "does good and should be continued." When critics tried to have boxing dropped at the University of Nevada last spring, the University Regents put the matter to a vote of the students, who supported keeping boxing by an overwhelming 10 to 1 margin.

As a boxing fan as well as a competitor for the University of California, I believe that the increasing popularity of the sport in college, and its hoped-for expansion to more schools in the coming years, is both a sign of a rekindling of the nation's interest in boxing and an aid to increasing boxing's popularity by helping to introduce more people to one of America's finest and most popular sports.

A typical league schedule is presented in the California chart, which includes the Navy invitation tournament at Mare Island on March 2.

ALONG THE V.B.A. TRAIL

By JACK LARKIN

Condolences to the family and many friends of Lou Cohen, president of Ring 4, Boston. Lou was fatally injured when hit by an automobile. He was a speaker at the recent National Convention in Philadelphia.

Jersey Bellows, of Ring 23, Allentown, Pa., recently celebrated his 82nd birthday. Bellows says he was Bob Fitzsimmons' last opponent. They fought in Bethlehem in 1914. In a career spanning 20-odd years, Bellows says he was never beaten. He still makes his home in Bethlehem.

Ring 9, Passaic and Bergen Counties, N. J., staged a Christmas party for the children of the Immaculate Conception Orphanage of Lodi. Two truckloads of food, clothing and toys were distributed. This writer was chairman, assisted by Al Rosen, Battling Odin, Ronnie Burns, Frank DiStassio, Jimmy Weldon, Phil Descalfani, Murray Flicker and Russell Spoto. The Ladies Auxiliary also was active in the festivities.

Phil Berman, former Paterson, N.J., light-heavyweight, member of Ring 9, is with the State Police in New Jersey. Ring 9 members Ronnie Burns and Joey Harrison are state referees.

In the Ring 9 elections, George Larkin was chosen president for 1965-66, with Pat Conte as vice president, Sal Scozaro 2nd v.p., Jimmy Weldon corresponding secretary, this writer as financial secretary, Mike Castano as treasurer and K.O. Jimmy Kollarik and Phil Terris as sergeants-at-arms.

Ring 14 of Hudson County also held elections, with Allie Tedesco chosen president. Bucky Keyes became vice president, Mickey Esposito corresponding secretary, Willie Mack financial secretary, Irish Tommy Brady treasurer and Johnny Ardito and Charley Korikorian sergeants-at-arms. Stanley Poreda, who fought the best of the heavies in the '30s, is a policeman in Jersey City. Poreda is honorary president of Hudson County's Ring 14.

The 1965 convention of the National V.B.A. has been definitely set for October 1-2-3 in Allentown, Pa.

The N.V.B.A. recently did some altering of its rules, regulations and by-laws. Originally, the organization admitted only ex-boxers, but through the years has gradually taken in promoters, managers, trainers, referees and others associated with the trade. Now it is accepting even boxing writers.

Harry Pegg of Philadelphia amassed a tremendous photo gallery during his 17 years as editor of the Veteran Boxers Magazine, and he is planning to assemble 50 or more camera shots of the more historic personalities and put them into an attractive pictorial that should have a popular appeal to boxing fans, old and new. His "art" display will feature fighters all the way back to Matty Matthews, and will include photos of Jack Johnson, Jim Jeffries, Gunboat Smith, Billy Papke, Georges Carpentier, Les Darcy, Philadelphia Jack O'Brien, Kid McCoy, Benny Leonard, Jack Britton, Lew Tendler, Stanley Ketchel, Willie Ritchie, and others who have contributed so much through the years to boxing lore and tradition. Pegg plans to sell his pictorial for $3.50. For those who may be interested, Harry can be contacted at 7345 North 21st Street, Philadelphia, Pa., 19138.

The slate of officers for Ring 25, embracing Essex, Union and Morris Counties in New Jersey, is headed by Charley Fusari, president. Dr. Max Novich is vice president; Benny Cross 2nd v.p.; Johnny Alessio, executive secretary; Bernie Hersh, corresponding secretary; Bill Poland, financial secretary; Eddie Durino, treasurer, and Paul Cortlyn and Roscie Manning, sergeants-at-arms.

BOXING WEIRDOS
(Continued from page 50)

● ● ● On March 18, 1955, Fred Powell was knocked out by Willie Hearn in a heavyweight bout at New Bedford, Mass. Fred certainly asked for it. Powell protested when the referee gave Hearn the decision after eight rounds. He insisted he had signed to box a ten-round bout. Hearn was willing to continue. He knocked out Powell in the tenth round.

● ● ● In 1961, when Ralph Dupas fought Guy Sumlin at Mobile, Ala., one of the officials turned in a scorecard that read: Dupas, 1 round; Sumlin, 7 rounds; even 3 rounds. This was a TEN round bout.

● ● ● Some years ago, Walter Wazel at the last minute withdrew from a bout with Ernie Memilli at Quincy, Mass. Wezel's manager substituted for him and knocked out Memilli in the second round.

● ● ● On Jan. 3, 1964, Jose Gonzales, middleweight, charged that during his bout with Jose Torres at Madison Square Garden, referee Zach Clayton continually scratched him when he broke the boxers.

● ● ● On March 29, 1957, in a preliminary bout at the Rollaway Arena in Revere, Mass., Al Rose, Brookline, Mass., and Dick McCarthy, Medford, Mass., saw their openings at the same time. Both tossed right hand blows. Both went down for nine counts. Both got up at the same time. Rose received a technical knockout at 1:10 of the second round.

● ● ● Some years ago in London, Alex Buxton weighed in at nearly an ounce over the limit for his British light-heavyweight title bout with Randy Turpin. Buxton made the weight limit after shaving off his mustache. Turpin won with a technical kayo in the fifth.

"College Boxing's Last Round" - March 1968

March 1968

COLLEGE BOXING'S LAST ROUND

All efforts to revive a long-dead sport seem to have failed. The final stand may be on the West Coast, where the California Collegiate Boxing Conference still slugs away. But it is only shadowboxing **by MARTIN KANE**

In a nation which accepts a bloody war in Vietnam and which fatalistically awaits the prospect of summer riots, it is paradoxical to discover that, except in four Far Western colleges, we have developed a squeamishness about intercollegiate boxing competition. Too brutal and dangerous, the explanation is, though that is not the full explanation. College boxing used to be a great and respected sport, with benefits to its participants far outweighing its dangers—just like football, lacrosse, hockey and so many others. But now it is done for in the East, the Middle West, the South and the Northwest, in all of which it once flourished. Its prospects for national revival, perhaps for survival, are just about nil.

The four U.S. colleges in which intercollegiate boxing still survives are the University of California at Berkeley, Chico (Calif.) State, Nevada and Stanford. Last weekend, after a season of dual meets, they participated, almost self-consciously, in the California Collegiate Boxing Conference Championships at Cal's Harmon Gymnasium and drew a total of 1,000 enthusiasts for the two nights of competition. This is not to be compared to football attendance, to be sure, but at Chico State and Nevada boxing outdraws basketball, attracting capacity crowds of 3,500 to their matches.

Boxing is a fully accepted and respectable sport at all four schools at which it persists on an intercollegiate basis. The conference was formed in 1959, in part because of discontent among the founders about the way intercollegiate boxing was being conducted nationally and because of a well-founded prescience that the sport was headed for disaster if certain practices were continued. (Nevada was not an original member but was invited in about the same time that California Polytech, the University of Santa Clara and the University of San Francisco dropped out. The word "California" nevertheless stayed in the title.)

Before the fall of national college boxing, signs of impending disaster were there, all right, though mostly ignored. It is hard to put a brake to the momentum of high-level competition. As boxing advanced in popularity and gates increased, ambitious coaches began to recruit highly experienced amateurs from the Golden Gloves and AAU clubs, some of the boxers with as many as 50 bouts or more behind them. Result: kids who wanted to take up boxing only after they entered college were sadly outclassed by the semiprofessionals—many of whom wanted to become full professionals after graduation.

Art Lentz, now executive director of the U.S. Olympic Committee, was once sports-news director at the University of Wisconsin, where boxing was very big a decade ago and now is discontinued. Lentz has this to say about the decline of intercollegiate boxing: "The pool room element had come in and changed the atmosphere of college boxing. People talked about going to see the fights, not bouts, when they went to college matches."

To counteract this trend, the CCBC effectively eliminated recruiting by adopting a rule that no student could compete in intercollegiate boxing who, after his 16th birthday, engaged in competitive bouts under auspices other than those of his school. Today a CCBC boxer may be awarded a grant-in-aid, amounting to $81.25 a quarter at the University of California, to pay his registration fees, but that is just about it. The grant is never promised as an inducement to go out for boxing. Instead, the varsity is chosen from the ranks of intramural boxers, all novices who box for the fun of it. College boxing nowadays is among the very purest of sports.

The rest of the college-boxing world was not impressed by dangers inherent in the situation until 1960, the year after CCBC got started, when Charlie Mohr, a star member of the University of Wisconsin boxing team, collapsed in his dressing room during the finals of the 23rd annual National Collegiate Athletic Association tournament at Madison. Eight days later he died of a brain hemorrhage.

Mohr and his opponent, Stu Bartell of San Jose State, wore padded headgear and the requisite 12-ounce gloves, which are supposed to be protective. In the eyes of those present, Bartell's punch, which landed on Mohr's left temple, was not a particularly good one, though it knocked Mohr down. He was up at the count of two, considered to be a good sign, and the referee found his eyes clear. He told the referee he felt all right. He moved around well for about half a minute. Then, as Bartell began to punch him once more, the referee moved in and stopped the bout, partly on the principle that Mohr had little or no chance to win. No one suspected that he was seriously hurt. But he was, and when he died college coaches saw what was coming. "I think college boxing is now finished," one said, and another chimed in with the prediction that "this will kill college boxing."

It pretty well did, even on an intramural scale. Daryl Talken, Chico State heavyweight of those days, now a high school English teacher at Fremont, Calif., recently undertook a national survey to find out what had happened to college boxing. He discovered that less than one-third of colleges have even an intramural program.

Nor is there any indication that the condition will improve. None of the four college coaches still functioning in intercollege boxing—Ed Nemir of California, who has been at it for 35 years, all at Cal, of which he is a graduate; Willie Simmons of Chico State; Jim Olivas of Nevada; and Ray Lunny of Stanford

Continued on Next page

53

1968

Continued from previous page

A diehard crowd of 500 watches as the home team takes four of the title bouts in Harmon Gymnasium at the University of California at Berkeley.

—has much hope that in their career time the sport will revert to its former glory. "Nobody will listen," said Nemir. "We don't try anymore."

Representatives of two Eastern universities where boxing once was big agree with Nemir. Roy Simmons, for 30 years the boxing coach at Syracuse, whose teams compiled a 107-49-14 won-lost record, has, at the request of Eddie Dooley, New York State's boxing commissioner, tried to revive the sport—with no takers. And William W. Cobey, director of athletics at the University of Maryland, says, "All in all, there is no talk of bringing boxing back, and I have no desire to see it come back."

It is all true and all too bad. The CCBC championships last weekend at California were both exciting to watch and a credit to those who conducted the program—with every possible protection for the athletes. At the same time it was no sissy exhibition. There were four knockouts in the 21 bouts of the finals and semifinals, but no one was seriously hurt. The victims, indeed, invariably walked out of the ring grinning sheepishly.

In the Olympic fashion, the meet does not recognize—officially, that is—a team winner, and only individual victors are honored with trophies. But it may as well be noted that Cal scored four victories in the finals, as did Nevada, and Chico had one. Stanford, which brought only three boxers to the tournament, went winless.

Despite the pessimism of intercollegiate boxing's adherents, the colleges might consider the wishes of their students in regard to the sport. At Nevada, when it was proposed to give up boxing, the question was put to a student vote. Boxing won 885 to 87, and some of the 87 said later that the question was phrased ambiguously or they would have voted otherwise. The faculty voted for it, too.

But at the University of Wisconsin where Charlie Mohr died, the faculty stand has not changed. Athletic Director Ivy Williamson says, "There have been no pressures or interest to restore boxing here. I have not even heard any interest recently expressed among other colleges."

It will take more interest and effort than seems extant to get college boxing off the canvas. **END**

February 1969

Cal Boxers to Continue After Coach Nemir's Death

By FRANK McDERMOTT

An atmosphere of shock and dismay pervaded the Cal Boxing Team's workout Monday afternoon, following the tragic death, Saturday night in Reno, of the Bears' long-time coach, Ed Nemir. Nemir died of a heart attack suffered at ringside moments after his son Phil had scored a decision over his Nevada opponent in the 139-pound bout. He was 58.

Funeral for the beloved dean of American collegiate boxing coaches will be held at 11 a.m. Wednesday at the Oak Park Hills Chapel in Walnut Creek.

Gary Evers, Junior letterman at 147 pounds, perhaps best summed up the feelings of his teammates. "Coach Nemir kept at this for 35 years," he said, "and I just don't see how I could quit now, even if I wanted to."

The entire Bear squad was quiet and subdued as they arrived for practice Monday afternoon. Ron Dell'Immagine, who takes over the reigns for the pugilists for the balance of the season, held a squad meeting before practice and told of his talk with Athletic Director Paul Brechler.

Brechler expressed belief to Dell'Immagine that Coach Nemir would have wanted nothing other than for the team to continue the season. "This is what he lived for," said the Bear's acting mentor, "and it's what he died doing. So we'll at least finish out the season."

Nemir had been boxing coach at California since 1933. Before that he had boxed as an undergrad for the Bears, winning the Pacific Coast Championship at 129 pounds. He entered UC Law School, eventually graduating with distinction in 1933.

While a law student, wrestling came to occupy an important part of his attention, and he went on to win a Silver Medal in the Olympic Games at Los Angeles in 1932, wrestling in the 134-pound division. Upon graduating from law school, Nemir decided that a career on the bar wasn't for him, and accepted the post that he held until his death.

The death of Nemir raises several questions regarding the future of collegiate boxing.

Ed Nemir fought for the existence of boxing in the collegiate ranks on a purely novice basis. In 1959, disturbed by the trend in collegiate boxing towards vigorous recruiting of Golden Glove boxers, Nemir broke away from the Pacific Coast Boxing Conference and became one of the dominant figures in the organization of the new California Collegiate Boxing Conference.

Nemir fought for and saw passed a novice rule for the new CCBC. The rule states that no student can compete in intercollegiate boxing who engages in competitive bouts other than under the auspices of a school after his 16th birthday. He was fond of saying that he looked first for enthusiasm in an athlete, and then to the skills of the sport.

Nemir was proud of the safety factors introduced by the CCBC. The gloves were made larger to absorb some of the impact and the headgear was improved to prevent eye cuts and "cauliflower ears."

Nemir's eyes used to glow with pride when he talked about the special mats under the canvas of the boxing ring. "Hitting your head on this mat would be like falling on a feather pillow," he said. "An egg thrown in the air will bounce rather than break when it hits the canvas."

Possibly the most important danger in boxing is the mismatch. If a boxer with ring experience gets into the ring with a beginner with little or no actual boxing experience, there is often a danger of injury. Nemir made no qualms about it, however, if he thought that one of his boxers was not ready to face his opponent the boxer wouldn't even be permitted in the ring.

Another factor in the CCBC policy was to stop a match quickly if one boxer was getting too much of an upper hand. Some people thought some of the fights were stopped a bit prematurely, but Nemir and the other coaches emphasized safety above everything else.

California became a power in intercollegiate boxing under Ed Nemir. His teams over the years compiled an excellent record of 120 dual meet wins against only 61 losses.

ED NEMIR

ED NEMIR ... Cal boxing coach for over thirty years is shown here as Pacific Coast Featherweight Champion during his intercollegiate days.

Dick Carter Article: Cal Boxing's Transition After Coach Ed Nemir

CAL BOXING'S TRANSITION AFTER COACH ED NEMIR
By Dick Carter - Cal Boxing, 1969
April 7, 2011

I knew that my 1968/69 senior year at Cal was going to be a year of transition, but, like so many things in life, it didn't go as I had envisioned. The Vietnam War was still extremely hot with high levels of American casualties, and protests were a regular feature on the Berkeley campus. The draft had been instated and life and death were part of our student concerns.

However, I was a Marine officer candidate in the Cal NROTC unit, so my future seemed to be pretty well defined. I would box on the Boxing team, complete my senior year, go to Quantico, Virginia to get my Marine commission and see what would happen next. Chances were good that it would be going to Vietnam.

All these expectations started to change on an early 1969 winter night in Reno, Nevada during the Cal boxing match with the University of Nevada. After 40 years that night is a blur for me today. I had finished my fight, and about midway through the card I noticed that something was happening in our Cal corner at ringside. Coach Nemir had collapsed. There was a frenzy of activity. The next thing I knew the rest of the match was cancelled and people were leaving the gym. It all seemed to happen very quickly.

The only other thing I remember of that night was us Cal boxers standing in front of our Reno hotel trying to make sense of what had happened. We knew that Coach had died of a heart attack, but we didn't know what was going to happen next. We flew back to the Bay Area to start picking up the pieces.

Coach Nemir was a wonderful man and coach. He loved his boxers and we loved him. I think like many Cal boxers he was like a second father for me. His death was extremely emotional for us. Preparations for Coach's funeral started and I remember going to it in Pleasant Hill during the following week. Lots of people attended, and again, it was emotional for all of us.

However, even before the funeral, the team had to make a decision. The next weekend we were scheduled to fight Chico State in Berkeley. Our emotions were extremely high. I felt like a tightly coiled spring. However, we knew the PE Department was not supportive of boxing and we didn't want to give them any opportunity to terminate our program. Additionally, we felt that Coach Nemir would want us to keep fighting. After all, that's what we did. So, we decided to box and did, but it was hard.

Ron Dell'Immagine, a former Cal Boxer who was in grad school getting his teaching credential, was our assistant coach under Coach Nemir. Ron became our head coach for the rest of the season. It was a difficult time, but Ron did a great job getting us through it.

I fought at 132 pounds, which was about ten pounds below my natural weight. We had Phil Nemir at 139 and Gary Evers at 147, both excellent boxers, so my spot on the team had to be at 132. Each week I had to go without meals and fluids to make weight. After each fight I would eat like a starving man. It was hard on my body, but I wanted to box and that's what I had to do.

As the season went on I became increasingly aware of a pain in my rib cage. I thought I had a slightly cracked rib, but it wasn't enough to stop me from boxing; especially after what we had experienced. We finished the season with the conference championships (I think they were at Chico) and the 1968/69 Cal Boxing season was finally over.

That weekend on Sunday night I came home to my parents' house, and felt like I was coming down with the flu, but I drove back to campus after dinner. By Monday night I knew I was really sick, and went back to my parents' house. Over the next couple of days, I was diagnosed with tuberculosis. The pain in my side had been the early symptoms. I had three weeks of fever, but it finally broke after hitting 104 and I got better. I was able to go to our team end-of-season lunch (I think it was at the Nemirs.) and it was great being with my teammates again.

However, TB is a medical condition that disqualifies you for military service, so I was not going into the Marines after all. During the next three months I was able to finish my incomplete winter classes, apply and be accepted to the Cal Business School's MBA program for the next fall. Truck Cullom in the Athletic Department (another great Cal coach) got me a summer job working as a laborer on a highway construction crew, starting the very next day after graduation.

When I returned I returned to Berkeley in the fall I was surprised when I walked into Harmon Gym and saw that "the Boxing Room" was no longer our room. The PE Department was not offering boxing classes and had turned our room into something else. The returning boxers, who included Phil Nemir and Gary Evers, wanted to continue to box, and we found other students who did too. Paul McNally, our 1969 teammate, had also graduated and was getting his teaching credential. We petitioned the Athletic Department to let us field a team for the 1969/70 season. The Athletic Director, Paul Breckler, agreed. Paul was the head coach and I was the assistant coach. Here's what the Blue and Gold had to say about our season.

"Boxing: And Then There Were Three Intercollegiate boxing is going down for the count. What at one time was one of the most popular collegiate sports now has only three colleges in the nation fielding teams. Last year there were four, but Stanford dropped out when lack of interest killed the team. Along with Nevada and Chico State, California forms the California Intercollegiate Boxing Association, the only such conference in the nation. For awhile, it looked like Nevada and Chico might be the only teams left. After Ed Nemir, coach and guiding force behind collegiate boxing, died at ringside last year, things looked dark. Paul McNally, a three year boxer for California and now a teacher in the area, assumed the job as coach, but found himself lacking almost everything but boxers with plenty of desire. Intramural boxing and boxing classes, the traditional source of talent, were dropped. The old boxing room was changed into a wrestling room, and the PE department seemed to turn deaf ears to the athletes. But Paul Brechler vowed to continue the sport if student interest remained. First the team moved into a tent on the roof of Harmon Gym, and then into a tiny room in the basement. Because of the room problems, the team had trouble training and was behind the other conference teams from the start. They did manage to win four while losing only three, for a winning record. Gary Evers and Phil Nemir, son of the late coach, battled to championships in the league tournament."

I remember how small our room in the basement of Harmon was. There wasn't room for a ring or bags. It was so small that some of the boxers had to spar in the hall outside of the room. It was not ideal, but with quality boxers like Phil and Gary we had a competitive, credible team.

However, the next season, 1970/71, was a real challenge. Phil and Gary had graduated and gone to graduate school. Athletic Director Brechler was under fire over the ineligibility of Isaac

Curtis, a football and track star. The NCAA didn't like the Berkeley campus much at the time and the issue resulted in Brechler stepping down. Paul McNally took a full time teaching position, and the PE Department didn't even give us the little room in Harmon. The one bright spot was that Brian Kahn, another 1969 teammate and a very good boxer, had returned to campus from a Sears Roebuck store manager training program to attend Boalt Law School. Sears suffered a huge loss, but it was great to have Brian back at Cal.

I had been attending the Athletic Department's coaches meeting and it was decided that since I was a "student of Ed Nemir," and had been the assistant coach the prior year, they would let me be head coach for 1970/71 and let us have a team. They even paid me $200 for the season. Ray Willsey, the Cal Football coach, had been named the interim Athletic Director. I remember Brian and me meeting with him and Coach Willsey telling us that the minor sports at Cal would someday have to have their "day of reckoning." Some of our loyal alumni including Sol Silverman, a prominent San Francisco attorney, kept the pressure on the Athletic Department to keep the boxing program.

Somehow we got the word out that there was still a Cal Boxing team and got a good group of inexperienced guys to come out for the team. We didn't have a room, but I was able to get my NROTC instructors to let us practice in the gun bay at the NROTC's Callahan Hall. We would roll out our mat and practice, and roll it up after practice. One of my concerns was that a boxer would get backed up and hit his head on one of the gun turrets in the bay. Thankfully, it never happened.

It was hard to field a team against Chico and Nevada. They still had full programs. Our inexperienced fighters didn't always fare well against them; but we did compete, and that what was most important. We had to keep Cal Boxing going in order to keep collegiate boxing alive. Here's how the Blue and Gold described the season.

"Pugilists' Inexperience Causes Subpar Season- The California boxing team did not have a very fruitful year for many reasons. Probably the most important was the lack of experience that plagued Coach Dick Carter all season. The season started off well enough, as the Cal pugilists slammed a Navy contingent from Hunter's Point by a 3-2 score. The Chico State Wildcats came to Berkeley overflowing with talent and experience—and a strange style both irritating to fight against and to watch. The Wildcats played it cozy and won 9-3. Nevada's Wolfpack simply outslugged the overmatched Cal men and defeated the Bears 2 ½ to 7 1/2. Again, lack of experience cost Cal dearly. In the return match against Chico State up north, the Bears felt lucky to be on the short end of a 1 ½ to 10 1/2 score considering the way the scoring went. The Laney Eagles stepped in over their heads and absorbed a 10-0 shellacking, even though their lack of experience matched the Bears' own. Playing it a little cagey at last, the boxers held their own against murderous Nevada in Las Vegas; losing 4 ½ to 6 1/2 in a match that saw three matches which could have gone either way."

My MBA program was suppose to last two years, but I stayed around for another semester in the fall of 1971 to take some additional classes and coach the team. Brian was in his second year at Boalt and continued as the assistant coach. The team was fortunate to have three good recruits from the football team. Paul Maurice Girody was a French Canadian from British Columbia. He was an exceptionally strong and athletic linebacker and heavyweight. Paul loved to hit people and had considerable fighting experience outside the ring. After Cal, Paul played in the Canadian Professional Football League.

Fortunately, Paul got his football teammate and fraternity brother, Stan Stenak, to be his practice partner and our #2 heavyweight. Stan was a delightful, good-looking guy and fierce competitor. He once was charged with 90 yards of personal foul penalties in a Cal JV football game. The only reason he wasn't ejected from the game was that there weren't enough other Cal players to continue the game if he was kicked out. Stan also saved me from a much-larger-than-me drunk with a broken beer bottle in a West Point, NY bar after a Cal/Army football game, but that's another story for another history.

Scott Stringer was a Cal football defensive back, who played football for the St. Louis Cardinals after Cal. Scott was our light heavyweight. These three and some other smaller, but equally fine young men comprised a solid squad.

We also had a terrific set of assistant coaches. Brian Kahn was a classic boxer in the Coach Nemir style. Brian is a wonderful person. It has been a great privilege to have Brian as a friend for all these years. In addition, two local professional boxers found our team and volunteered to work with us. One was Sonny Mills, a former California State Heavyweight Champ. It was terrific to have him work out with Paul and Stan because I didn't want to!

Another great resource and coach was former Cal boxer and longtime supporter, Paul Rein. Paul is one of the toughest boxers to ever put on a Cal jersey. Paul had finished law school at Boalt, but still wanted to put on the gloves. He worked our guys in practice like it was a bout and we were better boxers for it.

There was great joy the day that the Athletic Department said we could have a storage room on the west side of Edwards Track Stadium for a practice room. It was going to be our new home. We got a crew together with crowbars and ripped out all the pinewood storage shelves to clear the space to create our room. We put up our practice ring, and we even had running water right there in the room. You see the backs of the women's restroom toilet tanks were exposed in our room. We could wash out our mouthpieces whenever we wanted. We had our room and everything was great until the winter rains came. We then discovered that the seal in the Edwards concrete stands above our room leaked badly. Water poured into our room and on to the matt in our ring, but there was nothing we could do about it. We put on our sweats and practiced.

Fielding a team and practicing in our spaces were challenges, but so was finding other teams to fight. Our only competition was Chico, Nevada and the 12th Naval District. In 1972 to give our boxers an additional fight we decided to have an alumni versus varsity set of exhibitions. The feature of the night was our heavyweight, Paul Girody, against Cal Hall of Fame boxer, Tom Gioseffi. Tom had been out of school for about six years and was outweighed by 25 pounds, but he gracefully controlled the fight in what was an entertaining, but physical exhibition. The San Francisco newspaper reported on the bout and gave our boxing program some nice publicity.

Another memorable bout was in one in our match against Navy. It was an exhibition between our alum coach Paul Rein and a Navy fighter who had about a twenty pound advantage on Paul. We learned later that the Navy boxer was their district heavyweight champ. As you would expect with Paul, it was a take-no-prisoners affair and Paul more than held his own. To this day, Paul reminds me of the bout and the situation that I unknowingly put him in. However, I have no doubt that this fight was one of the highlights of Paul's boxing career and happiest days of his life.

I remember our inexperienced team going to Reno for a match with crusty old Jimmy Olivas' Nevada squad of seasoned boxers. Nevada's raised ring and full gym of yelling-for-blood fans were in stark contrast to what Cal boxers experienced at home, but we competed.

It is important to realize that keeping the Cal Boxing program alive was important not only for the Cal boxers and Cal, but also for the Nevada and Chico programs; and, as it turned out, the future programs at western US schools and their boxers. They needed Cal as a competitor to keep their programs alive. The future of boxing on the West Coast depended on us continuing to fight.

I had prolonged my MBA studies so that I could coach another season and find a real job. Towards the end of 1971 Procter & Gamble offered me a marketing position in Cincinnati. I know being Cal's Varsity Boxing Coach and what we had experienced were the primary reasons that P&G offered me a job. They let me finish out the season before I started work.

The conference championship was in Reno in March 1972. The team flew to Reno, and I packed up my belongings in my VW and drove to meet Brian Kahn and the team there. After the matches I said good bye to everyone and started driving to Cincinnati. Honestly, I don't remember how the team did at the championships, but it really didn't matter. Cal Boxing had fought a much harder fight for the prior three years and we had won this first round of keeping Cal Boxing alive.

Brian had another year of law school and he was the head coach the next couple of seasons; one of which he directed Cal to a conference championship. After Brian got his law degree and a full-time job, Phil Nemir returned to coach the team and then Mike Huff, a Cal Boxing conference champion, succeeded Phil for a set of seasons. This was a wonderful set of interim coaches for Cal Boxing.

When Mike moved on to more responsibilities within the Cal Athletic Department, the reins of Cal Boxing were turned over to another former Cal Boxing champ, Jim Riksheim. No one could have imagined how fortunate Cal Boxing and his hundreds of Cal boxers have been to have such a wonderfully steadfast and loyal leader as Jim Riksheim. I know Coach Nemir would have been proud of Cal boxers who continued Cal Boxing after his 30+ year tenure, and especially Jim. His devotion to Cal Boxing is truly remarkable and a great gift to all of us.

2004

Dick Carter and Paul Rein at the 2004 Cal Boxing Reunion

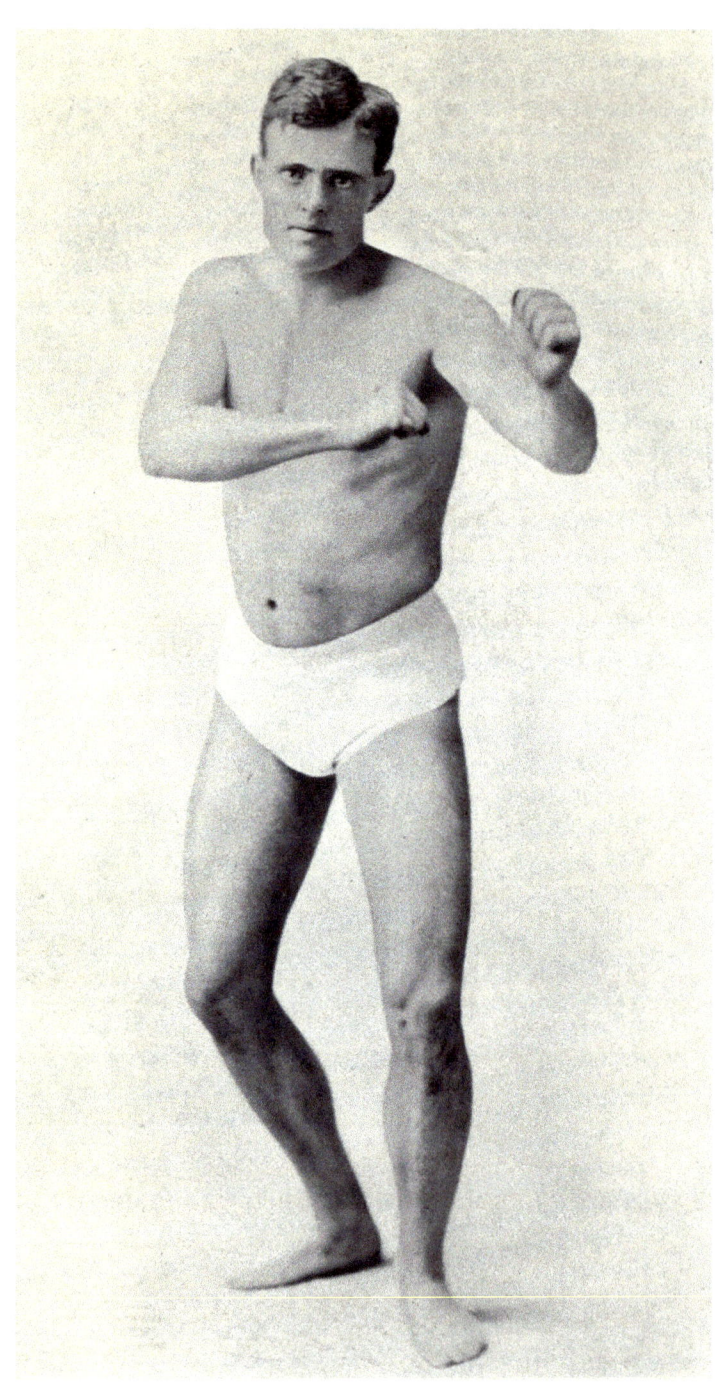

Boxing enthusiast Jack London in a 1904 photo by Arnold Genthe. Although Jack London attended Cal for at least one semester, there is no record indicating whether Jack London ever boxed at Cal.

1910-1915

The Beginnings of the Cal Boxing Team: The Polyducean Club

Prior to 1916, there was a club on campus, The Polydeucean Club, which was "devoted to the interest of boxing among the students of the University," and which focused on "the opportunity to receive some scientific training at the Club Quarters in the Gymnasium." In 1910, it held "two very successful boxing exhibitions...of several lively bouts by both Club Members and Professionals." The 1910 President was Marion Seevers. The 1911 President was M.W. Schuman, and the club boasted "nearly 30 members." In 1913, and 1914, the club continued its activities, with Walter Christie as a trainer, and "entertained with an exhibition of thirty-six rounds of boxing" in an effort in "increasing the interest of the University in the art of self defense." "It is through this organization alone that the sport of boxing is maintained." By 1915, there were "over forty members and the services of a permanent Coach have been enlisted."

By 1916, the club had added 15 new members. R.H. Sheridan, formerly middleweight champion of the Seattle Athletic Club, has taken hold of the instruction and made extensive improvements." The Club "was started in 1907 and has held forth in the basement of Harmon Gym ever since."

However, 1916 also marks the first verified Intercollegiate competition, and we therefore date the Boxing Team's creation from 1916. (See 1916 article by Donald Lawton, page 4.)

1910

Polydeucean Club

POLYDEUCEAN CLUB is, as its name implies, an organization devoted to the interest of boxing among the students of the University. A competent instructor has been secured by the Club, so that the members are now afforded an opportunity to receive some scientific training at the Club quarters in the Gymnasium. During the year two very successful boxing exhibitions were given, which consisted of several lively bouts by both the Club members and professionals.

OFFICERS

	First Term	Second Term
President	Marion B. Seevers, '09	Fred Searls, Jr., '09
Vice-President	Fred Searls, Jr., '09	Walter R. Johns, '09
Secretary-Treasurer	Clarence E. Black, '09	Hugh S. O'Neil, '10

Tribunal

Harvey L. Davis, '09 — Eugene L. Ickes, '09 — Milton H. Seelig, '09
Clarence E. Black, '09 — Roy E. Drake, '10

1915

Polydeucean Club Organized to enable its members to become more skilful in the art of boxing, the Polydeucean Club has taken long strides during the past year as is testified by the rapid increase in membership. There are now over forty names on the roll; the services of a permanent coach have been enlisted. Under his direction workouts have been held daily, resulting in encouraging gains in proficiency. In the Boxing and Gymnastic Carnival of last semester the members of the club gave some clean-cut exhibitions.

The officers of the club are: President, Carroll Searls '15; Vice-president, J. L. McKim '15; Secretary-treasurer, R. T. Hazzard '15.

1919

Boxing

The California glove men tied the Cardinals in the speediest game of fisticuffs that has been seen for years between the two teams. A. L. Picetti knocked out his man in the 115-pound go, while H. C. Whittlesey, a 125-pounder, decidedly outclassed his Cardinal opponent and knocked him out after a one-minute walk. Covington and Baker lost the 135- and 145-pound matches by decisions, as likewise did F. W. Huntington in the 158-pounder bout. The most interesting event of the evening was the battle between H. A. Mazzera and Kegley of Stanford. The latter received a doubtful decision after a hard exchange of blows. The heavyweight and lightweight bouts were forfeited by Stanford by lack of entries.

Wrestling

A long-delayed date for the meet with Stanford and the misunderstanding over the eligibility of one of the California men was the only thing that saved the Cardinals from a severe drubbing at the mat meet held in Harmon Gymnasium on the night of April 10th. The men had to be released from training before the meet, and it was not until a short time before the bout that it was known to Coach Andrews that George Iki was ineligible, due to his fourth year of competition. MacManus, who was in decidedly poor trim and had not planned to compete, was substituted and lasted his round out, but lost the decision. Stanford was represented in this and the 125-pound and 115-pound events by Japanese who were very much more mature than our lightweight men and captured all three events. A reverse came when Charles Farrel, 158-pounder, and Tom Gibson, 175-pounder, laid their Cardinal opponents on the mat in a little over one minute. Stanford forfeited the 145-pound and unlimited grapples to Brown and Gordon, giving both teams four matches.

Blue & Gold

1920s

The Cal Boxing teams of 1920-1923 were members of the "Wonder Teams" which did not lose a single intercollegiate match during the first four years of the 1920s.

THE BOXING SQUAD

BOXING

CALIFORNIA boxers, under the able training of the veteran conditioner and former phenomenal favorite of the middleweight ring, Stanley Jones, easily dominated all rival ringsters this year and captured the California intercollegiate championship.

Meets with Davis Farm, University of Southern California and Stanford provided excellent workouts for Jones' proteges. The first U. S. C. meet was held in the south on March 17th. California easily won by taking three of the four bouts. The return meet held in Harmon Gymnasium April 8th, proved even better for the Bears, two of the three matches won, being ended by the knockout route.

The "big meet" with Stanford on March 11th once more returned the California-Stanford intercollegiate title to the wearers of the Blue and Gold. As in all four big meets of the season, shifty footwork coordinated with lightning blows and excellent head work won the majority of the bouts for California. Coach Jones says he is more than satisfied. "We had some fights," he grins, "but I guess we showed them."

Page 284

THE BOXING SEASON

TO Stanley Jones goes the credit for turning out not only a winning boxing team, but one which has not lost a match all season. Two matches apiece were held with Davis Farm, Southern Branch, and University of Southern California; of these matches California won all but two by 5 out of 7 bouts.

As Stanford defaulted the boxing matches to California, the University of Southern California bouts were made the basis for Circle "C", awards, which were as follows; S. Silverman '23, captain; E. Jones '23 K. Gow '24, J. Moran '24, G. Reed '24, T. Thompson '24, R. Bowers '25, J. O'Donnell '24, R. Caldwell '25, F. Garner '25, S. Quackenbush '25.

Varsity Boxing Team

BOXING

CALIFORNIA has always been represented by a strong aggregation of boxers, especially during the last few years. This season was no exception to the rule which had previously been laid. Although winning one match with Davis and losing the other, the Bear fighters made a fine showing.

Kenneth L. Gow '24, captain of the squad, performed admirably, winning both of his bouts. Sammy Gold '27 also set a fine pace by carrying off the honors in his matches.

In the first Aggies-California bouts, which were held February 28 in Harmon Gymnasium, the matches were marked by speedy blows and fast footwork. A large crowd was in attendance, and the bleachers built up around the ring were packed. California won this meet by the score of 4 to 3.

The second match with the Aggies did not turn out so well for the Bears. After a somewhat slower program of boxing, the Bruin squad emerged with the short end of the score, 3 to 4. This meet occurred at Davis Farm on March 21.

On April 4 the team met the Southern Branch at Los Angeles. The Grizzlies put up plenty of opposition and gave the Bear squad hard fights in every match. The entire California team put up excellent fights. The clever footwork and shifty punching of Captain Gow were a treat to the large audience of boxing fans that thronged the Southern Branch gymnasium. This was the last match to be held this year. The Varsity boxing team defeated the Southern Branch squad by the score of 6 to 2, thus proving that California had produced another successful team. Much credit is due Manager Barlow for the fine way in which the matches were arranged and for the splendid way that the men were taken care of on the trip to Los Angeles.

Stanley A. Jones coached the squad, and it is through "Stan" that it received its spirit and technique. He will have a fairly large squad back again next year, and with additions from the Freshman Class, California should have another excellent season.

The following is the personnel: Kenneth L. Gow '24, George Reed '24, Raymond Bowers '25, William Meadows '26, Lewis Lecara '26, Lester Rapheld '26, Robert Tobey '26, Glenn Cherry '27, and Samuel Gold '27.

Fred Barlow '25 was manager, and he was assisted by Charles O. Busick '26 and William Sesnon '26.

Varsity Boxing Team

VARSITY BOXING AND FENCING TEAMS

THREE victories and one defeat mark the accomplishments of the California Varsity boxing team for this season. With a greater interest shown in the interclass bouts than ever before, Coach Stanley Jones was able to pick a winning squad. The team lost their first match to the California Aggies, but defeated the Davis Farm boxers later in a return match. The Bears won from the Southern Branch fighters both in Los Angeles and in Berkeley. Captain Bob Tobey '27 won the popularity of the crowds everywhere by registering knockouts in every meet. Coach Jones predicts another banner season next year.

Having defeated the Italian Club, and made a creditable display of swordsmanship in other preliminary matches, the California fencers hoped to win from Stanford, but although individual members showed up well, the Bruin foilsmen were beaten by the Cardinals on March 6th. Captain-elect A. Montin '27 and D. Antoshkin '26 were awarded circle letters for winning three out of five bouts. Coach B. Von Arnold '27 is responsible for a large part of the success that the team enjoyed in the American Amateur Fencing League bouts, the Bear fencers having placed second in the central California division championships.

Varsity Fencing Team

BLUE & GOLD

VARSITY BOXING TEAM

Moulding a winning team after many injuries and other setbacks, Coach Stanley Jones must be given a great deal of credit for the seasons success. The boxers lost their dual meet with U. C. L. A. by 4 to 3 but they took the measure of the California Aggies on two occasions. The meets with the Aggies were both won by a score of 5 to 2. California's big success came when they won the Pacific intercollegiate meet held at Stanford, where they gathered 16 points and their runner-up only obtained 12 points. In this meet California met and defeated the best from all the western colleges, and revenged themselves against U. C. L. A. for the previous defeat. Glen Cherry, a three year man, and Frank Ribbel proved themselves intercollegiate champions.

The men who received their Circle "C" awards were Cherry, Germino, Captain Gold, Grossman, Iserquin, Kobayashi, Parish, Ribbel, Rodriquez, and Manager Surenmosesian.

By virtue of winning the intercollegiate title, interest in boxing is greatly augmented for the coming year.

BOXING MATCH IN HARMON

1928

THE VARSITY BOXING SQUAD

VARSITY boxing started during the first part of the spring semester with the interclass boxing tourney, held February 16th. Led by Captain Frank Ribbel, last year's coast champion in his weight, and Coach Stan Jones, former middleweight champion, the California pugilists proved their worth in several bouts. Members of the California boxing team participated in the minor sports carnival held at Los Angeles on March 30th and 31st. The team met U. S. C. and U. C. L. A. in the South. The meet with Stanford, held March 9th, was won by the Bear team with a score of 5-2.

Varsity wrestling was coached this year by Henry Stone, who was captain of the wrestling team two years ago. Wrestlers contested with the University of Southern California and University of California at Los Angeles in the minor sports carnival.

THE VARSITY WRESTLING TEAM

1929

BOXING TEAM
Lewis (*Mgr.*), Ansberry, Nemir, Kindig, Dubecker, Ribbel (*Capt.*), Sherwood, Gribben, Garner, Nystrum, Jones (*Coach*)

BOXING California's boxing team lost its first match to Washington 4 bouts to 3. The feature bout was won by Captain Ribbel, Pacific Coast Intercollegiate champion, from Perdick, A. A. U. champion. Invading the Farm, the Bear mittmen defeated the Stanford boxers 4 matches to 3 in their first meeting. California's representatives in the bantam and light-heavyweight classes, scored knockouts in the first round. The following week the Bear sluggers trounced the Cardinals 6 bouts to 1. In their final tournament of the year the Bears won from U. C. L. A. 6 bouts to 1.

Ed Nemir third from the left.

MINOR SPORTS

VARSITY BOXING SQUAD
Jones, Walters, Nystrom, Hotopp, Magid, Garrity, Easterbrooks, Robinson, Mallory, McGrath
Searle, Davis, Dadigian, Valentine, Stevens, MacMillan, Hilton, Stone (Coach)

BOXING AND WRESTLING

WITH greater interest shown in intercollegiate boxing than ever before, the California Varsity started its tourneys during the early part of the spring semester. In the first Stanford match California boxers were defeated 4-3, but in a second meet with the Cards the Bears won 4-3. U. C. mittmen next broke into the win column when they took a 4-3 tilt from the California Aggies at Davis. The next engagement was with the University of Washington, and the Bear scrappers were forced to forfeit three bouts to the Huskies, making a score of 4-3 in the northerners' favor. The last important battle of the 1931 schedule was held with Nevada in the Stanford pavilion at Palo Alto. Earl Stevens '32 proved to be a capable captain of the Bear ringmen.

Bear wrestlers, under the tutelage of Coach Henry Stone, completed another successful season. In the past three years California grapplers have lost but one dual meet, and that occurred in a contest with Davis this semester. However, the Bear matmen twice vanquished Saint Mary's, and handed one defeat to the Aggies, the Olympic Club, and the U. S. S. Maryland. California also competed in the Far Western, P. A. A., and Intercollegiate championships. Foremost of the experienced Varsity men were Lanhanier '32, Handy '31, and Captain Libeu '31.

1933

VARSITY BOXING SQUAD
Jones (Coach), Goulard, Mazzetta, Smith, Thurston, Elvin, Mitchell, Pozzo, De Risi, Hogle, Boucher, Nemir, Pyles (Manager)
Nitta, Townsley, Dagdigian, Mierback, Jan, Louie, Moon

BOXING

VARSITY glove throwers scored five victories in matches with the California Aggies, Stanford, and S. F. U. Captain Jan, Pozzo, and Smith fought their way to decisions in the finals of the Pacific Coast Intercollegiates.

GYMNASTICS

COACH Pease's gymnasts placed third in the Minor Sports Carnival finals. In other competition, the Bears tied for third in the A. A. U. meet and unexpectedly lost a close 46-44 engagement with Stanford.

VARSITY GYM SQUAD
Janssen (Manager), Janes, Sturgess, Heeley, Tucker, Becker, Rowley, Maslin, Schultz, Rogers, Bradt
Howard, Jaure, Vaccariello, Chan, Hughes

1933 Cal Boxing team (original with Ken Elvin). Ken's father, Marshall Elvin, is 5th boxer from the left, standing. In light sweater, 2nd from the right, standing up, is Ed Nemir, starting as coach.

1936

BOXING

BOXING TEAM
Back row: Luker, McDowell, Wallstrum, Smith, Duggan, Stratton.
Front row: Norgard (Manager), Derr, Fisher, Glendinning, Schweizer, Morimitsu, Nemir (Coach).

BY WINNING THE LAST two encounters and placing sixth in the Pacific Coast Intercollegiates, the California mittmen concluded their 1936 schedule in a successful manner after a mediocre showing in early season matches. A decided improvement was shown by the whole team as the season progressed, as was evidenced by victories in the second matches with the California Aggies and Stanford.

The Bears were able to win but four matches from their first opponents, the California Aggies. Stratton and Francis were winners for California by decision in the 135 and 175 pound classes respectively, while Armstrong (165) made an impressive showing by scoring a knockout. The 118 pound match was won by the Berkeley team by forfeit.

Next the Bear scrappers journeyed to Palo Alto to lose a close 6 to 5 decision to the Stanford Indians. Fowler, Indian heavyweight, defeated Thomas by a slim margin in the final and deciding match. Armstrong made his second knockout in as many matches, sending his man to the canvas with a smashing left hook early in the first round. Derr and Heron won by technical knockouts, while Morimitsu and Duggan completed the list of victors for California by gaining decisions. The Bears made their poorest showing of the year against U. C. L. A. when they lost by a 7 to 3 count. California's only wins were by default in three matches.

In the first victory of the season, California won from the Stanford Indians by a score of 6 to 5, thus earning revenge for their defeat in the earlier match at Palo Alto. The two 147 pounders, Duggan and Heron, each made technical knockouts, while Morimitsu also won by a knockout. Thomas, Stratton, and Armstrong were the other winners of the evening for California, each by decision. California likewise upset the Aggies in the second battle, winning by a wide margin of 8 to 3. Bear points included six decisions, one technical knockout by Wallstrum, and one forfeited bout.

The Bears closed their season by placing sixth in the Pacific Intercollegiate Boxing Championships at Sacramento. Washington State and U. C. L. A. tied for first place with 29 points each, followed by the University of San Francisco with 28, Stanford 12, Cal Aggies 10, California 9, San Jose State 7 and Idaho 5. The Blue and Gold sluggers made a good showing in this final match when six men reached the semi-final bouts. Morimitsu, sole Californian surviving the eliminations, lost by a close decision in his final match.

Wallstrum was elected captain of the squad for the following season at the banquet held to conclude the year's activities.

1937

Back Row: White (manager), Folsom, Wallstrum, Thomas, Mead, Heron, Shell, Schweizer, Glendinning, Derr, Nemir (coach). Front Row: Kim, Boyce.

Thomas and Dakan trade punches in the Stanford match

Captain Andy Wallstrum

Coach Eddie Nemir

BOXING

WINNING FOUR out of five matches with intercollegiate rivals and showing well in the Pacific Coast Intercollegiate and National Collegiate meets, the Blue and Gold boxing squad had a very successful season in 1937.

The Bears opened their season at Stanford where they pounded out an 8-3 victory over the Indian mittmen. Kim, Derr, Glendenning, Wallstrum, Mead, and Thomas scored knockouts over their Stanford rivals, while California's only real upset occurred when Pease decisioned Milliron in the 159-pound division. The Californians also won their second match with the Cardinals, 10-1, featuring knockouts by Derr, Mead, Thomas and Wallstrum.

The only defeat of the season was at the hands of Cal Aggies in the second match of the season by a 7-6 score, but the Bears came back later in the year to gain revenge by slugging out a 9-1 decision in a return match and winning in every weight except 139.

In their other intercollegiate match of the season, the California battlers defeated the barnstorming Arizona State College ringmen by a score of 4 to 2. This meet was rather uninteresting and there were no knockouts.

In the Pacific Coast Intercollegiates, Derr won the championship in the 129-pound class and Captain Wallstrum was runner-up at 149, while Mead, Shell, and Derr were semi-finalists in the National Collegiates which attracted the best boxers from all over the country.

1939

ED NEMIR
Coach

VARSITY SQUAD
Back Row: DuBois, Swan, Mitchell, Lord, Mead, McDowell. Front Row: Green, Cho, Droubay, Mittler, Sakanari, Nemir.

BOXING

The Varsity boxing team salvaged one victory out of their five conference matches, losing two and tying two of their remaining bouts. The pugilists were most successful against Cal Aggies, whom they once defeated and once tied. Washington State drubbed the Bears 8 to 1, and against Stanford the Bears tied one and lost one match. Individual honors went to Paul Cho, who was Pacific Coast Conference Champion at 120 pounds.

Drachnik, who later won by a decision, lands a blow on Hovey of Stanford.

Ben Pavone, Bear grappler, on top of UCLA's Captain Bruce Roberts, the bout winner.

Led by Captain Ken McNamara, the California Varsity Wrestling Team opened the year by defeating the Olympic Club. Then followed a tie match with the UCLA Bruins, a tie with the Olympic Club for the Far Western Championship, and a loss to San Jose State. The final meet of the year was the National AAU Championships held at Treasure Island, where Matsumora Fujioka won second place in the 112-pound division.

WRESTLING

HENRY STONE
Coach

VARSITY SQUAD
Back Row: Scso, Spear, Wolohan, Kympton, Schneller, White. Third Row: Bennion, Knowlton, Macres, Thompson, McNamara, Enos, Sale. Second Row: Stone, coach, Crocker, Avila, Tashima, Kavin, Endicott, Jones. Front Row: Ikeda, Hopper, Hahu, Sugino, Wada, Raski, Coffey.

1940s

1942

BACK ROW: Ferguson Mitchell, Merrick Taylor, Seymour Lewis, Ray Greenwood, Jack Thorburn, Milt Cunha
FRONT ROW: Shiro Tokuno, Bob Torney, Bob Adams, Ewald Larson, Bob Shimoff, Ed Nemir (coach)

BOXING

Finding local competition fairly easy to whip, the Bears' leather slingers took on the Washington State Cougars and dropped a 5½ to 2½ decision.

Among the Bears' victims on the home front were Stanford and the Cal Aggies, each of whom the Bears took twice, and U.C.L.A., while in the P.C.I.C. California could do no better than a tie for fourth.

Captain and top man on the Bear squad was Milt Cunha who, for the second consecutive year, took the Pacific Coast 165 pound title. Honorable mention must also go to Ray Greenwood, 175 pounds, and Ewald Larson, 135 pounds, who lost but two matches in three years of competition.

ornia's Bob Adams chucks his opponent's chin with a dainty mitt as the two demonstrate how to keep trim and how to take a trimming.

It was open season on Aggies as the Bears defeated them 6 to 4 in a return encounter.

1942

CIRCLE "C"

Shadow-boxing in front of a mirror makes boxer RAY GREENWOOD doubly dangerous. The 175 lb. fist-flinger has had great success throughout his three year pugilistic career.

79

1943

The Boxing Team

BACK ROW: Clifford Misener, Brunel Christensen, Gordon Brittle, Donald Quinn

THIRD ROW: Paul Hillinger, Donald Bell, Dick Schoenig, Bob Broxholme, Bill Fothergill, Ray Cerles

SECOND ROW: Bob Torney, Andy McKelvy, Jim Cuthbertson, Jim Wigton, Paul Ward

FRONT ROW: Coach Tom Cureton, Gus Clarke, Kong Go

1944

BOXING

BACK ROW: Bill Nourse, Walter Reinholdt, John Wise, Hugh Curtis, Harry Mertens, Walt Fiedler, Donald Love, Myron Close, Brunel Christensen, William Young, Thomas Stuelpnagel, Mansfield Clinnick, Harold Walt, Floyd Pettit, E. N. Cureton, Coach. FRONT ROW: Tony Pia, Assistant Coach; Donald Bell, Manager; Robert Cole, Elia Long, Richard Groulx, Haden Reinecker, Louis Weldman, Gus Clark.

WRESTLING

BACK ROW: Ortlieb, Captain; Talsesian, Fulkerson, Maas, Elliott, Mumby. MIDDLE ROW: Skarin, Volber, Dorland, Ayres, Horn, Laughlin. FRONT ROW: Davis, Leonard, Elsbach, Petrofsky, Strugatz, Bangerter, Stone, Coach.

1945

Boxing

TOP: Coach Tom Cureton lets go a hard right.

CALIFORNIA'S Varsity boxing team engaged in only two matches during the 1945 season and in each case emerged the victors. Both matches were against the UCLA Bruins.

On January 27 Coach Tom Cureton took an inexperienced Bear squad down to Westwood where it responded by handing the heavily favored Bruins a 5 to 3 defeat.

That their first win over UCLA was no accident was proved on the evening of February 10 in the Bear gymnasium when Cureton's proteges handed the revenge-seeking Bruins a 4 to 2 loss in a rematch.

In both instances it was a case of too much strength in the 135 and 145 classifications so far as the Bruins were concerned. Bears Jack Bishop, 135, and Bob Howard, 145, were the only men to win their bouts in both matches.

In the first match, the Bears scored a knockout win when John Laughlin floored his opponent early in the second round. Bishop and Howard added to the California total by winning impressive decisions, while Bill Nash and Bill Bartley held their opponents to a draw. Homer Anderson, 127, and Heavyweight Joe Grothus both lost their bouts.

The rematch in the California gymnasium found Bishop knocking out his foe in the middle of the first round. Nash, Howard, and Grothus won their bouts while Al Nies, 145, and Veteran Tom Greathouse, 155, fought to a draw. Anderson lost his second straight to sensational Jose Poblete of UCLA.

VARSITY BOXING TEAM
BACK ROW: Jack Bishop, Joe Grothus, Thomas Stuelpnagel, Eldon Crump, Harold Kelton, Charles Welby, Bob Howard. SECOND ROW: Al Nies, Del Bartley, Bill Nash, Thomas Greathouse. FRONT: Homer Anderson, Coach Tom Cureton.

1945 VARSITY BOXING TEAM

127 POUNDS	HOMER ANDERSON
135 POUNDS	JACK BISHOP
145 POUNDS	BOB HOWARD
145 POUNDS	JOHN LAUGHLIN
145 POUNDS	AL NIES
155 POUNDS	TOM GREATHOUSE
165 POUNDS	BILL BARTLEY
175 POUNDS	BILL NASH
HEAVYWEIGHT	JOE GROTHUS

1946

Boxing

ED NEMIR
Coach

Nash and Bartley engaged in infighting.

BEAR mittmen boxed two matches this year, both of which were with UCLA.

Giving a thrill to the spectators February 2nd, the mittmen made a clean sweep by winning all the bouts, five with TKO's, two with decisions, and one with a forfeit at the Berkeley match. This was the last match for Coach Cureton who left March 1st when Ed Nemir, the prewar coach, returned.

Although the general opinion was that the outlook was good for the Bears for the March 23rd meet, the Bruins hit just hard enough to win five decisions and one forfeit.

BACK ROW: Walsh, Shaw, Chew, Shafer, Howard, co-captain, Bartley, Nash, co-captain.
FRONT ROW: Cureton, coach, Symonds, Moore, Harle, Fray, Welby, Walkotte.

1948

BACK ROW, left to right: Ed Nemir (coach), Jim Martin, Herb Bruce, Irv Tucker, Paul Ward (manager). SECOND ROW: James Johnston, John Keliiaa, Ed Farris, Warren Simmons, Jack Lamke. FRONT ROW: John Grennan, Leland Sapiro, Bud Smith, Rod Doerr.

aching the Cal boxing team through its 1947-48 season was NEMIR, who was a former PCC champ himself back in his undergraduate days at the University.

BOXING

THE Bear mittmen punched their way to four victories in six matches. The sluggers defeated UCLA 5-4 but were upset by Santa Barbara 6-4. The Blue and Gold fought Stanford to a favorable 8-3 win but later lost to the Cal Aggies 4-3. Meeting both their little brothers in the two final meets, the Bear leather-pushers tied UCLA, and downed the Aggies. Jack Lamke, Harry Schultze and Warren Simmons represented Cal at the PCI meet, while later Lamke was sent to the NCAA championships.

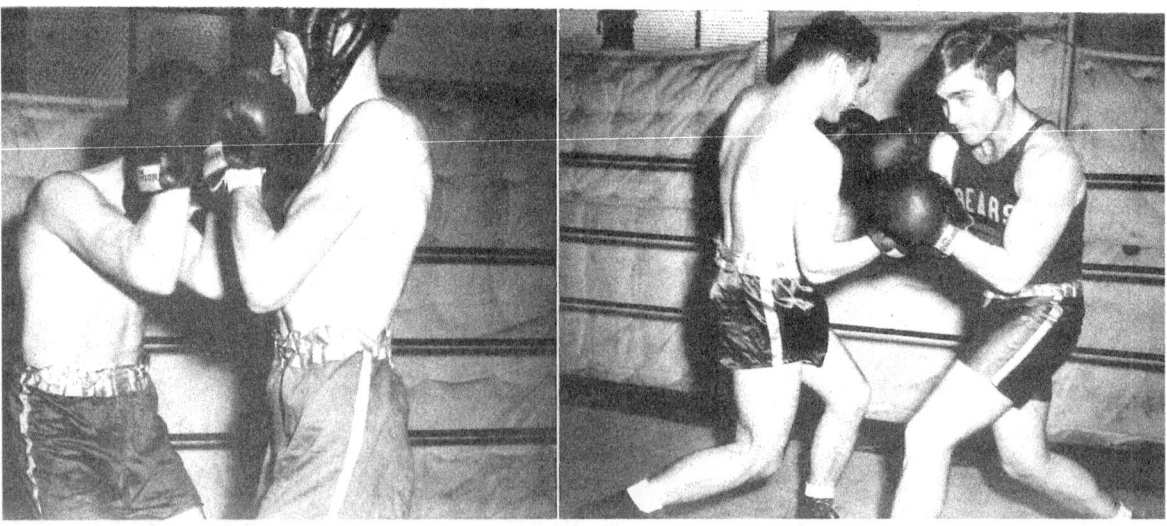

1949

Boxing

BOXING was a strong sport at Berkeley in 1949. In six encounters the Cal team won four of them. The one loss was to the Cal Aggies, while we beat the Aggies in a return match. We also took two from Stanford, one from the City College of San Francisco and then were forced to tie a hard-fought match with the UCLA Bruins, 5-5.

FRONT ROW, left to right: Parhan, Ong, Sapiro, Meiver, Lustig, Doerr. MIDDLE ROW: Nemir, Farris, Bartley, Sapris, Keith, Knesevitch, Harvey. BACK ROW: Galloway, Tucker, Lamke, Emerson, Groff.

The very best in California boxing was brought out by coach EDDIE NEMIR.

1949 Cal Boxing Team

1950s

Vincent Hallinan, father of "Butch" and "KO"

Legendary San Francisco lawyer, Vincent Hallinan, was the father of two outstanding San Francisco lawyers, Patrick "Butch" Hallinan and Terrence "KO" Hallinan, two excellent fighters on the Cal Boxing Teams of the late 1950s. Born in 1897, Vincent Hallinan was a 1948 Vice-Presidential candidate, running mate with Progressive Party Presidential candidate Henry Wallace, and in 1952 was the Progressive Party's presidential candidate.

In his autobiography, "A Lion in Court," Hallinan wrote of his own fantasy of boxing on the Cal team: "A few years ago, when I was suspended from the Bar, I wished to enroll at the University of California to study Russian. I had another secret purpose: I had watched four of my sons win, in succession, the middleweight intramural boxing championship at that school. I was about 60 years, but was certain that I could duplicate their feats. A transcript of my credits at St. Ignatius High School and College were duly transmitted to the Berkeley Campus. Altogether, including an AB and an LLB degree, they were insufficient to procure enrollment at the University of California as a freshman." (Pages 28-29)

Patrick (Butch) Hallinan and Terrence (Kayo) Hallinan (both 1956 and 1957), were both excellent criminal defense lawyers until "KO" decided to run for and be elected to several terms as San Francisco District Attorney!

George Pelonis

An outstanding fighter of the 50's, Ed Nemir is quoted as identifying him as one of the best fighters he ever coached. Marty Sammon, who boxed for Santa Clara University, and, for many years up to the present, has been a dedicated referee and judge of both college fights and professional matches, likes to tell a story about his fight against George Pelonis: "Before the fight, both Pelonis and I were undefeated. After the fight, Pelonis was undefeated."

SAN FRANCISCO EXAMINER, MONDAY, MAY 13, 1996

The man who taught 'Kayo' how to box

Tommy Egan and the Round House Boys swap tales of their glory days and welcome San Francisco's DA, an ex-pugilist who proposes bringing back an amateur boxing program for young people

By Edvins Beitiks
OF THE EXAMINER STAFF

In 1960, Terence Hallinan, *above left, got some pointers from boxer and coach Fred Apostoli as Hallinan prepared for the Golden Gloves tournament in Marin County. Below, Hallinan joked last month with his boxing mentor, Tommy Egan, at Monkey Murphy's Bar in Potrero Hill.*

DALY CITY — They sat across from each other at the table inside the Silver Moon, hands resting on the checkered tablecloth — the district attorney of San Francisco and the man who once taught him to box.

It was the third Friday in April, the monthly meeting of the Round House Boys, a collection of ex-boxers from the Bay Area with fighting credentials from the '40s, '50s and '60s.

They were honoring Terence "Kayo" Hallinan, district attorney of San Francisco, and there was standing room only along the bar.

The noise level was like a fight crowd on Saturday night as Hallinan came through the door, shaking hands with every boxer who walked up to him. He nodded, turning and turning again, saying to the men squeezing in, "My father told me, 'If you're going to fight, you might as well get paid for it,' so I became a lawyer."

Lately Hallinan has had to deal with a surge of unwanted publicity, including a Hall of Justice sex scandal and a push-punch match with developer Joe O'Donoghue. But when he met with the Round House Boys he was all smiles, happy to be in the company of friends.

Hallinan settled in the seat across from Tommy Egan, 71, who regularly went out to Ross in the '50s to teach boxing to the Hallinan brothers. "Good to see you," said Egan, who hasn't been in touch with Hallinan since those days.

As the crowd eddied around Hallinan, Egan nursed a vodka on the rocks and talked about boxing,

[See HALLINAN, A-16]

◆ HALLINAN from A-1

Round House Boys honor Kayo Hallinan

his memory settling on his title fight against Fred Apostoli in October of 1946. "My son was born in the second round," said Egan, adding with a grin, "Not in the ring. In the hospital."

Egan, who was born at 18th and Tennessee streets on Potrero Hill, never moved more than a few blocks away and now lives on 20th Street. He is losing sight in his left eye and is being treated for throat cancer, but Egan is still feisty — as feisty as he was as a youngster growing up during the Depression.

His first bout came on his 12th birthday in 1936, and he had 118 pro fights, losing only seven. He routinely stacked one bout behind the other, year after year.

"Fought every time I could," he said. "Pacific Auditorium on Monday, Sacramento on Wednesday, San Jose Friday. I figured, why go to the gym to get your brains beat out? Might as well get money every time you fight."

Fighting so often didn't take its toll on him, said Egan, matter-of-factly: "Not really — not when you're knocking 'em out."

"Know what I got for my first fight? Twelve dollars and fifty cents. The most I got? Two thousand, for Apostoli. It paid for my baby."

Don't mess with the baby sitter

Egan nodded toward Hallinan and said, "I taught him. Used to go across the Bay to their house in Ross. He had five other brothers and I baby-sat them all."

Terence Hallinan forged an amateur fight record of 85-15 and was solid enough as a middleweight and light heavyweight to be a contender in the 1960 Olympic trials. He was "a real good fighter," said Egan. "Aggressive, very aggressive. All the brothers were.

"I was at the house one Saturday when Butch — Patrick — did something at the table his old man didn't like. Vince got right up and started chasing him through the house, chased him from room to room."

Terence Hallinan was about 12 years old when Egan first started making calls at the Hallinan home, and he remembered sparring with the hard-punching pro. The district attorney leaned forward, smiled and said, "Tommy taught me how to take a punch, gave me my first lesson in the ring. Taught me a lot of other things, too."

Hallinan turned to Egan and said, "Remember when you took me to the 'Playboy' on Mission? Took me out to get me drunk in Butchertown?"

The two men laughed together as the Round House Boys meeting came to order. Big Al Ilardi gave boxer Sam Moratto, who died the week before, a memorial 10-count ("Rest in peace, Sam"), introduced Egan, and then said, "Let's give it up for that bomber, Terence 'Kayo' Hallinan!"

Recruiting more for the ring

Hallinan stood, nodded to the men along the bar, and talked about his first 100 days as district attorney.

His office has yet to lose a case, he told the boxers, adding, "I'd like to get into other things than just prosecuting people. There must be other things we can do."

One of those things would be to give boxing a rebirth in the Bay Area, said Hallinan — "I am determined to bring back amateur boxing in San Francisco."

Mayor Brown has indicated support for a boxing program, Hallinan said, and juveniles he has talked with also like the idea.

"I know kids want it. I talked to some of them at a meeting in Bayview, asked how many would be interested in boxing if we started something like that. Every one of them raised their hands, including the girls."

Hallinan looked around the room and said, "Dolph Thomas Gym, Newman Gym, what a really great fight town this used to be ... For kids who didn't have much, it was a chance to get some money, a chance to get some glory. We've lost that.

"I think we can do it again. I know I want to do it. We'll have to start slow, but I think the support is there."

The Round House Boys gave Hallinan an ovation and he sat down across from Egan as lunch was brought in from the kitchen.

One ex-boxer after another came over to say hello ("Kayo! Remember me?") until Egan, finishing another vodka on the rocks, frowned up at the crowd of faces and muttered out loud, "Hey, let him eat!"

SAN FRANCISCO EXAMINER, MONDAY, MAY 13, 1996

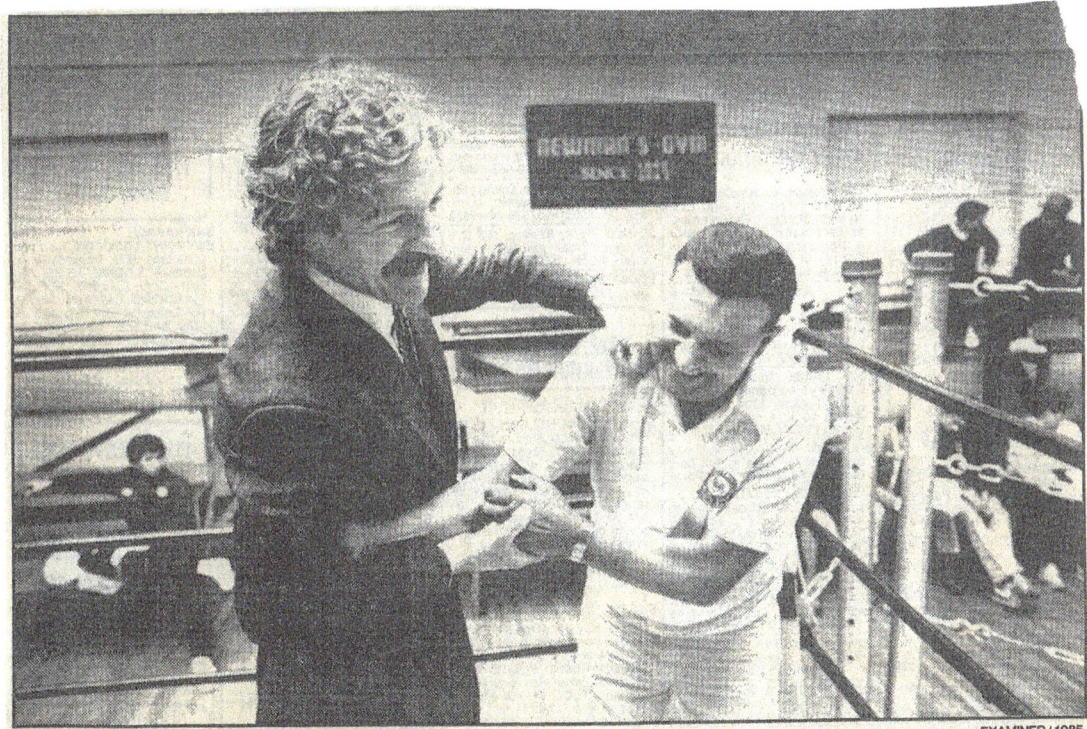

Terence Hallinan, *left, and coach Don Stewart posed at Newman's Gym in 1985 to promote Golden Gloves boxing.*

1950s

Pax Beale was Cal's Heavyweight for 1951 and 1952. He was undefeated at Cal, although he had numerous draws. He went on to box in the amateurs and was Air Force Heavyweight Champion and he had about a dozen professional fights. Later, he took up running and ran 26 marathons and, in his 50s, took up body building and won numerous championships in his age category. He was and is a successful entrepreneur in San Francisco, and author of "Body for the Ages."

Cal boxers turn back Indians in first go

By RUDIE TRETTEN

Led by t.k.o. winners Ken Hansen and Hank Harvey, Cal's previously untested boxing team dumped the Stanford mitmen, 5½ to 2½, in the Stanford pavillion Saturday night.

Cal's well drilled punchers possessed too much fire power for the Indians. Not one Bear made the trip to the canvas while three of the Stanfords went down and two of them out.

HARVEY SCORES

Hank Harvey came through with the most sensational performance of the night when he blasted Indian Bob Baldocci out of contention in 1:07 of the first round. Baldocci was down twice in that time. The referee didn't bother to count the last time but stopped the fight and awarded Harvey a technical knockout.

The other Cal t.k.o. came in the 130-pound class where Ken Hansen battered Stanford's Bob Neighbor from one end of the ring to the other for two rounds and finally put him away in the third. Hansen used a good left hook and a hard right hand to the head to uncouple Neighbor. It was Hansen's first varsity fight.

Bill Sapsis, Cal 155 pounder, turned in a workmanlike job as he handled Bob Colton. In the first heat Sapsis landed a left hook followed by a right to the head to send Colton to the canvas. Sapsis' hard punching to the body had a telling effect on Colton and at the end of the fight he was badly bruised.

BEST FIGHT

Best fight of the night was the 135-pound go in which Stanford's Bob White won a split decision from the Bears' Bruno Terreano. White used a snaky left jab to good advantage in combatting the heavier punching Torreano. The fight was loaded with action for the full three rounds with Torreano in pursuit of White for most of the distance. Several times Torreano caught up with White and the boys would stand and slug it out toe to toe—with Torreano generally having a little the better of these exchanges.

Heavyweight Paxton Beale was held to a draw by the Cards' Dave Anderson. Beale took the first two rounds handily but in the third Anderson came back with a series of left hooks to the head to even things up.

George Pelonis won his varsity debut easily by running after Bob Myers for three rounds. Pelonis forced what action there was but Myers was more intent on running than fighting.

GRIFFIN INJURED

Cal's only serious injury was sustained by Ed Griffin in a losing 145-pound match with Bob Baker. Griffin may have incurred a slightly broken nose. The doctor was not sure after the fight whether it was a full break or only a crack.

Here's what 'Unkle Oski' sez to you

i need u. learn a job with a footure. men under 5 ft. 5 in. of good karacter, who want a life of adventere, sine up now. commishuns open in the honorable order of Oski (that's mee). send an post card to George Heuer, 2254 San Jose Ave., Alameda, Calif.

1951

With Cal Squad Tonight

Cal Poly Boxers Seek Second Win Over PCC Opposition Here

Another outstanding boxing card is on the schedule for tonight when the very evenly matched Cal Poly Mustangs and California Bears clash in Crandall gym here for a knockdown-drag-out ring fest.

The 10-bout program as announced by Mustang Coach George Prouse—with no assurance that the usual number of forfeits and exhibitions will not be injected before the 8 o'clock bell time—follows (Cal Poly boxers listed first):

126—John Elder vs. Emmett Forrester; 132—Graf Shintaku vs. Ken Hansen; 139—Myron Moses vs. Myron Hansen; 147—Bill Feeney vs. Jay Slaybaugh; 156—Jack Bettencourt vs. Jim McCann; 156—Jim Kashiwage vs. Art Hillman; 165—Bill Lidderdale vs. Fred Shieman; 165—Jim Herra vs. Carl Koenig; 178—Charles Baca vs. Don Clawson, and heavyweight—Jack Shaw vs. Dick Tullsen.

Elder should give the Mustangs an opening victory against Forrester in view of earlier showings by the two boxers against a common foe, Stanford's Gary Seibert. Elder decisioned Seibert when Poly beat the Indians 5-4 while Seibert decisioned Forrester last Tuesday night when the Tribe fell before the Bears, 5-3.

Ken Hansen is favored to give the visitors a win in the second bout. The 132-pound Bear TKO'd Stanford's Bob Chalmers Tuesday night while Chalmers decisioned Shintaku in their meeting at Palo Alto. However, Shintaku has been improving steadily in recent weeks and could easily provide the surprise performance of the evening.

The 139-pound division has been a problem for Prouse all season and the Mustangs have been a problem for Prouse all season and the Mustangs forced to forfeit in previous outings. However, Moses was good enough to win the Poly novice championship in the 130-pound class and can possibly handle any extra weight which he may have to spot Hansen.

Feeney, Mustang novice champ in the 155-pound division, will be trying to fill the shoes of Paul Fischbeck in the 147-pound go against Slaybaugh. An 18-year-old freshman from Willows, Feeney looked sharp against San Francisco State fighting in his own class, but was TKO'd by Stanford's Tony Wynn when he tried to handle a 178-pound assignment. Slaybaugh decisioned Stanford's Ed Scarboro in his last ring appearance.

The Bettencourt-McCann bout should develop into a pier nine brawl. Both are experienced ringmen and both like to mix it up. Stanford's Eric Hansen has been a common victim of both. Bettencourt TKO'd Hansen but McCann put the Indian boxer away for the full count.

Kashiwage and Hillman have neither seen much action this season. Kashiwage gained a draw against San Jose and decisioned San Francisco State's Andy Ferrando. Hillman decisioned Stanford's Bill Millington in his last outing.

Lidderdale, veteran Mustang boxer, was late getting started this season and made his first appearance against Stanford. Meeting tough Bob Baldochhi, Lidderdale lost the decision but is favored to take his bout tonight since Baldochhi TKO'd Shieman when the Indians met the Bears.

Herra, whose somewhat awkward footwork keeps fans wondering how he wins any fights, will go after his second win against Koenig. Herra lost a decision to the veteran Darrell Dukes against San Jose State but TKO'd San Francisco State's Dick Storm. Koenig is tough, however. He decisioned Stanford's Tony Wynn in his last ring appearance.

Another Poly novice champ, Baca will make his first varsity appearance against Clawson. Baca, member of the Mustang basketball team, is big and tough and can be expected to throw plenty of leather at the Bear mittman.

Shaw and Tullsen are apparently evenly matched although there is no way to compare the two on past performances. Against the Indians, Shaw

JIM McCANN
Cal's Hope Against Bettencourt

MYRON HENSEN
Faces Novice Champ

1956

1956 Cal Boxing Team, including:
Top Row: Don Nemir (far left), Bob Ettinger (second from the left), George Pelonis (middle), Terrence "Kayo" Hallinan (second from right), Herb Davis (far right).
Middle Row: Dick Homuth (middle), Patrick "Butch" Hallinan (far right).
Front Row: Don Ricci (far left), Bill Holloman, Leo Gaspardone (second from right) Bill Homuth (far right).

1957

Top Row: Coach Ed Nemir, Herb Davis; Bob Ettinger, Charles Duncan, Clark Ide, Jim Vogt (second from right), Dick Homuth (far right). Bottom Row: Ken Kofman (far left), Bill Holloman, Leo Gaspardone, Bill Anderson, Don Buckman, Sammy Moreno (far right).

Boxing Stories by H.S. Davis

These boxing stories are dedicated to my father, the late Judge David E. Davis. Born in Neshin, Russia in 1905, he was the youngest of seven children. When he was five years old, his family immigrated to Boston, MA. He graduated Boston Latin School at the age of 16 and soon after became a professional fighter and manager. Later, he entered law school, passed the bar exam, and set up a law practice in Boston under his given name David Korisky. Since everyone knew him by his "ring" name, Eddie Davis, very little business came his way. For this reason, he had his name legally changed to David Edward Davis. Everyone called him "Eddie," but to his family he was always "Dave."

He had dozens of stories to share with me about his years in the ring. He followed boxing closely and never missed a bout on television. He was passionate about boxing and, to my good fortune, passed his love of the sport on to me.

Figure 1. My father's transition from boxer to lawyer (1929)

Boxing Stories by Herb Davis

Introduction
The other day, as I was foraging around in the attic, I came across a dusty and long-forgotten scrapbook. It was a collection of old, yellowed newspaper clippings and photos of my days as an intercollegiate boxer at the University of California, Berkeley. Rather than let those scraps of paper continue to rot away, I decided to organize them and document the events and memories of this aspect of my life. The following is result of that effort. I've also included some random, and hopefully interesting, comments on some of the people and places involved.

Boxing at Cal
My dad was a prizefighter back in his younger days. As soon as I was able to walk, he began teaching me the proper boxing stance and how to throw a great left hook. So, naturally, in my first year at Cal I took a boxing class and, at Coach Ed Nemir's request, I entered the Cal intramural boxing tournament. I won my weight division and also won the Cunha trophy for being voted the outstanding boxer of the tournament. I remember vividly when the announcement was made to a packed house in the Men's gym. More than 25 KNs, their cameras flashing, made a mad, noisy rush to the boxing ring to congratulate me. They tried to take the heavy, 3-ft tall permanent trophy from my hands and bring it back to the house, but the referee wrested it out of their hands.

Coach Ed Nemir giving me some boxing tips.

Darrell Sevilla was a big fan of my boxing. He assigned me a nickname—as he did with everybody. My "Sevilla" name was "Punch."

For the next two years I boxed on the Cal team. Also on the team was the previous year's runner-up in the NCAA finals tournament, George Pelonis, as well as the fearless Hallinan brothers, Terence (Kayo) and Patrick (Butch). I won most of my matches, including a 27-second, first-round knockout of my Stanford opponent with a great left hook. I retired in my senior year to focus on my physics studies

First Boxing Lesson
I was six years old the first time I put on a pair of boxing gloves. My friend Gary Riedel, who was two years older than I was, received a new pair of gloves for Christmas and brought them over to my house[1]. My father was going to give us a lesson in pugilism. He positioned me in the classic boxing stance: feet apart and balanced, head down, chin tucked into my left shoulder, both hands poised.

On my dad's "go," Gary was instructed to throw a left jab at me. I was told to block it with my right hand. Gary did everything right. Unfortunately, his jab sailed past my right glove and landed

---

1 We were living in a flat at 127 12th Avenue in San Francisco's Richmond District.

on my nose. So I did what any six-year old would do—I burst into tears! Somehow, I had neglected to block that jab. Immediately the gloves came off, my dad consoled me and Gary apologized

First Boxing Match

The second time I put on the gloves, the results were a little more satisfying. In 1944, when I was eight years old, my parents signed me up for a weeklong summer vacation at YMCA Camp Jones Gulch in nearby La Honda, CA. The campgrounds not only had a swimming pool, I discovered, it also had a boxing ring. I walked over to the ring and joined about five other boys my age that had gathered around it. Two pair of boxing gloves lay in a corner of the ring. One of the boys picked up the gloves, examined them, and tried them on. A boy next to him looked around at the rest of us and asked earnestly, "Does anyone here know how to box?" For some unknown reason, I responded, "I do." I didn't really have a desire to box, but I wasn't averse to the idea either.

The boy wearing the gloves asked me if I wanted to box with him. He looked like a reasonable type, so I agreed. We climbed through the ropes, danced around the ring and threw cautious left jabs at each other, clinching occasionally. He was African American, about my age, height, weight, as well as boxing skill. A camp counselor, who had been watching us spar, told us he thought we were pretty good boxers and invited us to give a demonstration to all the campers that evening.

That night, after dinner, amid the cheering throng of campers, the two of us were introduced. We boxed a friendly match and, when it was over after one or two rounds of unknown duration, the match was pronounced a draw. We congratulated each other on a good bout. We had both gained some small measure of status with our Jones Gulch peers

Learning the Ropes

Over the years my dad continued setting me in the proper boxing stance and taught me how to punch, block and move. He always emphasized the importance of a left jab. We often shadow boxed together and watched *Friday Night Fights* on television's *Gillette Cavalcade of Sports*. There were many great fighters to watch on TV in the late '40s, '50s, and '60s, including Rocky Marciano, Sugar Ray Robinson, Archie Moore, Rocky Graziano, and Willie Pep.

We also went to San Francisco's Civic Auditorium to watch the amateur fighters. I remember seeing future pro greats Johnnie Gonsalves and Maurice Harper, as well future middleweight champ Gene Fulmer. My dad always pointed out the fine points of their technique and strategy. I absorbed as much as I could. At the time, I had a pretty good left jab and hook—at least so it seemed to me in front of a mirror.

When I graduated George Washington High School in 1954, my dad asked me if I was *really* serious about learning how to box. I said I was, and I agreed to work out on a regular basis. This was the beginning of our Saturday morning boxing ritual.

Newman's Gym

Every Saturday morning we got up, ate a light breakfast and drove downtown to Newman's Gym. Newman's was San Francisco's elite boxing gym, located on Leavenworth St. in the Tenderloin district. It was established in 1924 and is where many great fighters trained, including heavyweight champions Jack Dempsey, George Foreman and local favorite, middleweight champion Carl "Bobo" Olson.

Entering Newman's gym, I walked down a short flight of stairs. Inside, were two full-sized boxing rings and several heavy punching and speed bags. One wall had a set of exercise ropes and pulleys. Another wall had bleachers for onlookers. There was an enclosed private office where the managers and trainers hung out. The lockers and showers were in the back.

I changed into my workout clothes and re-entered the gym. I heard gloves hitting punching bags, and grunts and groans from boxers sparring in the ring. There I was—a green, scrawny, 6 ft-150 lb 17-year-old kid—thrust in with, what seemed to me, gladiators in the ancient Roman Coliseum. To say that I was intimidated would be a gross understatement.

Training

I was hoping if I just started doing what all the other fighters were busy doing, no one would notice the new kid. So I stretched a little and pulled the pulley weights.[2] Then I wrapped my hands in tape, put on bag gloves and started hitting the heavy bag. I did a little footwork. Nobody seemed to be paying much attention to me so my confidence grew. After a few weeks, and with much urging by my dad, I finally stepped into a boxing ring to shadowbox. Things were going well, but my dad still didn't think it was time for me to begin sparring with anyone.

I worked out for about an hour, then showered and dressed. We crossed Leavenworth and ate lunch at Fosters—a now defunct, but at that time popular, cafeteria chain in San Francisco. I slid my tray along a chrome track, picking from the various prepared entrees and desserts behind a glass counter. My favorites were the chicken potpie and the rice pudding.

Some days I did "roadwork." I drove from my house in the Richmond District to the Polo Field in the middle of Golden Gate Park and ran around the dirt track. The Polo Field is a huge (4/5 of a mile around the outside track) grass-covered field used for, well, polo. It's also used for soccer and as a venue for rock and other concerts. I remember seeing the San Francisco 49ers practicing there in 1949. Running is a necessary evil for a boxer to develop stamina. It is very demanding and was always the least favorite part of my training regimen.

---

2   This was long before sophisticated fitness equipment was popular.

Entering College

After completing my freshman year at San Francisco City College, I enrolled at the University of California at Berkeley (Cal) in 1957 as a sophomore. I majored in physics and joined Kappa Nu fraternity, then one of four "Jewish" fraternities on campus[3]. The reason I decided to join Kappa Nu is simple: the president of the fraternity, Princeton Lyman, came by my house, presented me with a pin and invited me to join. He was very persuasive. Princeton was a friend from high school and a very bright guy. He went on to have a brilliant career as US Ambassador to South Africa and Nigeria and was Assistant Secretary of State under Clinton.

Coach Ed Nemir

One of the elective classes I signed up for at Cal was boxing. Ed Nemir, the long-time (since 1933) coach of the Cal boxing team, taught the class. Ed was a short, stocky, affable man with a square jaw and full head of graying hair. He was soft-spoken and modest. I learned later from others that he had been a championship boxer and wrestler at Cal and had won a silver medal in wrestling as a featherweight in the 1932 Olympics. He had also graduated Phi Beta Kappa from Cal and earned a law degree at Boalt Hall, Cal's law school.

In the last part of the 1957 boxing season Ed became ill with a liver ailment. The last few matches on our schedule that year were cancelled. Ed sat out the 1958 season. He returned to coach the team from 1959 to 1969.

On February 1, 1969, shortly after he had coached his son, Phil, to a victory at the University of Nevada, Ed Nemir suffered a heart attack and died at ringside.

The Truth About Intercollegiate Boxing

The powerhouses of intercollegiate boxing at this time were Idaho State, Washington, San Jose State, and Wisconsin. Cal light-heavy George Pelonis had lost two very close and controversial decisions at the NCAA finals the previous two years. Ed didn't want to bring his teams back east anymore—not because of these poor decisions, but because the schools back east had changed a rule which made it illegal for a boy who's boxed after leaving high school to box in college. The purpose of the rule was to keep schools from recruiting golden-glovers and other amateurs simply for their boxing ability. To quote Ed, " College boxing is for college boys. They can stay there and have their college matches between their own clubs. We'll stay on the Pacific coast where the old rule still applies."

Ed's decision proved to be prescient. In 1960, Charles Mohr—a boxer from the University of Wisconsin who was the 1957 NCAA 165 lb champion, as well as the winner of the "Outstanding

---

3 The others were Zeta Beta Tau, Pi Lambda Phi, and Sigma Alpha Mu. In 1969 KN merged with ZBT, today the only Jewish fraternity at Cal.

Boxer" award—*died* in his locker room after losing a decision to a fighter from San Jose State College.

There are many differences between college and other types of boxing, as shown Table 1.

	College	Olympic	Amateur	Professional
Glove wt, oz	16	16	12	8
Rounds	Three, 2 min ea	Four, 2 min ea	Three, 3 min ea	Four, 3 min ea
Judging	3 judges 10 pts/round	4 judges, pts count when 2+ judges score a 'hit' within 1 sec of each other	3 judges. 10 pt 'must'/round	3 judges, 10 pt 'must'/round
Headgear/Shirts	Yes	Yes	No	No
Middleweight Divisions, lb	156/165	156/165	154/160/168	154/160/168

Table 1. Rules of the various boxing types

The University of California Intramural Boxing Tournament

Ed Nemir encouraged me to enter the Cal intramural boxing tournament. I accepted the challenge and began to prepare. I worked out daily and (ugh!) ran regularly on Edwards Track Stadium. Edwards Stadium is located on campus and has a beautiful Olympic-class running track.

Because of my performance in preliminary bouts, Ed assigned me to the Senior 156 lb division. My opponent was Doug Young, a southpaw. The tournament was held in Harmon Gym (now Haas Pavilion) the evening of Dec. 6, 1955.

My First Match

I had never boxed a southpaw before. It can be a little awkward, as though you're boxing a mirror image of yourself. I recalled my dad telling me how to box a southpaw: circle to the left—away from his power (left hand)—and throw more rights. As nervous as I was, I managed to follow this strategy. I easily controlled the fight and finished the bout with a solid win. I was awarded the Cunha trophy[4] for being voted the outstanding boxer of the intramural tournament.

---

4   Named for Milton T. Cunha, who starred on the 1942 Cal boxing team and was killed in action in World War II.

Figure 2. My Cunha Trophy[5]

The award was announced over the loudspeaker to cheers from the crowd. I was handed the permanent Cunha trophy to hold in the ring.[6] A throng of over-exuberant Kappa Nus cheered wildly and swarmed the ring to celebrate my victory. They took so many pictures with their flash cameras, I felt like a celebrity.

---

5   In the 1958 San Francisco earthquake, the trophy fell off the mantle in my home and the figure snapped in two. My Dad replaced the figure with an identical one.

6   The permanent Cunha trophy was three feet tall and bore the engraved names of all of the previous winners. It was permanently displayed in a glass case in the lobby of Harmon gym with all of the other permanent sports trophies. Sadly, the permanent trophy vanished during construction of Haas Pavilion.

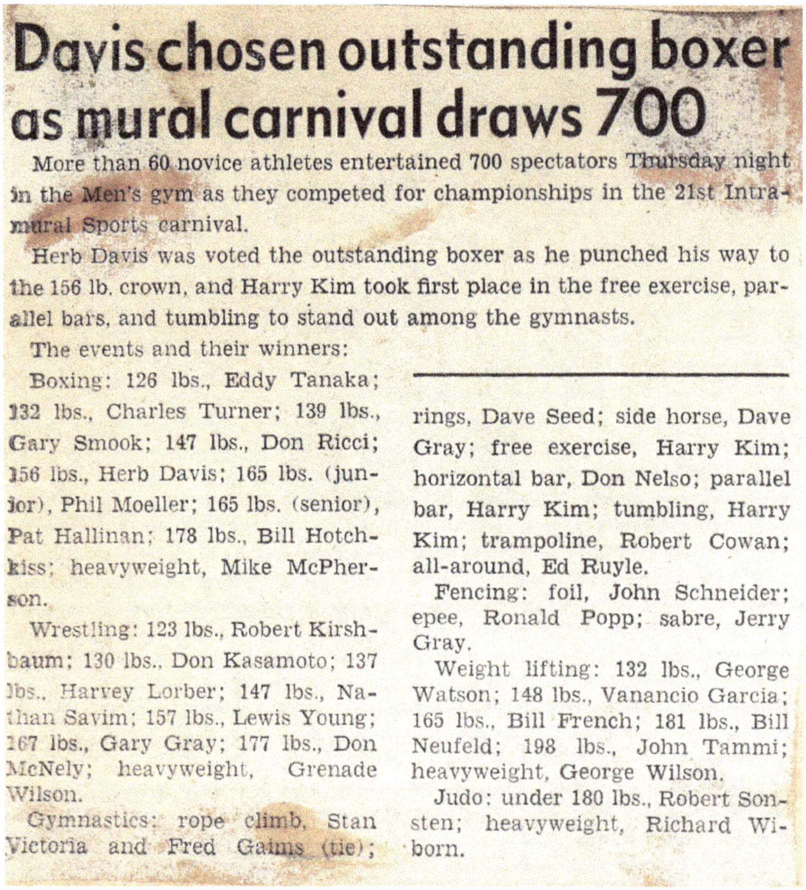

Davis chosen outstanding boxer as mural carnival draws 700

More than 60 novice athletes entertained 700 spectators Thursday night in the Men's gym as they competed for championships in the 21st Intramural Sports carnival.

Herb Davis was voted the outstanding boxer as he punched his way to the 156 lb. crown, and Harry Kim took first place in the free exercise, parallel bars, and tumbling to stand out among the gymnasts.

The events and their winners:

Boxing: 126 lbs., Eddy Tanaka; 132 lbs., Charles Turner; 139 lbs., Gary Smook; 147 lbs., Don Ricci; 156 lbs., Herb Davis; 165 lbs. (junior), Phil Moeller; 165 lbs. (senior), Pat Hallinan; 178 lbs., Bill Hotchkiss; heavyweight, Mike McPherson.

Wrestling: 123 lbs., Robert Kirshbaum; 130 lbs., Don Kasamoto; 137 lbs., Harvey Lorber; 147 lbs., Nathan Savim; 157 lbs., Lewis Young; 167 lbs., Gary Gray; 177 lbs., Don McNely; heavyweight, Grenade Wilson.

Gymnastics: rope climb, Stan Victoria and Fred Gaims (tie); rings, Dave Seed; side horse, Dave Gray; free exercise, Harry Kim; horizontal bar, Don Nelso; parallel bar, Harry Kim; tumbling, Harry Kim; trampoline, Robert Cowan; all-around, Ed Ruyle.

Fencing: foil, John Schneider; epee, Ronald Popp; sabre, Jerry Gray.

Weight lifting: 132 lbs., George Watson; 148 lbs., Vanancio Garcia; 165 lbs., Bill French; 181 lbs., Bill Neufeld; 198 lbs., John Tammi; heavyweight, George Wilson.

Judo: under 180 lbs., Robert Sonsten; heavyweight, Richard Wiborn.

Figure 3. From the Oakland Tribune

The Cal Boxing Team (1956, 1957)

I was now a member of the Cal Boxing Team. Also on the team were returning team members Sammy Moreno, the former 6th Army featherweight champ at 126 lb, Leo Gaspardone at 132 lbs, and George Pelonis, at 178 lb, the runner-up in the 1955 NCAA Intercollegiate Boxing Championships. Pat "Butch" Hallinan, at 165 lb was a new member of the team. Pat was the first of the Hallinan brothers on the Cal boxing team. His brother Terence ("Kayo") joined him the following year.

In 1956 Leo Gaspardone was the newly formed Cal boxing club's first president. In 1957, I was voted president of the club.

The Hallinan Brothers

Butch and Kayo are sons of legendary San Francisco attorney Vincent Hallinan. Like their father, they had a reputation for being scrappers. When they were in high school, they often got in trouble with the law. Their mother wrote a book about her family with the apt title, *My Wild Irish Rogues*.

However, my impressions of them were that, while they were tough fighters in the ring, they were nothing short of kind and compassionate everywhere else.

In 1956, Butch boxed in the 165 lb weight class. In 1957, I moved up to the 165-lb class and Butch moved down to 156 lbs. Kayo entered Cal in 1957 and fought first as a heavyweight, then as a light heavyweight, 178 lbs. He was a determined, fearless fighter. As a light heavy, he fought a few heavys in exhibition college bouts, as did also light heavyweight George Pelonis. I boxed on the Cal team in 1956 and 1957. In 1958, my senior year, I didn't box. I wanted to focus my attention exclusively on my studies. Because of a liver ailment, Ed Nemir didn't coach the team in 1958. That honor was given to my teammate Sammy Moreno. Sammy had a tough year coaching the team because, besides me not boxing, neither of the Hallinans did either.

Figure 4. George Pelonis, Ed Nemir, me, and Pat Hallinan

On several occasions during the year Sammy phoned me and pleaded for me to box "just one more time." If I did, he promised me, I would receive a Cal banner. I had already lettered twice. The banner was a reward for the third year. Determined to buckle down and study, I never boxed again. In those days, unlike football, basketball, and other "major" (read "money making") sports, boxing was a "minor" sport. This injustice was corrected some time after I graduated.

Coach Ed Nemir's season looks as rosy red as his boxing team's noses. Boasting nine lettermen, this year's squad could prove to be one of the best in the Pacific coast intercollegiate league.

The lettering returnees are Sam Moreno, 126 pounder; Leo Gaspardone, 132, who will be fighting his third year on varsity and Clark Ide, a rangy 139 pounder.

In the 156 class there are two returning lettermen, junior Dick Homuth and Ivan Polk, who is returning to the wars after a year's layoff; at 165 is Herb Davis, who coach Nemir calls one of the cleverest boys on the squad; a boy with the fitting name of Kayo Hallinan is fighting in the 178 lb. class, stepping down from heavyweight where he lettered last year. The heavyweight bossman is 217 lb. Mike McPherson.

The coach also cited the work of newcomers Jerry Pimintel, Del Krause, George Eshoo, Bill Anderson, Pat Bromfield and Bob Ettinger.

Nemir said that this season's team should do as well or better as the 1955 squad which placed fourth in the PCI. But he added a note of caution by saying that not only California, but most of the other teams in the league have the bulk of last year's varsity lettermen returning also.

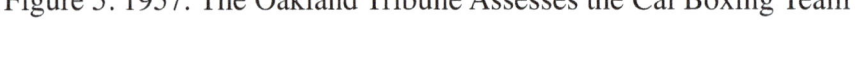

Figure 5. 1957: The Oakland Tribune Assesses the Cal Boxing Team

Figure 6. 1957 Cal boxing Team: Back Row, l to r: Ed Nemir, Herb Davis, Bob Ettinger, Charles Duncan, Clark Ide, Jim Vogt, Dick Homuth; Front row, l to r: Ken Kofman, Bill Holliman, Leo Gaspardone, Bill Anderson, Don Buckman, Sammy Moreno

Figure 7. 1957 Cal Boxers: l to r: Leo Gaspardone, Sammy Moreno, Ed Nemir, Herb Davis, Don Ricci, Dick Homuth, Clark Ide, Bill Holliman, Bob Ettinger

Boxing Matches, 1956 and 1957

Chico State College, 1956

I have no recollection about this fight, but clippings tell me I won my first bout at Chico State.

Chico State College Invitational Tournament, 1956

In the semi-finals, I was matched against Jim Richardson, a rough-tough plodding fighter. I kept my left jab going, but he kept coming after me. My father was in the stands opposite my corner moved his hand in a horizontal circle, signaling to me to move more. I tried to move more, but my legs just wouldn't cooperate. I lost, but it was a close fight. I simply ran out of steam. Maybe I could have won if I had taken my roadwork more seriously.

Figure 8. Excerpt from the Chico Enterprise-Record, March 10, 1956

In the consolation match, I faced Bernie Roberts of Stanford who stood about 6' 2". At one point in the fight Roberts' headgear started to slip and he used both hands to adjust it. I could have taken advantage of his vulnerability and laid into him, but I held back in a gesture of sportsmanship. It wasn't a particularly difficult fight and I easily won a decision.

After the fight, the referee, whom I believe was Fred Apostoli, the former middleweight champ, came over to my corner and told me I shouldn't have let Roberts off so easily. I guess that's the difference between a pro boxer and me. I didn't have a killer instinct.

In the finals Jim Richardson faced Rudy Brooks (Cal Poly), but I don't know who won.

Chico State College, 1957

The Chico Enterprise-Record reported on Jan. 14, 1957, "Chico State's…Ed Netherton (165) succumbed to experience and clever counterpunching that scored important points at just the right moments for…Davis."

Stanford University, 1956

My second bout of 1956 was held at Maples Pavilion on the Stanford campus. My dad was in the audience and brought his colleague Gerald Brown, the Regional Director of the National Labor Relations Board.

My opponent, Wally Honeywell, was very tall—about 6' 3"—for the 156 lb weight class. The bell rang for round one. I never had time to size him up early in the match, because he came out swinging. When he lunged at me, I stepped back and unfurled a left hook that caught him squarely on the chin. To my amazement, he immediately dropped to the canvas. The referee directed me to a neutral corner. I kept in motion, waiting for the ref to motion us to continue boxing. Then Ed, in my corner, signaled me to come to him. He threw a towel around my shoulders and told me to relax. My opponent was down for the count—and then some. Four people were around him, as he lay still. After a minute or so he got to his feet. I had knocked him out with a single punch in 37 seconds of the first round!

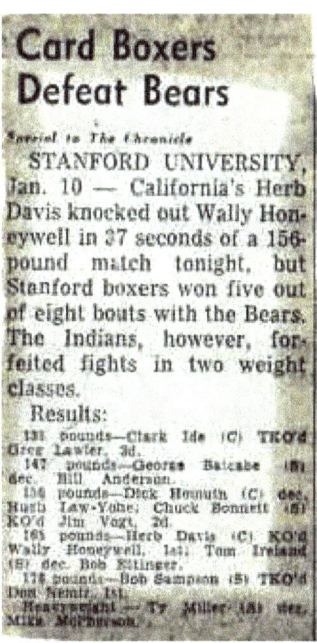

Figure 9. San Francisco Chronicle

My dad turned to his boss and asked "So, Gerry, what do you think of my son's boxing?" He replied, "I don't know—I still haven't seen him box!"

The following Saturday morning, as I was working out at Newman's Gym, my father was meeting with one of the fight managers in the office. He told me afterwards that the manager had seen the item in the sporting green about my fight and said he was interested in managing me! My father explained that I wasn't interested in becoming a fighter because I was on a different professional track. I was in complete agreement. Boxing is one hell of a hard way to make an easy living! To be a professional fighter you need to be crazy or desperate, or a little of both.

Stanford University, 1957

Stanford forfeited in my 165 lb division this year. Was this their response to my knockout the previous year?

University of Nevada-Reno, 1956

The venue for my fight in Reno was the spacious Reno Auditorium. They loved intercollegiate boxing in Reno and the auditorium was packed with two or three thousand fans.

My opponent Mike Marfisi, a southpaw, caught me off balance in the first round with a left hand. I stumbled backwards and fell—the only time I was ever knocked down. I got up right away and continued the fight unhurt and unfazed, but still lost by a controversial split decision. As I left the ring on my way to the dressing room, one of the spectators at ringside yelled to me a comforting, "*We* know who won that fight, Herb!"

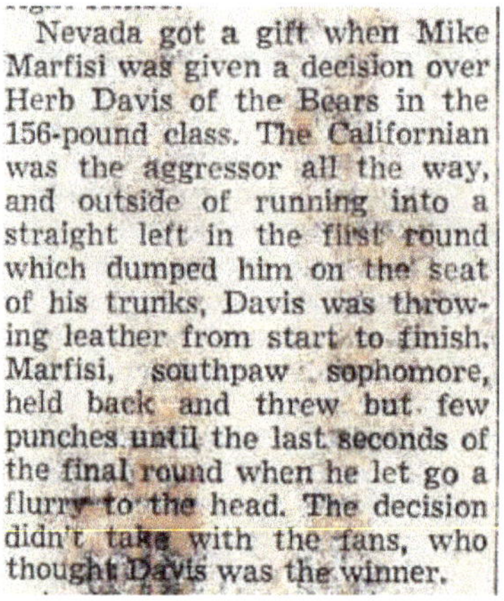

> Nevada got a gift when Mike Marfisi was given a decision over Herb Davis of the Bears in the 156-pound class. The Californian was the aggressor all the way, and outside of running into a straight left in the first round which dumped him on the seat of his trunks, Davis was throwing leather from start to finish. Marfisi, southpaw sophomore, held back and threw but few punches until the last seconds of the final round when he let go a flurry to the head. The decision didn't take with the fans, who thought Davis was the winner.

Figure 10. Nevada State Journal, Feb. 19, 1956

University of Nevada-Reno, 1957

This year my left jabs and hooks produced a win.

DEAD CALM

Cal's experienced and dead-calm Herb Davis had his hands full with straight-punching Chuck Smith. Davis kept hammering Smith with left hooks and Smith tried with jabs and a body attack. Davis held his right hand in reserve all the way through the first two rounds, but busted Smith's nose open the first time he threw the right in the third. Another Davis right spread Smith's nose all over his upper lip, but Smith, dazed and hurt, kept on banging. He lost it by a split decision, but earned an "A" for trying.

A snappy left hook won a decision for California's polished 165-pound veteran Herb Davis, who out-pointed Nevada's Chuck Smith in three fast rounds. It was the first of the season for the Smith Valley boy after two previous wins. Davis showed a lot of class and experience as his fast left counter-punches landed on Smith's head. Chuck's best round was the second, when he worked to close quarters and exploded both hands in a flurry which made Davis give ground.

But Davis took command again in the third with a long-range attack, spearing Smith's bleeding nose with both jabs and straight rights.

Figure 11. Nevada State Journal, 1957

Cal Poly, 1956

No data

Cal Poly, 1957

I was matched against Rudy Brooks, a very intimidating-looking, muscular African-American fighter who was runner-up in the Pacific Coast Intercollegiate Tournament in 1956. The judges scored the close bout 30-28, 30-27, and 29-29 in favor of Brooks.

Santa Clara University, 1956, 57

I won a decision over Art Crosetti in 1956. This was Crosetti's only loss in dual meet competition. I won another decision over Art Crosetti in 1957.

Sacramento State College, 1956

No data

Sacramento State College, 1957

This, the final match of the year (and my boxing career), was held in Berkeley in Harmon Gym. I fought Jim Flood, an Olympic finalist. Flood was very strong. I remember catching him with three successive left hooks. He backed up each time until he reached the ropes. It was very frustrating that my best punches had seemingly no effect on him. He was one tough, strong hombre. I lost a split decision.

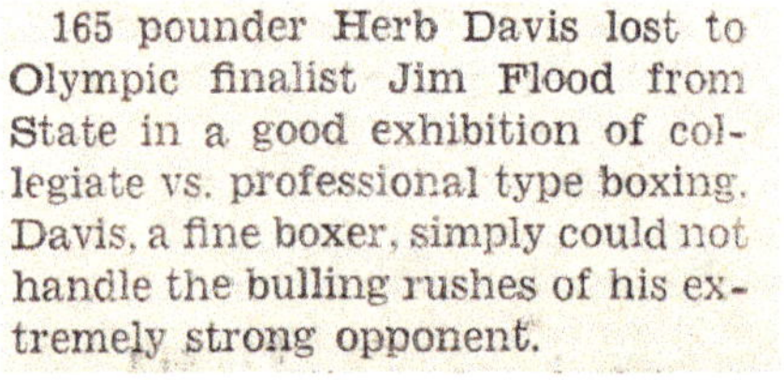

> 165 pounder Herb Davis lost to Olympic finalist Jim Flood from State in a good exhibition of collegiate vs. professional type boxing. Davis, a fine boxer, simply could not handle the bulling rushes of his extremely strong opponent.

Figure 12. Berkeley sports page, 1957

Three years later, I learned from a friend, Dick Weller, who grew up in Jim Flood's hometown of Pueblo, Colorado, that Jim was a well-known local athlete. Flood, who was elected to the Pueblo Sports Hall of Fame, remembered our boxing match—especially my left hook.

Flood dropped a weight class and won the national title in the 156-lb division in 1957. In 1958 he lost in the semi-finals of the 165-lb division (see next paragraph). In 1959 and 1960 he won the national title in the 165-lb division. He was later elected to the Pueblo, CO Sports Hall of Fame.

How Good Was I?

I was pretty good—for a college boxer. On the plus side: I was tall for my weight division and used my height to my advantage with a very good left jab and left hook; I moved fairly well around the ring and I was confident. On the downside: I had poor stamina, was not very strong and I had no "killer" instinct.

The "Battle of the Aged"

For my 50th birthday, Donne, my wife, surprised me by setting up a boxing match. We both attended Cal, but in different years. She had never seen me box and decided to conspire with Darrell Sevilla and Art Twain, two of my very creative Kappa Nu fraternity brothers, to make all the arrangements. On my birthday, we drove from San Francisco to Pittman's gym in Oakland, where dozens of friends and family had gathered for the occasion. I was led blindfolded from the car to the gym and climbed the stairs into the ring.

After a brief introduction and explanation to the audience (and to me!), I was led to the dressing room to change into my blue and gold trunks, which Donne had prearranged for me to wear. She also had my blue terrycloth bathrobe lettered with gold "Sonny KO Davis." I was then handed the plan for the evening: a detailed script of the match: three two-minute rounds, the third to be done in false slow motion with me knocking out my opponent in dramatic fashion.

My opponent turned out to be none other than Art Twain, who had been training for this event for over two months. My training was … zilch! Twain also reminded me with a note to take it easy on him because he had a bad neck—please avoid left hooks and body punches.

I had been set up!

There was a pre-fight analysis and a post-fight interview with Barry Tompkins (formerly HBO's fight announcer) and Darrell Sevilla, using his best Howard Cosell voice, as well as a stirring *a capella* rendition of the National Anthem sung in harmony by Art's son and a few of his friends. The match went on without a hitch and we were both happy to finish undamaged and *alive*! The match in its entirety is recorded on a DVD and a condensed version is on YouTube.

Figure 15. Photo from my 50th Birthday Party in 1987

Article From Sports Illustrated, April 20, 1959

Bachelor of Boxing's Arts

Biggie Munn, a man who has been around sports for a few years, said it was one of the greatest sports shows he had ever seen. Michigan State's athletic director and physical education head had just sat on the edge of his chair through 16 tumultuous semifinal bouts of the NCAA boxing tournament at the University of Nevada. Even the next night's finals, exciting though they were, could not match the memorable action of the semifinals.

Next day six out of seven coaches, assembled from some 20 colleges which recognize boxing as a sport, agreed that one semifinal bout, which pitted Washington State's Jesse Klinkenberg and the vaunted Jim Flood of Sacramento State in the 165-pound class, was the greatest fight in NCAA championship history. Through the three two-minute rounds it was toe-to-toe, each boy hammering with devastating skill and accuracy, each gaining in determination as the fight progressed and blood spattered from his heavily padded gloves. It was a magic six minutes, one of those rare occasions when athletes transcend their normal abilities.

Klinkenberg, who is an Alaska Indian, won and then, next night in the finals, lost a contrastingly routine bout to Charles Mohr of Wisconsin. But Klinkenberg was rewarded with the tournament's trophy for sportsmanship as Mohr took the title and the "outstanding boxer" trophy.

Figure 13. 1958 NCAA Semifinal Bout: Jesse Klinkenberg (l) vs. Jim Flood (r)

The crowd—mostly Nevada partisans, naturally—had other wild moments on the three nights of the tournament but none wilder than when it shook the gym, filled to its 4,500 capacity, with hysterical roars as another Indian lad, this time a Paiute, brought Nevada its first NCAA championship in history. Joe Bliss, a 139-pounder, outpressed and outslugged clever Darrel Whitmore of Washington State and so became immortal in the annals of his college.

San Jose State, coached by Julie Menendez, retained its team title, winning in two divisions and piling up 24 points. It suffered an upset loss of the heavyweight championship to Hal Espy of Idaho State, which placed second.

"It was tremendous," said Biggie Munn. "I can think of 10 of those fights which would be 10 times better than anything you see on TV."

Some representatives of TV's Wednesday Night Fights were impressed, too. They offered $12,000 to televise next year's finals and the coaches, totting up a mere $1,600 in their lean treasury, decided to seek NCAA approval.

1957

Bob Ettinger and Son

1958

Reno, Nev., Feb. 8, '58 ★ 7

California, Nevada Boxers Mix In Dual Meet in Reno Tonight

TONIGHT'S BOXING PROGRAM

Nevada		California
Dick Short	125	Ken Kaufman
David Hoy	132	Klaus Arons
Joe Bliss	139	Bill Holliman
Bill Short	147	Al Adams
Stan Davis	155	Dick Homuth
Jim Sloan	165	Bob Ettinger
Angus McLeod	178	Andy Lockwood
Carl Looney	Hvt.	Terrance Hallinan

University of Nevada Gym, North Virginia St., 8:15. Extra freshman bouts may be added to program. Admission, $1.50 ringside reserved, $1.00 general admission.

Collegiate boxing for 1958 in Reno bows in tonight with the traditional California-Nevada dual meet.

University of California's most promising squad in several years appears at the University of Nevada gym against a Wolf Pack team which has been hard-hit by illness, injury and the scholastic axe — yet is strong enough to boast several individuals who will be strong contenders for Coast honors.

The regular card begins at 8:15, preceded by an intra-squad bout between light-heavies Murdock Smith and John Genasci. It'll wind up with what promises to be a rib-snortin' heavyweight brawl between free-swinging Terrance "KO" Hallinan of the Golden Bears and Nevada's sharp-shooting Carl Looney.

steal the show will be the lightweight tilt between Bill Holliman of Cal and popular Joe Bliss of Nevada. Several of the Bear boxers have appeared here before, such as Dick Homuth, Bob Ettinger, and others. Their new coach is Sammy Moreno, himself an ex-Cal ring regular.

Coach Jimmy Olivas of the Nevada team has been plagued by misfortune among what appeared to be his most promising squad of all time. Nevertheless, such veterans as Bliss, Dick and Bill Short and Looney should go a long way this year; and he has some good-looking newcomers, topped by light-heavy Angus McLeod.

BOB ETTINGER

1958

1959

ED NEMIR
Boxing Coach

Cal's boxers had a successful year under the direction of veteran coach Ed Nemir. The Bears tied for third in the California Collegiate Boxing Conference with the aid of a win by Don Ricci in the 156-lb. division, a second by Gordon Van Kessel in the 147-lb. division, and a second by Fred Weaver in the 178-lb. division. All three boxers are Juniors, so will be back to strengthen next year's team.

The Bears finished the season with a three win, two tie, three loss record. They tied Cal Poly, tied then lost to Chico State, placed second in the CCBC, lost twice to Stanford, CCBC champions, and defeated Fresno State, Santa Clara and USF, who tied for third in the CCBC tournament.

Cal sent Don Ricci and Fred Weaver to the NCAA championships in Madison, Wisc.

Ed Nemir and the Cal boxers discuss an upcoming match.

FIRST ROW, left to right: Chuck Eastman, Don Ricci, Jack Kawamoto, Ed Killbride, Ed O'Dea, Mike Huffman. SECOND ROW: Coach Ed Nemir, Jack Damich, Fred Weaver, Pat Newell, Jim Santag, Don Kennedy, John Wylie, Jim Hagenderin, Gordon Van Kessel.

1960-1969

Introduction: Cal Boxing in the 1960s

The 1960s was a particularly pivotal time for Cal Boxing. In the 1960 NCAA Championship tournament, a middle weight boxer, Charles Mohr, from Michigan State, the previous year's National Champion and Outstanding Boxer Award winner, died a few hours after his fight and loss to Stu Bartell of San Jose State. The NCAA bowed to public criticism and dropped the sport.

However, on the West Coast, four or five dedicated coaches, led by Ed Nemir of Cal and Jimmy Olivas of Nevada, formed a new league, the California Collegiate Boxing Conference (CCBC) and boxing continued as an intercollegiate sport for Cal. However, this decade was the last in which the University funded boxing as a "Big C" sport - like Football, Basketball or Baseball -- and it was transformed into a "Club Sport," privately funded, but still heavily competitive.

Despite continued efforts to ban all boxing after the deaths of Professional Boxing Champions Davey Moore, in 1962, and Benny "Kid" Paret, in 1963, California Governor "Pat" Brown distinguished College Boxing from Professional Boxing (which he sought to outlaw) and students at the University of Nevada (Reno) voted 10-1 to keep boxing.

This decade saw the emergence of a superb fighter who won 3 Intercollegiate Championships: Tom Gioseffi. In 2008, Tom became the first Boxer to be admitted to the Cal Athletic Hall of Fame, and more than 40 years after he had boxed, had been awarded the Conference "Outstanding Boxer Award" 2 of the 3 years he boxed, and was CCBC champion (1963, 1964, 1965). He lost one fight, his first year, then drew with the same fighter (Skip Houk of Nevada, who was otherwise undefeated), then beat Houk in their third fight to win the 147 pound championship. In his third year, Tom and his teammates won championships in six of the 9 weight divisions, and won every dual meet. (The other Cal champions were Jerry Knapp (178) and Paul Rein (165) (both undefeated), Paul Bell (139), Pete Cowen, (139 lbs), and Phil Walson (a converted wrestler, 125 lbs). Other outstanding boxers that year were Dale Chamblin (125), Dave Weiner (147), Dell'Immagine (heavyweight and later, a coach), Walt Cunningham (heavyweight). In 1965, Ed Nemir's assistant coach was Bill Harrison, who boxed at Cal in 1959, then boxed in the Army. Bill was assistant coach in 1965, supporting Ed Nemir on a team that won six of nine weight division Championships, and then went to "coach" the Santa Rosa College Drama Department for the next 30 years! Bill also acted in "summer stock," playing the lead in "My Fair Lady," "Death of A Salesman," and "Krapp's Last Tape," a one character play by Samuel Beckett.

Other 60s boxers who went on to success after the ring were Bill MacAdam (1961-1962) who became a San Diego Superior Court Judge; Dave Archibald (1966), who got by on strength and determination as a boxer after previously being such a great a track runner that he was admitted to the Cal Athletic Hall of Fame the same night as Tom Gioseffi. Defense lawyer Dennis Natali boxed from 1960-1963), was teammate and long time friend of Tom Gioseffi and Paul Rein (1963-1965). Unfortunately, Natali, a well loved criminal defense attorney known to his teammates as "Bird Legs," was gunned down and murdered in his beloved San Francisco. This was a notorious crime that was never solved, even though his close friend, District Attorney Terrance "KO" Hallinan, made every possible effort to find the killer.

Bob Winter (1964) wrote of his 1967 Golden Gloves Heavyweight fight with George Foreman (1968 Olympic Gold Medal Winner and two time World Heavyweight Champion), which Bob lost on a split decision. However, in Round One, Bob knocked Foreman down, the only time *anyone* knocked Foreman down until Mohammed Ali did in 1974, taking the World Championship in the "Rumble in the Jungle," in Zaire, Africa. Before his 1973 knockout victory over Joe Frazier, Foreman told the press that the only time he'd been knocked down was by this guy Winter, who "walked out and clobbered me with a left hook. Knocked me flat." Bob, who boxed in 1964 for Cal, was an excellent Heavyweight at 6' 3" 230 lbs. However, he dropped out of Cal after the December 1964 "Free Speech Movement" political battles, and didn't fight in 1965.

Bob, a popular alumnus who later operated a popular Berkeley Bar known in the 60s Vietnam War era as the "Draught Board," wrote and described his first round 1967 knockdown of George Foreman; "At the bell we met midring, straight up, hands high. Sure enough, he led with a jab, short, then followed with another. Within that very moment, an impulse erupted from the canvas into the ball of my right foot, traversed ankle, calf, knee and thigh, torqued at the hip, shot up my spine, compounded at the shoulder, snaked through upper arm, elbow, forearm and rigid wrist, and exploded from my flat fist upon the point of George's jaw, propelling him off his feet and onto his back. Now, striding to a neutral corner, I heard the roar of the crowd. This had been too easy, effortless, like a snap shot that you know will hit the target before you touch the trigger."

"Suddenly, the crowd went silent, and I turned to see the kid on his feet. Damn! ... By the round's end he had recovered. While I had stumbled into a tarpit..."

Bob Winter

On February 1, 1969, the 60s decade ended on a tragic note, when Ed Nemir, Cal Boxing's legendary coach for 37 years, suffered a heart attack and died at ring side in Reno, Nevada, after cheering his son Phil Nemir on to victory. Ed Nemir's prestige and ability to gain admiration from all who knew him had helped keep the boxing program at Cal alive for the 60's, but after Ed passed, opponents of the boxing program nearly killed it. Fortunately, over the next 5 years, a series of former Cal boxers stepped in as interim coaches and saved boxing as a Cal sport: Ron Dell'Immagine, Dick Carter, Brian Kahn, Mike Huff, Paul McNally and Phil Nemir stepped up and saved the day. Since then, however, while nationally the sport has flourished so that Intercollegiate Boxing has been taken up by more than 30 universities which have teams that can fight their way to the National Championships, Cal, with diminished funding and less than enthusiastic support from the University Administration, struggled on. The UC "Boxing Club" team was allowed only the most primitive practice facilities and given no scholarships or other incentives to encourage students to join the sport. But the program survived, though at times Cal fighters with one or two bouts under their belt had to face the likes of Nevada Reno - where boxing matches have always been heavily attended and generously supported, and powerhouses such as the United States Naval Academy, West Point (Army) and the Air Force Academy, which often fielded fighters with twenty or more bouts experience.

1960 NCAA Champions

1960 NCAA CHAMPIONS
Back row (left to right): Heiji Shimabakura, Ron Nichols, Dave Nelson, Brown McGhee, Steve Kubas, the 1996 NCBA Honorary Tournament Director Mills Lane, Jerry Turner, Stu Bartell.   Front row: Archie Milton, John Horne.

1960

Included below: Gordon Van Kessel, Don Ricci, Dennis Natali, Bill Holliman

1960 CCBC Champions

1960

ED NEMIR
Boxing Coach

Boxing

Cal's boxers had a successful year under the direction of veteran coach Ed Nemir. The Bears tied for third in the California Collegiate Boxing Conference with the aid of a win by Don Ricci in the 156-lb. division, a second by Gordon Van Kessel in the 147-lb. division, and a second by Fred Weaver in the 178-lb. division. All three boxers are Juniors, so will be back to strengthen next year's team.

The Bears finished the season with a three win, two tie, three loss record. They tied Cal Poly, tied then lost to Chico State, placed second in the CCBC, lost twice to Stanford, CCBC champions, and defeated Fresno State, Santa Clara and USF, who tied for third in the CCBC tournament.

Cal sent Don Ricci and Fred Weaver to the NCAA championships in Madison, Wisc.

Ed Nemir and the Cal boxers discuss an upcoming match.

FIRST ROW, left to right: Chuck Eastman, Don Ricci, Jack Kawamoto, Ed Killbride, Ed O'Dea, Mike Huffman. SECOND ROW: Coach Ed Nemir, Jack Darnich, Fred Weaver, Pat Newell, Jim Santag, Don Kennedy, John Wylie, Jim Hagendorn, Gordon Van Kessel.

1961

Boxing

ED NEMIR
Coach

Coached by Ed Nemir, who entered his 25th year of coaching at Cal, the boxing team had one of their best seasons. After their opening loss to Chico State, the California boxers won three straight, defeating Cal Poly, Santa Clara and Fresno State. Last Year's 156-pound title winner, Don Ricci, and veteran welterweight Gordon VanKessel gave this year's team added strength. Last year the California Collegiate Boxing Conference was organized, stimulating boxing interest on the West Coast. Conference members include: Cal Poly, Stanford, Chico State, Fresno State, Santa Clara and California.

VARSITY BOXING TEAM—FIRST ROW, left to right: Dennis Natali, Stewart Nyholm, Bill McAdam, Jack Kawamoto, Larry Costa, Shiori Sakamoto, Don Ricci. SECOND ROW: Coach Ed Nemir, John Wylie, Roger Kent, Fred Weaver, Tobey Cornsweet, Dave McCullough, Dennis Treadway, Gordon VanKessel.

Cal boxers replace their gloves after a practice session.

Bear pugilists work out on the bags in preparation for their match against the Navy at Mare Island.

Coach Nemir gives some "fistic" tips at a sparring session.

1961

Daily Californian Sports

Sports Editor, ELLIOT STEINBERG; Assistant Sports Editor, WILLIAM HAND
LOWELL HICKEY, Sports Night Editor

Bear Boxing Bombers Bring 4 State Titles Home to Cal

By LOWELL HICKEY

California's varsity boxers finished off the 1961 season with a bang Friday and Saturday nights at Chico in the California Collegiate Boxing Conference Championship. The Bear bombers won four of the eight weight divisions, while Chico State took three and Santa Clara one.

Cal's two big men, Gordon Van Kessel and Don Ricci, won the 147 and 156 pound championships. Gordy won his two bouts with little trouble. Friday he stopped Clayton Oilar, of Cal Poly, in the second round and in the finals, Saturday, received a unanimous decision over Will Moule of Chico State.

RICCI WINS 4th LETTER

Ricci had a little more trouble. He drew a bye Friday, then Saturday defeated Chico's Jim Perry, 7-1 up 'till then, in a very even fight. Perry earned his way into the finals with a 56 second, first-round knock-out over Bob Gow of Cal Poly Friday.

Ricci, a senior, earned his fourth varsity letter this season, the first Cal boxer in history to do it. Van Kessel became a three-year varsity letterman.

Other California first places came in the 139 and heavyweight divisions.

NATALI WINS BOUTS

In the former the Bears' Denny Natali won both his Friday and Saturday bouts by a decision. He defeated Frank Godinas, of Cal Poly, the first night and won a very close split decision over Chico's Will Baker in the finals. Denny got ahead early in both fights and never relinquished his lead in either.

In the heavyweight finals Saturday, Clark Dooley repeated an earlier season win over John Jellison, of Chico State. Dooley earned his way into the finals with a victory over Al Muro, of Cal Poly, Friday.

CHICO WINS THREE

Chico State's three wins came in the 125, 165 and 178 pound divisions. In the featherweight finals Chico's John Rivers went up against Cal's Shori Sakamoto. The fight was real even until the third round when Sakamoto was pounded with such heavy artillery that the Bears were forced to throw in the towel.

Cal's John Wylie, 165, lost to Chico's Dave Borjon in the preliminaries and Borjon went on to win the 165-pound championship the next night.

The same thing happened to Fred Weaver in the 178-pound class. Weaver was beaten Friday by Chico's John Mundell, who won a split decision over Cal Poly's Tessier, Saturday.

SANTA CLARA WINS ONE

The 132-pound title went to John Willett of Santa Clara. The Bears' entrant in this division, Jack Kawamoto, lost a decision to Willett in the preliminaries.

Coach Ed Nemir was very pleased with his team's performance, not only in this tournament, but throughout the year. "I'd say this team has had a better record than any team we've had in years," he said. Cal also won more dual meets than any school on the West Coast.

The teams competing in this weekend's championships were Cal, Stanford, Chico State, Cal Poly and Santa Clara.

NEMIR: 'BEST IN YEARS'

STANDING: Coach Ed Nemir, John Wylie, Roger Kent, Fred Weaver, Toby Cornsweet, Dennis McCullough, Dennis Treadway, Gordon Van Kessel. KNEELING: Dennis Natali, Stew Nyholm, Bill McAdam, Jack Kawamoto, Larry Costa, Shiori Sakamoto, Don Ricci.

Tommy Gioseffi, A Boxing Legend
"First Fight" (1961) by Paul Rein
(Practice Match Against Boxing Legend Tommy Gioseffi)

"He's a lefty. Don't throw any left jabs!" This was the advice from my cornerman, Bill McAdam, an experienced member of the University of California Varsity Boxing Team, as I stepped into the ring for my first boxing competition. (This was a non-elimination "practice" fight, before the intramural tournament's elimination bouts.) My opponent, Tom Gioseffi, who would be competing as a welterweight (147 lbs.), while I was a "light Middleweight (156 lbs) was also entering his first fight. Unknown and unknowable to me at that time, Gioseffi was destined to become one of the finest intercollegiate boxers of his era.

My corner's advice to <u>not</u> use the left jab startled me: I was in my <u>first</u> month of a "<u>beginning</u>" boxing course at Cal, a half-unit physical education course, and the only punch we had been taught so far was throwing the left jab!

Fortunately, Gioseffi was as wild and inexperienced as me. We traded punches for three rounds, proving to each other how good we were at <u>taking</u> punches, and we fought to a "draw." That fall, Tom and I went on to win our respective weight division Championships in the 1961 Intramural Boxing Tournament competition. We continued to fight as teammates on the Cal Berkeley Intercollegiate Boxing Team for the next three years, from 1963-1965. Tom won the intercollegiate championships all three years, with a record of 22 wins, 1 loss, and 1 draw.

Tom's toughest fights were the loss and draw with Nevada's Skip Houk during Tom's first Intercollegiate year. Houk was an experienced and excellent fighter, the 147 lb. Conference Champion in 1962, as well as a "2 mile" runner on the Nevada track team. (Fifteen years later I picked up a Runners' World magazine and found that Skip Houk was the current national 50 mile running champion!)

But Tom avenged his only loss by beating Skip Houk in the 1963 Championship Tournament and winning the award for the Conferences' "Outstanding Fighter."

Skip Houk was undefeated at 147 lbs. the next year because Tom had moved up to 156 lbs! Tom also motivated me to move up to a heavier weight division: When Tom moved up to the 156 lb. level, I decided it was a good time for me to move up to 165!

I didn't win my championship until 1965, when I was 7 and 0. Sparring hard with Tom in practice prepared me well for fighting intercollegiate opponents. I'd joke that the competition matches were easier than the "practices."

As a college boxer I "peaked" in my senior year, 1965, and would have had to train intensely for the next three years to have a fantasy chance to even compete in the tryouts for the 1968 Olympics. My teammate, master boxer and three time Intercollegiate Champion Tom Gioseffi did keep training and fighting, twice winning the San Francisco Golden Gloves 165 lb. Championship (and twice winning the tournament's Outstanding Boxer award). However, he finally lost a controversial split decision to Jerry Quarry's younger brother, Mike Quarry, in the 1968 "Western States" Olympic elimination finals. (As a professional, Mike Quarry was later the No. 1 professional light-heavyweight contender in the World, losing in 1972 to the great light heavyweight Champion Bob Foster.) As for me, I went to law school instead, trading the physical punishment of the fight world for the psychological punishment of practicing law.

In 2008, more than 40 years after he had boxed, Tom Gioseffi was selected for the Cal Athletic Hall of Fame, the first Boxer to be so honored. (Ed Nemir had been selected as a "Coach.")

1965

Cal Belters Paul Rein and Tom Gioseffi, 1965

1965

Gioseffi Seeks Third Ring Title To Close Undefeated Season

By SID BERGER

The Bear boxing team is blessed with one of the bruisingest boxers in the country: Tom Gioseffi. Fighting in the 156 pound category, Gioseffi has gone two successive seasons undefeated, and, including his sophomore year, he has compiled a record of 16-1-1.

As a soph Tom met and drew Skip Houk of Nevada, and later on that year Houk beat him. So in retaliation he was pitted against Houk in the finals of the 147 pound bracket that same year, and took the championship by conquering this old nemesis.

Since then, he hasn't lost a bout.

Boxing coach Ed Nemir has only praise for his star. "He's a good leader," he said, "and just last week he was chosen captain of the squad." And he's one of the best 156 pound boxers in the nation, Nemir asserts. The coach goes so far as to say that he is probably one of the top four amateurs in the country.

TREMENDOUS DESIRE

Why is he so good? Nemir stated that Tom's greatest innate ability is his desire. "He just wanted to fight."

Of course, this isn't all. He is fast, strong, clever, and he has a great concentration when he boxes, both intellectually and physically.

Not only is he fast, but he is also quick: that is, exceptionally fast to take advantage of his opponents' slightest tactical error. It takes brains as well as brawn to be a good boxer.

This was demonstrated this semester when Tom was awarded the Wheeler Scholarship because of his academic and athletic achievements. He is, incidentally, an engineering major, taking 16 units, is especially interested in metallurgy, and hopes to continue in this field after graduation.

OLYMPIC BID?

When asked about his future in boxing he said that he does not want to be a professional, but would like a try at the Golden Gloves, and maybe the '68 Olympics.

And with the rate of his improvement as it is, this is possible. As a soph he was "very good," and as he matured, so did his boxing. He says that when he was just beginning, he would get into the ring with the idea that he was just going to land punches, and he would swing until he was pooped.

He won with this method, but he also learned that this wasn't the way to box. He began taking more time, using more strategy, and, according to Nemir, his boxing improved tremendously. "He began throwing fewer punches, but they were landing harder."

Nemir states that one of Tom's greatest assets is the fact that he is in superb condition. He works out about two hours every day, skipping rope for his footwork, running to improve his stamina, and hitting the bag to increase his strength and concentration. He says that boxing is probably the best sport by which to get into top physical condition. It takes nearly every muscle of the body, and it requires stamina and mental concentration.

VICTORY BY OPPORTUNITY

Tom says that there is really no such thing as "planning an attack"; the way to victory lies in being able to take advantage of every opportunity, and a good boxer creates his own opportunities.

"Experience helps," he points out. With experience a boxer tends to be less nervous before each fight, and can concentrate more on his fighting. He tries never to be overconfident. "All it takes is one punch," and you can lose a bout to a boxer who is definitely your inferior.

As a matter of fact, Gioseffi is a very modest person. He is also easy-going, and, he says, "I'm not made angry easily." He relies on the coach to pick out his errors and bad habits, and he tries to correct them immediately.

He claims that "guys don't take a beating in college boxing." The two main reasons he cites are first that the gloves used in college boxing are considerably bigger and more padded than those used by professionals, and that college boxers must wear head-guards to protect the eyes and ears.

WANTS MORE COLLEGE BOXING

He is dissatisfied with the lack of intercollegiate boxing in the United States, considering that it is a superb conditioner and it is not very dangerous when fought under collegiate officiating and rules. In fact, there is only one intercollegiate conference in the country, composed of only four schools: Cal, Chico State, Stanford, and Nevada. Because of men like Gioseffi, Cal is the conference champ.

On March 19 and 20 the CCBS Championships will be held in Harmon gymnasium, and Gioseffi should take his third consecutive conference championship.

He has the power, he certainly has the experience, and he has the desire. With these attributes, he is justifiably rated among the best in the country in his class.

This 5-11 senior will be detracting from the world of boxing when he quits, but he will be an asset to the world of metallurgy.

TOM GIOSEFFI
Terror at 156 lbs.

1965

THIS IS Cal ATHLETICS.

DAVE ARCHIBALD
Men's Track & Field

Archibald was the 1964 Pac-8 champion in the 440-yard dash and NCAA and Pac-10 champion in the mile relay in both 1964 and '65. In 1964, he was fourth at the NCAA meet in the 440 (46.0), while he took third at nationals a year later in 46.4 seconds. Archibald was part of Cal's mile relay that went undefeated, winning 28 consecutive races against collegiate, national and international competition. In 1966, he set an unofficial world record in the straight 440-yard dash in Santa Rosa. In addition, Archibald was a member of the U.S. National team that faced Poland (in Chicago) and the USSR (in Palo Alto) in 1962.

JACK HART
Football

A first-team all-conference selection in 1958, Hart served as co-captain of Cal's team that won the Pacific Coast Conference and played in the 1959 Rose Bowl. As a running back for the Bears, he led Cal in receiving (396 yards) and scoring (58 points) his senior season, which was capped with two touchdowns vs. Iowa in the Rose Bowl. He also paced the Bears in scoring as a sophomore (36 points) and in rushing (395 yards) and scoring (36 points) as a junior. Hart has remained close to Cal and college football since graduating, serving as executive director of the annual East-West Shrine Game and as committee chairman for the Glenn Seaborg Award, which is presented to a distinguished former Cal football player each fall. He is also a past president of Pappy's Boys, an organization of players who played for head coach Pappy Waldorf that continues to support the Golden Bears.

TOM GIOSEFFI
Boxing

Gioseffi captured three consecutive California Collegiate Boxing Conference titles from 1963-65. The Bears also won the 1965 team championship by claiming six of the nine weight divisions. Gioseffi compiled a 22-1-1 record during his three years with the Cal boxing program, which began in 1916, and he was twice voted the CCBC's outstanding boxer. He is the first boxer to be elected to the Cal Athletic Hall of Fame.

DON JAMES JR.
Rugby

James played both football and rugby for the Bears, but is best known for his exploits on the rugby pitch. A four-time All-American, he helped Cal to four national championships and later served as a member of the U.S. National team from 1987-94. James is one of only three Cal alumni to have earned a "Blue" at Oxford University. He was selected to the national championship tournament team four times, helped the Old Blues win two national club titles and earned nine international caps with the U.S. squad. As a football player, James was a two-year starter along the defensive line, earning second-team All-Pac-10 honors in 1983 and playing in the Japan Bowl All-Star Game in 1984.

Cal Athletic Hall of Fame Inductee, 2008

1965

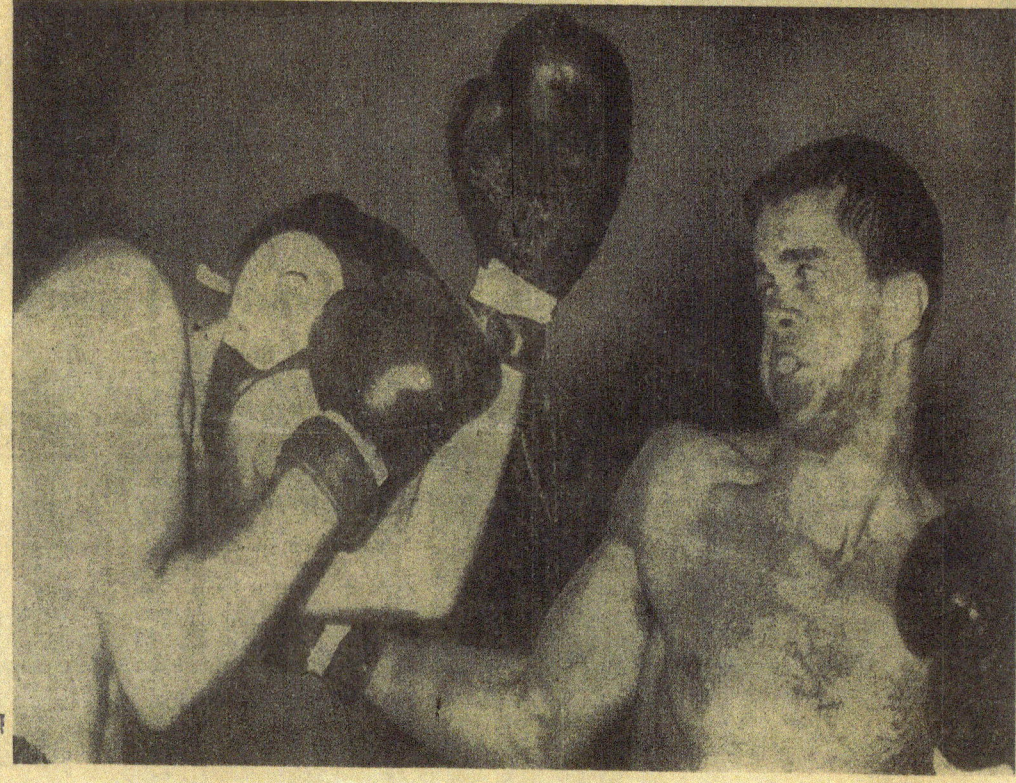

2 Years after graduating, Tom won the Outstanding Boxer Award at the Golden Gloves in San Francisco.

1961

Fall Intramurals

Phelan Wins Cunha Trophy With TKO Over Weiner In 2nd

John Phelan won the Milton Cunha trophy in the intramural boxing finals Thursday night in Harmon Gymnasium. The perpetual trophy goes to the best boxer in the annual tournament.

Phelan, representing Sigma Phi, earned the award with a second round TKO over Dave Weiner in the 139 pound, senior division.

The team award went to Theta Xi fraternity. John Barnard was the only finalist representing Theta Xi.

There was eleven bouts in all and boxing coach, Ed Nemir said, "The caliber of the fights was as good as we've ever had." All but one fight was won by decision, but there were three other knockdowns.

Dave Licata, of Deutsch, won the opening fight of the evening with a close split decision over Thep Himathongham, of Thai Students. That was in the 125 pound class.

Dale Olson defeated Allan Jacobs in the 132 pound junior division and Justin Firenze won a split decision over Tom Bulgin in the senior division of the same weight class. Olson, of Ehrman Hall, scored a second round knockdown.

Park Trefts, of Pi Kappa Phi, won a unanimous decision over Theta Xi's Barnard in the 139-pound, junior division. Barnard was knocked down once in the second round.

Lowell Hickey and Tom Gioseffi were the victors in the 147-pound weight class. Hickey, of Navy and Theta Chi, won a split decision over Skene Moody, of Sigma Alpha Epsilon. Gioseffi's victory over Duke McConnon was by unanimous decision.

Ken Balcomb, of Delta Sigma Phi, was saved by the bell in the third round of his 156 pound match with Paul Rein, of Piedmont, but Rein had enough points to win unanimously. Balcomb was still on the canvas when the fight ended.

Joe Alvarez's aggressive style led him to a unanimous decision over Walt Foskett, of Zeta Psi, in the 165-pound junior division.

In the senior division of the same weight class John Parks slugged out a decision over Greg Goddard, of the Vat 69ers.

Ken Budman, of Kappa Nu, defeated Don MacAdam in a powerful slugfest between two heavyweights. Neither fighter scored a knockdown, however.

Graeme Forrester won the 179-pound intramural championship by default. In the semi-finals he defeated Don Bell in a split decision.

In the ceremonies after the bouts each winner received a belt buckle with "California Intramural" and a boxing insignia engraved on it. Mrs. Cunha awarded the Cunha trophy to Phelan.

1961 Intramural Championships - Never Give Up!
by Paul Rein

A snapshot of the conclusion of a "championship" boxing match decorates my office wall. It's from the Cal Berkeley Intramural middleweight boxing championship in late October, 1961. One boxer is walking away from the body of the other fighter, lying in the center of the ring. The photo reminds me to "Never give up."

As a 17 year old Cal freshman, I had signed up for a "beginning" boxing class to fulfill my academic requirement for a half unit "physical education" course. After a month's classes, I had learned little besides using the straight left jab and maintaining a rudimentary <u>defense</u>! (I *never* did get the "defense" part down too well, possibly on the theory that the other guy would get tired of hitting me.) At the coach's urging I signed up for the Intramural Boxing Tournament. Having never boxed before, I expected to fight in a "Novice" division. However, for some logistical reason all sixteen of us at 156 pounds competed in one "Senior" division.

I was trying to improve my boxing and find some other claim to fame besides having so hard a head that it could damage my opponents' knuckles. (My friend and teammate, Dennis Natali, later nicknamed me "Hard" Rein.) Somehow, much more by effort than by skill, I fought through three elimination bouts, working my way up to the middleweight finals of the Intramural Championship Tournament, held in Cal's Harmon Gymnasium.

My opponent turned out to be my "best friend" in the "beginning" boxing class, Ken Balcolm. We <u>both</u> knew that Ken was the better "boxer," as we had learned through numerous sparring sessions. I realized that I might need a knockout to beat Ken, as he was very likely to outpoint me due to his superior boxing skills. So I gave a request to my "corner man," varsity veteran Bill McAdam: "When there's only 30 seconds left in the fight, <u>if</u> I'm way behind on points and <u>need a knockout</u> to win, yell the word 'Tiger' to me as a signal."

Sure enough, after 2½ rounds of Ken using his better boxing skills to outpoint me, I heard Bill's voice from my corner yell, "Better go get 'em, <u>Tiger</u>!" I threw caution to the wind and traded wild punches with Ken until one of mine hit his jaw and he crumpled to the canvas.

After the fight, while he held an iced towel against his still bleeding nose, Ken introduced me to his wife: "I want you to meet my good <u>friend</u>, Paul Rein." His wife did her best to accept that <u>this</u> was one way that "friends" played together.

Never Give Up : 3rd Round KO

1962

Ed Nemir
Coach

A solid punch lands on an unguarded jaw.

Boxing

This was a year of rebuilding for California's Boxing Coach, Ed Nemir. Graduation took conference champions Gordon Van Kessel and Don Ricci and veterans Fred Weaver, John Wylie and Jack Kawamoto. Returning boxers, however, included conference champion Dennis Natali, and lettermen Mike Huffman, Dennis Treadway, Larry Costa, Bill McAdam, and Roger Kent. Promising newcomers included Tom Bulgin and Dave Weiner. The fall intramural tournament, the main source of varsity boxing material, had well over 100 participants. Inasmuch as conference rules forbid schools to recruit boxers who have had experience in the Golden Gloves match, AAU tournaments or in Armed Forces competition, the member schools, to a large degree, begin the season on an equal basis. The schedule was full of hard-fought dual meets and the season ended in the team's 3-3-2 finish.

Members of the Boxing team don their protective gear before a practice session.

BOXING TEAM — Left to Right, **Row One:** Dave Weiner, Dennis Natali, James DiGrazia, Cliff Sarko, Mike Huffman, Dennis Treadway. **Row Two:** Ed Nemir, Coach, Larry Costa, Bill McAdam, Roger Kent, Tom Bulgin, Roger Baker, Don Bell.

1963

Ed Nemir
Coach
Former 129-lb. Pacific Coast champion; Olympic silver medal wrestler.

Boxing

Ed Nemir's Bear battlers wound up the 1963 season with a very satisfactory record, defeating all their opponents except Nevada in dual meets. Since the CCBA forbids competition by men with previous boxing experience, the Bears were not at a disadvantage to other schools in the league. Stanford and Chico State fell to the Californians twice, while Nevada swept the league undefeated. Outstanding in competition were Dennis Treadway, who remained undefeated for the season, and Tom Gioseffi whose only non-wins came at the hands of Nevada's Skip Houk in a draw and a TKO. Gioseffi later had the satisfaction of defeating Houk and was chosen the outstanding boxer of the league.

BOXING TEAM — Row One: Dave Licata, Brian Loveman, Bill Corrigan, Steve Ricketts, Josh Tofield, Jim Moore, Paul Alpert, Dennis Treadway. Row Two: Ed Nemir, Coach, Terry Timmins, Max Levine, Frank Welsh, Tom Drewek, Rod Marraccini, Tom Gioseffi, Paul Rein.

Dennis Treadway throws a left at Stanford's Roger Smith. Dennis went undefeated this season in the 139-lb. division.

Max Levine gets the victory sign in the heavyweight division.

What's the matter, Mike? Flunk a mid term?

1963

Nemir's Boxers Deep Despite New Faces

Despite the fact that the 1963 version of the Cal boxing team will have only two returning lettermen it will have an abundance of new faces that will give it its greatest depth in many years.

The pugilists will have two men in each weight division except 180-pounds and coach Ed Nemir said, "We haven't done that well in a long time."

The returning lettermen are Dennis Treadway, 139 pounds and Dave Weiner, who has boxed in both the 139 and 147 pound classes. And neither has his job completely secured.

Steve Ricketts, co-winner of the Cunha trophy in this year's intramurals, will be battling it out with Treadway for the starting berth in the 139 pound division.

This leaves Weiner in the 147-pound category along with Tom Gioseffi, 1960 intramural champion. This is sophomore Gioseffi's first year of varsity eligibility.

The heavyweight division, which was very sparse last year, will have Frank Welsh and Rod Maracini vying for starting roles this season.

Welsh is a senior from Palo Alto and is the top heavyweight on the varsity wrestling team.

Jim Moore and John Parks will make the 165-pound division an especially strong one for the Bears this year. Both are intramural champions.

All these boxers plus a host of other as yet unproven youngsters will be in Harmon Gym Saturday night for Cal's opening CCB meet with Chico St.

1963

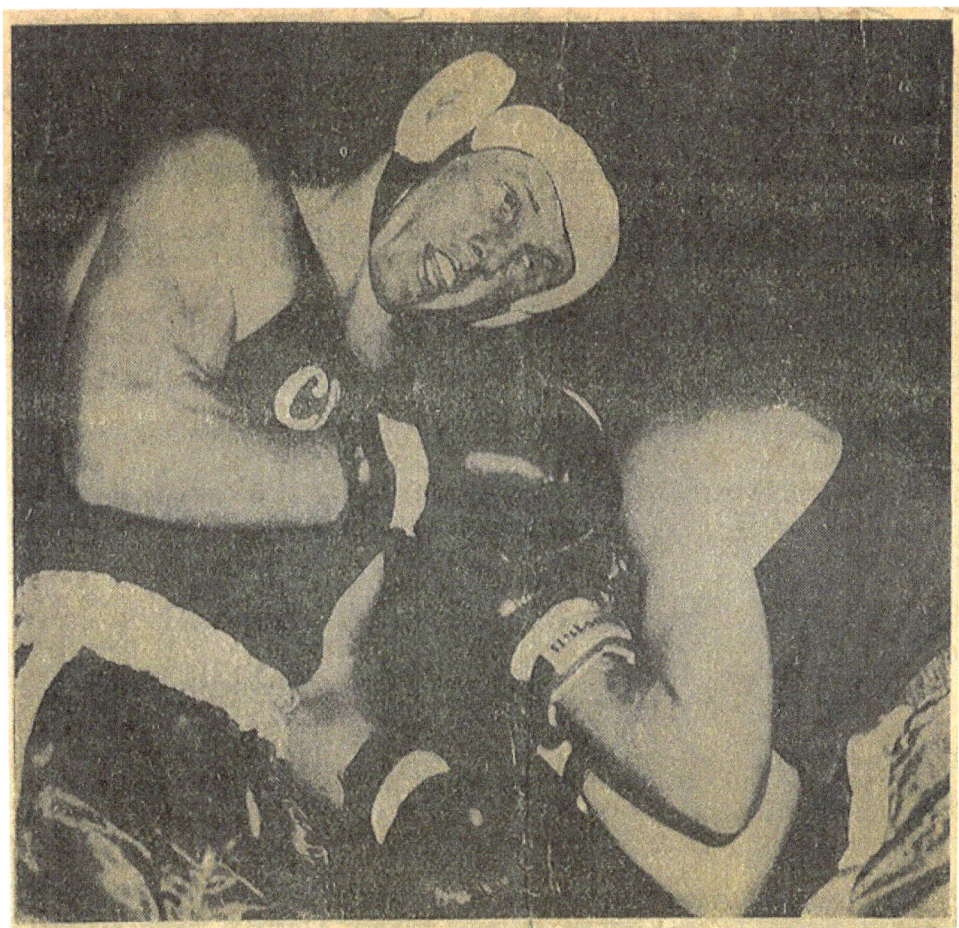

BODY BLOW—Chico State's John Thompson (left) grimaces after absorbing a body jab from University of Nevada boxer Dave Stix in Saturday night's 156 lb. bout in North Gymnasium. Stix won this bout but Chico State edged the Wolfpack 5½ to 4½. The local boxers will host the University of California team in North Gymnasium tonight.
—Bruce Harris Photo

Chico Tops Nevada
Cal to Box Here Tonight

Top flight ring action will be on tap in North Gymnasium tonight at 8 o'clock as the Chico State College Wildcats host California's Golden Bears.

THE UNIVERSITY of California squad, coached by Eddie Nemir, registered a 7-4 decision earlier this season in Berkeley.

Expected to see action for the local mitt team are Carlin Jardine (132), Robby McSpadden (139), Paul Guedet (147), John Thompson (156), Ron Duval 165), Doug Paul (178) and Ed Burton (heavyweight).

SLATED to enter the ring for the Berkeley Bears are Paul Albert, Dennis Treadway, Tom Gioseffi, Terry Timmons, Paul Rein, John Parks, Rod Marracainni, Max Levine and Frank Welsh.

Saturday night, Chico State picked up its first victory of the season in beating University of Nevada 5½-4½.

another point as Courter TKO'd Mike Gottschalk. The final one-and-one-half points came via Ron Duval's draw with Chris Wilson and a forfeit in the 132-pound class.

UNIVERSITY of Nevada winners included Skip Houk (147), Dave Stix (156) and Jim Evans (heavyweight). The Wolfpack's final tally came when Chico forfeited the 123-pound bout.

1963

Parks-Duval Top Cal-Chico Boxing Card

There will be a full card of 11 fights, 10 of which will count in the scoring, tomorrow night at 8 o'clock when Chico St. brings its boxing team into Harmon Gym.

One of the top billings of the evening will be in the 165-pound division between Cal's John Parks and Ron Duval. Neither have a varsity letter, but they were each chosen number one in a division which is three or four meen deep at both schools.

Little Paul Alpert will be boxing Chico's conference champion in Carlin Jardine in his 132-pound bout.

Denny Treadway, 139 pounds, will be the Bears' only letterman in the meet. He will face Robby McSpadden.

SATURDAY'S CARD:

Chico		Cal
Forfeit	125	Loveman
Jardine	132	Alpert
McSpadden	139	Treadway
*Katsumoto	139	Ricketts
Guedet	147	Gioseffi
Thompson	156	Timmins
Courter	156	Rein
Duval	165	Parks
Maurer	165	Moore
Paul	178	Marracini
Burton	HW	Welsh
Anderson	HW	Levine

*Extra bout

Cal Boxers in Win Over Chico

The University of California boxing team defeated Chico State, 7-4, in the opening match for both teams Saturday night in Harmon Gym.

Cal's John Parks decisioned Ron Duval in the 165-pound feature match, almost decking his foe on three occasions.

Three Bears won by knockouts. Denny Treadway, 139, stopped Robby McSpadden in the first round; Tom Gioseffi, 147, flattened Joe Guedet in the second and Paul Rein, 156, stiffened Jerry Corter in the second.

Boxers Go In Mare Island Invite; Four Cal Fighters Still Unbeaten

California's four undefeated boxers stay at home tonight, as four other pugilists journey to Mare Island to take part in the Navy Invitational Tournament.

Brian Loveman (125), Steve Ricketts (139), Paul Alpert (132) and Jim Moore (165) will make the trip to the Navy base. Terry Timmins is a possible entrant in the 156-pound division.

Loveman is paired up with Tom Santos of Mare Island, Alpert is scheduled to meet Ron Moseley of Alameda, Ricketts will square off with Sherwood Gehris of Concord, and Moore tangles with Jim Gibauitch, who is stationed on Treasure Island.

The rest of the squad will continue preparations for the Bears' final home boxing show of the year against the University of Nevada, Saturday night.

Paul Rein, Max Levine, Denny Treadway and Tom Giioseffi will try to extend their win strings against Nevada. Levine, Treadway and Giosseffi are 3-0 while Rein has won one and drawn two.

Rein will have a job to do this week in preparing for his match with Nevada's highly rated letterman Skip Houk.

Paul Rein, sophomore boxer who has been moved to number one position in the 156 pound class, will meet Nevada letterman Skip Houk this Saturday at 8 p.m. in Harmon gym. He won't fight in tonight's match at Mare Island.

1963

Daily Cal - February 18, 1963

Rein, Butts Draw as California Boxers Maul Stanford 7-2-1

California's boxing team mangled arch-rival Stanford, 7-2-1, at Harmon Gym Saturday night to extend its unblemished season record to 2-0.

The Bear maulers capitalized on three forfeits in easing to its victory.

Paul Rein of Cal and Jerry Butts, two superb boxers, drew in the feature match of the evening. Both fighters were dripping with blood at the conclusion of the even bout.

Dave Weiner, Denny Treadway and Tom Gioseffi earned decision wins in 147-pound fights for the Bears. Heavyweight Max Levine was the only other Cal winner. He decisioned Mike Dowling.

Stanford's John McMains was the only TKO winner of the night. He stopped Rod Marraccini in the third round.

Brian Loveman (125), John Tofield (125) and Steve Ricketss (139), all of Cal, won exhibition bouts.

Boxing

At Berkeley

California vs. Twelfth Naval Dist.:

125—Brian Loveman, Cal., dec. Richard Kline, Mare Island; Josh Tofield, Cal., dec. Tom Santos, Mare Island.

139—Steve Ricketts, Cal., dec. Tom Planeni, Treasure Island.

156—Joe Rubio, Treasure Island, dec. Terry Timmons, Cal.

California vs. Stanford:

125—Forfeit to Cal.

132—Rudy Oberzon, Stanford, dec. Paul Alpert, Cal.

139—Forfeit to Cal.

147—Dave Weyner, Cal., dec. Bruce Stadel, Stanford; Denny Treadway, Cal., dec. Roger Smith, Sanford; Tom Tioseffi, Cal., dec. Al Taylord, Stanford.

156—Paul Rein, Cal., drew Jerry Butts, Stanford.

165—Forfeit to Cal.

178—John McMain, Stanford, dec. Rod Marraccini, Cal.

Heavyweight—Max Levine, Cal., dec. Mike Dowling, Stanford.

1963

Wednesday, March 6, 1963

Seek Sweep
Boxers Go for Indian Scalps

By Marylinda Morrison

California boxers journey to Stanford today to attempt a sweep of this year's home and home series with the Indians. In the first meeting at Harmon last month, the Bears destroyed Stanford 7 to 2 with one draw.

This meet finds the Indians forfeiting two matches to Cal in the 125 and 139 lb. classes leaving the Bears needing only three wins for a triumph.

Cal will be handicapped in the heavyweight division by the loss of Max Levine, winner of the last meet. Levine will be out for at least the next three days with a bruised shoulder. He will be replaced by Frank Welsh who will face Indian Mike Dowling.

In the 132 class Cal's Bob Arevelo will meet Rudy Oberan, winner of the 147 class last meet. Tom Gioseffi, undefeated this year, will seek a second win against Stanford's Al Gaylord.

A rematch between Paul Rein and Jerry Butts at 165 lbs. will find the two seeking to remedy the draw situation resulting from their last meeting. Rein is undefeated this season and tied only by Butts.

Terry Timmons will meet Brett Brenaman in the 165 division and Jim Moore boxes Tim Steele at 178 pounds.

The boxers, having dropped one and tied one meet since last they met Stanford, are seeking the season's third win.

This will be the next to the last meet of the season leaving the boxers only a journey to Reno to meet the University of Nevada maulers. The Wolfpack is the only team to have bested the Bears, winning by only one point when they visited Harmon.

Daily Cal - March 7, 1963

Thursday, March 7, 1963 • THE DAILY CALIFORNIAN • Page

Boxers Sweep Series Defeat Stanford Again

California boxers took a second straight win from Stanford to sweep this year's home and home series. The boxers journeyed to Stanford to return the Indian's visit to Harmon.

The final score of five to three in California's favor was assisted by Stanford forfeits in both the 125 pound and 139 pound divisions.

Both teams scored technical knock-outs as the 165 pound class match between Terry Timmons of Cal and Bob Brennaman of Stanford was halted in Timmons favor in the third round.

In the heavyweight class Stanford's Mike Dowling scored one of Stanford's three bout wins when the fight was stopped in the second round. Loser Frank Welsh was a last minute entry when Bear favorite Max Levine had to be withdrawn.

In the 156 pound division a rematch between Indian Jerry Butts and Bear Paul Rein resulted in Rein's first defeat of the season. The last time the two met the result was a draw.

Stanford's only other win came in the 132 pound match when Rudy Oberzan decisioned Bear Bob Arevello.

Cal's three wins out of the six matches actually boxed included the 147 and 178 weights as well as Timmon' TKO. At 147 Cal's Tom Guseffie retained his undefeated record by decisioning Al Gaylord.

In the 178 pound division it was Cal's Jim Moore winning the decision over Tim Steele.

The win yesterday extended the Bears' winning total to three out of five attempts this season with one loss and one draw.

Only one more outing awaists the Bears when they travel to Reno next weekend ot meet the University of Nevada Wolfpack, the holders of the single win against Cal boxers this season.

Bear heavyweight man, Max Levine should be restored to action fully recovered from a bruised shoulder that sidelined him yesterday against the Indians. With his help the Bears hope to be able to reverse the loss by one point to Nevada at Harmon Gym.

1963

4-Way Battle For National Crown; Boxing Team vs. Chico Tomorrow

By Lowell Hickey

There's a California varsity team that, believe it or not, is a strong contender for a national championship.

It's the boxing squad coached by Ed Nemir.

All that is required to be national boxing champions is to be the best of four teams, because that's all there are competing in intercollegiate boxing.

But the way the Bear pugilists have stomped over the only two opponents they've faced it may be that they would be national champs if the whole country still competed.

The Bears defeated Chico State in Harmon Gym, 7-4, two weeks ago and Stanford, 7-2-1, last Friday in the same place.

Cal travels to Chico tomorrow night for a rematch with the Staters that should be closer than the last meet. Nemir said that his team had the advantage of being better conditioned than Chico for the first meet, because Cal started training earlier.

Several Cal boxers have looked especially impressive in their first two bouts.

Tom Gioseffi, at 147 pounds, is without a doubt the best welterweight to hit the Cal campus since Gordon Van Kessel and is possibly the best boxer the Bears have had in any weight class for the last several years.

The 147-pound class is the Bears' strongest, as both Denny Treadway and Dave Weiner, the only two lettermen on the squad, are in that division.

Yet Gioseffi, only a sophomore, got the nod over both of his seniors in the Stanford meet when Nemir chose to go with the young left-hander against the Indians' Al Gaylord, a two year letterman.

Gioseffi decisioned Gaylord quite easily.

The time before that, against Chico, the southpaw fighter decked Joe Guedet in the first varsity bout of his life.

Another Cal boxer that has looked especially good in his first two bouts is Paul Rein, 156 pounds.

Rein KO'd his Chico opponent Jerry Courter in the second round. That was Rein's first varsity match.

Against Stanford's Jerry Butts, Rein could only earn a draw, but that fight was the best of a very good card. Both boys were very aggressive and were bleeding profusely from the nose at the end.

After the Chico State meet tomorrow night the Bears box only four more times and just one of these is at home. That is against the University of Nevada at 8 p.m., Saturday, March 2.

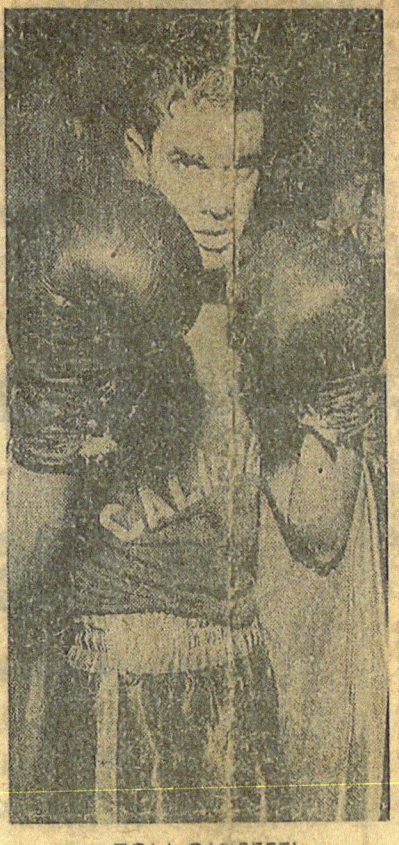

TOM GIOSEFFI
149-pound champ?

March 23, 1963 - Chico Enterprise-Record

A GOOD ONE, BUT... —California's Terry Timmins applies a solid right to the face of the University of Nevada's Chris Wilson in last night's 165-pound clash in the California Collegiate Boxing Conference Tournament in North Gymnasium here. Wilson, un-shaken by the blow, went on to decision Timmins and moved into tonight's finals. He will box Chico State College's Ron Duval for the 165-pound championship. (Enterprise-Record Photo)

1963

Seven 'Cats in Finals

Thomson, Anderson Capture First Night Wins In CCBC Tourney Action

By TED BLOFSKY
(Enterprise-Record Sportswriter)

Thanks to the luck of the draw and opening night victories by John Thomson and Roger Anderson, Chico State College's host Wildcats will have seven boxers in tonight's fourth annual California Collegiate Boxing Conference Tournament finals.

Six bouts were held last night in CSC's North Gymnasium and three of them ended before the regulation three rounds expired.

CSC coach Willie Simmons, University of California mentor Eddie Nemir and University of Nevada tutor Jim Olivas took part in the afternoon drawings and the Wildcats drew five byes.

The only bout on the eight-match program tonight in which a Wildcat boxer will not be performing will be in the 147-pound class. There were only two entries for that class—the same as for the 132-pound division.

Last night's card was a quick one. It took an hour to get in the six bouts and an intermission. The sparse gathering at the North Gymnasium hardly had a chance to settle back into their seats before it was intermission as two of the first three bouts went only a round.

Nevada's Larry Williamson moved into tonight's finals when he quickly disposed of the University of California's Brian Loveman in the opening bout of the evening in the 125-pound class.

Williamson went to the attack from the opening bell, throwing caution to the wind and wading in on his opponent. Loveman went to the canvas after a hard right hand from Williamson and Nemir called a halt to the affair when the count reached five.

The Bears' Denny Treadway needed only a round to dispose of the Wolfpack's Gene Montrose in the 139-pound bracket. Treadway countered well against the pressing Montrose early in the round, then caught the Nevadan with two straight rights and a left hook.

Referee Bill Moule gave Montrose a mandatory eight - count near the end of the round, although the Wolfpack boxer did not go down. Olivas would not let Montrose come out for the second round.

The first bout of the evening to go the full route came when Thomson utilized a straight left jab to overcome Cal's Paul Rein and gain a berth in the 156-pound division finals.

Thomson opened strong in the first round with his left jab continually setting Rein back. Rein countered well and midway the round caught Thomson with a good right.

Thomson continued to press the attack and his stiff left and occasional right made the difference in the fight. Rein tired in the second round and his mouth and nose were bloodied from Thomson's punches.

Thomson won the bout going away with his third round showing. Using the left hand exclusively, Thomson was in complete command in the third frame and Rein's nose and mouth were bleeding badly when the scrap came to an end.

Nevada's rangy Chris Wilson simply had too much reach and savvy for Cal's Terry Timmins in the 165-pound fracas. Timmins was the aggressor early in the fight but continually walked into stiff punches from Wilson. Wilson won the final two rounds easily as Timmins tired and could not keep the pace.

The only close fight of the evening came in the 178-pound division where the Bears' Jim Moore copped a split decision from Ne-
(Continued on Page 9A, Col. 3)

March 23, 1963 Chico Enterprise-Record

Thompson, Anderson Take Wins in CCBC Tournament

3/23/63 Chico Enterprise

(Continued from Page 8A) vada's John Curry.

Moore utilized a left hook for a major portion of his assault and forced the attack throughout the fight. Curry countered well and rallied in the closing seconds of each round.

Moore tired in the third round as Curry came on strong. However, Moore's point margin was not overcome on two of the judges' ballots and the California boxer won the decision.

Sugar Ramos Will Stay In LA a While Longer

LOS ANGELES (UPI) — Newly crowned world featherweight champion Sugar Ramos today planned to remain here until Monday, or until there was more definite news about the condition of stricken Davey Moore, the man he defeated Thursday night.

Ramos decided Friday to forego a celebration scheduled for him in Mexico City today because of his concern about Moore. His manager, Cuco Conde, said they intended to return to Mexico City for the big ceremony but would stay here a while longer.

The Wildcats' Anderson gained sweet revenge when he stopped Cal's Max Levine in the brief heavyweight encounter.

Levine owned a pair of regular season victories over Anderson. Anderson's early strategy obviously was to stay away from Levine and he circled his opponent while flicking left jabs.

Anderson began to force the attack even more and then came a big right hand that caught Levine flush on the jaw. Levine did not go down but he was walking on "easy" street when Moule gave him a mandatory eight count.

Moule called a halt to the bout at 1:25 of the first round.

Tonight's finals get underway promptly at 8 o'clock. Only Carlin Jardine, CSC's 132-pounder, will be defending his title. New champions will be crowned in all other weight divisions.

Following are last night's results and the pairings for tonight:

LAST NIGHT'S RESULTS
125—Larry Williamson (N) stopped Brian Loveman (UC), 1:50 first round.
139—Denny Treadway (UC) stopped Gene Montrose (N), halted after first round.
156—John Thomson (CSC) dec. Paul Rein (UC).
156—Chris Wilson (N) dec. Terry Timmins (UC).
178—Jim Moore (UC) dec. John Curry (N).
Hwt.—Roger Anderson (CSC) stopped Max Levine (UC), 1:25 of first round.

TONIGHT'S PAIRINGS
125—John Ulmer (CSC) vs. Larry Williamson (N).
132—Carlin Jardine (CSC) vs. Bob Arevalo (UC).
139—Robby McSpadden (CSC) vs. Denny Treadway (UC).
147—Skip Houk (N) vs. Tom Gioseffi (UC).
156—John Thomson (CSC) vs. Dave Stix (N).
165—Ron Duval (CSC) vs. Chris Wilson (N).
178—Doug Paul (CSC) vs. Jim Moore (UC).
Hwt.—Jim Evans (N) vs. Roger Anderson (CSC).

1963

Enterprise-Record
SPORTS

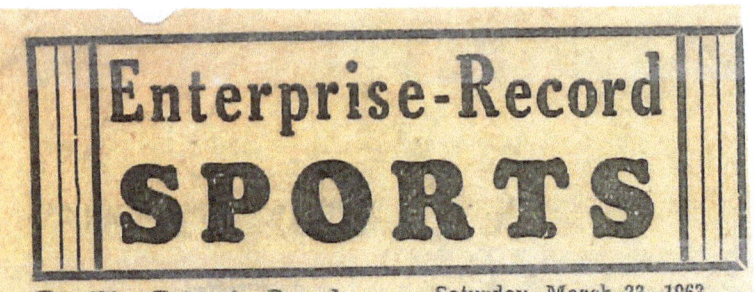

8A Chico Enterprise-Record Saturday, March 23, 1963

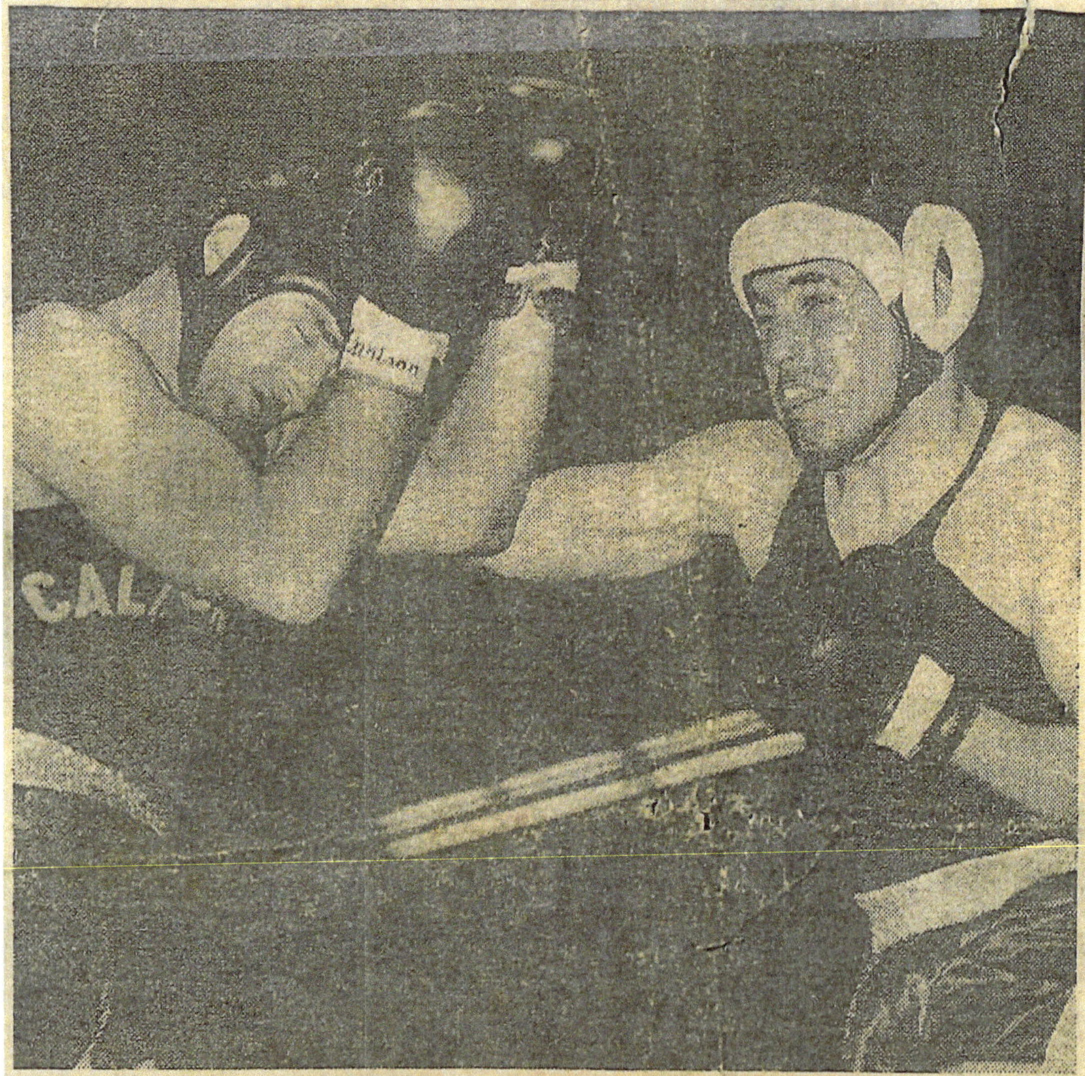

ANDERSON AT THE ATTACK—Chico State College's Roger Anderson (right) throws a right hand at the University of California's Max Levine, but the Bear boxer thwarts the blow with a shoulder. Levine did not get out of the way of a right hand a few moments later and was stopped by Anderson in 1:25 of the first round of their heavyweight bout in the fourth annual California Collegiate Boxing Conference Tournament last night at North Gymnasium. Anderson's victory placed him in tonight's finals against the University of Nevada's Jim Evans. Seven other bouts also are slated for tonight's finals. (Enterprise-Record Photo)

March 1963

Gioseffi Takes 147-Pound Title; Voted Loop's Outstanding Boxer

Cal sophomore Tom Gioseffi was voted the outstanding boxer of the California Collegiate Boxing Association tournament held at Chico State Friday and Saturday.

Gioseffi scored a revenge victory over Nevada's Skip Houk in the 147-pound championship bout. All three judges gave the fight to Gioseffi by scores of 9-6, 9-7 and 9-8.

After being stopped in the third round by Houk in Reno two weeks ago, Gioseffi decided to change his style for Saturday's match. He went into more of a crouch and was more aggressive than usual.

The crouch puzzled Houk and the Nevada fighter was unable to score with the left hook, his main weapon in the two previous bouts with Gioseffi.

The Californian took a lot out of his opponent with a good flurry in the second round and, although Houk tried to come back in the final frame, much of his usual punch was gone.

The only other Bear to win a championship was veteran Denny Treadway in the 139-pound class. Treadway defeated Gene Montrose of Nevada Friday night and Chuck McSpadden of Chico State Saturday.

In the 132-pound division Cal's Bob Arevalo lost a one point decision to Chico's Carlon Jardine in the finals. Coach Ed Nemir was very pleased with Arevalo's performance despite the loss. "He has come a long way this year," said Nemir of his sophomore boxer. "He should be a big help to us for the next two years."

Nevada's Larry Williams decisioned Brian Loveman, of Cal, Friday night and went on to win the 125-pound championship Saturday.

The Wolf Pack's Dave Stix won both the 156-pound class and the good sportsmanship award by defeating Chico's Jack Thompson Saturday, after Thompson had bested the Bears' Paul Rein the night before.

Nevada's Chris Wilsen won the 165-pound division by defeating Cal's Terry Timmins Friday night and Chico's Ron Duval in the finals.

The Bears' Jim Moore earned his way into the finals by taking a split decision over Nevada's Jim Curry in the 178-pound class, but dropped his match with Doug Paul, of Chico State, on Saturday.

Cal's Max Levine was knocked out by Chico's Roger Anderson in his heavyweight fight Friday night. Then, in the finals, Nevada's Jim Evans beat Anderson for the championship.

1964

Boxing Against Stanford: "Alice in Wonderland"
by Paul Rein

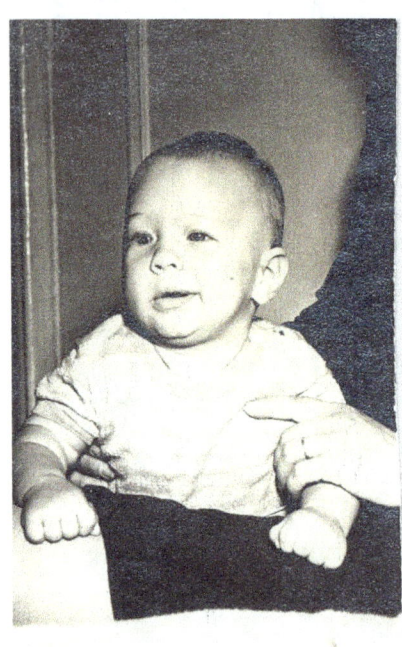

Early 1945. Punching Paul's first pugilistic pose. His mother, Erma sent this photo to Mel Rein, who was on a WWII ship, somewhere in the Pacific, with the caption "Dem's fighting words, Pa. Do ye wanna fight?"

In 1964, I was a 165 lb. middleweight on the Cal Boxing team, scheduled to fight against Stanford at the Palo Alto campus. Stanford's middleweight was Al Simmons. Before the scheduled time for the fight, both teams were transferred from one arena to another with a larger crowd capacity. We wound up sharing a single dressing room with the Stanford fighters. Because of the delay (which occurred after we had already gotten into our gear and started warming up), I ended up lying on my back on a wooden bench in the locker room while the Cal and Stanford fighters circled around the room.

I always carried a book with me in case I had "waiting" time to kill. Lying on my back, I began reading the book I had brought with me, which happened to be "Alice in Wonderland" by Lewis Carroll, a book I had loved as a child and was re-reading. I leaned back and fell asleep on the bench, "Alice in Wonderland" folded, cover up, on my chest. The sight of a sleeping Cal fighter absorbed in reading "Alice in Wonderland" probably terrorized the Stanford fighter.

At fight time someone woke me and, still in a deeply relaxed trance, I shuffled lazily out onto the gymnasium floor. Because several fights before mine had been shortened by knockouts, my turn came unexpectedly early, and I never had a chance to "warm up" or break a sweat. Fortunately I was so relaxed that I boxed in an unusually flowing and coordinated manner (although without my usual high emotional drive) and thoroughly out-pointed my Stanford opponent.

Just before the final bell I hit him on the chin with a right cross. His eyes glazed, his hands dropped to his sides. Because he appeared helpless I didn't hit him again, and I stepped out of the way expecting him to fall to the canvas. Unfortunately he didn't fall; the bell rang, and I had to settle for a decision!

Apparently the Stanford fighter didn't want to fight me again the next season; he dropped weight so that he could fight at 156 lbs. At this weight he leaped "out of the frying pan and into the fire" to fight the best boxer in college competition, my teammate Tommy Gioseffi, who cut the Stanford fighter's misery short by knocking him out in the second round.

(Are we simply over-eager Blue and Gold Bear loyalists, enjoying any opportunity to tease Stanford? Or are we seeking revenge for the Stanford treatment of Walter Gordon back in 1916? Please see "Please see Beating Up Stanford story by Donald Lawton, at page 4.)

Paul blocks punch with his face

1964

"Remember Me?"
by Paul Rein

In 1964, when I had the "experience" benefit of being in my second year of intercollegiate competition, I managed to outbox and outpoint University of Nevada football hero John McSweeney in a fight at Reno, refereed by the illustrious Mills Lane.

> The Daily Cal article by Howard Sanger described the fight:
> "Cal letterman Paul Rein found himself in the wildest fight of the evening when he locked up with newcomer John McSweeney, a Nevada gridiron hero."
> "The third and final round of the bout had the spectators on their feet."
> "At the end of the fracas the fighters were battling toe-to-toe along the ropes, exchanging sharp hooks. Rein got the nod in the wild fray."

McSweeney was only about 5'8", but was an All-Conference football guard at 190 lbs. He managed to get down to 169 lbs. (165 plus a 4 lb. "weight allowance") in order to fight me as a middleweight. The Nevada sports writer describing the fight said that "tall, lanky Paul Rein used his superior reach and boxing skills to outpoint Nevada football hero John McSweeney." I was 5'10" tall. Two weeks later I was still 5'10", but this time I fought a Nevada light heavyweight named Joe Curry in a fight designated as the "172 lb. championship." (I was 162 lbs., he was 182 lbs. I guess the coaches decided to split the difference, calling it a "172 lb." match!)

Joe Curry was 6'4" tall. This time the same Reno writer wrote that "short, stocky Paul Rein was unable to overcome the reach advantage of Nevada's Joe Curry and lost a split decision." In just two weeks I had gone from "tall and lanky" to "short and stocky!"

Because I was required to fight out of my weight division for the championship, John McSweeney won the championship tournament at 165 lbs. and became the 1964 "CCBC" middleweight champion. His only loss had been to me.

Exactly 25 years later, in March, 1989, my best friend, John Kolar and I traveled to Reno to see a featured professional "title" fight between two boxing legends, Hector "Macho" Camacho and Ray "Boom Boom" Mancini. I found out that John McSweeney, now a schoolteacher, was working as a boxing judge for some undercard fights. I was told that I might find him outside, near the restrooms, smoking a cigar. I came up behind a man fitting his description and called out, "John McSweeney, do you remember the name 'Paul Rein'?" McSweeney whirled around, and without missing a beat shouted, "Rein, you son-of-a-bitch! I always told Mills Lane he should have given the decision to me!"

1965

PUNCHING PAUL—California's rugged 165-pound boxing champion Paul Rein places his unbeaten 1965 record on the line tonight in the California Collegiate Boxing Conference Tournament at Harmon Gym. Semi-finals will be staged tonight with the championship bouts scheduled for tomorrow. Both cards get underway at 8 p.m.

1964

Boxing

A vastly better Bear boxing team was able to improve on their 1963 record of 3-2-1 by finishing 4-1-1. The loss and tie both came at the hands of the University of Nevada, always a power in boxing. Three Bears went into the California Collegiate Boxing Conference championships at Reno undefeated. Outstanding among these was junior Tom Gioseffi, a 156-pounder who had six straight victories throughout the season. Also undefeated were veterans Jim Moore and Paul Rein both of whom had draws to slightly mar their records.

Ed Nemir
Boxing Coach

BOXING TEAM — Row One: Kunio Inoue, Dave Weiner, Paul Bell, John Barnard, Bill Corrigan, Don Worden. **Row Two:** Ed Nemir, Coach; Jerry Knapp, Bob Winter, Dave Newhouse, Paul Rien, Tom Gioseffi, Larry Lusardi, Rod Marraccini, Manager.

Page Four • THE DAILY CALIFORNIAN • Tuesday, February 11, 1964

The Daily Californian Sports

L.C. WELL HICKEY Sports Editor   **RICHARD HOLMES** Sports Night Editor   **BILL ROWEN** Assistant Sports Editor

Bear Novice Winners to Start Against Veteran Nevada Boxers

John Barhard (140), Kunio Inoue (125), and Bob Winter (heavyweight) scored wins for California in the first collegiate fights of their careers at the recent California Collegiate Boxing Conference Novice Tournament.

Novices Bill Corrigan (136) and Jerry Knapp (178) fought their opponents to draws.

In three very close decisions, Don Worden (147), Larry Lusardi (155), and Dave Newhouse (170) all went down to defeat.

Win, lose, or draw, boxing coach Ed Nemir believes that his charges gained "valuable ring experience." He expressed a definite satisfaction with the novices' over-all performance.

Although the novice tournament does not go down in the official standings, it could be a very important meet for California.

In the match with Nevada tomorrow, Nemir will be relying primarily on first year men. Inoue, Bell, Corrigan, Knapp, and Winter will be starting against Nevada, but the only experience under their belts is intramural competition.

The only returning Cal boxers are Dave Weiner (147), Tom Gioseffi (156), and Paul Rein (165).

Nemir thinks that conditioning will be the biggest factor in the Nevada match. The new boxers will have to go from the one and a half minute rounds of novice boxing to the regulation two minute rounds.

To the layman, this may not sound like a difficult change. But those added thirty seconds in the ring will be a severe test of the boxers' endurance.

Nevada is perennially loaded with tough fighters. The Nevada team has more experience and more returning lettermen than Cal.

Nevada's Larry Williamson (125) and Jim Evans (heavyweight) are 1963 conference title holders. So novice victors Inoue and Winter will be faced with the fights of their lives.

After the Nevada match, Nemir's charges will return to their home gym to face Chico State on Saturday night. By then, Nemir will know whether he simply has a bunch of novices or a potential conference champion.

Following is the card for the Cal-Nevada battles:

Nevada		Cal
Williamson	125	Inoue
Breese	134	Bell
Jarvis	139	Corrigan
Houk	147	Weiner
Stix	156	Gioseffi
MacSweeney	165	Rein or Moore
Guynor	178	Knapp
Evans	HW	Winter

1964

Novices Come Through
Boxers Surprise Nevada, Tie 4-4

BY HOWARD SANGER

Coming off an encouraging 4-4 tie against Nevada at Reno, California's boxers will face Chico State tomorrow in Harmon gym at 7:15 p.m.

Two of the five novices, on whom Coach Nemir was counting so heavily against Nevada, came through with clutch victories.

Tom Corrigan (139) stopped Tom Jarvas in two, while Cal teammate Jerry Knapp, belting his opponent along the ropes, likewise scored a TKO in two rounds.

Veterans Paul Rein and Tom Gioseffi scored the other two Cal victories.

Two of Nevada's wins came by way of the TKO route. Larry Williamson belted out Kunio Inoue (126), and Skip Houk (147) stopped Dave Weiner. Nevada's Chuck Breese (132) and Jim Evans (HW) got decisions over Cal's Paul Bell and Bob Winter.

From the opening bell, the battle which was not decided until the last bout of the evening, had the large Reno crowd on its feet.

Attempting to battle it out with conference champ Williamson, Inoue tried to match the power of the experienced Williamson.

In the first round Williamson dropped Inoue with smashing rights; the end came in the third when Inoue was dropped by a punch to the stomach.

Williamson has now won his last 8 straight bouts, 7 by TKO's.

Powerful Skip Houk (147), biding his time in the first two rounds, caught Cal welterweight Dave Weiner with a vicious shot to the head. Weiner went down and Coach Nemir moved in to stop the fight against Weiner's wishes.

Cal letterman Paul Rein found himself in the wildest fight of the evening when he locked up with newcomer John McSweeney, a Nevada gridiron hero.

The third and final round of the bout had the spectators on their feet.

At the end of the fracas the fighters were battling toe-to-toe along the ropes, exchanging sharp hooks. Rein got the nod in the wild fray.

Novice Tom Corrigan (139), methodically boxed Nevada's Tom Jarvas at long range in the opening round, landing to the head and body.

In the 156 pound bout, Tom Gioseffi, handily whipped Nevada boxer Dave Stix. Stix was last year's 147 lb. Conference champion.

Going into the last bout of the card, an upset was in the making as Cal led 4-3. However, it was not to be.

This Week In Sports

TODAY
SWIMMING—Varsity vs. Long Beach City College, Harmon pool, 10 a.m.
WRESTLING—Varsity vs. UCLA, Harmon gym, 3 p.m.
BASKETBALL—Varsity vs. Stanford, Harmon gym, 8 p.m.

TOMORROW
RUGBY—Varsity at SC.
WRESTLING—Varsity vs. Oregon and Washington at Eugene, 2 and 8 p.m.
SWIMMING—Varsity vs. Cal Poly and Arden Hills, Harmon Pool, 10 a.m.
BOXING—Varsity vs. Chico State, Harmon gym, 7:15 p.m.
GYMNASTICS—Varsity vs. Long Beach State, Harmon gym, 9 p.m.
BASEBALL—Varsity vs. alumni, Edwards Field, 3 p.m.
BASKETBALL—Varsity vs. Stanford, 8 p.m.

TOM GIOSEFFI
and veteran comes through

1964

Nevada State Journal—SPORTS — Thursday, February 13, 1964

Nevada Boxers Tie Cal Bears in 4-4 Action

Jim Evans Heavy Verdict Earns Draw for Wolves

University of Nevada's boxing team came from behind to earn a 4-4 tie with visiting University of California in Reno Wednesday night on the heavyweight victory of Nevada's Jimmy Evans over big Bob Winter in the final and decisive bout of the evening.

The Berkeley Golden Bears, with one of their best balanced boxing teams in many seasons, held a 4-3 edge going into the windup fray, but Evans' sharp boxing performance provided Nevada with a deadlock. It was a standout card all around and well enjoyed by one of the biggest crowds in a long time.

It was the second home dual meet for Nevada, which last week beat Chico State 5-3. The Wolf Pack has away-from-home cards at California, Chico and 12th Naval District before the conference championship tournament in Reno, March 20-21.

Highlights of last night's affair saw Cal's Tom Gioseffi surprise with a win over Dave Stix, along with smashing TKO victories by the Wolf Pack's Larry Williamson and Skip Houk.

The crowd-pleaser of the night came in the 165-pound class where Nevada's green but scrappy John McSweeney came close to dumping California's experienced Paul Rein in a real rouser. The hard-hitting McSweeney belted tall Rein around in the first round but appeared to have punched himself out. Rein used his long reach to jolt McSweeney's head with straight lefts and hard hooks throughout the second frame. McSweeney made a sensational comeback in the third, meeting Rein punch for punch, had making him give ground,

smoothly away from Winter's leads, later moved to close quarters. Winter's best punch was a rousing straight right in the second round, but Evans snapped back with one of his own. Evans came on strong in the last round, several times scoring one-two-three combos to the button. In the closing seconds he bashed the Californian with a tremendous clout, reaching up to plant the left hook on Wonkers' jaw.

The other Nevada win was gleaned by promising Chuck Breese. Tall for a 132-pounder, Breese made a strong last round rally to earn the nod after Bell's rushing tactics had kept command in the third and the point. Bell frequently ran into hard counter flurries, although he had the better of the long range boxing. But Breese took persistent Bell could only walk into a series of long straight lefts and rights to the face.

Tom Gioseffi was Cal's standout. The erstwhile conference 147-pound king decisioned Nevada's Dave Stix by using his superior reach and southpaw style. Gioseffi was able to ward off the persistently crowding Stix with long jabs and uppercuts, and landing footwork. Actually, he seldom jolted the Nevadan...

egiate clouters got things off to a flying start in last night's opening bout in the da gym. Undefeated Larry Williamson t) mowed down fiery Kunio Inoue in two rounds of furious action. Williamson, 126-pounder from Hawthorne, scored his eighth straight win for the Nevada Wolf Pack. (Journal Photo)

(Continued on next page)

1964

20-21.

Highlights of last night's affair saw Cal's Tom Gioseffi surprise with a win over Dave Stix, along with smashing TKO victories by the Wolf Pack's Larry Williamson and Skip Houk.

The crowd-pleaser of the night came in the 165-pound class where Nevada's green but scrappy John McSweeney came close to dumping California's experienced Paul Rein in a real rouser. The hard-hitting McSweeney belted tall Rein around in the first round but appeared to have punched himself out. Rein used his long reach to jolt McSweeney's head with straight lefts and hard hooks throughout the second frame. McSweeney made a sensational comeback in the third, meeting Rein punch for punch and making him give ground. Rein rallied with a volley to the body but McSweeney rocked the Cal middleweight with three crashing left hooks. The decision didn't win any popularity poll with the Nevada student rooting section, but it could have gone either way.

Williamson Again

Nevada got off to a rousing start in the opener with sensational little Larry Williamson winning his eighth straight bout over two seasons, seven of them by the TKO route. The dynamic 126-pound junior from Hawthorne triumphed over Cal's scrappy Kumio Inoue in two rounds, although the Nippon native was a battler while he lasted. Inoue flailed at Williamson from the opening bell and they traded leather furiously until the Nevadan landed a smashing straight right. Inoue was given the count, resumed action and was dumped again, from a left hook. A violent right to the stomach early in the second made the Californian sag, and he went down in a corner from two rights to the head. Referee Sammy Macias stopped it immediately.

Houk Patient

Nevada welterweight Skip Houk waited until the third round for a good shot at elusive Dave Weiner, and put away the Cal 147-pounder with an overhand left. Up to that time Weiner had given a good account of himself against the veteran Nevadan, his fast reactions getting the Bear welterweight out of trouble in the first and second rounds. Weiner's best blow was a straight right to the face when Houk missed in the second. However, in the third, Houk opened up a vigorous flurry and the looping left sent Weiner down on his knee. Coach Ed Neimer signalled for a halt at this point.

Jimmy Evans, as usual, gave away about 30 pounds to a heavyweight opponent and boxed his way to a decision in the windup fracus. His short jolting punches at close range compensated for Bob Winter's and weight.

The other Nevada win was gleaned by promising Chuck Breese. Tall for a 132-pounder, Breese made a strong last round rally to earn the nod after Bell's rushing tactics had kept the Nevadan busy up to that point. Bell frequently ran into hard counter flurries, although he had the better of the long range boxing. But Breese took command in the third and the persistent Bell could only walk into a series of long straight lefts and rights to the face.

Tom Gioseffi was Cal's standout. The erstwhile conference 147-pound king decisioned Nevada's Dave Stix by using his superior reach and southpaw style. Gioseffi was able to ward off the persistently crowding Stix with long jabs and retreating footwork. Actually, he seldom jolted the Nevadan who caught most of the leads on his own gloves. Stix, last year's conference 156-pound champ, made a strong bid to get inside the frustrating long arms of the Berkeley veteran, and occasionally he flurried to the midsection.

Tall and apparently more experienced Tom Corrigan of Cal outboxed Nevada 139-pounder Tom Jarvis at long range, catching him with pot shots the midsection throughout first round. Suddenly switching his attack to the head, Corrigan jarred Jarvis with hook in the second. You...TKO.

John Gaynor, subbing temporarily sidelined ry, lost in two rounds 178-pounder Jerry Knapp nor made a fast st ping lefts to the face ing an edge in the op to. But Knapp began him at long range second and then se vadan lurching int with a hard straight was it.

1964 - Cal at Nevada (Reno)

Weekend Scoreboard

Gymnasts Win; Boxers, Matmen Maul Tribe

It was victories number 45, 46, and 47 in a row as the mighty California gymnastic team, under the leadership of Coach Hal Frey, defeated San Fernando State, Sacramento City, and Los Angeles State colleges over the week-end.

The Cal still ring teams, perhaps the best in the nation, swept all three top places both Friday and Saturday nights. The still ring men are Rich Field, Steve Zahm and Rich Golden.

Friday night the Bears won over San Fernando Valley State college by a score of 84-44 before a home crowd in Harmon Gym. Besides winning the still rings competition, Field also won the side horse.

Saturday the Bears recorded victories 46 and 47 with a 99-29 rout of Sacramento and a 78-50 win over Los Angeles State. Paul Newman was one of the outstanding Cal men as he scored a 9.35 on the high bar.

WRESTLING

Despite beating Stanford 21-13 Friday night in Harmon Gym, Cal's wrestlers succumbed to a strong Cal Poly team 16-18 Saturday.

The Stanford results: 123—Walson (C) dec. Anderson (S), 5-2; 130—Sylvester (C) pinned Davis (S); 137—Siegel (C) pinned Smith (S); 147—Takemoto (C) pinned Bridgewater (S); 157—Kendall (S) pinned Barker (C); 167—Kay (S) dec. Kuhlman (C), 8-5; 177—Allen (S) pinned Killman (C); Hwt—Garamendi (C) dec. Duncan Ross (S), 14-5.

Cal Poly results: Walson (C) pinned Franklin (CP); 130 — Teem (CP) pinned Sylvester (C); 137—Forfeit to Cal; 147—Takemoto (C) dec. Taberma (CP); 157—Creceres (CP) dec. Barker (C); 167 — Kuhlman (C) dec. Dillascrusta (CP); 177 — Wool (CP) pinned Kleeman (C); Hwt. —Doupler (CP) dec. Garamendi (C).

BOXING

California's boxers defeated Stanford 6-3 Friday in Harmon Gym and by remaining undefeated paved the way to a league championship at the same time.

The Stanford ring results: 125—Forfeit to Cal; 132—Bell (C) and Oberzan (S) drew; 139 — Corrigan (C) dec. Bob Miller (S); 147—Weiner (C) and Gaylord (S) drew; 156—Gioseffi (C) dec. Gans (S); 167—Rein (C) TKO'd Lippman (S); 178—Moore (C) dec. Winters (S); 178—Knapp and Konker drew; Hwt — Pettigrew (S) dec. Winter (C).

SWIMMING

Cal's varsity swimming team pulled an expected victory over UCLA (58-37) and went down to defeat to the nation's number one swim team, USC, (65-30) last weekend in Los Angeles.

Bear Grady Romine set a new Cal 100-yard freestyle record with a clocking of 50.9 at UCLA.

Cal winners at UCLA: 400-yard medley relay, (McCreary, Gage, Goode, Baker); 50 yd. free, first—Romine, 23.1, second — Kagan; 200 yd. free, second—Knight, third—Teele; 200 yd. individual medley, second—McCreary, th... —Ed Duncan; 200 yd. butter... first — Goode, 2:13.2, secon... Darney; 100 yd. free, firs... mine, 50.9, second—Kaga... yd. back, second—McCrera... —Voorhees; 500 yd. free, ... —Baird, third—Teele; ... breast, first—Gage, 2:28.3... —Stanley; 400 yd. fre... first, disqualified; divin... Rodrigo, second—Pletch...

GOLF

The California golf tea... Cal State 14-13 Friday in ... meet of the season.

The Bears' John Einl... the medalist with a 73 o... 72 Mira Vista Count... course.

FENCING

Last Saturday the fenc... of UC Berkeley and UC... display their skill ... ship. Cal won ... epee 7-2 to sh...

1964

Bear Boxers Seek 1st Place Against Nev.

3/13/64

California's boxing team has a chance to finish the season undefeated when it meets Nevada tomorrow at 1:30 p.m. in Harmon Gym in a battle for first place in the California Collegiate Boxing Conference.

Both teams have 4-0-1 records. The Bears and the Wolfpack tied 4-4 in an earlier meet in Nevada.

Tom Corrigan, Jerry Knapp, Tom Gioseffi and Paul Rein were the four Cal winners in that meet.

Rein and Nevada gridiron hero John McSweeney engaged in a real wild affair in the 165-pound division last time and tomorrow's bout should be equally action-packed.

Probable card:

Nevada	wt.	California
Williamson	125	Inoue
Breese	134	Bell
Jarvis	139	Corrigan
Houk	147	Weiner
Stix	156	Gioseffi
McSweeney	165	Rein
Guynor	178	Knapp
Evans	Hwt.	Winter

CCBC Tournament
Cal Favored in Two Divisions

March 1964

Trying to redeem a second-place finish in CCBC dual meet competition, California's boxers will travel to Reno today for the CCBC individual championships.

Three undefeated boxers will lead the Bear contingent.

In the 156-pound division, Tom Gioseffi will try to make it seven straight victories for the season. Gioseffi was CCBC 147-pound champion last year and was voted the outstanding boxer of the championship tournament.

Both Jim Moore and Paul Rein have draws on their record, with five victories apiece. Rein started out as a 165-pounder with Moore at 178, but they swapped at mid-season and were still successful.

Rein will have one of the toughest fights of the night when he tangles with Joe Curry of Nevada in the 172 division, a class not usually fought in dual meets. According to coach Ed Nemir, "This match is a toss-up."

A team is usually considered CCBC champion of the tournament if it can register one-half of the final winners. According to our handicapping, Nevada can be favored for three winners, Cal for two, and Chico State for one.

The remaining three bouts are definitely toss-ups, so any one of the three teams is capable of taking the title.

Cards for the two-night championships (X indicates favored for champion):

Friday night: 132 — Jardine (CS) (X) vs. Bell (Cal); 150—McConnell (CS) vs. Clark (N); 147—Skip Houk (N) (X) vs. Dave Weiner (C); 156—Hayes (CS) vs. Stix (N); 165—Moore (C) (X) vs. McSweeney (N); 180 — Nicholas (CS) vs. Evans (N) (X); Hwt—Anderson (CS) vs. Winter (C).

Saturday night: 126—Williamson (N) (X) vs. Inuoe (C); 132—Briese (N) vs. Friday winner 139 — Katsamoto (CS) vs. Corrigan (C); 147—Tollete (CS) vs. Friday winner; 156—Gioseffi (C) (X) vs. Friday winner; 165 — Duval (CS) vs. Friday winner; 172—Rein (C) vs. Curry (N); 180 — Knapp (C) vs. Friday winner; Hwt. — Landon (N) vs. Friday's winner.

PAUL REIN
165-pound class

1964

Nevada State Journal—SPORTS   *Friday, March 20, 1964—15*

Collegiate Boxing Tournament Opens in Nevada Gym Tonight

Pack, Chico, Cal Entered

Boxing fans will trek to the University of Nevada campus gym tonight prepared to see eight bouts launch the 1964 conference championship ring tournament.

It's a three-school, two night affair as the California collegiate Boxing Conference climaxes a busy season.

Competing are teams from University of California, Chico State College and the host University of Nevada. Stanford University was prepared to enter until it found a conflict with final examinations.

First bout tonight answers the gong at 7:30. Saturday night's finals are billed at 7:30 but may be delayed so that the fans can see Reno's downtown St. Patrick's Parade. Coaches attending the Nevada grid clinic will be guests Saturday night.

First Since NCAA

This is the first boxing tourney in Reno since 1959 when Nevada staged the Pacific Coast Intercollegiates in Reno.

Nevada has no 139 - pounder, but Chico and Cal are each entering two, so tonight it'll be Bill Corrigan and John Barnard of California vs. Kent Katsumoto and Rich Plimpton of Chico.

Popular Skip Houk of Nevada, who has lost but three bouts in three years and is winding up his collegiate competition this weekend, mixes with Cal 147 - pounder Dave Weiner, the winner meeting Rich Tolotti of Chico in the finals.

Another Nevada senior, Dave Stix, risks his conference title this weekend. The 156-pounder tonight faces Glen Hayes of Chico, while undefeated Tom Gioseffi of Cal meets Rich Nunes of Chico.

McSweeney Ready

John McSweeney, 165, of Nevada, faces former conference champ Tom Moore of California, while Chico's Ron Duval drew a bye into the finals. Chico's John Nichols hurt his nose this week, leaving the new 172-pound class open for a Saturday final between Joe Curry, Nevada, and Paul Rein, California.

Slick Jimmy Evans of Nevada, conference heavyweight champ, has pared down to the 178-pound class and battles Jerry Knapp of Cal tonight. Bob Pyatt of Chico faces the winner Saturday.

Nevada heavyweight Dale Landon drew a bye into the finals, and meets the winner of tonight's brawl between two huge rivals, Roger Anderson of Chico and Bob Winters of California.

Saturday finals will include Nevadan Larry Williamson vs. Cal's Kunio Inoue for the 126-pound crown, and two - time conference champion Carline Jardine, Chico, vs. Paul Bell of California for the 132-pound title.

California's undefeated Paul Rein (above) tomorrow night will fight Joe Curry of Nevada for the 172-pound title in the California Collegiate Boxing Conference Tournament at the University of Nevada. Action will begin at 7:30 tonight and tomorrow in the two-day tourney.

Tournament

Wolf Pack's Skip Houk Lands Top Boxer Award

University of Nevada picked up five individual titles, Chico State four and University of California one as the 1964 California Intercollegiate Boxing Conference tournament concluded in Reno Saturday night. In addition, Skip Houk of Nevada and Carlin Jardine of Chico State were voted the NCAA's top national boxing trophies.

Champions crowned in the two-night tourney hosted by University of Nevada were: heavyweight — Roger Anderson, Chico; 180 — Jim Evans, Nevada; 172 — Joe Curry, Nevada; 165 — John McSweeney, Nevada; 160 — Rich Nunez, Chico; 156 — Tom Gioseffi, California; 147 — Skip Houk, Nevada; 139 — Ken Katsumoto, Chico; 132 — Carlin Jardine, Chico; 125 — Larry Williamson, Nevada.

Collegiate boxing's highest honor, the John S. LaRowe Trophy for "the athlete whose sportsmanship, skill and conduct perpetuate the finest attributes in collegiate boxing" was voted to Nevada senior Skip Houk. Chico senior Carlin Jardine was voted the DeWitt Portal Memorial Trophy, based on sportsmanship and desire.

Nevada veteran Skip Houk realized the goal of three years when he carried off the 147-pound championship in his last bout for the Wolf Pack. He punched out a clean-cut decision over out-gunned but gritty Rich Tollette of Chico State in the title fracas. Tollette's speed afoot kept him away from trouble in the initial round although he had to shake off a smashing left hook to the head. Houk's powerful lefts to the body weakened Tollette in the second and left him open for short right hands. Few fans expected Tollette to last out the third round but he survived a continual pounding and was still banging back at the final bell.

University of California's classy Tom Gioseffi who was the conference champ at 147 last year, dethroned defending 156-pound king pin Dave Stix of Nevada with a well-earned decision. Throughout the fifth, the shorter Stix tried vainly to pierce the long-armed defense of the lanky California southpaw. Stix never stopped boring-in, trying to get close for his favorite in-fighting tactics. But Gioseffi kept him away with a stream of long right jabs. Stix took most of them on the shoulders and gloves, and in the third round was able to get through with a few sharp rights, but Gioseffi was far from being in trouble at any time.

Fiery little Larry Williamson of Nevada was the first champion crowned as he defended the conference 125-pound title he won last year with a two-round knockout over University of California's Kunio Inoue. The UN junior from Carson City overpowered the game Cal featherweight with sheer punching power and speed. Williamson had trouble with sharp-shooting Inoue in the early moments as the Berkeley boxer's spearing straights kept catching the Nevadan coming in. But Larry slammed a rousing right to the stomach noticeably slowing down Inoue.

Inoue counter-punched cleverly early in the second as Williamson missed haymakers. But they did not all miss and the Nevadan drove a crushing right to the stomach, Inoue sagged against the ropes, took an eight count, then went down from a looping right to the chin. Referee Sammy Macias stopped it without a count.

There was thrilling action in the two rounds it took veteran Carlin Jardine of Chico State to win his third consecutive conference 132-pound championship. He stopped plucky Chuck Breese of Nevada, but had to climb off the canvas to do it. Breese dropped face down after taking a hard hook at close quarters in the first round. He got up but was floored by an overhand right. Coming off the deck after an eight count the Nevadan brought the fans to their feet with a game rally. He tore into Jardine with both hands winging and surprised the champ by dumping him for an eight count.

Jardine Jarred

Breese started the second in the same fashion, shaking Jardine with two rights. But that was as far as he got. The heavy-punching Chico vet floored Breese with a left hook and promptly dropped him again, ref Macias halting proceedings right then.

Chico State's super-aggressive Ken Katsumoto shook off first-round tumbling to wear down California's 139-pounder, Bill Corrigan, and eventually stop him late in the third round. Corrigan's long rights continually caught the boring-in Katsumoto during their wild first round and for some of the second. But the California lightweight began to tire badly under the relentless pressure.

Katsumoto continued to swarm all over him with both hands swinging. Finally late in the third, a long right staggered the weary Berkeley-battler and the referee called a halt to the proceedings.

Switching his customary ring

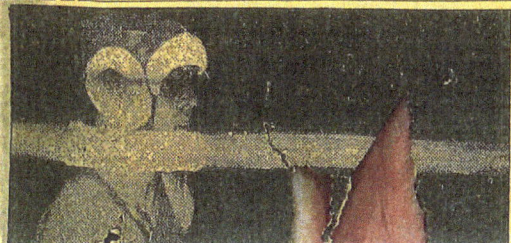

1964

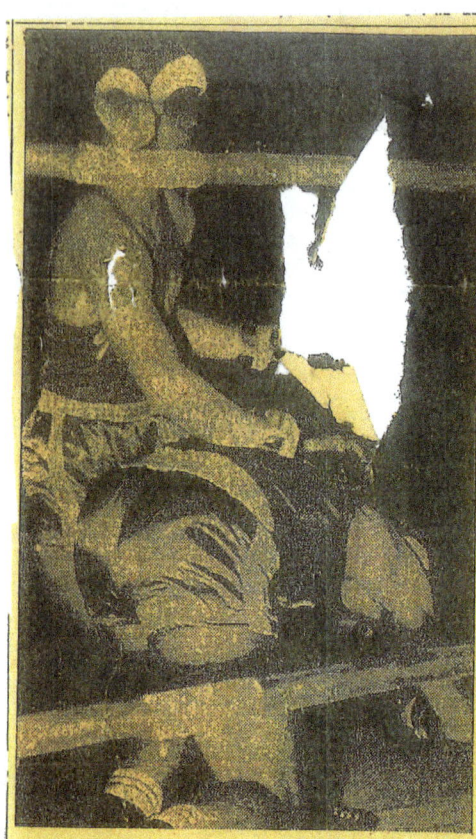

Cool and sharp-boxing Jim Evans of Nevada dumps Chico State's Ron Pyeatt in the second round to carry off the conference 180-pound division title. Evans, unbeaten in two seasons of college boxing, was the conference heavyweight champ last year. (Journal Photo)

ing their wild first round and for some of the second. But the California lightweight began to tire badly under the relentless pressure.

Tatsumoto continued to swarm all over him with both hands swinging. Finally late in the third, a long right staggered the weary Berkeley-battler and the referee called a halt to the proceedings.

Switching his customary ring tactics Nevadan John McSweeney scored the upset of the tourney by outboxing experienced Ron Duval of Chico State for the 165 - pound championship. If the Chico corner had expected McSweeney to come storming in with his usual windmilling, his change of tactics must have upset their strategy. The stocky McSweeney turned southpaw, backed away to entice Duval into leads, and then banged him with authoritative counter punches. Throughout the bout it was Duval who was wading in and was receiving hard, long lefts from the Nevada junior biology student.

Clean-cut Decision

McSweeney paced himself well and fought off Duval's desperate late flurry for a clean-cut decision.

Another upset was hung up by the Nevada team when tough Joe Curry came on strong in the last round to outpoint seasoned California 172-pounder Paul Rein. It was a grueling bout and the nod could have gone either way. A fine series of left jabs by Curry broke up Rein's last ditch rally in the final round and earned him the nod. Curry dominated the first round with left-hooking tactics but Rein started catching him coming-in during the second. Late in the round Curry set the Californian back on his heels with a crackling left to the button but was too tired to follow. Rein came out swinging for the last round, pumping to the body of the tall Nevadan from Lake Tahoe. Curry rallied with his timely series of straight lefts to glean the decision.

Nevada's Jimmy Evans, who was the conference heavyweight champion last year, scored an easy victory to win the 1964 crown in the light-heavyweight (180) division. Robert Pyeatt of Chico went down for a TKO in the second round. A right to the body, so short that some of the spectators missed it, made Pyeatt grunt and double up in the bout's very first exchange. He went down from a short right a little later and Evans coasted the rest of the round. A short right early in the second sent Pye-

Brawny Roger Anderson of Chico State won the heavyweight title in the tourney finale, making a strong last-round finish to outpoint big Dale Landon of Nevada. Anderson laid back through the first round as the Nevadan's one-two combos kept him on the defensive. Each got across a good flurry during an even second frame. Anderson came on strong in the third, beating the tiring Nevadan to the punch and shaking him with several hard rights to the head.

UNIVERSITY OF CALIFORNIA BOXING SCHEDULE 1964-1965

JANUARY

Friday	8	California Collegiate Boxing Conference at Chico 8:00 p.m.
Thursday	14	Stanford University at Palo Alto 8:00 p.m.

FEBRUARY

Saturday	6	University of Nevada at Berkeley 8:00 p.m.
Saturday	13	Chico State at Chico 8:00 p.m.
Friday	19	Stanford University at Berkeley 8:30 p.m.
Thursday	25	Chico State at Berkeley 8:00 p.m.

MARCH

Tuesday	2	Navy Invitational at Mare Island 8:00 p.m.
Saturday	6	University of Nevada at Reno 8:00 p.m.
Friday	19	California Collegiate Boxing Conference at Berkeley 8:00 p.m.
Saturday	20	California Collegiate Boxing Conference at Berkeley 8:00 p.m.

1965

Boxing Season Opens; Bears Enter CCBC Novice Tourney, Face Cards in Dual Meet

The sound of clashing flesh and leather will fill the Chico State gymnasium Friday night at 8:00 p.m. as Cal's beginning boxers travel there to compete in the California Collegiate Boxing Association novice meet.

The Bear yearlings will get their first taste of intercollegiate competition against novices from Stanford, Nevada, and Chico State. According to the rules, no novice must have had any formal competition after the age of 16. This eliminates any golden glove or semi-profesional boxers and keeps the competition on an even keel.

The competition will be held in five divisions. At 139 pounds is junior Pete Cowan, an intramural champion, and sophomore Jim Rodgers. At 147, sophomore John Sobczyk. At 156, junior Terry Holberton, who won the outstanding boxer trophy in the intramural meet. Also at 156 will be Paul Hasen. Junior Ray Kropp, also an intramural champ, will be in the heavyweight division.

Cal's first dual meet of the season is against Stanford on January 14 in the Stanford gym.

In the varsity competition, nine bouts will be held. At 120 pounds, wrestling champion Phil Walson with one year of experience. At 132, junior letterman Paul Bell, and the 139-pound class will be filled in from the group of novices. Don Worden with four bouts of experience will compete in the 147-pound class. At 156, Tom Gioseffi, the conference champion for two years is the backbone of the team. Jim Moore and Paul Rein fight in the 165-pound class. Dave Newhouse at 172, Jerry Knapp at 180 and heavyweight Bob White round out the staff.

According to Coach Ed Nemir, the competition in the conference is on a relatively even level.

"We are at least as good as any of the other teams," stated the Bear mentor.

Nemir confides that intercollegiate boxing is held on a non-professional level. The goal is not to pile up numerous records but rather to spread the interest in boxing to other schools. As of now there are only four schools in the nation which hold competition in boxing: Chico State, Stanford, Nevada and Cal.

This year's home schedule boasts three dual meets in addition to the conference championships, which will be held in Berkeley for the first time.

THE DAILY CALIFORNIAN • Wednesday, February 3, 1965

Cal Sport Teams Have Successful 'Break'

The Daily Californian SPORTS

BILL ROWEN, Sports Editor
JOHN RODGERS, Ass't Sports Editor
GEORGE BAKER, Sports Night Editor

The Ol' Perfesser

Spring Brings Better Sports

By BILL ROWEN
Sports Editor

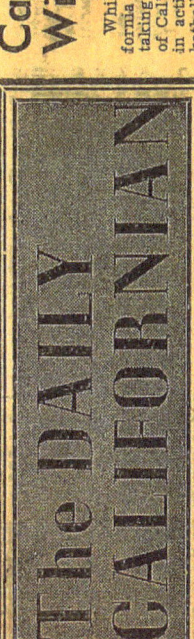

Welcome (or welcome back) to the sports capital of the West Coast. True, Cal's performance in THE college sport—football—was not the greatest last year. But if you take a look at the sports menu which will be offered up this semester, you will discover that there isn't a greater variety and quality of athletic action anywhere.

California's total sports program is one of the largest of any University in the world. Last year, 765 men took part in all the official intercollegiate sports for which Block C's are given. Anyone who complains that sports at Cal are all spectating and no participating doesn't know what he's talking about.

This spring, Cal will compete in 10 "major" sports, and this does not include important activities such as fencing, yachting, skiing and cricket which compete in well-organized intercollegiate leagues.

California is one of the last four schools in the U.S. which still compete in boxing, and this is a fact which Bears fans can feel proud about. A boxing fatality at Wisconsin in 1957 caused almost every school in the country to buckle under public pressure and abolish the sport (you'll notice that no one screams for the abolition of football, even though the mortality rate is tremendously higher).

But Cal boxing coach Ed Nemir, a former Phi Beta Kappa, stuck behind the sport he loves, however, and amateur boxing still flourishes in Berkeley.

The ringsters' first home meet of the year will be against Nevada this Saturday at Harmon Gym, and if you want to see a clean, fast, exciting, and really sportsmanlike event, this is it.

Cagers, Gymnasts and Boxers Win, Swimmers Finish Fourth

By JOHN RODGERS

While most University of California students were studying, taking finals, or going home, four of Cal's spring sports teams were in action—gymnasts, boxing, basketball and swimming—and compiled a sparkling 40 dual meet record. The Cal swimmers finished fourth in the Stanford relays.

Last January 16, the Bear swimming team competed in the six team Stanford relays on the Farm and thanks to two first place finishes they finished fourth behind outstanding Foothill College, the amazing Stanford Varsity, UOP and San Jose State followed the Bears in the standings.

The Bears first placed came about in the free style relay and the team diving. The relay team posted a new university mark of 1:31.4 as George Vigue, Jim Gage, Terry McNally and Ed Duncan covered the 200 yards in record time.

In diving, Del Pleicher and Lloyd Davidson combined to take the first place medal.

The tankmen go into action again this Saturday at 2:00 when they meet Stanford in the "Big Swim" at Harmon pool. At the same time the frosh will be meeting the Stanford frosh in a bout "Big Swim" in the same location.

travels north this weekend where they will be meeting Oregon State and Oregon as they resume competition in the AAWU. They will be without the services of razzle-dazzle guard Charles Kennedy who has been declared scholastically ineligible.

GYMNASTICS

The gymnastics team, under the capable eye of coach Hal Frey, registered consecutive victories number 53 and 54 in dual meet competition since being defeated seven years ago as they banged San Jose State 92-28 and San Francisco State 97-17.

In the SJS meet sophomores Danny Millman scored three victories as he won his specialty, the trampoline, plus free exercise and the long horse. Juniors Rick Field and Lonnie Kapp were also outstanding for Cal.

Field and Kapp also sparked the Bear victory over the Gators last Saturday as they each collected two victories.

The gymnasts travel to Long Beach State this weekend where they will try for victory number 55.

BOXING

In their only meet of the season, the Cal boxing team went down to Palo Alto where they edged the Stanford Indians 5-4.

Leading the Bears to victory were division winners Tom Gioseffi, 156; Paul Rein, 165; and Walt Cunningham, heavyweight. Phil Walson at 125 won his match by a forfeit.

Other Bears who saw action but were defeated were Tim Rodgers, Paul Bell and Don Worden.

The Boxing Bears will host Nevada Saturday night at 8:00.

TOM GIOSEFFI
Victory over an Indian

1965

Matmen Face Class of Conference in OSU; Boxers Lose Walson for Meet With Nevada

By JOHN STAAB

Both wrestling and boxing matches will take place in Harmon Gym at the same time tomorrow night as the Cal grapplers tangle with UC Davis in the wrestling room and the Bear ringmen square off against Nevada at 8:00 on the main floor.

The wrestlers will have a tune-up tonight against UC Davis, also at 7:30 in the wrestling room (118 Harmon).

Phil Walson, a 123-pounder who is a member of both the boxing and wrestling squads, will forfeit his boxing match in order to concentrate on his mat efforts.

As a result, the ringmen will go into the crucial tilt already one point behind, but there will be 11 matches instead of the ordinary nine to give the Bears plenty of room to catch up.

Co-captain Haruki Takamoto will wrestle for the first time this season against UC Davis, and his added strength should help the Bears tremendously.

Takamoto, who wrestled his way to the third spot in the AAWU tournament last year, was sidelined with a knee injury for the first half of this season, but according to Coach Martell, now "He's ready." Those two words will mean a lot to Cal grapplers this weekend when they face the number ten team nationally, Oregon State.

"OSU will give us a pretty go[od] indication of our toughest co[m]petition in the conference," sa[id] Martell. "They're skilled, stro[ng] and don't make many mistake[s.] If Cal is to beat the Beav[ers]

(Continued on page 5)

PAUL REIN
Bear bomber faces Nevada

1965

Friday, February 5, 1965

Gioseffi Leads Cal Pugilists Into Tossup Match

(Continued from page 4) they'll, have to wrestle hard all the way, but the Bears are "in the best shape we've been in all year, physically and personnel-wise," said Head Bear Martell.

California's lineup for the Davis and OSU matches is: Phil Walson 123, Alan Tabor 130, Alan Siegel 137, Takamoto 147, Don Schlotz 157, Dave Kuhlman 167, and Jim Porter, heavyweight.

Martell is still undecided about the 177 spot, probably because of Oregon State's Len Kauffman, all-American and U.S. Olympic competitor. OSU's coach Dale Thomas describes Kauffman, a junior, as the best wrestler he's ever had at OSU, and he's seen a few—Oregon State has nabbed the Pacific Coast Championship 7 out of the last 8 years, and has placed at least one wrestler on every U.S. team for 8 years, including the two Olympic teams. Either Bob Fisher or Steve Shook will face the big Beaver.

Davis should prove easy victims for the Bears by comparison, but Siegel and Takamoto will have their hands full in the 137 and 147 pound classes.

The California-Nevada rivalry, which produced two exciting matches last year, should be just as action-packed as ever.

Last season, the Bears staged a tremendous upset by tying the Wolfpack in Reno as two novice boxers came through with wins. When the Wolves returned to Harmon Gym, they revenged the upset by edging past the Bear ringmen 4½-3½ in a match which was not decided until the final bout.

As a result, Nevada won the CCBS dual meet title with a 5-0-1 record, with the Bears breathing over their shoulders at 4-1-1.

Regarding Cal's chances for victory, Nemir expects a very close match with some excellent bouts, and a probable 6-5 score one way or the other. Both Cal and Nevada beat Stanford in previous clashes, and both had 4-1-1 records last year.

The three best bouts, according to Nemir, should be between Cal's Paul Bell and Nevada's Chuck Brees at 132; two time conference champion Tom Gioseffi and Gordon Browning at 156 (both lefties beat their Stanford opponents); and heavyweights Walt Cunningham and Dale Landon.

Other starters for the Bears are Pete Cowan and Tim Rodgers 139, Paul Rein and Terry Holberton 165, Dave Newhouse 172, and Jerry Knapp and Ray Kropp, 180.

There are only four universities in the country that have boxing teams: Cal, Nevada, Stanford, and Chico State. The reason for the survival of boxing in these four universities is the common philosophy that no man who has ever boxed before coming to the institution can compete. This keeps the competition on an even level and keeps the danger of the sport down.

1965

B
O
X
I
N
G

CALIFORNIA vs. UNIVERSITY OF NEVADA

Saturday, February 6, 8:00 PM.

Blue Corner   Red Corner

	125 lbs.	
	Forfiet to Nevada	
Paul Bell	132 lbs.	Chuck Breese
Lee Phillips	139 lbs.	Gary Parsons
Pete Cowan	139 lbs.	Dave Widmer
Don Worden	147 lbs.	Bill Georgeson
Tom Gioseffi	156 lbs.	Gordon Browning
Terry Holberton	165 lbs.	Riley Beckett
Paul Rein	165 lbs.	Tony Schullor
Dave Newhouse	172 lbs.	Mike Parman
Jerry Knapp	180 lbs.	Bob Hall
Walt Cunningham	Heavyweight	Dale Landon

Coach: Ed Nemir   Coach: Jim Olivas
Assistant Coach: Gordon VanKessel

Referee: Frank Carter

Judges: Jim McDowell
        Ed Roberts

Timekeeper: Snort Winstead

Announcer: Chuck Turner

Physician: Dr. Bob Weyand

NEXT HOME MEETS: Friday, February 19, 8:30 P.M.   STANFORD
                 (GYMNASTICS at 7:00 PM with Stanford)

                 Thursday, February 25, 8:00 P.M. CHICO STATE

1965

```
CALIFORNIA    165    NEVADA
  REIN                SCHULLER
1
2     K.O
3
_____        _____

                              McD

CALIFORNIA    165    NEVADA
  REIN                SCHULLER
1     KO
2
3
_____        _____

                              EHR

CALIFORNIA    165    NEVADA
  REIN                SCHULLER
1
2         KO
3    Carter
_____        _____
                              FC
```

These cards are for Rein's 1st round knockout, 1965. The following year, Tony Schuller was conference champion at 165 lbs (1966).

1965

Weekend Scoreboard — 2/8/65

'Minor' Teams Compile 2-2 Mark

California boxers moved another step along the road to a position of supremacy in the CCBS by soundly trouncing Nevada 7½-2½ Saturday night.

The Bears captured six bouts, fought to a draw on three and lost one in amassing a large margin for their victory. Tom Gioseffi, 156, looked strong in his first round knockdown of Gordon Browning. Both lefties had defeated their Stanford opponents.

ALAN SIEGEL
wrestler's 'shining light'

Pete Cowan, 139, and Paul Rein 165, each scored knock down victories in the first round, while Lee Phillips 139, Terry Holberton 165, and Jerry Knapp scored decisions. Paul Bell 132, Don Worden 147, and Dave Newhouse fought to draws, scoring ½ point each for the Bears. Walt Cunningham, heavyweight, boxing Nevada's best, lost a nine to eight decision.

Coach Ed Nemir singled out Bell's, Gioseffi's and Rein's bouts as exceptionally good ones, and praised Cunningham for his good effort and improvement. "The team looks strong, and they're all out to win," said Nemir.

A victory over Chico State Feb. 13, would put the Cal boxers on top of the four-school conference, but each of the opponents will get a second whack at the Bears in return matches before the conference championships here in Berkeley March 19.

WRESTLING

California's matsters split a weekend doubleheader squashing UC Davis 16-12, and losing hard to Oregon State 25-7 Feb. 5 and 6.

Alan Siegel 137, the only Bear who managed to emerge from the weekend's activities unscathed, decisioned both his opponents.

Against Davis, Jim Porter, heavyweight, pinned his man for five team points, Alan Tabor decisioned his man 4-0, and Phil Walson won by a forfeit. Hauri Takemoto, Don Schlotz, Dave Kuhlman, and Bob Fisher all lost decisions.

Oregon State, perennial Pacific Coast champions, romped over the Bears, allowing only two draws besides Siegel's decision. Phil Walson tied Ron Iwosaki 1-1, and Dave Kuhlman tied Gordy Lowell 1-1.

Alan Tabor had to forfeit his match because of a leg injury, Takemoto and Porter lost decisions 4-3 and 6-2, and Fisher and Schlotz were pinned.

SWIMMING

Despite six individual victories by Golden Bear tankmen, the varsity squad was defeated by the Stanford swimming team 53-42 in the "Big Swim" Saturday in Harman pool.

The meet was highlighted by a superb performance by Ed Duncan who set two California varsity records when he captured the 200 yard freestyle in 1:52.6, breaking the old record by three tenths of a second, and the 500 yard free in 5:15.4 which is 9.2 seconds better than the previous Cal best.

Other men registering victories for Cal were: Del Fletcher, diving; Terry McNally, 50 and 100 yard freestyle; and Jim McCleary in the backstroke.

1965

Friday, February 12, 1965

Boxing Team Seeks Third Consecutive Win In Battle With Chico St. College on Saturday

Seeking a third consecutive dual meet victory, the Bear boxing team voyages to Chico to take on the Chico State College team Saturday afternoon.

With wins over Nevada and Stanford already, the Cal team is withing reach of last season's 4-1-1 record, and Coach Ed Nemir feels that Saturday's match will give a good indication of just how well the team will succeed.

"We are going to have more experience and more lettermen than Chico, but they still have some good men," commented the coach.

A real tussle is expected in the 139-pound class when Chico's Ken Katsumoto, defending conference champion, will take on Pete Cowan. Tom Gioseffi, perhaps Cal's best boxer and a two year letterman, will give Cal added strength in the 156-pound division.

"Chip" Bell, seeking his first victory, will battle in the 132-pound class and Phil Walson, wrestling captain, will be making his first start as a boxer in the 125-pound division.

Another exciting bout will be in the 172-pound division when Chico's Gary Sitton tangles with Dave Newhouse. And Paul Rein and Terry Holberton in the 156 and 165-pound class respectively will each be seeking their third straight win.

1965

Friday, February 19, 1965 — THE DAILY CALIFORNIAN — Page Five

Unbeaten Boxers Battle Stanford

California's undefeated boxers enter the ring with Stanford with the advantage of three forfeits out of the ten bouts tonight at 8:30 in Harmon gym.

At the last clash with the Indians, the Bears emerged five to four victors on the strength of one forfeit. Tonight Stanford is offering no opponents to Cal veterans Tom Gioseffi and Paul Rein, and the Indians have no man to face Phil Walson at 125 pounds. The remaining seven bouts should be close ones, probably decided by a few points according to Coach Ed Nemir.

Of the six bouts Cal and Stanford boxers fought earlier this year, two bouts ended in draws, and one ended in an Indian victory. Cal's Paul Bell, 132, who lost to Rudy Oberzan last time, faces the Redskins again with an even 1-1-1 record.

Pete Cowan, also 1-1-1, will do battle for a decisive finish with Stanford's Jim Conti in the 139 pound class, and Jerry Knapp, 2-0-1 will face Phil Zengker at 180. Both fought to draws in their bouts.

Other bouts are: Jerry Olson, 1-0, versus George Bellows, 147; Dave Newhouse, 0-1-1, vs. Barc Johnson, 172; and Walt Cunningham, 1-1, vs. Tom Yanger, heavyweight.

Nemir's Unbeaten Blasters In Final Bouts Here Tonight

The undefeated California Boxing team will make its final dual meet appearance this evening at Harmon Gym when it takes on the rugger Chico State Squad at 8 p.m.

Coach Ed Nemir's Bear leatherslingers have rolled through four opponents without a hitch, and included in that is an 8-4 win over the Wildcats earlier this month in the Chico ring.

Heavyweight Walt Cunningham will watch this match from the sidelines due to an injury, and Jerry Knapp has been elevated from the 180 pound class to fill in for the hard-punching Cunningham on he 11 bount card.

Despite the win over the Wildcats, Nemir is not looking for a pushover tonight. "They are always stronger in the second match," he said cautiously, "some of our decisions up there were by one point and could have gone either way.

Nemir looks for the best bouts to come in the 139, 165 and 180 pound class. In the 139 class Cal's Pete Cowan will have his hands full with defending California Collegiate Boxing Association Ken Katsumoto, who decisioned Cowan in their earlier meeting in a close match.

Unbeaten Paul Rein of the Bears and Mike Jones of the Wildcats are expected to stage a slugfest, Jones topped Terry Holbertson in Chico and Nemir rates the Wildcat an "extremely strong puncher."

Jerry Knapp of Cal and John Luallen are expected to renew their torrid 180-pound battle which saw Knapp pull out a close decision.

Nemir referred to this year's group of Bear pugilists as one of the best balanced groups he has had. "They have real good ring presence,' 'the graying mentor in the art of self defense commented, "they know what they are doing and they are almost at their peak."

1965

CALIFORNIA VS CHICO STATE

THURSDAY, FEBRUARY 25, 1965

8:00 P.M., HARMON GYM

/California/		/Chico State/
Forfeit to Calif.	125 lbs.	
Forfeit to Calif.	132	
Lee Phillips	139	Denny Helms
Pete Cowan	139	Ken Katsumoto
Don Worden	147	Joe Viscuso
Jerry Olson	147	Dave Dohn
Tom Gioseffi	156	Jack Farmer
Terry Holberton	165	Joe Madrigal
Paul Rein	165	Mike Jones
Dave Newhouse	172	Tim Fitzgerald
Jerry Knapp	180	John Luallen
Ray Kropp	Heavy	Jerome Circo

Coach: Ed Nemir
Assistant Coach: Gordon VanKessel

Coach: Willie Simmons

Referee: Jack Downey

Judges: Ed Roberts
        Jim McDowell

Timekeeper: Snort Winstead

Announcer: Chuck Turner

Trainer: Jack Williamson

Physician: Dr. Bob Weyand

*******NEXT HOME MEET: CALIFORNIA COLLEGIATE BOXING CONFERENCE CHAMPIONSHIPS, ********
        Friday and Saturday, March 19 & 20, Harmon Gym, 8:00 P.M.

Cal Boxers Paced to Win By Groseffi

By DAVE BUSH

Paced by Tom Gioseffi's spectacular knockout win, the Cal boxing team wound up its dual meet season still unbeaten with a 9-3 win over Chico State last night in Harmon Gym.

The Bears are now 5-0 for the year.

Gioseffi, Cal's veteran 156-pounder, had trouble solving the peek-a-boo style of Chico's Jack Farmer for the first two rounds. In the third however, Gioseffi caught Farmer with a terrifying right hand that sent the visitor plummeting to the mat.

Cal's 139-pounder Pete Cowan turned in the upset of the night by narrowly decisioning defending CCBA champ Ken Katsumoto. Cowan served notice as to what was to come by stunning the Wildcat momentarily with a sudden right to the nose seconds after the opening bell.

The most entertaining bout came in the 172's with Cal's Dave Newhouse and Chico's Tom Fitzgerald trading punches through three even rounds and ending in a draw. To the delight of the spectators, both fighters threw caution away and stood and threw punches with abandon during the third round.

Paul Rein, the Golden Bears' 165-pound ace, maintained his undefeated skein with a technical knockout win over tough Mike Jones. Both fighters came out throwing leather and each scored second round knock downs before a shattering combination by Rein knocked the Chico fighter down in the third and stopped the fight.

Other Golden Bear winners were Jerry Olson, Terry Holbertson and Jerry Knapp, while Don Wordon battled to a draw.

1965

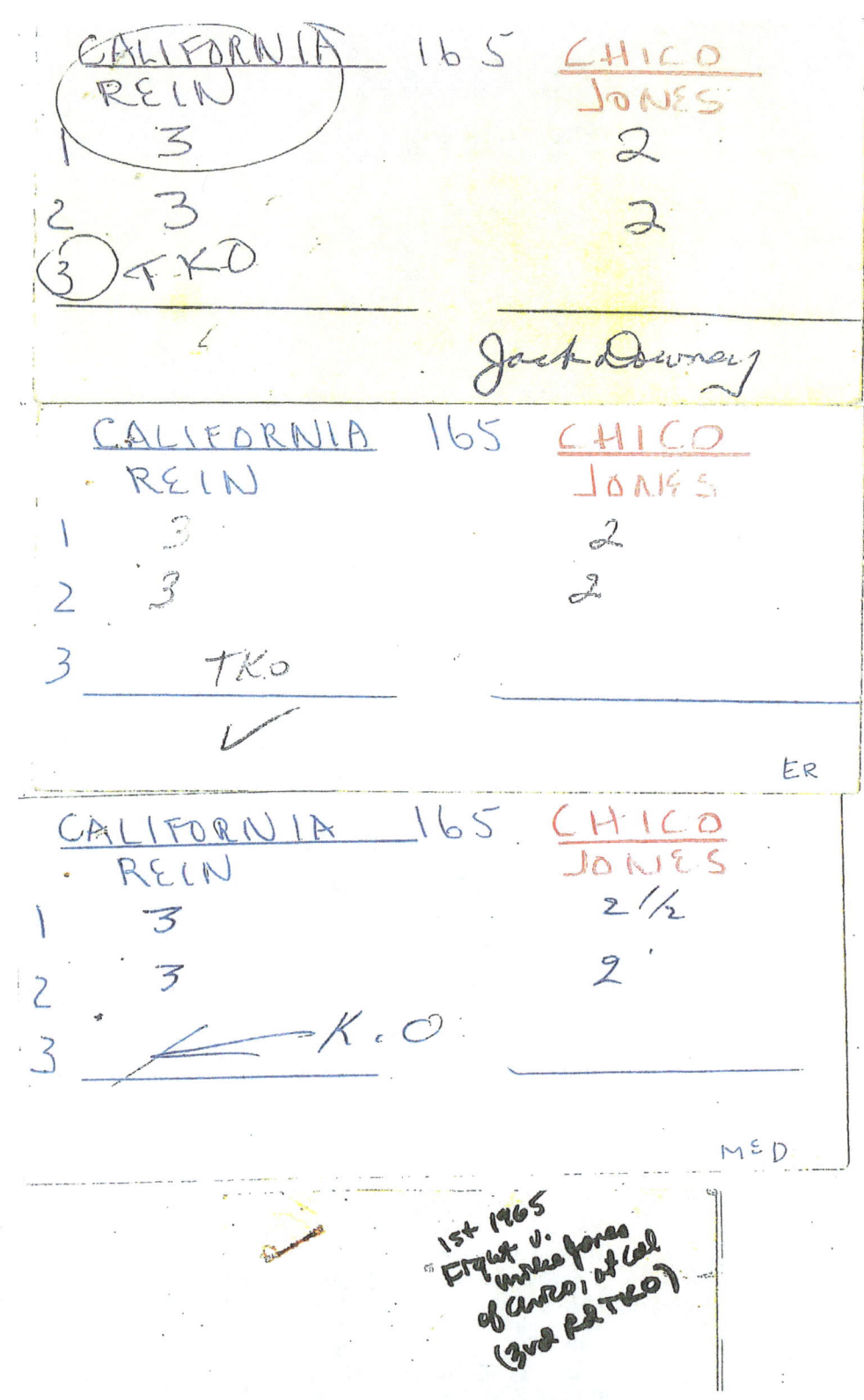

First 1965 fight v. Mike Jones of Chico, at CAL. (3rd Round TKO)

1965

BOXING TEAM — Row One: Jerry Olson, Tim Rodgers, Pete Cowan, Paul Bell, Phil Walson, John Sobczyk, Lee Phillips. Row Two: Coach Ed Nemir, Tom Gioseffi, Paul Rein, Walt Cunningham, Jerry Knapp, Dave Newhouse, Con Worden, Terry Holberton, Ray Kropp, Assistant Coach Gordon Van Kessel.

Lee Phillips connects with a hard right to the mouth.

wolves,

injuns,

wildcats

mauled by

bear boxers

Ed Nemir
Head Coach

1965

Cal's Jerry Knapp connects with a low blow against his Nevada opponent. He gets a fist in the face in return.

Two boxers flail away at each other during the Nevada contest. Cal won the match 7½-2½.

To say that the 1965 season was a successful one for the Cal boxing team would have to be an understatement. Competing in the four-team California Collegiate Boxing Conference, the only collegiate boxing league left in the nation, the Bears blasted each of the three other teams in two different season encounters. The result was a perfect 6-0 season for the Bears, as well as an impressive first place finish in the CCBC championship tournament at Berkeley. Probably the most important factors in this year's success were the performances of Tom Gioseffi, Jerry Knapp, and Paul Rein, who ended the season without a defeat. In regular season competition, 156 lb. Gioseffi and 165 lb. Rein compiled perfect 6-0 records, while Knapp who fought in the 178 lb. class, was 5-0-1. Other top men on this year's team were sophomore heavyweight Walt Cummingham, and Pete Cowan, who lost only one match all year in the 139 lb. class. Although coach Ed Nemir will lose five standouts from this year's squad, next year's team will be bolstered by the return of two-year letterman Jim Moore as well as the fine sophomores and juniors from this year's team.

1965

Scenes from the CCBC Tourney

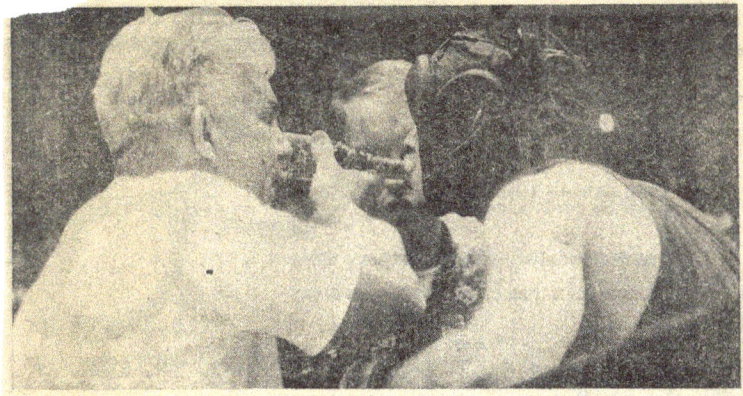

CHAMPIONS... Here you see how Cal's pugilists clobbered the cream of the CCBC boxing talent last weekend. The Bears won six of the eight bouts to win the conference title. Above, Coach Ed Nemir stimulates an unidentified Bear between rounds. Right, Paul Rein belts his opponent on his way to victory. Note the extra-large gloves and protective headgear which makes collegiate boxing as safe a sport as any on the schedule.

—Photo by Chuck Harp

1965

"I Was a Cal Boxer"
by Paul Rein

In 1965, my senior year at Cal, I had gone undefeated on the Cal Boxing Team through the season and was looking forward to the CCBC championships, held that year at Cal. On Friday night I had gone through an exhausting semi-final fight with Reilly Beckett of Reno, and in the Saturday night finals I would face "tough" Mike Jones from Chico State.

Cal boxer Terry Holberton, the other middleweight on our team, had been the 1964 middleweight Cal "intramural" champion and had also been voted the "Outstanding Boxer" in the intramural tournament. While he was #2 to me on the team, because of my experience, I didn't know if I was a better fighter than him. Then, in our "dual meet" at Chico, Mike Jones had knocked Terry out cold with his first overhand right in 15 seconds of the first round!

Although I had fought Mike Jones once before and beaten him, Jones had a "bye" on Friday night, whereas I had to fight Riley Beckett, of Nevada, that night, then fight Jones in the Saturday "finals." My parents had driven up to Berkeley from Los Angeles to see both of my bouts, the first time that they'd ever seen me fight. This further energized me, although fighting at home was always more fun; I had never lost a fight at home in Harmon Gym, although I had two "draws" my junior year.

As the result of my fight with Riley Beckett, I felt exhausted on Saturday; my shoulders were so sore I couldn't lift my gloves above shoulder level. Although three "two minute" rounds may not sound very long, the Championship bout against Mike Jones was so grueling it seemed to last forever. But I boxed well enough to win the fight lopsidedly on the judges' scorecards, and was "runner-up" to my super teammate, Tommy Gioseffi, in voting for the "outstanding boxer" in the tournament.

1965 CCBC Champions from Cal, from left, back row: Tom Gioseffi, Paul Rein, Mike Parman (Nevada), Jerry Knapp; Front row from left: Pete Cowan, Paul Bell, Phil Walson.

Perhaps because I'd never been a competition-level athlete until boxing, the Cal boxing experience was extremely positive for me, and has given me strength over the last 50 years of my life. It was good preparation for being a trial lawyer. My association with boxing was so positive that in 1991 I married Brenda Keith in a boxing ring as part of a Boxing History exhibition at the Oakland Museum. (I had helped collect materials for a "College Boxing" portion of the exhibit). I wore my Cal boxing "uniform" for the marriage, and we actually sparred one round, sporting 14 oz. gloves and wearing protective mouthpieces.

When people ask me, "What did you do in college?" I rarely say that "I was a political science major" or "I was Phi Betta Kappa" or that I was "pre-law;" I say that "I was a Cal boxer." However, 24 years after my college boxing career ended, I "came out of retirement" to box a three round "exhibition" at a 1989 "Alumni Night" fundraiser for the Cal Boxing Team. I got my weight *down* to about 205 lbs. and boxed against Jason Julian, a recent Cal graduate who had fought at "cruiserweight" and weighed about the same as me. (I bragged I held the World Record as the "World's Heaviest Middleweight.")

However, I had a distinct 2 to 1 advantage over my opponent: I was 44 and he was "only" 22! I thought I did pretty well, and I treasure a video of that fight as a souvenir. Not learning from that experience, three years later, I helped organize another alumni fight, and Reunion, and personally fought a 3 round exhibition fight against James Walker, Cal's 195 pound fighter. Due to a ring rope coming loose, there was a five minute break between the first and second rounds. I called out to the announcer, in vain, to give me a similar five minute break between the second and third rounds! Parenthetically, most college boxers at Cal seem to have survived their head traumas with most of their brains intact. In my senior year at Cal I was one of several athletes who earned a 4.0 for that year, and learned that the boxing team had the second highest grade point average among men's sports teams - second only to the Crew Team.

In 2004, San Francisco criminal defense lawyer Chris Morales and I organized an alumni dinner for ex-Cal boxers and family members, and about 80 former Cal boxers showed up. Among them was my "corner man," Bill McAdam, now a San Diego Superior Court Judge, and my friend, Sam Gold, who had fought for Cal 80 years earlier - 1924 to 1927 - before going on to Boalt Hall School of Law and a 64 year legal career. I discovered that at least one-third of the boxing alumni had become lawyers. Maybe there's a connection between pugilism and trial law! Terrence Hallinan and Patrick Hallinan, two famed San Francisco criminal lawyers, fought in the late 1950s; Bruce Simon, Claude Wyle, and George Choulos, prominent San Francisco trial lawyers, boxed in the 1970s; and Rod Maricini, an excellent Bay Area defense lawyer, was my teammate in the mid-1960s, and kept boxing despite breaking his nose multiple times. (Although he wore a catcher's mask when sparring in practice, he couldn't use it in competition!)

Is there an element of masochism in being a trial lawyer?

When my younger friend, Joey Gilbert, a three time national champion from the University of Nevada Reno, decided to turn pro boxer while also completing law school, he told me that his mother was very concerned that he'd suffer brain damage from boxing. I told Joey to "reassure" his mother by reminding her of San Francisco 49er quarterback Steve Young, who had also studied law while playing football. When too many concussions forced Steve Young to retire from football, he practiced law instead. "The moral of this story, is that you can have too much brain damage to play football or box, but still have enough brains to be a lawyer!"

Joey Gilbert had a successful professional boxing career till he suffered a serious broken nose injury, and decided to limit his fighting to the courtroom. He's still a local favorite in Nevada, and has a successful practice as a trial lawyer, who promises to "fight" for his clients. A large billboard with his advertisement greets you as you drive into Reno on U.S. 80.

1965

BOXING TEAM — **Row One:** Jerry Olson, Tim Rodgers, Pete Cowan, Paul Bell, Phil Walson, John Sobczyk, Lee Phillips. **Row Two:** Coach Ed Nemir, Tom Gioseffi, Paul Rein, Walt Cunningham, Jerry Knapp, Dave Newhouse, Con Worden, Terry Holberton, Ray Kropp, Assistant Coach Gordon Van Kessel.

**The 1965 team had one of the best records of all Cal teams:
Cal won 6 of the 9 weight divisions, and three of the fighters (Tom Gioseffi, Paul Rein, and Jerry Knapp) went undefeated.**

1965

BLOW-BY-BLOW KNOCKDOWN PICTURE—Tom Gioseffi of California, right, starts a deadly barrage on Nevada's Gordon Browning in the second round of a scheduled three-rounder Saturday night in the California Collegiate Boxing Conference at Harmon Gym. In sequence, top row, left to right, Gioseffi starts a right, lands it, throws a left, and bottom row, lands another right, a left, and Browning is down and out.

March 1965, 156 lbs CCBC Champion Tom Gioseffi also won the CCBC Outstanding Boxer Award

Reunion of 1960-1965 Boxers (1989)

From left to right: Tom Gioseffi, Paul Rein, Bob Winter, Bill Harrison.

From left to right: Bill Harrison, Dennis Treadway, Dennis Natali, Paul Rein.

1965-1966

THE DAILY CALIFORNIAN • Thursday, December 9, 1965

Commuters Take Intramural Boxing Title

BY JAY BERNSTEIN

Last night at Harmon Gym before a large turnout, the Commuter boxers walked off with the team championship. The C-Is edged SAE 14-13 in the final point standings.

The Milton T. Cunya award for the outstanding boxer of the tournament went to Greg Monahan of Alpha Tau Omega. He gained the individual laurels with an impressive decision over Dave Archibald of Theta Delta Chi.

Other victories:

127 lbs; Mike Jay of Pi Alpha Phi, TKO in 1:28 of the third round, over Steve Rein of C-Is.

134 lbs; Richard Carter of Phi Kappa Sigma, unanimous decision, over Bob Sakai of Norton.

141 lbs; junior div.; Bruce Megna Dal Porto of Lambda chi Alpha.

141 lbs. senior div.; Freeman Harris of Lambda Chi Alpha, TKO at the end of the second round, over Jim Sobczyk of Phi Kappa Psi.

144 lbs. junior div.; Rick Bently of Phi Delta Theta, unanimous decision, over Bill Swift of SAE.

149 lbs. senior div.; Dick Weinbrandt of Phi Sigma Kappa, unanimous decision, over Randy Munro of Zeta Psi.

158 lbs. junior div.; Phil Nyborg, TKO at the end of round one, over Dan Schimenti.

158 lbs. senior div.; Terry Stewart of SAE, unanimous decision, over Bill Neyland.

168 lbs. junior div.; Jim Hoobler of A Chi Rho, TKO in 1:28 of second round, over Richard Marliave of Bowles.

180 lbs. junior div.; Jack Boot of Fijis, unanimous decision over Dick Brannin.

180 lbs. senior div.; Larry Taylor of C-Is, split decision, over Gary Buckingham of C-Is.

Heavyweight; a draw between Tom Born and Tom Garrity of Theta Delta Chi.

INTRAMURAL SPORTS

INTRAMURAL BRUISERS BATTLED IT OUT LAST NIGHT .. First Row, left to right: Rick Carter, Mike Jay, Dick Weinbrandt, Bill Swift. Second row: Randy Munro, Bob Sakai, Jim Sobczyk, Steve Rein, Bruce Megna, Phil Nyborg, Jim Hoobler, Freeman Harris, Jim Dal Porto. Third row: Jack Roof, Gary Buckingham, Rich Marliave, Tom Garrity, Dave Archibald, Terry Stewart, Larry Taylor, Greg Monahan, Dan Schimenti.

Intramural Boxing at Cal Produced many fighters who later joined the Cal Intercollegiate Team.

For example, this article about the December 8, 1965 Intramural Finals included: Dick Carter, Dick Weinbrandt, Mike Jay, Bob Sakai, Dave Archibald and Greg Monohan, who won the Milton C. Cunha Award as "Outstanding Boxer" in the Tournament.

1966

Action in the corner: A short left to the body.

Punishment for a Chico State boxer. . . .

cal boxers bid for undefeated season
under the direction of coach ed nemir

A pressbox view of the ring is seen.

1967

VARSITY BOXING — Row One: Dirk Noyes, Tim Rodgers, Jim Hoobler, Bob Sakai, Dick Carter, Bill Neyland, Dick Weinbrandt, John Cowart, Phil Nemir, Dale Chamblin. Row Two: Ed Nemir, Ron Dell'Immagine, John Chappell, Greg Monahan, Bruce Tichinin, Bob Hink, Terry Stewart, Troy Cox, Webb Loyd, Steve Spreiter, Walt Cunningham (assistant coach).

Boxers Win Dual Meet Championship -

Ed Nemir's Boxing Bears ended another outstanding season this year by capturing the Dual Meet Championship. The Bears finished with five wins, one loss and a tie in dual competition. They also took second place in the California Collegiate Boxing Championship Tournament, ending only below Chico State who had three wins and three second places in the tourney. The Bears took two firsts—Jim Hoobler and Troy Cox—and four seconds—Dale Chamblin, Bob Sakai, Phil Nemir, and Greg Monahan. Senior and team captain Greg Monahan, accumulating the highest point total as far as wins go of any Cal boxer, was undefeated in dual meets and won six matches this season while tying one.

Next season the Bear Boxers will have to regroup and start afresh as they are losing seven lettermen while only five are returning.

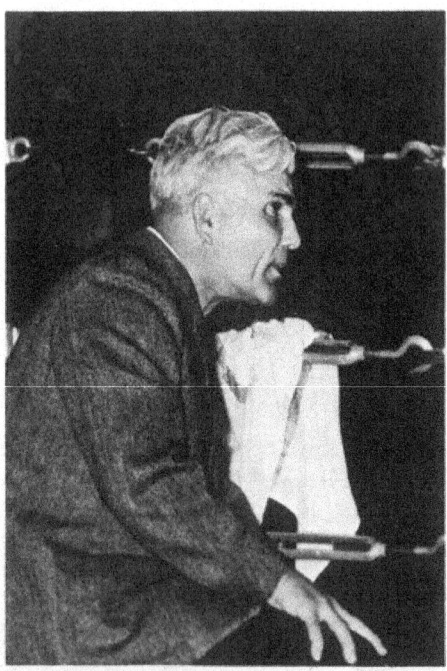

Boxing coach Ed Nemir watches anxiously as his son Phil Nemir takes on his Nevada opponent.

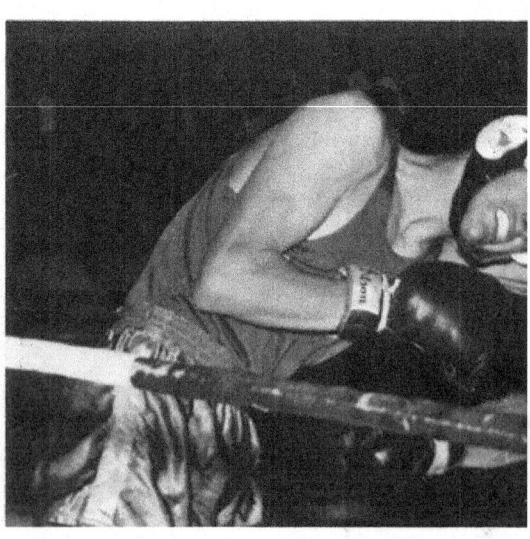

1967

One hundred and thirty-nine-pound sophomore Phil Nemir jabs his Nevada opponent Dennis Humphreys with a right. Nemir won the decision 9-7.

A left hook by senior and heavyweight Ron Dell'Immagine helps him win a draw with Smithwick of Nevada.

Bantomweight Dale Chamblin fights to a draw with his Nevada opponent Larry Williamson.

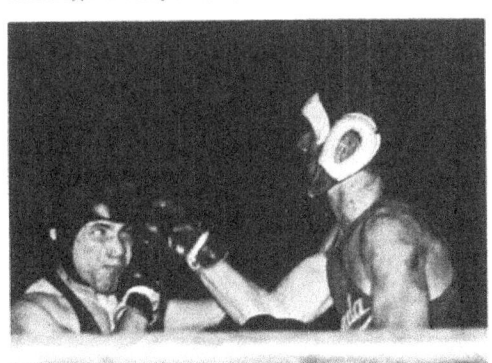

1967

Life Lessons from Cal Boxing
By Dale Jeong

At 135 lbs, too small to participate in the normal sports of football and baseball, and too scrawny for wrestling…I came to Cal with an open mind. My reflexes were good and I had had an introduction of boxing from some PE classes in high school on the peninsula. In 1967 the team sport of boxing was mostly for the juniors and seniors at Cal. At that time I was a freshman and fortunately found intramural boxing coached by the late Eddie Nemir (Phil Nemir's dad). Intramural boxing was competition for those in their freshman and sophomore years between the dorms, fraternities, and for those who lived at home. This turned my life around! Coach Nemir believed in me and gave me confidence where None existed before. Emotionally I felt insecure coming to such a big university and was challenged by the tough course work at the time. At the end of classes each day, I couldn't wait for my boxing workouts in the exercise room adjacent Harmon Gym. Coach Nemir would be patient and could analyze what I was doing right and especially what I was doing wrong. He was very direct, supportive, and very immersed in all of his boxers. Success in sparring and in the ring became immediately evident. I loved it! I even encouraged many of my friends to join as well.

Boxing gave me an excellent foundation for both working out and improving my abilities. I learned to take a chance, if I could, in the ring. Sometimes it worked and sometimes it didn't. It taught me to be reserved when winning and to be humble when beaten. It taught me restraint. It taught me to always do my best. I learned to read body language, character, and have confidence where I felt I had some. We all worked together to improve each other and to enjoy the camaraderie. You learned the limits of the human body, at least of mine; and that you'll reap the most reward after having tried your best in all that you do.

All of the lessons learned above have helped me through my entire life and professional career. I feel fortunate I have a rich past to reflect upon and am grateful for all that boxing has provided me. Boxing influenced me to have confidence and patience in those around me. It introduced me into a lifelong brotherhood that gave back more than I had put in. If I had to do it all over again I wouldn't change any of it!!

Dale Jeong, DMD
Cal Grad 1971, BS

1967

Coach Nemir and Dick Carter get ready for a bout.

1968

troy cox is best in league - five knockouts

This sequence shows Cal's star boxer Troy Cox knocking out his Nevada opponent John Rodgers. Cox went on to win the CCBC Championship in the 172-pound division the next night by knocking out Luis Hernandez of Chico State in the first round.

four cal boxers win championship titles -

Webb Loyd of California defends himself from a jab by Merv Matorian of Nevada.

The California boxing team, one of only four intercollegiate boxing teams in the United States, ended the season with a disappointing 1-3-1 record, but fared much better in the California Collegiate Boxing Championship Tournament held in Harmon Gym. Four Cal boxers—Dan Burnstein, Gary Evers, Troy Cox, and Webb Loyd—won titles giving the Bears a tie with Nevada for the championship. Senior Troy Cox led the team scoring five knockouts to end a fine collegiate career. Coach Ed Nemir remarked at season's end, "Losing only three men off this year's squad makes prospects bright for 1969."

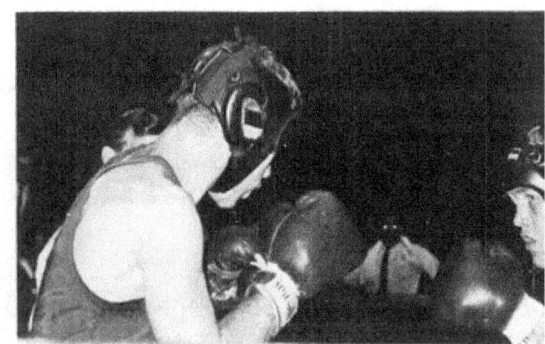

1968

VARSITY BOXING TEAM — **Row One:** Dirk Noyes, Dick Carter, Mike Hogan, Jeff Stewart, Dave Clement, Gary Evers, Pete Morris, Phil Nemir, Sol Quintero, Jon Bedri, Bill Holmes, Dan Burnstein. **Row Two:** Ed Nemir (coach), Rick Aftergut, Ray Koch, Steve Fallai, John Chappell, Webb Loyd, Rod Ott, Mike Ramsey, Troy Cox, Ron Dell'Immagine (assistant coach).

prospects "bright" for 1969 team

Gary Evers of Cal grits his teeth and swings at Sam Simmons of Chico State in the championship bout of the 139-pound division; Evers won.

Bear coach Ed Nemir, one of the founders of the California Collegiate Boxing Conference and Cal's boxing coach for 35 years, shouts encouragement to a Bear boxer.

Dirk Noyes of Cal and Joe Pedrojetti of Nevada fight it out for the 147-pound division championship.

1969

Ed Nemir—Competitor, Coach, Champion

Ed Nemir, a landmark in the rolls of California collegiate boxing for thirty-six years, has fought the final bout. Nemir died of a heart attack during the season while at ringside in a match between Cal and Nevada.

Nemir was a fiery competitor in whatever he undertook. As a result, he broke away from the Pacific Coast Boxing Conference and fought vigorously as one of the prime movers in organizing the California Collegiate Boxing Conference in 1959. He was instrumental in having a novice rule passed—no students can compete in intercollegiate boxing who after a sixteenth birthday engages in competitive bouts other than under the auspices of a school.

In his thirty-six years of coaching, he compiled a record of 120 wins and 61 losses in dual meets. Perhaps the greatest tribute that can be made to such a man as Ed Nemir is the living monument of the four schools that still possess boxing programs in the country. He fought long and hard to keep boxing programs at Cal, Stanford, Chico State and Nevada. They will truly miss this champion who is responsible for the sport's existence at the college and university level.

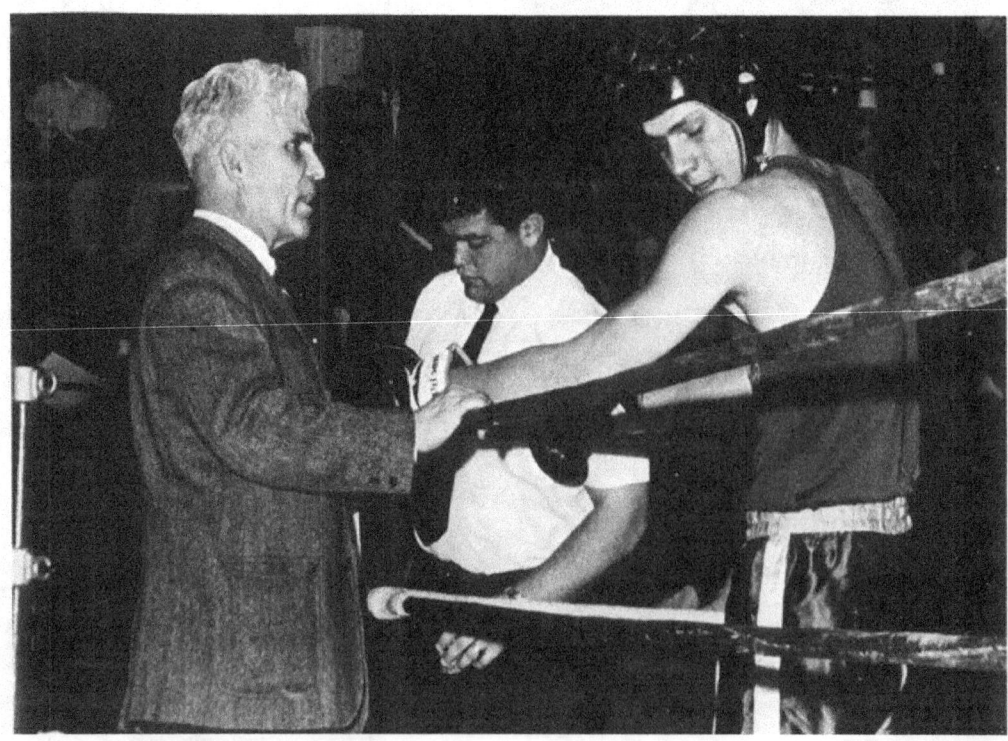

1969

VARSITY BOXING TEAM — Front Row: Dick Carter, Gary Evers, Phil Nemir, Glen Takei, John Incerti, John Yamamoto. Middle Row: James Walsh, Boyd Alexander, Greg Felice, Dirk Noyes. Row Three: Greg Monahan, Steve Fallai, Rod Ott, John Wilson, Brian Kahn, Webb Loyd, Ron Dell'Immagine, coach.

The 1969 California boxing team finished out a long and deeply saddened season with a frustrating 1-2-2 record. Cal's team, one of only four intercollegiate boxing teams in the United States, scored a satisfying 7-3 opening win over the Stanford pugilists, but then suffered back to back losses to Nevada, 5-1, and Chico State, 10-3. A rematch against these same two teams saw the Bears tie Chico State, 7-7, and Nevada 3-3. The Cal ringmen then competed in the California Collegiate Boxing Championships Tournament held in Nevada and placed third. Phil Nemir, in the 131 pound class, was the only Cal boxer to take first in any weight category. Gary Evers, 147 pounds, Brian Kohn, 165, and Webb Lloyd, 180, finished as runnerups for the Bears.

The results of this season never really concerned anyone after the sudden death of Cal coach, Ed Nemir at ringside in a Nevada dual meet. Just a week before leaving for his match he had said, "It's always great to box in Reno." There is a lot of enthusiasm for college boxing and there is always a large turnout at every bout.

Page 212, Upper Right: Coach Ed Nemir. Nemir died suddenly during the season after having led the Cal boxing program for 36 years. **Lower Left:** Late Coach Ed Nemir talks over fight strategy with 165 pounder, Brian Kahn. Assistant Coach Ron Dell'Immagine is in the background. **Page 213, Left:** Bear Webb Loyd (180 pounds) lands a smashing right against his Nevada opponent. Loyd won the match in convincing style.

1970s

Introduction

By 1977, there were seven "varsity" boxing teams in the CCBC (California Collegiate Boxing Conference), including: Cal, CSU Sacramento, More University, University of Santa Clara, Chico State University and UC Santa Cruz. There was also now a "National Conference," and the CCBC won six of the twelve National Titles. Cal also had fights against the 12th Naval District.

Intramural Champions Claude Wyle, George Choulos, Coach Mike Huff

CAL BOXING 1968-75
Brian Kahn

Most of what I learned at Berkeley I learned by boxing.

In the rural environment in which I had grown up, male-on-male violence was limited to boyhood scraps. Even in high school, real fights were rare. As a freshman I was once "chosen out" by an upper classman. Unprovoked, he slapped me and challenged me to fight. I agreed to meet him, but instead told my parents. The principal was called, the boy chastised. But I felt ashamed, a coward. I knew I had acted out of fear.

That fear was aggravated by my upbringing. I knew what racists did to black people in the South. And although I do not remember thinking consciously about it, I knew that behind the hatred of the Reds lay the threat of violence. I still remembered the crazed, screaming faces in the photographs of the Peekskill riots, the overturned cars and smashed windshields, and the leering police.

At the beginning of my junior year at Cal I walked through Harmon Gym, and looked through an open door. Young men in gray sweats were working out. Several hit heavy leather bags suspended from the ceiling. Others skipped rope on the dark cork floor. Two boxers stood at opposite corners of a black-roped ring. A bell rang and they moved toward each other, gloved hands raised. Whap! One man's left hand snapped across the potent space between them. The other boxer countered with his own jab, then moved in, throwing a right and a left hook. The first man blocked the punches and danced gracefully away. They moved with honed skill and the contradiction of relaxed, intense concentration.

I stepped into the room, leaned against a wall, watching.

"You ever box?"

The voice was soft, and I turned to see a short, stocky man, maybe sixty, with startlingly white wavy hair combed straight back. His tanned face was lean and heavily lined.

"No I haven't. My dad boxed in college and we've fooled around some. That's all."

"Would you like to learn?" His dark eyes held steadily on mine, assessing but comfortable.

I hesitated. "Well, I don't know. These guys look pretty tough."

"They're the college team. We offer a P.E. class for beginners. If you're good, you can move up. I'm Coach Nemir", he said, extending a hand.

There was something about him, the easy softness of his voice, the comfortable smile and the distinctive way he stood—fully relaxed, weight back of center, legs slightly spread. He conveyed the sense he knew and liked just where he was and would be hard to move.

"I'd like to think about it."

A week later I stood in the same room wearing gym shorts and feeling nervous. I visualized gloved fists coming fast at my face. Bang! Bang-bang! Jesus...

"Good afternoon, gentlemen. I'm Eddie Nemir. This is a Physical Education course in Elementary Boxing. If you successfully complete this class, you will learn the fundamentals of the manly art of self-defense. We emphasize safety at all times. We teach defense first, so you will learn how to fend off blows in a controlled environment before you face them in the ring. You will learn balance, movement, how to deliver effective blows. Success in this class will require physical and mental discipline. If you enjoy boxing, and develop your skill, we offer Intermediate and Advanced Boxing. And after that, we have an intramural program, and finally, the varsity Cal Boxing Team."

Standing there, feeling uneasy as I watched and listened to him, I had no idea what was unfolding, an experience that would change my understanding of other men and myself.

From the beginning I felt fear. I was afraid of being hit in the face, afraid as I watched other boxers hit the heavy bag hard and imagined them hitting me. I felt fear in the blocking drills, tense as I raised my glove to stop a blow. I felt the fear in my stomach learning each new technique, facing the jarring right hands most boxers threw, and again at unrestricted sparring. I felt fear when the bell rang and I stepped from the safety of the corner to face another man determined to hit me. Fear of being knocked out, fear of losing, fear of being conquered.

But the controlled environment that Coach Nemir imposed gave me and the other young men just enough security to face our fears incrementally. And so each time I was afraid, I stepped forward. The punches came, some hit me hit hard. But the hardest ones, the punches that shook you, jarred your sense of balance, were nothing compared to the *fear* of being hit.

I don't know when Coach Nemir saw I had unusual talent. But I remember the day he stood in front of me, one glove held behind the other alongside his face, his eyes keen.

"Jab!"

I drove off my back leg and struck his gloves sharp and fast. He took the punch smoothly, sliding backward.

"Jab!"

Again. Again.

"Relax. Don't think. Quick hands. Jab!"

Again. Again. Again. I was sweating.

"Don't drop the left. Jab! Jab, right, hook!"

My eyes were on his hands, but I could see eyes, watching. I drove forward with each punch and he moved away, light on his feet, establishing that unique rhythm between offense and defense. At the bell, there was something different in his gaze as I stood unsure, breathing hard.

"Good," he said with a nod, then turned away. And I knew something had changed.

* * *

I stared across the ring, ready for the third round, and could hear my opponent's corner man urge him on: "Go after him. Hard right hand!"

It was the intramural title fight, and Brady had bored in throughout the bout, his thick arms high, driving forward with the jab, winging over with the right hand. I had hit him again and again with my jab as he came, snapping his head back. But he kept coming.

Harmon Gym was packed with the fraternity crowd, beered up and roaring. They were chanting for Brady now. "Sigma Ki! Sigma Ki!" "Kill him!" I'd felt tense before the first round, sweat trickling from my armpits, but with the bell the fear had fallen away and I stepped forward, fully focused on the other man.

The bell rang for the final round, and he came on faster now. He lunged with a jab and I hit him hard, rocking him back. He stood, uncertain, then came again. I knew he would throw the right, putting everything behind the punch, and when he did I leaned back, making him miss short, his weight coming fully to his front leg. He was immobile as I stepped in, my full weight shifting forward, snapping the left hook. I hit him on the jaw, and it felt like swinging a bat fast and smooth and hitting the pitch just right, the strange soft feeling of the hard ball going off the bat. Only it was Brady's head snapping to the side. He fell straight backwards, his arms stretched out like a man on a cross, and his head bounced when it hit the mat. Then he was still.

I stood frozen above him, caught between full combat and seeing a human being helpless at my feet. And a different fear swept up from my stomach and into my throat as I watched the ringside doctor cradle his head and gently remove his mouthpiece. It was a full minute before Brady moved. Half an hour later when I came up awkwardly to him in the shower he said softly that he had a headache, but would be all right. I stood alongside, wondering if I had damaged his brain.

Through a week of vacation I thought about that. I thought about the danger to another man, the danger to myself. How much risk *was* there? Knockouts were rare in college boxing. We wore headgear, used big fourteen ounce gloves. Were the safeguards enough? And how could I feel so different about Brady from one instant to the next? How could that make sense?

The first day after vacation I passed Coach Nemir in the hall. "You're going out for the intercollegiate team," he said.

And I did.

* * *

The first day of varsity practice I sparred with the coach's son, a two-time West Coast champion. I stood six foot one and weighed a hundred sixty-five pounds; Phil weighed 143 and was five foot seven. When I learned we would box, I was worried for him, he was just too small. Inside the ropes I was relaxed as I looked across the ring to see Phil staring at me. I flashed a smile and he did not respond, his face blank. At the bell he closed quickly, throwing a jab. I countered with mine, fully confident of stopping him. But he sidestepped my punch, and hit me very fast three times. I danced back surprised and he came again. Again I jabbed and again he hit me three times. Within thirty seconds my whole sense of ringmanship, of controlling the fight, of effective counterpunching, was in shambles. Coach Nemir pulled me out after one round. "It's not like intramurals, is it?" he said.

He had me train with Phil and welterweight Gary Evers. They were the best boxers on the team and when we sparred it was war. They hit me, pressed me hard, forced me to learn. There was no place to hide. So every day I fought, learning and relearning to push through fear, to focus on what must be done, and to do it. And in the doing, I learned to relax, and found to my amazement that relaxation was the key to enabling one's body to perform to capacity. In the small, real world of the boxing ring I learned that fear is paralyzing, and that moving past it liberates the body and the mind.

I learned to read my sparring partners, the nuances of their stance, the rhythm of feints and counters, the timing of their combinations. And I learned about them as men.

What does a man do when he's been hit hard, his back is to the ropes and the punches keep raining down? When his breath is ragged, his legs heavy, hand speed gone? Does he turn aside or retreat into a shell, primordial surrender? Grab and desperately hold? Or does he slip or duck, block and counter, the mind still focused, looking to fight back? You can find out a lot about a man in twenty seconds.

And so we came to know each other in a way only known to men who have faced direct physical combat. And during the course of the season I came to feel I had earned a place as one of them.

* * *

Coach Nemir straddled the bench in the basement of the University of Nevada gym. He handled the gauze rolls fast, the soft white cloth spinning from his fingers as he wrapped my hands. He wove the gauze carefully and precisely over the back of my hand, around the wrist, between each finger. It took perhaps sixty seconds per hand and when he finished my clenched fist felt solid and comforting.

While he wrapped he talked in his easy way. He knew you were tense, knew you were in some way afraid, knew that just by talking he could help.

"If I had four bits for every pair of hands I've wrapped, I'd be a rich man," he said, his dark eyes sparkling. "Just relax out there. Fight your fight. You'll do fine."

An hour later I stood in the arena, warming up in my blue satin robe. I shadow boxed easily, watching as the fight before mine came to a close. My arms and legs were light and very fast, the easy looseness of top conditioning. It was bright there under the ring lights, and Coach Nemir's white hair gleamed as he stood, waiting for the decision. Then he fell, his head bouncing off the floor, and his whole body shook in spasms and his head kept banging on the floor. Then someone was kneeling beside him, holding his head while his body spasmed.

I turned and saw his son Phil, frozen. Dick Carter was kneeling in his dark robe, his eyes closed, his hands clasped in prayer. Behind him the crowd was standing. No one moved.

It seemed a very long time before they slid Coach Nemir onto a stretcher, his head rolling loose to the side, his white hair still brilliant in the lights. And they carried him out dead into the night.

* * *

Coach Nemir's death cut the heart out of our team. We practiced hard, finished the dual meet season, prepared for the championship tournament. But it was all going through the motions. The intense camaraderie was gone, the solid feeling of accomplishment at the end of a workout, the lightness in the room.

I don't think any of us other than his son knew him well enough to love him. But we all had come to understand that he was teaching us things of value as young men, that he approached us with respect, that he cared for each one of us, and that unlike so many athletic coaches he would never risk our safety for the sake of winning. We knew it was Nemir, in the aftermath of the death of an intercollegiate boxer, who had forced the "amateur" rule on college boxing. It banned all boxing scholarships, and barred from collegiate competition men who had fought in Golden Gloves, high school or the military. This eliminated gross mismatches of skill, and heavier gloves and headgear became mandatory. But for us it was not his boxing reforms that mattered, but who Nemir was as a man. He never raised his voice, never bluffed or postured, always looked you in the eye, always said directly what he had to say. And each of understood, without articulating or perhaps even fully grasping the idea, that we could trust him with our safety, and our lives.

* * *

When I'd returned to Berkeley to go to law school, the boxing program was still alive, but barely. We had lost much in the aftermath of Coach Nemir's death. Our room in Harmon Gym had been taken; Nemir's salary as a P.E. instructor was diverted elsewhere. With boxing's support system severed, any rational assessment would have predicted its demise. But the members of Coach Nemir's boxing team were not rational about it. We were determined that the program would survive.

That determination had been fueled by our bureaucratic opponents. Had they been honest in dealing with us in the aftermath of Nemir's death in January, 1969, I do not think we would have rallied so fully to try to save the sport. But they were not. Professor Van Dalen, chairman of the P.E. Department, had the ultimate decision. He told us how much he respected Coach Nemir, what an outstanding coach he had been; he said that the decision on the future of boxing would be made based on objective data, particularly student demand. He assured us that we would be kept fully informed and given opportunity for input.

Friends in the department warned us that the decision had already been made, that Nemir's salary was to be divvied up for teaching assistants, and the boxing room eliminated. Tipped off about a faculty meeting scheduled to discuss boxing, we asked to make a presentation and were informed that was not necessary. We submitted ten years of student enrollment data for P.E. classes which showed that boxing ranked near the top in student interest.

In March we headed home for spring break, having been assured no decision had been made. When we returned ten days later all the equipment —- the heavy bags, speed bags, lockers, the ring, had been removed from the boxing room and its doors locked.

People react to perceived injustice. The boxing team as a whole was politically more conservative than average Berkeley students. But the administration's deviousness infuriated us all. We held a meeting, decided we would fight, and developed our strategy.

In the next two months we forged on unorthodox coalition: We rallied the leftist student government by stressing that bureaucrats were thwarting student will; we appealed to the alumni on the basis of loyalty to Coach Nemir and Cal tradition; we won over media with the human interest story of students fighting for their sport and in honor of their beloved coach. Feeling the pressure, P.E. agreed to give us its boxing equipment and allow us one year's use of a tiny basement room while the Athletic Department assessed the feasibility of taking over the elementary and intermediate classes. (During Nemir's tenure, the Athletic Department was responsible for only the intercollegiate team.) Both departments would provide minimal funding for a year. My former teammate Dick Carter, pursuing his MBA on campus, became head coach. He, Coach Nemir's son Phil, and others kept things going, recruited newcomers and coached the intercollegiate team.

During the 1971 and '72 seasons, I served as assistant coach. I believe I was paid a hundred fifty dollars each year. When Dick Carter graduated at the end of that second season, I became head coach.

In pursuing space for a training facility, I learned that a track stadium storage room leaked so badly that nothing could be kept there. We obtained permission to use that room for boxing. It was small -— barely enough room for a twenty-foot ring and two heavy bags, but for us it was heaven-sent. We even had the luxury of water to clean mouthpieces. A bathroom occupied the space behind one wall, and the open-topped toilet reservoirs had been installed on our side.

The support we had cobbled together had saved us from destruction, but was not potent enough to generate real commitment from the Athletic Department. Dave Maggard, former Olympic discus thrower, was its director. His job was difficult -— to please the alumni by developing winning, money-making programs in basketball and football while maintaining credible academic performance by the Cal athletes. With chronic financial pressure, the "minor sports" like baseball, track, wrestling, swimming, boxing, gymnastics, were all viewed through the prism of revenues: they "lost" money. Maggard, unlike the emerging breed of fully business-oriented athletic directors, had a personal commitment to the ideals of amateur athletics. This placed him in a tough position, constantly having to choose between the money-driven imperatives of what were in fact semi-professional athletic programs and the truly amateur sports.

In relation to boxing, he was a lukewarm ally. He agreed to take jurisdiction over the sport, and allowed us to teach the elementary and intermediate programs vital to recruitment. He gave us minimal funding. But he refused to leverage up the program with a quality training facility and realistic funding for a coach.

By 1973 it was clear that the boxing program could not be sustained without a major change. I asked around: Who at Cal controlled the purse strings and who, if anyone, had leverage over Maggard?

The answer: Robert F. Kerley, Vice Chancellor for Administration. I did not know him, and I didn't want to: Kerley had been there during the time we had been shafted by the bureaucracy, and he was one of them. Still, what choice did I have? I made an appointment.

On a spring afternoon I walked to the center of the campus and entered the Chancellor's building. The ceilings were very high as I walked up marble stairs and came to a sitting room with dark walls and large couches. A receptionist greeted me and said Mr. Kerley would be available in a few minutes. I sat, looking over the large sterile portraits of past Chancellors. Mothballs would not have been out of place.

"Mr. Kerley will see you now."

I entered a small office dominated by a heavy wooden desk. Behind it sat a jowly man with slicked back grey hair and bags under blue-gray eyes. He looked tired.

"Jesus…" I said to myself as he rose heavily to greet me with a puffy hand and a gravelly, "Hi, I'm Bob Kerley." He motioned to the only chair.

"What can I do for you?" he said, looking intently at me over half-rimmed glasses.

Seeing him, I _knew_ it was hopeless. And that removed any hesitation about being completely frank. I would tell it like it was.

I told him of my experience boxing at Cal, what I had learned about myself and my teammates; I told him about Coach Nemir, why he was a great coach, and how his team had rallied to try to save the sport. I told him how we'd been lied to; how we had kept things going, how Maggard was weak in his support. I told him why I believed this purely amateur sport was good for young men. I told him that unless the University decided it was serious about maintaining boxing, it would die.

His expression never changed. He watched me, breathing slowly and heavily. When I finished there was a long pause.

And then he said, "You're an honest guy, aren't you?"

I was dumbstruck. I sat for several seconds before saying, yes, I thought so.

"What are you going to do after law school?"

I said I didn't know, that I still had a few months to think things though.

"How would you like to work for me?"

I had heard him clearly, but it made no sense. "Work for you??"

"Yeah. For me." His voice was flat. "I hire two graduates each year as administrative interns. You get a modest salary — I think it's three hundred bucks a month. You come to a monthly meeting of the Chancellor's council to learn how the University runs.

"I don't care what you do with the rest of your time, so long as it's connected with the University and you keep me informed." He paused again. "I thought you might want to coach the boxing team."

I took the job and for the next year devoted myself to promoting and building the boxing program. For his part, Bob earmarked funds for first class equipment and adequate travel. Dave Maggard's attitude changed immediately, saying he'd see what he could do to get adequate training quarters.

Able to coach full-time, I recruited more students, including the first women for the program; we increased training for the intercollegiate team. And we were lucky: We had some good and determined athletes during the 1973-74 collegiate season.

Cal won the west coast boxing championships in 1974, taking titles in five of the nine weight classes. It was Cal's first championship in more than a decade. Chancellor Bowker came to see the finals, since his student chauffer, Bill Stanley, was fighting for the 125 pound title. Bowker liked Bill, and the Chancellor invited the team to his house for a formal victory celebration. Maggard made a large room available at the track stadium. The political wind had shifted. As I write this more than forty years later, Cal Boxing is thriving on the Berkeley campus. And dozens of colleges and universities nationwide, all following Coach Nemir's strict amateur rules, now participate in collegiate boxing.

History is the product of large forces that almost always overpower human feelings, desires. But sometimes not. In this small and not small case human commitment won out. It took the sustained efforts of a dedicated core, but when push came to shove the outcome hinged on Bob Kerley. One principled man.

Boxing:
And Then There Were Three

Intercollegiate boxing is going down for the count. What at one time was one of the most popular collegiate sports now has only three colleges in the nation fielding teams. Last year there were four, but Stanford dropped out when lack of interest killed the team. Along with Nevada and Chico State, California forms the California Intercollegiate Boxing Association, the only such conference in the nation.

For awhile, it looked like Nevada and Chico might be the only teams left. After Ed Nemir, coach and guiding force behind collegiate boxing, died at ringside last year, things looked dark. Paul McNally, a three year boxer for California and now a teacher in the area, assumed the job as coach, but found himself lacking almost everything but boxers with plenty of desire. Intramural boxing and boxing classes, the traditional source of talent, were dropped. The old boxing room was changed into a wrestling room, and the PE department seemed to turn deaf ears to the athletes. But Paul Brechler vowed to continue the sport if student interest remained. First the team moved into a tent on the roof of Harmon Gym, and then into a tiny room in the basement.

Because of the room problems, the team had trouble training and were behind the other conference teams from the start. They did manage to win four while losing only three, for a winning record. Gary Evers and Phil Nemir, son of the late coach, battled to championships in the league tournament.

Boxing Roster

Ted Blankeburg
John Cosly
Gary Evers
Gus Felice
Orb Greenwald
John Incerti
Dale Jeong

Ray Koch
Dan London
Phil Nemir
Frank Roesch
Glenn Takei
Jim Walsh
Dan Yamamoto

Cal	2	Chico State	7
Cal	4	U.S. Navy	1
Cal	3	Chico State	6
Cal	3	Nevada	8
Cal	5	12th Naval District	1
Cal	6	U.S. Navy	1
Cal	5½	Nevada	4½

1970

opposite: Ray Koch lands a hard right against a Chico State opponent. Chico was the only team to defeat Cal twice this year. above: Paul McNally, taking over for Ed Nemir who died last year, gives some pointers to Glenn Takai. Assistant Coach Dick Carter listens in. left: Big Dan London finds his mark on the head of a boxer from the 12th Naval District team.

1971

Pugilists' Inexperience Causes Subpar Season

Roster

Sam Bort
Hank Davalos
Gus Filice
Paul Giroday
Fred Gusman
John Incerti

Jeff Karp
Mike Ramsey
Scott Roberts
Sid Strickland
Glenn Takei
Rick Taylor
Jim Walsh

The California boxing team did not have a very fruitful year for many reasons. Probably the most important was the lack of experience that plagued Coach Dick Carter all season.

The season started off well enough, as the Cal pugilists slammed a Navy contingent from Hunter's Point by a 3-2 score.

The Chico State Wildcats came to Berkeley overflowing with talent and experience—and a strange style both irritating to fight against and to watch. The Wildcats played it cozy and won 9-3.

Nevada's Wolfpack simply outslugged the overmatched Cal men and defeated the Bears 2½-7½. Again, lack of experience cost Cal dearly.

In the return match against Chico State up north, the Bears felt lucky to be on the short end of a 1½-10½ score considering the way the scoring went.

The Laney Eagles stepped in over their heads and absorbed a 10-0 shellacking, even though their lack of experience matched the Bears' own.

Playing it a little cagey at last, the boxers held their own against murderous Nevada in Las Vegas; losing 4½-6½ in a match that saw three matches which could have gone either way.

1971

opposite above: A Cal boxer explodes a shot to the midsection of his Nevada opponent. opposite below: A vicious left hook is hammered home as a Bear pugilist squares off with his adversary. top left: A judge looks on as a Cal man lands a solid right hand to the head. top right: Coach Dick Carter confers with one of his charges between rounds. below left: A double exchange of right crosses between a Chico State foe and his Cal opponent.

SEASON RECORD

California	3	Navy	2
California	3	Chico State	9
California	2½	Nevada	7½
California	1½	Chico State	10½
California	10	Laney	0
California	4½	Nevada	6½

2-4

1971

The 1971 Cal boxing team. (The first team that Dick Carter coached as head coach. Carter was also the Assistant Coach to Paul McNally for the 1970 team.)

1972

Boxing and Wrestling

My Heavyweight Battle (1972) by Paul Rein (1963-1965)

I fought as a Cal Berkeley intercollegiate boxer from 1963 to 1965. (Our California Collegiate Boxing Conference (CCBC) was the only conference in the country since 1960, when the NCAA dropped boxing after a death in the National championship tournament.) In my senior year I was undefeated and won the "CCBC" Conference Middleweight Championship, fighting against Stanford, Chico State and Nevada (Reno). Yet the fight that I remember most vividly was a fight I fought 7 years later, a fight that didn't officially count, and a fight that I did not win.

"They've got an out of shape Marine, 5'11", 195, not much experience. Do you want to fight him?" "Great, let's go! What have I got to lose?" I was a 27 year old lawyer and hadn't boxed competitively for seven years. I was 5'10", 180 lb. and had last fought in college at 165 lbs.

I'd been working out with the University of California Boxing team during the spring of 1972, sparring, teaching and playing "assistant coach" with the younger boxers, seizing the opportunity to stay in shape and share my experience. Dick Carter, the Cal Boxing Coach, told me about an upcoming Cal bout against the 12th Naval District at Hunter's Point Naval Shipyard. The Navy coach wanted boxing experience for as many of his fighters as possible. My fight would be scored, but officially it was an "exhibition."

I drove over to Hunter's Point with the coach and four Cal boxers. I joked about my advanced age and being "over the hill" at age 27. At Hunter's Point I got into my gear and began shadow boxing. It was great to put on the Golden Bear "Blue and Gold" uniform. I was excited and looking forward to the challenge when the Navy coach delivered the bad news. "The marine you were supposed to fight didn't make it. Your fight's off." When I expressed my disappointment, he said, "Well, there's another heavyweight you might fight, if you're really anxious to fight." "How big is he?" I asked the Navy coach. "Well, he's inexperienced, but he's learning; he's strong, but he's only had a few fights." "How big is he?" I asked again. "6'3", 235. But he's an older fighter; he's 27."

I saw the guy. A large black man with broad shoulders, at least four inches taller than me. Well, I thought, maybe I could psych him out, "out tough" him. He must think I'm some kind of "ringer" to be willing to fight him at this size difference. Maybe he knows I'm a former college champion. (Maybe he just thinks I'm crazy!)

The Navy heavyweight came over with a big smile and a handshake. "Hey, I hear you're a lawyer! My wife and I got this problem. Maybe you could give us some advice?" There went my chance to "psych him out!"

We were introduced to the referee ahead of time, Frankie Carter, a top professional. He had refereed some of my Cal bouts, and remembered me. I must have been the model of confidence:

"Frankie, could you do me a favor? You know I'm an experienced boxer. I'm not going to get hurt. Please, don't stop the fight unless it looks like I'm really going to suffer *serious* damage." High hopes!

Showtime! I touched gloves with my opponent and got ready to fight, searching for a strategy. There *must* be something *wrong* with this guy or they wouldn't put a 6'3" 235 lb. fighter against a 5'10" 180 pounder. (But maybe they felt I must know something or I wouldn't be agreeing to get into the ring!)

I waited in my corner for the opening bell, and looked across the ring. My opponent looked very large and very muscular. ("At least if he's *that* muscular, maybe he won't have a good left jab," I thought. "Maybe he won't use that long reach.")

The bell rang and we met at the center of the ring. He reached down and snapped out a left jab and my head snapped back from the punch. Instant whiplash! He stung me with three more left jabs. (So much for my theory!) A poor start, but then the first round went downhill from there.

I figured he'd present a large target for body blows: I crouched down and hit him, thud, thud, left, right, left, right into the bread-basket. No response except a couple of solid counterpunch blows to my head. Then he threw a hard right at my head. I raised my left shoulder in a "shoulder roll" defensive move, whereby the opponent's right cross is blocked by the proponent's left shoulder. I blocked his punch and took such a smash to my shoulder that I lost most of the power in my left arm for the rest of the fight. I could still stick out a jab, but
could no longer throw a left hook! His left, however, worked well enough and caught me on the chin, which cut and bled. (I had never been cut before.) The bell rang, and the longest first round in boxing history came to a close. I managed to find my corner, on the second or third try.

Coach Carter encouraged me between rounds. "Keep up the good work, champ. You're wearing out his knuckles on your chin! He'll probably tire soon."

With the arrival of the second round, I had a moral revelation, and remembered that great axiom of human behavior, "It is better to give than to receive." I threw some thumps to his solar plexus. (It felt like hitting sandbags.) I tried to throw hooks around his forearms. As he looked down upon me from his greater altitude, his blocking arms looked and felt like 2x4s against my wrists. However, my perseverance and adrenalin-based temporary insanity finally paid off: Goliath began tiring, and my punches kept landing.

By the third round I was working him over, trying for a fight-ending knockout. "Navy" was running out of gas and I was too numb and crazy to stop punching; I kept hitting until he was saved by the final bell. I had survived!

The professional referee scored the fight in my favor, but the two Navy judges voted for the sailor. I lost the "split decision," but emerged with a genuine smile on my face. I shook hands with my opponent, congratulated myself upon my relatively good health, and drove back to the East Bay for a midnight visit to the Oakland Kaiser Hospital. I had a big grin on my face as the emergency room doctor sewed up my chin with seven stitches. "Looks like you've been in a fight, Tiger," said the doctor. I grinned again. "You should'a seen the other guy!"

Three weeks later, my Navy opponent came to Berkeley for a Cal "home" bout and knocked Cal's 230 lb. heavyweight champion out cold in the second round, leaving him draped across the ropes. I then learned that I had fought against the undefeated Heavyweight Champion of the 12th Naval District! This increased my joy at having survived. What a way to have fun!

Oakland Tribune, Sunday, January 9, 1972

Tribune photo by Howard Erker

PAUL GIRODAY LASHES OUT WITH RIGHT TO TOM GIOSEFFI'S FACE
It was a close, no-decision bout between Cal's best of past and present

A Giroday, Gioseffi Punch Out

It was a series of exhibition bouts between California's varsity boxing team and the alumni, not something to stir up much interest normally.

But there was a special attraction in this case — 200-pounder Paul Giroday, rated by many to be the Bears' best in recent years, against lanky lefty Tom Gioseffi, a 175-pounder who was the dominant figure in the early 1960s.

There were no judges, and therefore, no decision. The opinion of Harmon gym spectators was mixed as to yesterday's winner.

Giroday fought an unusually conservative fight, but staggered the ringwise Gioseffi in the third round. Gioseffi, on the other hand, used his reach to good advantage and scored well with combinations.

There were 14 bouts and perhaps the star was Old Blue Jim Handel.

Still a trim 125-pounder, Handel, a 1952 graduate, bloodied Mel Menda and the bout was finally stopped in the third round.

The exhibitions tuned the Bears for their first matches of the season, which will be held against a Navy team Friday night. Chico State provides the first college competition for the Bears, Jan. 22 at Harmon.

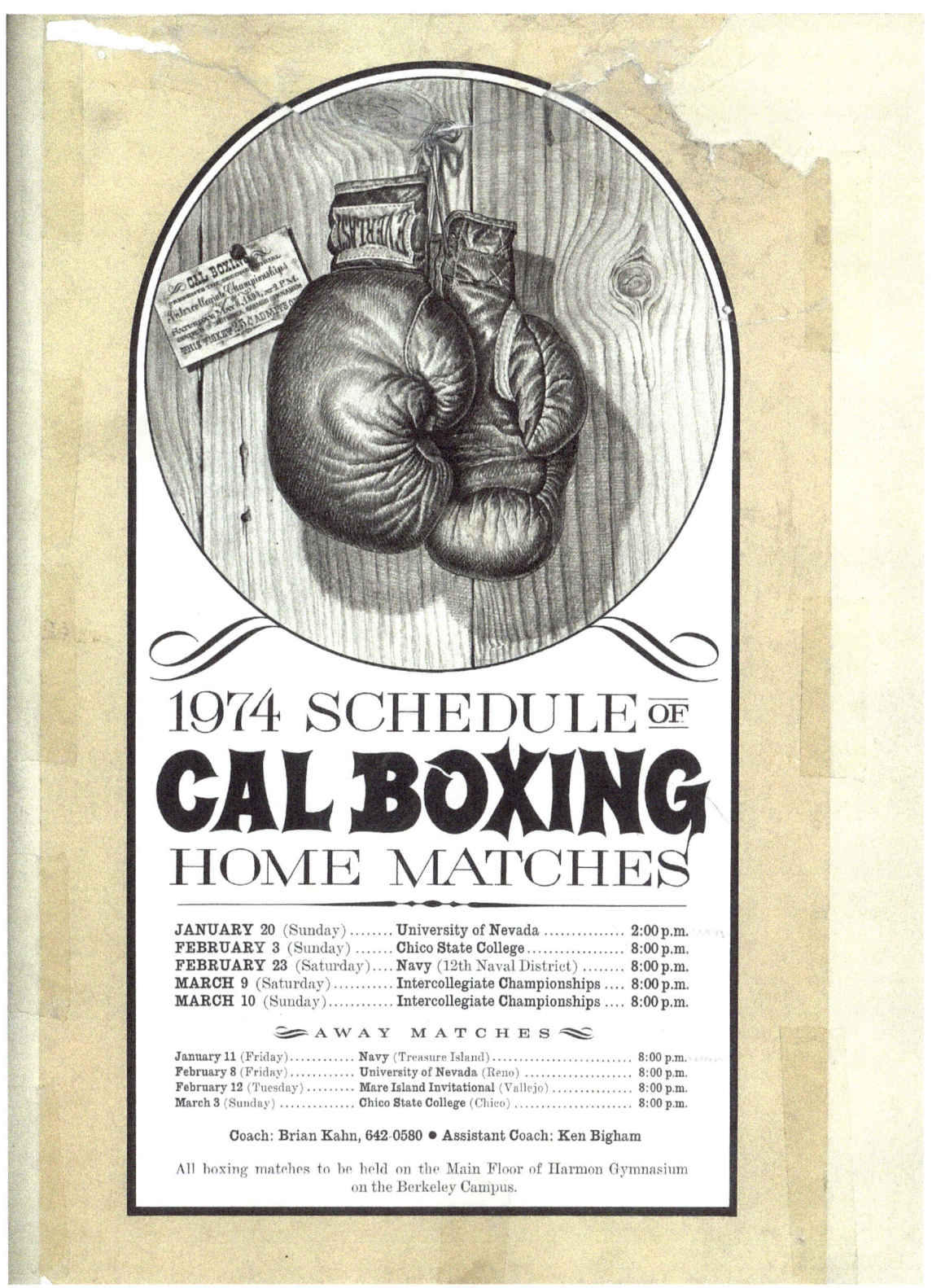

1976

Cal Athletic News
WEDNESDAY, JANUARY 28, 1976

Cal Boxers Now 1-0 in Early Season

The California intercollegiate boxing team got off to a good start in its 1976 schedule by easily beating a Navy team, Saturday. The Bears won five bouts, four by technical knockouts, lost two bouts and had one draw.

"We really have a very strong team. There really aren't any weak spots," said head coach Ken Bigham.

The Cal team has three returning lettermen from last year's squad along with a host of talented newcomers.

Saturday, knockouts were recorded by Bill Sandoval in the 147 pound division, Lyon Rathbun in the 156 pound division, Tom Pedamonte in the 172 pound division, and by heavyweight Bob Black. Cal's Antonio Aguirre won a unanimous decision over Amado Evangelista of the Navy in the 132 pound division.

Bigham said he was quite pleased with his team's performance and said he thought they were ready for the start of league competition. The Bears compete in a league composed of the University of Nevada at Reno, Chico State, and Cal.

Thursday the Bears travel to Reno to box their arch-rivals from the University of Nevada. Nevada has a number of returning lettermen from last year's team and looks to be Cal's chief competition for the league title.

The Bear's next home match will be February 7 against Chico State in Harmon Gym at 3 pm, and then on February 21 at 2 pm against the University of Nevada. Admission is free.

Cal's boxing team is an intercollegiate sport organized on the club level. It is supported by the athletic department, which provides money for travel and equipment.

HEAD BOXING COACH KEN BIGHAM cuts an impressive figure here, overseeing the action in Cal's new boxing quarters beneath the track stadium. The Bears, now 1-0 on the year following a victory over Navy last week, fight again February 7 against Chico State in Harmon Gym.

ANOTHER ALI? ... Boxing coach Ken Bigham surveys two of his boxers working out in the new boxing facility located under Edwards Stadium. Cal is one of only three West Coast schools that have boxing programs.
Photo by Michael Hill

College Boxing: Just for Fun?

By MARK MELTON

To most people familiar with only the pro version, boxing is considered a brutal sport fought by unthinking, gargantuan hulks whose IQ's wouldn't rival that of a pet rock. That popular stereotype and pro boxing's supposed "underworld" connections and influences have detracted from the reputation of the sport and given it a rather unsavory image.

But the gentlemanly art of fisticuffs does still exist, though presently obscured by the big money of professional heavyweights and dwarfed by vast programs of amateur boxing and Golden Gloves competition. It's called intercollegiate boxing.

Interest in intercollegiate boxing experienced a precipitous downfall several years ago when a boxer was killed in a college bout. Many schools dropped their programs at that time, but Cal continued its team and is now in a league with Chico State and the University of Nevada, Reno, the only other schools on the West Coast with boxing teams.

Why does Berkeley still have the program? That question was posed to athletic director Dave Maggard. "Basically, we have continued our program to serve the broad interests of the student body," he said.

According to Maggard, boxing is a "varsity intercollegiate club sport," which means the eligibility requirements differ from a recognized NCAA sport. The crucial difference in college boxing is that one can't have participated in the sport, even as an amateur, before attending college.

(see page 10)

Boxing Without Glory

(from page 7)

Thus all of the boxers are beginners when they enter the program. That is also the reason why the college sport is different in emphasis. Unlike the pros there is no big money involved (the entire program is run on $6,000), and unlike amateurs it's not a farm league for the pros.

Ken Bigham is the new boxing coach, replacing Brian Kahn after assisting him last year. He is an anomalous figure in a sport associated with run-down gyms and "street tough" personalities. He writes plays and poetry, attended Cal, and hopes to enter San Francisco State's creative writing program.

Bigham said. "People aren't in this program to make it in the pro's. They learn self-discipline, how to handle themselves, and work into great physical shape."

The boxers fight three one-minute rounds, wear protective headgear and 14-ounce gloves to pad the blows, and referees immediately stop a fight if it's too one-sided. "The matches aren't designed to see if one guy can beat up the other," Bigham said. "They are designed to show boxing skill."

Who participates in intercollegiate boxing and why? Ed Mitchell, a senior, boxes because "it helps your confidence and the workouts are tough and satisfying." Dave Skruggs looks at it this way: "I'm too small to play football, and I don't play any other sport, so I tried boxing. It's a chance to participate, and I get a letter." Pete Lindstrom said, "I enjoy the contact."

But for whatever reason, boxing at Cal has experienced a resurgence of interest and participation. There are many returning lettermen, and Bigham says there are some new, inexperienced people with great promise.

And this year, the Cal boxers will be developing their skills in a new facility at Edwards Stadium. Bigham thinks the new room is great. "If people could see it," he said, "they might be more inclined to look into the program." He welcomes anyone interested in boxing, including women.

"A lot of it is confidence,"

1976

INTERCOLLEGIATE BOXING 1976

U C BERKELEY VS NAVY

Weight	Cal			Navy	
118	TOM BRADFIELD	(Cal)	vs	MIKE THOMPSON	(Navy)
125	JOE CHAIREZ	(Cal)	vs	HAROLD PATTERSON	(Navy)
132	ANTONIO AGUIRRE	(Cal)	vs	AMADO EVANGELISTA	(Navy)
139	ED MITCHELL	(Cal)	vs	BILL ADAMS	(Navy)
147	BILL SANDOVAL	(Cal)	vs	ROYCE CRAVEN	(Navy)
156	LYON RATHBUN	(Cal)	vs	MARK DABBS	(Navy)
165	DAVE SCRUGGS	(Cal)	vs	JIM MONTOYA	(Navy)
172	TOM PEDAMONTE	(Cal)	vs	TO BE ANNOUNCED	
180	PETE LINDSTROM	(Cal)	vs	KEVIN HARVEY	(Navy)
Hvywt	BOB BLACK	(Cal)	vs	MIKE ALDRIGHETTE	(Navy)

REFEREE: RON DELL-IMAGINE

JUDGES: MARTY SAMMON

ED ROBERTS

DALE CHAMBLIN

COACHES: KEN BIGHAM (Cal)

NELSON DUNKLE (Navy)

1976

EAST vs WEST
College Boxing

THURSDAY, MARCH 25, 1976
8:00 P.M.
CENTENNIAL COLISEUM

EAST

COLLEGE OF CHARLESTON
Location: Charleston, S.C.
Enrollment: 4,000
Athletic Director: Alan LeForce
Coach: Henry T. Nielson
Colors: Maroon and White
Nickname: Cougars

PENN STATE
Location: University Park, Pa.
Enrollment: 24,322
Athletic Director: Edward M. Czekai
Coach: Ed Sulkowski
Colors: Blue and White
Nickname: Nittany Lions

SOUTH CAROLINA
Location: Columbia, S.C.
Enrollment: 27,000
Athletic Director: Harold Hagan
Coach: Chris Hytopoulos
Colors: Garnet and Black
Nickname: Gamecocks

TEMPLE
Location: Philadelphia, Pa.
Enrollment: 16,397
Athletic Director: Ernest C. Casale
Coach: Mike Foley
Colors: Cherry and White
Nickname: Owls

TORONTO
Location: Toronto, Ontario, Canada
Enrollment: 28,000
Athletic Director: A. Dalton White
Coach: Anthony Canzano
Colors: Royal Blue and White
Nickname: The Blues

VILLANOVA
Location: Villanova, Pa.
Enrollment: 5,895
Athletic Director: Dr. Theodore Aceto
Coach: Jim McMillin
Colors: Blue and White
Nickname: Wildcats

U.S. NAVAL ACADEMY
Location: Annapolis, Md.
Enrollment: 4,200
Athletic Director: Cpt. J.O. Coppedge
Coach: Emerson Smith
Colors: Navy Blue and Gold
Nickname: Midshipmen

WEST CHESTER STATE
Location: West Chester State
Enrollment: 7,200
Athletic Director: Robert W. Reese
Coach: Alan E. McChesney
Colors: Purple and Gold
Nickname: Rams

WEST

CALIFORNIA
Location: Berkeley, Ca.
Enrollment: 27,500
Athletic Director: Dave Maggard
Coach: Ken Bingham
Colors: Blue and Gold
Nickname: Golden Bears

NEVADA
Location: Reno, Nevada
Enrollment: 8,150
Athletic Director: Dick Trachok
Coach: Jimmie Olivas
Colors: Silver and Blue
Nickname: Wolf Pack

1976

The 3 on right bottom sporting the blue and gold Cal boxer champions from the *1976 East-West tournament at the Lawlor Center at UNR with Mills Lane the referee:
Warner Gysin, Jose Ortega, & Tom Bradfield.

Boxers 1976:
Warner Gysin
Ed Mitchell
Tom Pedemonte
Pete Lindstrom
Bill Sandoval
Jose Ortega
Tom Bradfield
Lyon Rathbun
Dave Scruggs
Bob Black
Joe Charrez
Antonio Aguierre

(Coach: Ken Bigham)
(Dave Maggard was the Intercollegiate Athletic Director at the time)
*1st National Collegiate Championship since 1960

1976

Nevada State Journal — Friday, March 26, 1976

Nevada-led West Boxers Batter East

By DAN McGRATH

The first national college boxing championships in 16 years gave a Centennial Coliseum crowd of 1,700 a night's worth of entertainment and the West team a tenuous claim to superiority by virtue of its 8-5 victory Thursday night.

The West team, composed of boxers from the University of Nevada-Reno, the University of California and San Diego State, got five victories from UNR fighters and three from Cal's representatives to claim the team trophy. UNR heavyweight Dave Jarstad's victory came via a forfeit when his scheduled opponent, West Chester State's Bruce Blair, was a last-minute cancellation because of surgery to correct an injured nose.

The East team consisted of conference champions from the Eastern Collegiate Boxing Association.

The butterflies which kept Bob Kimberlin, UNR's 112-pounder, from eating all week and had him at 111 pounds at the afternoon weigh-in were gone within the first few seconds of his bout with Jason Lo, a University of Toronto sophomore. Kimberlin, in command throughout, floored Lo with a big left hook midway through the third round and won a unanimous decision.

The Tom Bradfield-Lenny Ermak bout at 118 pounds featured nine minutes of non-stop offense. The five-judge panel awarded Bradfield a split decision.

If an award for most courageous fighter had been given, the presenters would have been hard pressed to keep it away from Warner Gysun, Cal's 125-pound senior. His nose was split wide open by South Carolina's Robby Collingwood early in the second round, but Gysun refused to fold. Instead he scored consistently with a straight right that slowed Collingwood's charges, and was awarded a well-earned split decision despite his gruesome appearance.

Tom King, a cherubic-looking Temple University sophomore, played boxer to Jose Ortega's role as slugger in their bout at 132. The Cal junior was wild, but caught him often enough to win a narrow split decision.

UNR freshman Dave Morgan ran afoul of Villanova sophomore Juan Montez, a San Juan, Puerto Rico native with monogrammed trunks, a baleful stare and a snappy, aggressive style, at 139 and the West's string of four straight successes came to an end. The combination of Montez' aggressiveness and considerable reach advantage was too much for Morgan to overcome, and he took a standing eight-count after a particularly fierce Montez barrage in the third.

The towel was thrown in shortly thereafter, at 1:46.

West Chester State's Ed Skalamera, who had to sit in the sauna and ride an exer-cycle for nearly an hour Thursday afternoon to make 147-pounds, then gave the East its second straight win. Skalamera's tightly-muscled physique gives him the appearance of being much heavier, and he threw some heavyweight punches at a weary Bill Sandoval of Cal on the way to a split decision.

The 156-pound matchup between Penn State's Mike Benelli and Cal's Lyle Rathbun, lived up to expectations. The two unbeaten, ask-no-quarter sluggers started trading punches at the opening bell and never stopped, even after Benelli's split lip began spewing blood all over both of them. But Benelli, somehow, came up with his third wind after exhausting his second, and a strong third round carried him to a split-decision victory that could hardly have been closer.

The crowd had barely settled back into its seats before UNR's Dave Billing and Ty Venable of College of Charleston had them on their feet again. Venable, perhaps the East's classiest boxer, used his reach advantage and a slick left jab to bloody Billing's nose in the first round, but midway through the second he walked into a Billing right and never recovered. The two-time ECBA champ attempted to cover up and weather the storm but couldn't, and referee Mills Lane stopped it after Billing landed several additional strong rights.

Billing was named outstanding fighter.

Jim Krtinich, UNR's unbeaten 172-pounder, started slowly against Jimmy Jones, understandably wary of the West Chester State fighter's big guns. But a sneaky right hand hurt Jones late in the first round, and he seemed reluctant to engage Krtinich at close quarters thereafter. Krtinich was content to bang away from long range and piled up a tidy lead.

Stan O'Conner from the U.S. Naval Academy decisioned Bob Kerry of San Diego State at 180.

Clay Griswold, UNR's freshman 185-pounder, stayed away from Joe Gery's long, strong right through the first round, but the West Chester State sophomore bloodied Griswold's nose and dropped him with two rights in the second. Griswold, a real crowd-pleaser owing to his tenacity, made it close with a good third round, but Gery was a clear-cut winner.

Another toe-to-tow slugfest in the Benelli-Rathbun mold was provided by UNR's Dave Schuster and West Chester's Joe Bucelli at 190. Neither fighter bothered with such niceties as jabs, and three rounds of roundhouse swings had both men out on their feet at the end. Schuster, making his first appearance of the year, rallied from a slow start to gain a split decision victory which brought a smattering of hoots from the audience.

'I Won.'
Warner Gysun of the University of California leaps in the air after defeating Robby Collingwood of South Carolina in the East-West Collegiate boxing championships at Centennial Coliseum. The West dominated the meet. At right Bob Kimerlin of UNR wins an exchange with Toronto's Jason Lo.
(Journal photos by Marilyn Newton)

14—Reno Evening Gazette Friday, March 26, 1976

Diehard boxing fans shoul

By DAN McGRATH

Mike Benelli was having some trouble talking, since his lower lip had been split open and sewn back together. A painful-looking little mouse adorned his right eye, and his overall appearance suggested that what he'd been up to lately wasn't in the best interests of his health.

But he was smiling broadly, and it didn't seem he could be much happier.

"What'd you think of it?" he demanded of a reporter.

"I'm supposed to ask you that."

"Yeah, I know, but I know what I think. I thought it was great. Make that terrific. What'd you think?"

The world will little note nor long remember what went on in Centennial Coliseum Thursday night, but diehard boxing fans in the crowd of 1,700 are likely to. They saw 12 highly spirited, tightly competitive fights between champions from the Eastern Collegiate Boxing Association and representatives of the University of Nevada-Reno, California and San Diego State.

It was the first national college boxing competition since 1960, and it was well received, particularly since the West team — UNR and company — walked off with the team trophy by winning seven bouts and getting an eighth on a forfeit.

Benelli, unbeaten in 16 fights as a collegian, met an equally tough customer in Cal's Lyon Rathbun, undefeated this year at 156 pounds. The two ask-no-quarter sluggers exchanged teeth-rattling punches for the better part of three rounds, even after Benelli's split lip began spewing blood over both of them. Somehow they were both on their feet at the final bell, and the Penn State senior was awarded the decision by the narrowest of margins.

"God he was tough," Benelli acknowledged afterwards. "But how'd I look -- pretty good?" To say the least.

For constant action, the Benelli-Rathbun fight had only one rival — a win by Dave Schuster of UNR over Joe Bucelli of West Chester State at 190. The appearance was Schuster's first this year, and by his own admission he was not quite with it.

"And the guy was a little tougher than I thought," he admitted.

Bucelli, a West Chester State football player, was fighting for only the fourth time in his life, and though he was literally out on his feet at the end, he was within two points of the two-time California Collegiate Boxing Conference champ on all five judges' scorecards.

"I've got nothing to be ashamed of," Bucelli noted, quite correctly, it seemed. "I gave it my best. It was a helluva fight."

For sheer explosiveness, Dave Billing's performance was in a class by itself. The UNR sophomore has been through some lean days (1-3 this year) after going undefeated as a freshman, but it took him less than four minutes to erase a lot of frustration.

Ty Venable, a two-time ECBA champ, was Billing's opponent at 165, and the College of Charleston junior

1976

Fistic action

In picture on left University of California boxer Jose Ortega, left, gets ready to send a punch to the body of Temple sophomore Tom King. Ortega won a narrow split decision in the 132-pound fight. Cal's Warner Gypsun, right, lands a solid left to the jaw of South Carolina's Robby Collingwood during their 125-pound fight during East-West college boxing championships at Centennial Coliseum Thursday night in above picture.

(Gazette photos by Marilyn Newton)

d remember all-star card

used his reach advantage and a stiff left jab to bother Billing in the first round.

"I knew I had to start getting underneath him, work on the body to get his hands down," Billing observed.

And he did just that early in the second round, hurting Venable with some body shots, then dropping him with a straight right to the jaw. Venable took an eight-count to clear the cobwebs, but no sooner had referee Jim Evans continued the fight than Billing's right was at it again. Evans stopped it at 57 seconds.

"I was really up for it. The season hasn't been what I expected it to be, probably because it came pretty easy for me last year and I didn't think I'd have to work too hard," Billing noted. "I'm feeling pretty good right now. I did the job."

The judges were impressed enough with Billing's job to name him the evening's outstanding fighter.

The West's other victories came from UNR's Bob Kimberlin, who dropped Jason Lo of Toronto in the third round and won a unanimous decision at 112; Cal's Tom Bradfield, who won a slugfest from West Chester's Lenny Ermak at 118; Warner Gysun of Cal, who ignored a freely-bleeding nose to take a split decision from Robby Collingwood of South Caroline at 125; Cal's Jose Ortega, on target with enough roundhouse punches to get a split decision over Temple's Tom King at 132; UNR's Jim Krtinich, who hurt West Chester's Jimmy Jones early, then scored from long range on the way to a unanimous decision at 172; and Nevada heavyweight Dave Jarstad, who was awarded a forfeit victory over West Chester's Bruce Blair when Blair submitted to surgery to repair cartilege damage to his nose suffered in a workout back in Pennsylvania.

Besides Benelli the East winners were Villanova's Juan Montez, a classy Puerto Rican who used his superior reach to bang away at UNR's Dave Morgan and stopped him in the third round; Ed Skalamera of West Chester who outmuscled Cal's Bill Sandoval at 147; Stan O'Connor of the Naval Academy who floored San Diego State's Bob Kerr in the first round and hung on for a unanimous decision; and West Chester's Joe Gery, whose only weapon was a big right hand which he used to hammer out a close but unanimous verdict over UNR freshman Clay Griswold.

Both Jimmie Olivas, who helped assemble and coach the West team, and Al McChesney of the East, expressed satisfaction with the program and are hopeful of doing it again next year. New York's Madison Square Garden has expressed interest in staging it.

But Benelli, who impressed everyone he met with his ability to put things in perspective, summed it up best.

"Was it a success? You better believe it," he stated.

"Just the fact that they could have it after all these years, get this many people interested and involved and pull it off, makes it a success."

Oakland Tribune sports

Cal Boxers Hanging on Among Last In the West

Alan Pryor gets a tip from instructor Ralph Salas

By PAUL McCARTHY

BERKELEY — Time was when intercollegiate boxing packed the arenas, offered scholarships and served even as a spawning ground for the pros.

Death of Wisconsin's boxing captain, following an NCAA tournament bout in 1960, left the sport hanging on the ropes. Critics said it was brutal and had to go.

One by one, West Coast powers dropped out. Schools like San Jose State, Gonzaga, Washington State and Idaho gave it up. Stanford, Santa Clara and Chico State finally followed suit.

Cal and Nevada-Reno are now the last survivors.

The unexpected death in 1969 of Ed Nemir, Cal's beloved coach for 35 years, might have signaled the end even at Cal. In fact, only dedicated former Bear boxers among the alumni, plus a series of part-time coaches, has kept it alive.

Nemir died at ringside in Reno eight years ago Tuesday, only moments after his son, 139-pound Phil, had won his bout against Nevada. Staunch defenders of college boxing were numbed by the loss, but somehow carried on.

Fittingly, Ed Nemir's son Phil coaches this year's team — no longer a Big C sport with full recognition, but still active in the Nemir tradition.

"I'm a forester by profession, and would normally be out in the woods now," says the 29-year-old Nemir who graduated from Cal in 1970. "But I agreed to coach for one year. Yes, I'm paid something so I don't lose out financially, but I really don't gain from it, either, except from the satisfaction these kids give me in the ring."

Athletic Director Dave Maggard, building Cal's program toward excellence in other, more glamorous sports, has agreed to help the boxing orphans.

"But to assure financing for the 1977-78 season," Nemir explained, "we must be able to compete against five other schools in the area. We have a real solid alumni group, which

Continued Page 24, Col. 5

Bearded coach Phil Nemir exchanges punches with Livermore veteran Bill Sandoval

Nemir

Cont. from 1st Sports Page

has helped us fund 60% of our budget. Now we hope they can influence other schools, like Santa Clara, UC-Santa Cruz and possibly Sacramento State, to return to boxing."

Cal has a hard core gang of 28 young boxers — the remnants of an original turnout of "somewhere around 100" who signed up for an introductory boxing class, Nemir says with pride.

'Saves'

"It's a great way to keep in shape," says slender Alan Pryor, at 24 an industrial hygiene student from Santa Cruz by way of Atwater. "I wrestled in high school, and just wanted to try boxing."

Sandoval, who suffered from the flu just before losing his title bout last year, "took some lessons in the spring of 1974, and liked it enough to try out for the team."

The Bears go on public view

Boxing

for the first time tomorrow night at Harmon Gym when, with entries from Mare Island's Navy program and others from Nevada at Reno, Nemir presents his novice tournament.

The schedule includes four home meets and, if funds can be raised by alumni and friends, a trip to the collegiate nationals at the U. S. Naval Academy in Annapolis, Md., March 30-April 1.

Tribune photos by KENNETH GREEN

1976

Cal Athletic News
WEDNESDAY, FEBRUARY 11, 1976

Kahn Connects

Brian J. Kahn, for five years Cal's boxing coach, was sworn in last month as the youngest supervisor in the history of Sonoma County.

Kahn, 29, a former legislative aide to Assemblyman John Vasconcellos, took the oath of office January 22 of this year to assume the duties of First District Supervisor of Sonoma County.

A 1965 graduate of Sonoma Valley High School where he was number one and valedictorian of his class, Kahn attended the University of Oregon for two years and the University of California at Berkeley for his final two years. He graduated with honors in 1969 with a degree in political science.

In 1970, he entered the University of California's Boalt Law School, graduating in 1973.

While studying law, Kahn (who had been UC Berkeley's "outstanding boxer" in 1969) became the school's boxing coach. Kahn took over when the death of long time Coach Ed Niemer, threatened to jeopardize the boxing program. Kahn continued to coach throughout the three years he attended law school and for the two years following graduation from Boalt Law School. Incidentally his 1974 and 1975 Cal boxing teams won the conference championships.

During 1974, Kahn served as an administrative intern to Vice Chancellor Robert Kerley while during the period July 1974-75 he served as a district representative for Assemblyman John Vasconcellos of San Jose.

In July 1975, Kahn came back to Sonoma County to work on the county's federally funded Criminal Justice Self Assessment.

This unique in-depth study will involve all the local criminal justice agencies and interested citizens in dialogue to determine future policies and objectives for criminal justice in Sonoma County.

Kahn, in commenting on his appointment, said, "My experience in working with state government at the local level taught me how hard it can be for citizens to get government to respond to their needs."

"The majority of my time, in serving Assemblyman John Vasconcellos," Kahn continued, "was spent helping people fight bureaucracy and cutting red tape. I don't believe that government has to work that way ... instead, we have to develop new ways to meet public needs and get people involved in making and carrying out the decisions which affect their lives."

"We started down that road together 200 years ago. We believed in people — in ourselves and in each other. We faced problems then and we face other problems now. In order to solve the problems we face today I believe we must return to the basic principles we began with ... Some people regard the idea of a working democracy as unrealistic. I disagree, and so did the people who founded this country."

Kahn, who replaces 11 year board veteran, Ignazio Vella as First District Supervisor, will have to run for re-election this year.

Vella, whose third term ends December 31, 1976, resigned the board seat to accept the position of General Manager of the Sonoma County Fair.

BRIAN KAHN, shown here after his 1974 boxing team won the conference championship.

1977, 1978

LA Road Trip, by Paul O'Neil

Boxing matches were not plentiful in 1977-78. Mind you, those of us with young man's disease were not complaining. Mike Huff, using some creative desperation to find us some "action", picked a venue in LA.

Normally you would expect competition in a school or military facility, you know, "normal" places, but not when Mike picks 'em. Once we hit town we were passing all these small tiny homes in what seemed to be a semi-neglected 1950's type East LA neighborhood. I'm thinking to myself, where the hell are we going? Suddenly, the Van stopped, and we unloaded into a perfectly square grey cinderblock flat roofed building in the Hood. I couldn't figure out whether this was a gym for "smoker fights", or what else. You entered through a narrow hallway that led into the Ring Room with the mirrors. The hallway was lined with angry faced, but curious home boys & girls that you had to pass, more or less "through" to get in. I recall that I sensed an odd unexpected feeling of relief once we go into the ring room. Well, ...it seemed safer.

(This was my second fight, the first being under Phil Nemir the prior year).
My tall opponent and I had a definite mutual wariness of each other, but perhaps he a little more wary of me than I of him on this particular day; this gave me the license for me to drive in to score points and dart away to avoid his height. He seemed to want to get away with throwing the big towering shot from above with only a moderate work rate. This allowed a comfortable decision in my favor, I think it was unanimous; however to be honest, this bout was more like a sparing session than a high energy, high effort "fight". This LA trip was one of those experiences where the actual boxing had become secondary, at least for me, to the entire road trip itself.

I can remember (then teammate, and now famous Cal Coach) Jim Riksheim with a few cocktails under his belt; that's probably a rarity! And Floyd Salas, infamous unofficial assistant coach, was Rapid Fire Jittering & shadow boxing to Disco music in the front seat as he drove the Van on the return trip up I5; plus I got away from Engineering School for a while—no complaints, only appreciation.

1979

BOXING

The Cal Boxing team, under Coach Mike Huff, finished second in the California Collegiate Boxing Conference. They were third at the Western Regional tournament. Dave Oster and Jim Riksheim qualified for the National Collegiate Boxing Association tournament in Chicago.

1980s - Introduction

The 1980s were an exciting time for Cal Boxing; including winning numerous Regional Championships and several National Championships in competition which included more than 39 schools, by 1981, including West Point (Army), The Air Force Academy and Annapolis (Navy).

In 1982, Cal won five individual Western Regional Conference Championships and took Fifth Place in the Nationals. Regional Champs included: Frank Delzompo, (1982 Team Captain) Chan Kim (139 lbs), Norris Moore (147 lbs), Paul Templin (180 lbs) and Heavyweight Kurt Heffernon (3 times Regional Champ and 1984 National Champ). The team was 13-0 in individual bouts at Harmon Gym.

In 1982, Jim Riksheim, a former CCBC Champion started his long career as an outstanding Head Coach, assisted by former Cal Boxers Floyd Salas, Albert Sandell and Mike Huff (a former head coach).

1n 1983, an article referred to Floyd Salas, as a "Novelist and Poet" who was in his 8th year as Assistant Coach," author of "Tattoo the Wicked Cross."

In 1984, the National Championships were held in Harmon Gymnasium at Cal. Cal won two championships in extremely exciting fights: Chris Morales beat an excellent former National Champ at 125 lbs, winning by decision and ending his Cal career with an 11-1 record. His only loss was in the 1982 National Finals. Kurt Heffernon, considered an underdog to the huge and powerful fighter from Shippensburg, Mike Regan, amazed the crowd by knocking the "Tornado" out in the first round, bringing everyone in the crowd to their feet. [See articles: "Hometown Hero Tackles Tornado," by David Darlington, "Just Gutting It Out Offers Satisfaction," by Francis Kane and "Cal's Morales, Heffernon Win Titles," by Dave LeVecchio for the Oakland Tribune.]

Western Regional Champions were Hariberto Fermin (119 lbs), Chris Haddawy (132 lbs), who won the Western Conference Championship and the Eddie Nemir Memorial Award, and Mark Fowler (156 lbs), who won the Western Conference Championship and the Outstanding Boxer Award.

1980

CAL BOXING NEWSLETTER
April 28, 1980

Hello! This is the fourth of five newsletters to keep Cal Boxing friends informed about club activities.

APOLOGIES TO ALUMNI - Many of you were unable to attend the California Collegiate Boxing Conference Championships held at Harmon Gymnasium March 23,24, because our last newsletter advertising the event did not arrive until after the event. The newsletter was submitted to bulk mailing over two weeks before the event, but was not processed for 2½ weeks. WE APOLOGIZE.

CCBC CHAMPIONSHIPS - An exciting championship tournament was held at Cal with Nevada, Reno winning the team championship. Chico finished 2nd and Cal third in the team competition. Individual honors for the Bears went to David Oster (112), and Bo Mitchum (125), each conference champions in their respective weight class. Oster went unopposed while Mitchum had his finest hour as a collegiate. He decidedly beat Vic Vicari from Nevada with an impressive offense. Cal's runner-ups were Jeff Rubin (139) and Tim Potter (190). The CCBC 1980 Conference Champions are as follows:

```
112 Dave Oster (Cal            156 Kevin Johnson (Nev)
119 Dirk Vitto (Nev)           165 Maurice Kilpatrick (More)
125 Bo Mitchum (Cal)           172 Don Francesconi (Chico
132 Vic Alegria (Nev)          180 Mark Romero (Nev)
139 Dave Morgan (Nev)          190 Paul Cimino (Chico)
147 Mike Cusick (Chico)        HWT Jim Quillicci (S. Clara)
```

NCBA NATIONALS - The Air Force Academy won the National team title with 4 champions and 50 team points in front of 7,200 cadets in two days of tournament action at the Academy in Colorado Springs. David Oster (112) was the most successful Bear finishing second to Ray Fernandez of Westchester State. Oster scored a stunning 2nd. round KO victory over Bob Navarro (Air Force) in his semi-final bout. However, the classy Fernandez only let the powerful Oster get close once in the third round when Dave scored with a strong right hand. Fernandez, recovered and had the stamina to keep moving and outpoint Oster for the championship. Bo Mitchum (125) fought well but fatigued because a nagging knee injury had interferred with his training. Bo lost a unanimous decision to Greg Ebert of West Chester, who eventually won the title at 125 lbs. Cal's Jeff Rubin received an invitation to participate in the Nationals, but lost a very close semi-final decision to Dave Werkhiser of Penn State. The West only won one championship as Mike Cusick (Chico) pounded out a close decision over Aaron Swanier (Air Force) at 156 pounds. NCBA National Championship finals:

April 5, Finals

```
112  Ray Fernandez (West Chester State)   Dave OSter (CAL/Berkeley )           points
119  Denny Grunstad (Air Force Academy)   Curt Vitto (NEVADA/Reno)             points
125  Greg Ebert (West Chester State)      Dave Garman (Penn State)             points
132  Billy Koltnow (Dickinson College)    Victor Alegria (NEVADA/Reno)         points
139  Ricky Graham (Air Force Academy)     Dave Werkhiser (Penn State)          points
147  Mike Cusick (CHICO State)            Aaron Swanier (Air Force Academy)    points
156  Tony Thornton (West Chester State)   Paul Frappier (Air Force Acacemy)    points
165  Alex Cline (Air Force Academy)       Maurick Kilpatrick (More Univ)       points
172  Shelton Redden (Naval Academy)       Don Francesconi (Chico State)        points
180  Larry Steuck (Air Force Academy)     Tim Hill (Ohio University)           points
190  Harry Nixon (Ohio University)        Paul Cimino (Chico State)            points
HWT  Ken MacDonald (Naval Academy)        Curt Lanzel (Air Force Academy)      points
```

1981

CAL BOXING NEWSLETTER
March 23, 1981

This is the fourth of five newsletters designed to keep Cal Boxing Enthusiasts informed about our program in 1981.

BOUT RESULTS @ MORE The Bears scored two wins and one loss at the More Invitational on February 28. Frank Delzampo (156) and Paul Templin (190) each picked up a victory by virtue of a TKO and unanimous decision, respectively. Mike Valli (147) suffered Cal's only loss at the hands of Chris Hernandez of Navy. NEVADA @ CAL Frank Delzampo and Bert Sandell (180) chocked up victories for the Golden Bears against Nevada, each by virtue of second roud TKOs. Delzampo, Cal's "Italian Stallion," was too strong and aggressive for the heavier Duff Stewart. Sandell and Rick McGough of Nevada hooked up in one of the most exciting fights Harmon Gym has seen since the Mid seventies. Reminiscent of the great bouts between Lyon Rathbun (CAL) and Dave Billings (Nevada) and Stan Staneck (Cal) and Jack Abbott (Chico), these two fought a seesaw battle that Sandell won with an impressive barrage of punches. Delzampo and Sandell were the only Cal boxers on the card. CHICO @ CAL The Bears sent five into the ring on March 6, winning two, losing one, while two were non-scored exhibitions. Raul Pardo of Cal, a slick 139 pounder, and Albert Sandell (180), won by decison. Mike Valli (147) lost on points to Frank Venegas of Santa Cruz while Nick Radetsky (147) and Paul Templin boxed in exhibitions.

BEARS TO ENTER FIVE BOXERS IN WESTERN REGIONALS UC Berkeley will enter five boxers in five weight classes in the California Collegiate Boxing Conference Championships at the Richmond Auditorium on March 28 and 29. Senior Albert Sandell is the Bear's most solid contender at 180 pounds. Sandell has had three impressive wins and has shown great improvement over the course of the season. Frosh boxers Mike Valli (147) and Frank Delzampo (156) are solid contenders as well. Valli, started fast but stagnated in mid-season. He has looked good in recent work-outs, however, and is protecting himself much more. Delzampo could be a big surprise as he is learning the necessary skills to compliment his great power. Other possible surprises include Raul Pardo (139) and Paul Templin (190). Pardo is a slick boxer who came into the program late. His level of conditioning is the question. In contrast, Templin is strong and in great shape. Coach Mike Huff believes that if "Paul can relax and fight on his terms he can be very effective." In rating his squad, Huff states: "Realistically, we are very young, but our kids are tough and in good shape. I'm hoping we can sneak up on the Conference fat cats, Reno and Chico."

NATIONALS @ RENO The 1981 National Collegiate Boxing Association Championships will be held on April 3 and 4 at the University of Nevada, Reno. Cal Boxing Backers invites all interested alumni to join the fun in the "Biggest Little City in the World." Accomodations will be available at the Gold Dust Hotel. Prices and reservation information were not available at press time. However, interested alumns should phone Mike Huff or Nora Dowley at (415) 642-8342 for information.

COME ENJOY 2 NIGHTS OF BOXING AND A LITTLE GAMBLING ON THE SIDE!!!!!!!!!!!!

1981

CAL BOXING NEWSLETTER
May 5, 1981

This is the fifth of five newsletters...

APOLOGIES - Our sincerest apologies to those who were inconvenienced by the sudden shift in location of the CCBC Championships from Richmond, California, to the University of California. More University was unable to secure the Richmond Auditorium and informed the Conference one day before the event. Disciplinary action has been taken. Please forgive us.

CCBC Championships - Cal finished a disappointing fourth in a field of six at the CCBC Championships, March 28 & 29, at Cal's Harmon Gymnasium. Senior Albert Sandell (180) captured the Bear's only individual Championship defeating Mark Romero (Nevada) in the semifinals and Bob Berenschott (Chico) in the Championship. Sandell was named the victor over Romero when the ringside physician stopped the bout due to a cut over Romero's eye. In the championship bout Sandell scored repeatedly with varied combinations soundly drubbing Berenschott. The referee stopped the contest in round three. Sandell's performance earned him the award as the Tournament's Most Outstanding Boxer. Cal's Frank Delzompo (156) and Paul Templin (190) were tournament runner-ups while Raul Pardo (139) and Mike Valli (147) lost in semi-final bouts. The University of Nevada won its seventh straight CCBC title. Chico State finished second while More University finished third. Santa Clara's Mark Ansami (125) won the Eddie Nemir Sportsman Award.

NCBA Championships - The Golden Bears finished sixth of seventeen at the NCBA Championships at Reno, Nevada, April 3 and 4. Freshman Frank Delzompo garnered the highest honor capturing second at 156 pounds. Delzompo, selected as an NCBA alternate, lost an extremely close bout to Bob Steigerwald of the Air Force in the championship. Albert Sandell (180) and Paul Templin (190), also selected as an alternate, lost in the semi-finals. The Air Force Academy won its second consecutive national title thoroughly dominating the tournament. West Chester State finished second while Nevada faired third. Thirty nine school competed on the intercollegiate level in 1981.

Edgar Nemir Outstanding Boxer Award - Albert Sandell has been selected as the recipient of the 1981 Edgar Nemir Outstanding Boxer Award. Sandell only boxed for Cal in his senior year, but his accomplishments were substantial. He accummulated a 5-1 record, winning a CCBC Championship at 180 pounds. In addition, he captured the Outstanding Boxer Award at the CCBC Championships. Sandell's achievements were not limited to the boxing ring. President of the Chi Psi fraternity, Albert was responsible for reinstating the Intrafraternity Boxing Tournament this spring. Sandell majored in Industrial Engineering and has maintained a 3.4 GPA. Albert is the grandson of the late amateur boxing organizer Al Sandell. It is hoped that he will remain in the Bay Area next year as he wishes to contribute more to the development of collegiate boxing.

Intrafraternity Council Boxing Tournament - After an extended absence, the IFC Boxing Tournament returned to Berkeley on April 24, 1981. Thirty six contestants tested their skills on the deck of the Chi Psi Fraternity in an afternoon of sun, beer, and boxing. Chi Psi won the team title with Fijis taking second and SAEs capturing third. Thanks to all those who helped rejuvenate this great event.

1981

YOU CAN HELP CAL BOXING maintain its place among the top college boxing programs in the United States by becoming a **CAL BOXING BACKER**. Organized in 1977, Cal Boxing Backers is composed of alumni and friends who are keenly interested in maintaining the sport on the Berkeley campus. Cal Boxing Backers provides funding for all phases of Cal's boxing program: instruction, intramurals, intercollegiate competition and recreational exercise. Alumni donations comprise approximately 60% of the annual budget and give more than 100 students per year the opportunity to experience this unique sport.

CAL's PROGRAM IS ON THE RISE following a **SIXTH PLACE** finish in the National Collegiate Boxing Association championships in 1981. Three freshmen (Frank Delzompo, Raul Pardo, Michael Valli) and two juniors (Paul Templin, Tim Potter) return from last year's squad to provide a core of tough, determined competitors for the 1981-82 season. Reinstitution of the Interfraternity Boxing Tournament last April should increase participation and spectator interest on campus. New interest coupled with the standard instructional program should furnish an exciting year for the Golden Bears in 1981-82.

BOXING HAS BEEN A TEAM SPORT AT CAL SINCE 1919, when students from Stanford and Cal squared off in one of college boxing's first matches. Cal now boasts the oldest continuous program in the country. Since 1919, literally thousands of Cal students have participated at various levels of programming ranging from instruction to highly skilled intercollegiate competition. In the late sixties boxing enjoyed only moderate student support and participation was limited to a small group of individuals. But the mid-seventies marked a resurgence of interest with more than 40 institutions sponsoring intercollegiate teams under the auspices of the NCBA. Cal's program is now housed in the Sports Club Program with 31 other "small sports." The UC Boxing Club is responsible for all boxing activities on the Berkeley campus.

1982

1982

WELCOME TO THE CAL INVITATIONAL! Tonight's card feature both novice and experienced boxers from CAL, SANTA CLARA, SANTA CRUZ and the 12th NAVAL DISTRICT. Hope you enjoy the bouts.

12th NAVAL DISTRICT

John Dorsey	125
Mike Sims	132
Otto Frye	132
Bill McBride	132
Paul Hernandez	147
Ron Foultz	147
Rod Martin	156
Melvin Gorland	156
Tyrone Clay	190
Dave Graves	190

SANTA CLARA

Mark Ansani	125
Andrew Sakai	132

SANTA CRUZ

Jeff Arnett	139
John Ribiero	147
Peter Heimerdinger	156
Joe Delgadillo	165

CAL

Chris Morales	125
Garrell Kirtley	132
John Halbrook	139
Dennis Kehoe	147
Frank Delzompo	156
Stan Pierchoski	165
Tim Potter	190
Scott Rasmussen	190

REFEREES AND JUDGES:

- Jack Campbell
- Jack Downey
- Dick Rall
- Jack Scheberies

ANNOUNCER:

- Ed Mitchell

TIMEKEEPER:

- Bill Treseler

COACHES:

Nelson Dunkle	Navy
Duke Drake	S. Clara
Dave Nelson	S. Clara
Yankee Glendon	S. Cruz
Bob Bishop	S. Cruz
Jim Riksheim	Cal
Mike Huff	Cal
Floyd Salas	Cal
Al Sandell	Cal

PHYSICIAN:

- Earl Mitchell MD

1982

Cal Boxing looks to national championships

By JIM CARSON

In one of the oldest organized sports at Cal, the boxing club has started its season in top form and looks to once again rank as one of the best teams in the country.

The club, which up until 1975 was a part of the department of physical education, has won 75 percent of its fights. The team hopes to improve upon last year's sixth place finish at the National Collegiate Boxing Association Championships.

Like last year the team is dominated with novice boxers, yet through the course of the season, the coaching staff provides enough training to lead a majority of the boxers to the national championships. The use of novices at Cal reflects the National Boxing Association's prohibition of recruiting and scholarships, believing that institutions should teach skills to novices rather than recruit the experienced amateur.

But in addition to just skills, the program at Cal works on developing character in the students participating in boxing. Coach Floyd Salas explains this character that is developed as one of confidence in themselves. "No matter what happens during the season each one of the boxers comes out a winner."

Another point which is emphasized is safety. "We stress safety first and if one of our boxers looks overmatched in the ring we take him out," says Salas. The coaching staff further emphasizes that the common belief that boxers are in the ring to destroy their opponents is false.

In truth, many of the boxers on the team who have lost in at least one of the two bouts so far, say they box simply because the activity is fun. This may seem odd to many people, but the challenge of conquering the fright and possibility of being knocked out pushed the boxers to extremes in exertion and physical ability.

Currently the team has 10 boxers with no less than six competing against any one team. The team is really a trimmed-down version of the fall boxing club program which competes on the intramural level.

Unfortunately, a majority of the fall boxers drop out of the program after the intramural season concludes in December and a surprising number of walk-on students fill the gaps for the team that competes at the intercollegiate level during the winter quarter.

The team fields seven of 12 weight group classes and will be putting everything on the line this Friday when they host the traditionally bigger and stronger Nevada Las Vegas team at the Cal Invitational tournament.

Coach Michael Huff says his team looks better than last year and thinks the club can beat Nevada. The Cal Invitational will serve as a conference preview as all the conference teams will participate. Other teams in the conference include Cal State Chico, UC Santa Cruz and Santa Clara.

Outside of the eastern schools which dominate collegiate boxing, the state of California is one of the biggest boxing states. Nationally there are 39 teams, representing a steady increase since 1975 when only five teams existed. It was this same year that a tragic event occurred that nearly collapsed the college sport.

During the national championships of 1975 an eastern boxer died in the ring and it was later determined the cause of death was a poor heart condition. Nevertheless, the stereotype reached epidemic levels and many institutions including Cal dropped the sport as part of the varsity program.

The boxing club is run and financed by the students involved and donations are contributed by the boxing alumni directly to the club.

Coach Salas said on the outside there are no motivating factors to make a person want to join the team. "These guys get no letter or scholarship," says Salas, "and the only recognition they receive is being a part of the club."

Junior Boxer Chris Morales (125 pounds) says he decided to come out for the sport after watching the Olympic Games in 1976. Fellow boxer Dennis Kehoe (147 lbs), simply says he always wanted to try boxing and walked on just December.

The team is very dedicated to a vigorous training schedule which includes two-a-day runs with weight lifting, shadow boxing and sparring sessions in the afternoon. This dedication has led to many conference champion boxers in the past as well as All-American boxers. In Los Angeles, for instance, professional boxer Jose Ortega was a graduate of UCLA, and member of the boxing club.

Returning this year after a one-year layoff is Tim Potter (190 lbs), the 1980 conference runner up in his weight category. Joining Potter will be heavyweight Roger Scott Rasmusson, who is a transfer from West Point, where he went undefeated in intramural competition, and Frank Deljonpo (156 lbs), who placed second in the 1981 Western Regionals and National Championships. Several freshmen and JC transfers will be giving the team much-needed depth to match the highly recruited boxers of Nevada Las Vegas.

Coach Floyd Salas concludes, "the outlook for the season should be better, for we are much sharper and skilled than last year." The fast regular season, which spans five weeks, concludes with two Friday evening bouts, the first coming this week at 7:30 in Harmon Gym. Following these matches, the team will travel to Reno for the California Collegiate Boxing Conference Finals and then back east at the beginning for April for the national championships.

1982 California Boxing Newsletter

Coaches: Jim Riksheim, Mike Huff

January 19, 1982

HAPPY NEW YEAR!! Welcome back for the 1982 Cal Boxing campaign. This is the first of five newsletters designed to keep alumni abreast of Cal Boxing activities.

THE 1982 SEASON promises to be an exciting one for California Boxing enthusiasts. The Bears will field a team of seasoned veterans and impressive novices lead by Frank "The Italian Stallion" Delzompo. Delzompo, a fierce competitor at 156 lbs., finished second last year at the NCBA nationals with only two months of boxing experience. Delzompo is just a Sophomore and will be joined by fellow Sophomore Mike Valli (139) from the 1981 team that took sixth at the NCBA nationals. Valli, nicknamed the "missle", is a flashy, skilled boxer who should do much better down from the 147 lb. class. Also adding punch to the Cal attack is 190 pound veteran Tim Potter. Returning from a one year layoff, Potter is a skilled scrapper who is clearly in the best shape of his life. Coach Jim Riksheim smiles over such a core of tough competitiors for the 1982 team. Coach Mike Huff adds, "These kids don't mess around. In fact, they genuinely like a good fight."

Top newcomers to the Cal squad include Garrell Kirtley (132), Chris Morales (125), and Scott Rasmussen (HWT). Kirtley is a Junior transfer from Cerritos J.C. in Orange County. Cerritos has an excellent instructional boxing program under the direction of Lefty Pendleton. Romero received similar instruction at U.C. Santa Barbara while Rasmussen is the standout of the Fall classes. All three are well schooled and should add quality and depth to this year's squad.

CAL INVITATIONAL - The Bears will open the 1982 CCBC season with the Cal Invitational on January 29 at HARMON GYM. Boxers from Cal, Santa Clara, Santa Cruz and the Central Pacific Naval District will compete in both novice and senior bouts. The Cal Invitational traditionally begins the Western collegiate boxing season and always features a highly entertaining card. Bouts begin at 7:30pm and admission is $1.00.

A pre-bout cocktail hour is scheduled for Cal Boxing Backers from 6:30 to 7:30pm in Room 175E Harmon Gymnasium. Complimentary passes are available to all Cal Boxing enthusiasts. To obtain your passes please call Mike Huff/ Nora Dowley at 642-4028.

1982

1982 California Boxing Newsletter

Coaches: Jim Riksheim, Mike Huff

February 22, 1982

RESULTS - The Golden Bears are off to a fast start this year winning nine of nine in two home bouts and taking two of five at Mare Island. The early season standout is 125 pounder Chris Morales. Morales, a Junior transfer from UC Santa Barbara, has compliled a 3-0 record including decisive victories over 1981 Nationals participants Mark Ansani (S. Clara) and Kirk Vitto (Nevada).

Other early Bear standouts are Garrell Kirtley (132) and Frank Delzompo (156). Each sports a 2-1 record having dropped bouts at Mare Island. Kirtley rebounded from a devastating first round KO loss at Mare Island to fight his best bout last Friday. Garrell was somewhat cautious in rounds one and two against the powerful Andy Sakai of Santa Clara. But he turned it on in round three with impressive left hooks, overhand rights, and quick flurries which turned a close bout into a unanimous decision in favor of Kirtley.

Delzompo, Cal's "Italion Stallion", turned in his finest effort as well on Friday. After dropping a close decision to his "clone" at Mare Island, Frank and the coaches decided he needed to start faster. Frank executed perfectly, integrating boxing skills and control to defeat the heavier Joe Delgadillo of Santa Cruz. Delzompo worked the body in the early rounds and caught Delgadillo with his hands down late in rounds two and three. The referee stopped the contest in round three giving Delzompo his second consequtive TKO at home. Coach Huff noted that " Frank is finally fighting with 'controlled aggression.' We've been after this for two years."

UPCOMING BOUTS - The Bears travel to Nevada this Friday, February 26, for a meet with the Wolfpack. They will return to Harmon Gym March 5 and try to keep their unblemished home record intact at the Cal Open. Boxers from Chico, Santa Clara, and Santa Cruz will square off with Cal at the Open. Starting time is 7:30pm. CONTINGENTS FOR FRANK DELZOMPO AND GARRELL KIRTLEY HAVE MADE HARMON GYM THE PLACE TO BE ON FRIDAY NIGHTS. COME JOIN THE FUN!

CCBC SCHEDULE CHANGES

(added)	Feb. 26 (Fri)	Cal @ Nevada	Old Gym	7:30pm
	Mar. 5 (Fri)	Cal Open	Harmon	7:30pm
(previously	Mar. 19 (Fri)	CCBC Semi Finals	Old Gym	(Reno, NV) TBA
Mar. 26&27)	Mar. 20 (Sat)	CCBC Finals	Old Gym	(Reno, NV) TBA
	Apr. 2-4	Nationals		East/TBA

MID TERM ANALYSIS - The Bears have experienced a rash of injuries and illness at the mid-point of the 1982 season. The list of disabled boxers is incredible: Robert Mee(125) inactive, 2 months illness, recently passed physical; Mike Valli (139) inactive, 2 months, still out; Dennis Kehoe (147) strained ligaments, inactive; John Holbrook (139) inactive, 10 days flu; Adlai Jourdin (180) inactive, broken nose; Scott Rasmussen (190) inactive, 2 weeks brochitis; Tim Potter (190) inactive, 2½ weeks strained back; Stan Pierchoski (156) inactive, 6 weeks, stress fracture, foot.

Despite the mid season blues, the coaches feel that the Bears should be very competitive at the Western Regionals. "For the first time in years we have some depth in several weight classes," states coach Jim Riksheim. "If we can get through this and get some of our kids healthy again, we'll be very competitive in eight of the twelve weight classes."

1982 California Boxing Newsletter

Coaches: Jim Riksheim, Mike Huff

March 22, 1982

BEARS COMPLETE PERFECT HOME SEASON - Cal pugilists finished a perfect 13-0 at Harmon Gym this season when they swept all four bouts with Cal men at the Cal Open on March 5. Winners included Chris Morales, Raul Pardo, John Halbrook and Scott Rasmussen. The overall regular season team record was an impressive 18-6-1.

CAL WINS FIVE TITLES AT WESTERN REGIONALS - The Golden Bears took five individual championships and finished a close second in team scoring to Nevada at Reno at the California Collegiate Boxing Conference Championships in Reno last weekend. Chris Morales (125), Garrell Kirtley (139), Frank Delzompo (156), Scott Rasmussen (180), and Kurt Heffernon (HWT) won championships out of the eight Cal entries. Raul Pardo (139) and John Holbrook (147) lost in the finals while Craig Jordan (165) lost a "horrendous" decision in his semi-final bout. Nevada led the team scoring with 37 points followed by Cal-32, Chico-11, Santa Clara-11, and UC Santa Cruz-6.

The most impressive performance came from Frank "The Itallian Stallion" Delzompo. Delzompo, angered by a questionable decision and unfriendly press in Nevada three weeks earlier, displayed his wrath against Dan Holmes of Nevada. "The Stallion" opened the fight with savage right hands to the body early and then caught Holmes with an overhand right which sent him reeling and terminated the bout 1:28 into the round. Delzompo ran his collegiate record to 7-4-1 with six KOs.

Heavyweight Kurt Heffernon showed vast improvement winning a unanimous decision against Rich McGough of Nevada. Heffernon, nicknamed "Tiny" by his teammates, repeatedly scored with left jabs and short right hands resulting in two standing eight counts during the course of the bout. Scott Rasmussen and Garrell Kirtley both won "wars" against tough physical opponents; Rasmussen defeated a "tough Nevada Cowboy" named William Routsis with repeated straight 1-2s, and Kirtley scored enough hard rights to dominate Andrew Sakai of Santa Clara in a sloppy wrestling match. Sakai's strategy was to stay close after seeing Kirtley stop Chris Moser (Nevada) with a sharp left hook in the first round of their semi-final bout. As usual, Chris Morales of Cal calmly outpointed Kirt Vitto of Nevada raising his record to a perfect 5-0.

The Tournament's Most Outstanding Boxer was Chris Yach of Nevada while the Edgar Nemir Sportsman Award went to Jim Quillicci of Santa Clara. Western Regional champions will travel to West Chester, Pennsylvania, for the NCBA nationals April 2,3.

1982

1982 California Boxing Newsletter

Coaches: Jim Riksheim, Mike Huff, Floyd Salas

April 30, 1982

BEARS FINISH FIFTH AT NATIONALS-Cal finished fifth out of a field of sixteen (40 nationally) at the National Collegiate Boxing Association Championships on April 2 & 3 at West Chester State College in Pennsylvania. The Golden Bears finished one point behind Lock Haven State, more than doubling their point total in 1981 when Cal finished a distant sixth. Host school West Chester State won the championship with 41 points. The top ten schools, individual champions and point totals are as follows:

1 West Chester State(3)	41pts.	6 Chico State(1)	10pts.
2 Air Force Academy(3)	39pts.	6 Xavier(1)	10pts.
3 University of Nevada(2)	22pts.	8 Virginia Military Inst.(1)	9pts.
4 Lock Haven State	12pts.	8 Army-West Point(1)	9pts.
5 UNIVERSITY OF CALIFORNIA	11pts.	10 Lehigh University	8pts.

California's Chris Morales (125) and Scott Rasmussen (180) faired the best of the five Cal entrants finishing second in their respective weight classes. Morales outscored Keith Dixon of Lock Haven State in his semi-final bout while Rasmussen defeated hometown favorite Tim Dever of West Chester State. Both Cal men suffered their first intercollegiate defeat in their championship bouts. Morales fought an outstanding bout against West Chester State's Ray Fernandez. However, Fernandez' relentless aggression, superior style and leverage, and punching power caused the referee to stop the contest in round two. Rasmussen suffered a similar fate against Bill Akers of VMI. Rasmussen's shabby defense finally cost him as Akers impressive power resulted in a standing eight count in the second round and termination of the bout in the third round.

Cal's Garrell Kirtley (132), Frank Delzompo (156) and Kurt Heffernon (HWT) lost in their semi-final bouts. Kirtley boxed Lynn Mack of Air Force. Kirtley fought well in the first round but Mack scored with hard rights to the body and left hooks to the head leaving Kirtley unable to answer the bell for round three. Delzompo was the Bear's biggest disappointment losing a unanimous decision to southpaw Rob Revercomb of Lock Haven State. Delzompo looked confused and puzzled by the southpaw and threw only three lefts the entire bout. Heffernon boxed well against West Point's Jeter Barnhill. However, Barnhill's superior skill and power got Heffernon in trouble in the second round and Coach Mike Huff stopped the bout. Both Mack and Barnhill went on to win NCBA championships.

HOME BOX OFFICE TELEVISION COVERAGE-HBO Television will show the NCBA Championships (1½ hour presentation) from three to five times throughout the United States starting on the 19th of May. Check your local papers for dates and times.

1982

CAL BOXING BACKERS
California Boxing Alumni

Dear Friend of CAL Boxing,

We wish to express our gratitude to all CAL BOXING BACKERS for your enthusiastic support during the 1981-82 season. This was a banner year for California Boxing. Briefly, we accomplished the following:

(1) Cal finished the home season undefeated, a perfect 13-0.

(2) Cal won five individual Conference championships.

(3) Cal finished second in the Conference close behind Nevada.

(4) Cal finished fifth in the nation one point behind fourth place Lock Haven State.

(5) Cal Boxing Backers raised $5262.

(6) Cal taught instructional boxing to more than 70 students, faculty, and staff.

(7) Cal placed two runner-ups at the NCBA Nationals.

(8) Cal placed five individuals on the NCBA All American Team.

(9) Cal Boxing Backers instituted pre-bout events and the first Student-Alumni Golf Tournament.

Thank you for helping us achieve our most outstanding year in over a decade.

Frank Delzompo
Team Captain

Mike Huff
Coach

Floyd Salas
Coach

Jim Riksheim
Coach

1983

The sport of boxing in certain circles is a very violent endeavor. This is the image the media is giving since the death of Korean boxer Kim. However, the world of amateur boxing maintains strict rules to prevent incidents such as Kim's. Cal's Boxing team is one of the finest in the state, stressing the attributes of the athlete. It is the sense of athletic competition that makes boxing appealing to the athlete. The one-on-one competition that boxing provides is as intense as any sport. It is the goal of the Cal boxing team to keep the sport a competition between men and not dollars.

Don Roper

1983

1983

Boxer Profiles

WEIGHT	NAME	HOMETOWN
119	Chan Kim	Los Angeles, Ca.
125	Chris Haddawy	Reno, Nev.
125	Kevin Octavio	San Francisco, Ca.
132	Garrell Kirtley	Cerritos, Ca.
132	Heriberto Fermin	Los Angeles, Ca.
132	Steve Pugh	Pasadena, Ca.
139	Raul Pardo	Los Angeles, Ca.
139	Jim Dedelow	W. Lafayette, In.
139	John Shimmick	Woodside, Ca.
147	Norris Moore	Salisbury, Md.
156	Alphonso Quintor	Guadalajara, Mex.
156	Sean Mockler	San Francisco, Ca.
156	Wolfe Birkie	San Rafael, Ca.
165	Jim Fardeen	San Mateo, Ca.
165	Carl Orsi	San Francisco, Ca.
172	Adlai Jourdin	Washington, D.C.
172	Dan Carr	Orinda, Ca.
180	Paul Templin	San Diego, Ca.
190	George Straggas	Oakland, Ca.
190	Scott Rasmussen	Sacramento, Ca.
HVY	Kurt Heffernon	Albany, Ca.

NATIONAL COLLEGIATE BOXING ASSOCIATION

The National Collegiate Boxing Association (NCBA) in 1976. It is a non-profit organization whose goal is to provide a safe, positive educational experience for student athletes. NCBA philosophy and rules seek to provide a boxing outlet for students with little or no boxing experience. It encourages widespread participation at the instructional, Intramural, competitive, and recreational level.

To insure safe participation of boxers having roughly equal ability and strength the NCBA eligibility rule states: "Any student, in or out of college, who after his sixteenth birthday, participates in a boxing contest other than one sponsored by his college or university, shall be rendered ineligible to compete in collegiate boxing." This rule tends to equalize competition and reduce injuries resulting from mismatches. By reducing the variation of skill among and between competitors, the rule insures that young men of different abilities do not face each other.

The decline of college boxing in the 1960's was mainly due to an overemphasis on recruiting and providing scholarships for experienced boxers in order to build winning teams. This emphasis on winning often produced dangerous mismatches in boxing contests. As a result the NCBA adopted a rule to protect the student competitor in college boxing.

Tonight's Card

Tonight's boxing card features representatives from the Central Pacific Naval District, Santa Clara University, and the University of California, Santa Cruz (UCSC), pitted with the Golden Bears of CAL. The Cal Invitational traditionally "kicks-off" the intercollegiate boxing season on the West Coast and serves as a first test for athletes who hope to culminate the season with regional and national championship competition in late March and early April. Tonight's bouts will provide an exciting blend of both novice and experienced competitors.

Nationals will take place this year in Colorado Springs at the United States Air Force Academy. CAL finished fifth at the championships last year, just one point behind fourth place finisher Lock Haven. The Golden Bears landed five regional champions in 1982 and placed a close second to Nevada-Reno for the team championship.

The outlook for the 1983 season is good for the Bears since regional champions Garrell Kirtley (132) and Scott Rasmussen (190) will be joined by a host of talented newcomers and veterans. Raul Pardo (139) and Paul Templin (180) add experience while novices Chan Kim (119), Norris Moore (147), and Carl Orsi (165) will be quality performers in their respective weight classes. In addition, for the first time in almost ten years the Bears will have quality depth in most weight divisions.

There are currently seven schools competing in the Western Collegiate Boxing Association (formerly the California Collegiate Boxing Conference) with newcomers Nevada-Las Vegas and Sacramento State joining Nevada-Reno, Chico State, Santa Clara, UCSC, and CAL. There are over forty schools nationally which field intercollegiate boxers.

Recruiting and scholarships are illegal in the NCBA because it is felt that highly skilled experienced boxers have other, more serious, avenues through which they can pursue their boxing. The elimination of experienced boxers through recruitment and scholarship restrictions, and the "sixteen year old rule" forces schools to develop their instructional and intramural programs because the emphasis is on teaching fundamentals to novices.

COLLEGE RULES

The following rules and safety features distinguish college boxing from other amateur and professional programs:

Twelve weight divisions diminish mismatches due to size and strength advantages.

Boxers wear mandatory headgear, mouthpiece, and supporter.

Boxers use twelve and fourteen ounce gloves.

Bouts consist of three two-minute rounds with one-minute rest period between rounds. (Novice bouts feature 1½ minute rounds).

Referees administer standing eight counts if a boxer is stunned or unable to effectively defend himself.

Boxers of roughly equal caliber are matched according to skill, strength, conditioning, and number of competitive bouts.

1983

California Boxing Newsletter

Coaches: Jim Riksheim, Mike Huff

CAL BOXERS AT REGIONALS!! The Cal Boxing Team will face its "final exams" on Friday, March 18, at 7:00, and Saturday, March 19, at 8:00 in the Santa Cruz Civic Auditorium. With its largest squad in years, the Bears will field entrants in 11 of the 12 weight classes. Competition promises to be fierce-- both Nevada-Reno and Chico State have strong teams, and the team title looks to be literally up for grabs. Coach Riksheim is cautiously optimistic about Cal's chances: "We have a couple of weight classes seemingly in our pockets, but others are so close that the deciding factor could be the luck of the draw and the matchups of individual skills. Unfortunately, Cal invariably faces a double obstacle at this time, with final exams immediately preceding Regionals. Just when we want to peak in our training, our fighters have to cope with the primary demands of school, as well. Hopefully, the stress we've placed on running and conditioning will carry us through. One thing's for sure, the Regionals will be one heck of a tournament."

RECENT BOUTS On February 18, the Cal Team boxed against Cerritos JC in Cerritos, California. Facing a seasoned group of fighters coached by Lefty Pendleton, the Bears posted an excellent record of 5-5. "I was very pleased by the bouts," says Riksheim, "because even when we lost, we lost moving forward. I think we really surprised them with our conditioning and desire. We didn't have experience on them, but our squad fought their hearts out." Individual champs include: 119-pounder Chan Kim, in a stunning knockout win against a 125 pound opponent; Norris Moore at 147, who quickly dispatched his tough and experienced foe; 180-pound Paul Templin, working his man over with a relentless attack; and heavyweight Kurt Heffernon, who outpointed a heavier opponent with clean and effective punching. An added highlight to the bouts was the presence of several Cal Boxing Alumni, both at the fights and afterwards at a local restaurant, who live in the Southern California area. Included in the evening were such well known personages as Don Flaherty, Sal Moreno, Larry Costa, Don Crane, and John McClay. It was a real pleasure for the boxers and coaches to renew ties with these standouts of Cal Boxing history.

On March 4, the Cal Bears hosted one of the largest bouts in recent memory at Harmon Gym. With a total of 19 matches, the action extended for over three hours in front of an enthusiastic crowd. With 11 fighters in contests, and 4 in exhibition matches, the Bears won a majority of their bouts against opponents from WCBA member schools, Nevada-Reno, Chico State, Santa Clara, and UCSC. Cal winners included: Garrell Kirtley, in a knockout win at 132 pounds; John Shimmick solidly outpointing his man at 139; 156 pound Wolfe Birkie, in a convincing display of firepower; and Jim Fardeen at 165, winning a tough scrap. Preceding the bouts was an alumni dinner held at the Haas Clubhouse at the Strawberry Canyon Recreational Area. The fete was a huge success with over 35 alumni and friends of the program in attendance. The highlight of the evening was the presentation given by the guest speaker, Jack Downey. One of boxing history's greatest names and an authority on the subject without rival, Jack spoke about the sport's colorful past and some of his own experiences. We only wish there was more time to listen to the wonderful stories Jack could tell.

In attendance were, among others, Sam Gold, Sol Silverman, Charles and Phoebe Paccagnella, Jim and Magaret Hansen, Dale and Pat Jeong, Tim and Marilyn McCarthy, Jim Koszinski, Dale Chamblin, Phil Nemir, Warner Gysin, Mark Devincenzi, Pat Ferdon, John Halbrook, Chris Morales, Bert Sandell, Ginny Wisdom, Margie Williams, Maureen Morison-Meshot, Kathy Rittler, Floyd Salas and Leslie Woodd, Linda Dezzani, Craig Jordan, and "Round Girl" Jeanette Williams.

A 'thunderous' finale
Late KO leads Cal to first-place finish

Boxers claim western title; look to nationals

WE DID IT !!!

For the first time in eight years, CAL BOXING broke Nevada-Reno's hold on the team title for the Western Collegiate Boxing Association Championships. Utilizing the depth of their squad, the BEARS sent an 11 man team to the Regionals in Santa Cruz on March 18 and 19, gathering in four second place finishes as well as four individual champions to best the defending Wolfpack team by one point! Winners who will go to the Nationals in Colorado Springs are: Chan Kim, at 119, in a walk through; defending Regional champ Garrell Kirtley, at 132, who scored two convincing victories including a second round TKO in the finals; Norris Moore, at 147, who fought two tough opponents and avenged his only loss of the season to earn the title; and, returning champ Kurt Heffernon, at heavyweight, scoring a third round TKO to advance to the National squad. Cal placed eight men in the final round and gathered points from all its competitors to carry them through to this hard won and satisfying victory.

WISH US LUCK AT NATIONALS!

Cal boxers in bid for national titles

1984

Challenge to Attain Excellence

THE GOLDEN BEARS FACE THE YEAR OF CHALLENGE in 1984 as they attempt to defend their Western Collegiate Boxing Association (WCBA) Championship and host the National Collegiate Boxing Association (NCBA) Championships this Spring. Cal won the WCBA Team Championship in 1983 over the University of Nevada, Reno (UNR), when Heavyweight Kurt Heffernon defeated Wolfpack Heavy Pete Enart in the night's final bout. The Bears defeated UNR 35-34, with just one point separating the two schools when the final points were tallied. Helping Heffernon accept this year's challenge are Chan Kim, 1983 WCBA Bantamweight Champion, and 1982 Champions Chris Morales (125) and Frank Delzompo (156). Both Morales and Delzompo sat out the 1983 season after winning WCBA crowns the previous year. Each of the four returning champs has had extensive experience at the Nationals which should provide an edge when the Golden Bears challenge the nation's finest boxers here at Berkeley next April.

NATIONAL CHAMPIONSHIPS COME TO BERKELEY this Spring as individuals representing over thirty-five schools in four regions will square off in Harmon Gymnasium for the 1984 National Collegiate Boxing Association Championships. Forty-eight regional champions will vie for individual titles next April 6-7, in what is college boxing's most outstanding event. The Golden Bears have never hosted this event in their sixty-one year history and become the second sports club to hold an event of this magnitude. The National Championships provide the biggest challenge to date for the Boxing Club administration and Cal Boxing Backers. The UC Boxing Club is obligated to house all competitors and officials and to provide all of the amenities for the tournament. The University administration has been extremely supportive; however, your help is needed to insure the success of this event.

YOU CAN HELP US MEET OUR CHALLENGE by making a pledge or donation to California Boxing Backers. Our ability to conduct the NCBA Championships is predicated on our ability to raise funds. Cal Boxing Backers is committed to raising $10,000 to help pay operational team costs and to fund a portion of costs for hosting the Nationals. Profits from the event itself will be used in 1985 to establish an endowment for the Boxing Club and to purchase equipment for a new boxing facility dedicated to the late Edgar Nemir. Anticipated expenditures for fiscal 1983-84 are $21,990. Anticipated revenue is broken down as follows:

University Allocations	$2550
Student Fund Raising	6440
Alumni Fund Raising	10000
Gate (does not include Nationals)	3000
Total	$21990

Please make a generous donation today and help us take the first step in accepting our challenge.

1984

CAL BOXING NEWSLETTER

FEBRUARY 24, 1984

HAPPY NEW YEAR!! California Boxing hopes you had a wonderful holiday season and wishes you a great New Year!

1984 Boxing Schedule - Due to the Universities' recent conversion to the semester system, the 1984 season will begin Wednesday, February 8, at the Collegiate Invitational at Mare Island. The schedule will feature two home bouts on Friday, February 17, and Thursday, March 8, both at 8pm at Harmon Gymnasium. The season will be culminated at Cal with the National Collegiate Boxing Association Championships on April 6 and 7, 1984. Our complete schedule is enclosed.

Outlook for the Defending WCBA Champs - The Golden Bears return a squad of seasoned veterans in their quest of their second straight Western Collegiate Boxing Association team championship. Cal returns six "number-one" men from last years squad which won the team championship from Nevada 34-33. Heriberto Fermin (125), Jim Fardeen (165), and Dan Carr (172) were runner-ups last year in their respective weight classes. Defending WCBA champions Chan Kim (119) and Kurt Heffernon (HWT) will be joined by 1981 champions Chris Morales (125) and Frank Delzompo (156) to give the Bears their most experienced line-up in years. Coach Jim Riksheim has a fine crop of novices which should "complement the experience and make this year's squad very competitive."

NCBA Championships - Arrangements have almost been completed for the National Collegiate Boxing Association Championships at Cal on April 6 & 7, 1984. Our efforts will now be concentrated on promotion and ticket sales. Our thanks to the many individuals who are helping us with the championships. Ticker information will be available to Cal alumni shortly.

Fund Raising - Cal Boxing Backers has collected $5880 and generated $725 in pledges for a total of $6605 towards our $10,000 goal. It is essential that we reach our goal this year. If you have not yet contributed, please do so today. We are thankful to those who have already contributed including: Sammy Moreno, Warren Simmons (Eddie Nemir Club); Terry Holberton III, Mike Huff, Dale Jeong D.M.D., Dirk Noyes, Glen Takei M.D., Danny Yamamoto (Champion Circle); Paxton Beale, Tom Bottorff, Richard Carter, Dale Chamblin, Ewald Larson, Tim McCarthy, Sol Silverman (Golden Bear Boxing Backer); Robert Birkie, Timothy Chew, E.L. (Dick) Derr, Dick Glendinning, Warner Gysin, Joe Lehman, Jonah Li M.D., Earl Mitchell M.D., Ed Mitchell, Don Nemir Phil Nemir, Al Pryor, Albert Sandell, Shiro Tokuno (Old Blue Bear Boxing Backer).

***SPECIAL TICKET INFORMATION FOR MARE ISLAND BOUT--Due to recent terrorist activities at United States Military Installations, security at all bases in and out of this country have been tightened. Individuals must purchase tickets in advance in order to obtain admission to the naval base at Mare Island and the boxing matches. Advanced ticket may be purchased from Cal coach Jim Riksheim or in front of one of the main gates at Mare Island.

For further information please call Jim Riksheim at 642-8342.

1984

CAL BOXING NEWSLETTER

MARCH 2, 1984

Results from Mare Island and Cal Invitational - Cal has split victories and losses in its first two bouts to date. Cal, with a large group of new fighters augmenting a solid core of returning competitors, has divided its emphasis in order to provide seasoning and experience for its novices, as well as fine-tuning for the veterans.

The fast-paced action at Mare Island culminated in two Cal victories in four bouts: Frank Delzompo, a two-year Nationals competitor at 156 lbs., hammered out a unanimous decision over an elusive Navy counter-puncher, scoring repeatedly with body shots and looping rights. Kurt Heffernon, another two-time Western Regional Champion, sized up his heavyweight opponent in the first round and then stopped him in the second with crushing right hands.

At the Cal Invitational Cal took three of seven fights with veteran performances from: Chris Haddaway, at 132 pounds, gaining a split decision from his Nevada foe by using a relentless body attack on his backpedalling opponent; Jim Fardeen, at 165, who won in a war with a bruising Santa Clara fighter by landing powerful uppercuts and hooks with both hands; and, again, Kurt Heffernon, stopping his Nevada rival in the second round with a non-stop barrage of punches.

Schedule Revision- Cal's boxing schedule was revised at the collegiate invitational at Mare Island. There are no changes in Cal's home schedule but two changes have occured in the Bears' road schedule.

THURSDAY	MARCH 8	CALIFORNIA OPEN	HARMON GYM	8PM
Saturday	March 17	California @ Navy	Lemoore, CA	TBA
Saturday	March 24	WCBA Championships	Reno, Nevada	TBA
FRIDAY	APRIL 6	NCBA SEMI-FINALS	HARMON GYM	7PM
SATURDAY	APRIL 7	NCBA CHAMPIONSHIPS	HARMON GYM	8PM

Reduced Ad Rates For Alumni - California Boxing is appreciative of the loyalty and generosity which has been demonstrated by our alumni since the inception of Cal Boxing Backers in 1977. Fr this reason we are providing alumni with the opportunity of purchasing priority advertising space in our "National Championship Program" for reduced rates. Individuals may promote business interests or send private messages ranging from business card size ($100 reduced to $90) to full page ads ($700 reduced to $625). If you would like more information please return the enclosed form or phone Mike Huff at 642-5575.

Tickets for the NCBA Championships - Tickets for the National Championships at Cal will go on sale March 8. Tickets will be available through the National Championship Committee on that date and at BASS ticket outlets soon thereafter.

Fund Raising - Cal Boxing Backers has raised $7565 towards our fundraising goal of $10,000. We have collected $6790 and have $775 remaining in pledges. We have attracted $3835 in contribution increases or new monies. There are still $1830 in monies that alumni havecontributed in previous years

1984

CAL BOXING NEWSLETTER
MARCH 26, 1984

FIVE BEARS ADVANCE TO NATIONALS - The Golden Bears won five individual titles and placed second at the Western Collegiate Boxing Association Championships at Reno, Nevada. Heriberto Fermin (119), Chris Morales (125), Chris Haddawy (132), Frank Delzompo (156) and Kurt Heffernon (HWT) qualified for the National Championships next week at Cal by capturing Western Regional crowns. Chris Morales was the Bear's most outstanding competitor as he thoroughly drubbed 1982-83 Champion Carl Gatson of Nevada. Morales scored repeatedly with jabs and straight rights which kept the shorter Gatson at long range. Morales reclaimed the title he vacated last year and set the tone for the Bears by winning a tough and tense bout.

Cal's Chris Haddawy was Cal's most resourceful competitor winning two bouts on Saturday to win the 132 pound championships. Haddawy defeated Ken Prager of Nevada Saturday morning and returned the same evening to overwhelm Andy Saiki of Santa Clara. "I felt sluggish Saturday morning, but tonight I could have gone another three or four rounds," commented Chris. Coach Jim Riksheim noted that Haddawy was "by far the best conditioned Golden Bear."

Junior Middleweight Frank Delzompo turned in a workman-like performance outpointing Nevada's Jack Smith in a unanimous decision. Delzompo scored often with quick straight punches mixed with left hooks which resulted in two standing eight counts in the second round. Delzompo will advance to the Nationals for the third time. Another Bear advancing to the Nationals for the third time is Heavyweight Kurt Heffernon. Heffernon and Cal Bantamweight Heriberto Fermin were unopposed in the Tournament. Jack Light (147) and Jim Fardeen (165) placed second while Dan Carr (172) lost his semi-final bout. Nevada-Reno also had five regional champions and outpointed the Bears 35-32 primarily because they were able to fill two more weight classes than Cal.

NATIONAL CHAMPIONSHIP TICKET INFO - Advanced ticket orders for the National Collegiate Boxing Championships on April 6 & 7 at Cal should be mailed to:

> U.C. Boxing Club
> 195 Harmon Gym
> University of California
> Berkeley, CA 94720

Ringside tickets for the Championships are $8.00, while General Admission is $5.00 (Student General-$3.00). All tickets for the Semi-Finals are General Admission and cost $3.00. CHECKS PAYABLE TO: U.C. BOXING CLUB.

ALUMNI REUNION DINNER - Cal Boxing Backers is organizing an Alumni Reunion Dinner prior to the Championships on April 7. The Dinner will be held in the HEYN ROOM of the MEN'S FACULTY CLUB (near the Great Hall) on the CAL campus at 4:45 pm. The menu includes prime rib, vegetable, potato, soup or salad, rolls, dessert, and coffee. Dinner will cost $15 per person (cost includes tax, gratuity, and room rental). Individuals may purchase wine and other alcoholic beverages. Please fill out the attached form and submit a check by Monday, April 2, 1984.

SPECIAL DEDICATION TO EDGAR NEMIR - Cal Boxing will DEDICATE THE NEW BOXING ROOM TO EDGAR NEMIR on Saturday, April 7, immediately preceding the NCBA Finals. This special ceremony will celebrate boxing's move back into the "old boxing room" in Harmon Gymnasium. The dedication will take place in the room 185 Harmon (North-east corner of Harmon Gym) at 6:45 pm. All boxing enthusiasts who knew Coach Nemir are invited to attend.

NATIONAL COLLEGIATE BOXING CHAMPIONSHIPS - 24 Semi-Final Bouts Friday, April 6 at 7 pm, 12 Championship Bouts Saturday, April 7 at 8 pm, at Harmon Gymnasium, U.C. Berkeley. COME SUPPORT THE BEARS IN THE QUEST FOR THE NATIONAL CHAMPIONSHIP.

1984

Continued on next page.

Friday, Saturday — Harmon Gymnasium

Today, 2:30 — Evans Diamond

SPORTS

TUESDAY, APRIL 3, 1984 — THE DAILY CALIFORNIAN

EDITOR: PETE DANKO ASSISTANT EDITOR: RON KROICHICK

Just gutting it out offers satisfaction

By FRANCIS KANE

I got to see some amateur boxing last month when the University of California held its first Invitational of the year. Boxers from Santa Clara University, the University of Nevada at Reno, San Jose State, and the Mare Island Naval base all showed up with some very vocal fans.

In the final bout of the evening, Cal heavyweight Kurt Hefferman fought a blonde, chubby, apple-cheeked fellow from the University of Nevada. Comparisons to Little Big Horn could be heard in the crowd: the fighters were introduced. Hefferman — tall, well-muscled and looking like a fighter — walked right into the boxer from Nevada, jabbing, hooking and throwing straight rights. The fight did indeed seem a mismatch. But for a while the heavy fellow gave as good as he got and occasionally looping a funny left hook that went all the way around Hefferman's guard and landed somewhere above his right ear. A punch that looked like it was invented on the spot.

Despite the Nevada fighter's valiant efforts, his bell tolled for him in the third round. Hefferman had bloodied his nose and backed him into a corner. He fought back, but Hefferman was able to hit him too easily and the referee stopped the bout. Although the losing fighter protested, there was a general feeling of relief in the crowd. The referee's quick actions typified the concern for safety that all the officials had that evening. Cal coach Jim Riksheim stopped an earlier bout when his fighter seemed to be in trouble, and a doctor conferred with both corners in more than one match.

Intramural boxing is one of the oldest and least publicized sports at the University of California. The Cal Boxing club has existed since 1939. Every year, one article about it appears on the Daily Californian sports page. This article usually comes out midway through March, as well. Boxing is an arduous sport in which people suffer to succeed. The rewards for such sacrifice must be intensely personal and probably are unsuited to the celebration or pep rallies.

Still, this year's team is the largest in recent history. There are nearly 30 fighters in the club. Of that group, 12 fought last year, and four fought in the National Collegiate Boxing Association tournament. Returning fighter Chris Morales boxed competitively for the first time last year, went undefeated, picked up the Pacific Coast Regional title, and found himself fighting for the NCBA championship against a senior fighter with three previous titles to his credit. There was standing room only for the fight at Westchester State. It was, as they say in the fight game, a real donnybrook. The boxers exchanged hard punches throughout the fight and each had the other reeling at different times. But experience paid off and the triple champion won. Morales, though, is expected to do well this year in the NCBA tournament.

The NCBA is the organization that was created in 1968 after the NCAA deemed boxing unsuitable for college athletes. Several recruiting scandals and a ring death led to this decision. The way it is practiced in the NCBA, boxing is as safe as it will ever be. No one with boxing experience after age 16 is allowed in the program. A serious effort is made to match fighters according to ability and a doctor examines all who compete. Fights consist of three two-minute rounds — shorter than the three-minute rounds fought in Golden Gloves, AAU and Diamond Belt competition. This reduces fatigue-related injury. Thumbless 14-ounce gloves are used and headgear is mandatory. Scoring is based on blows landed and not knockdowns, and emphasis is placed on skill and conditioning rather than brute power. A genuine aura of sportsmanship seems to surround all matches.

Precautions aside, the question might exist as to why educated men at one of the best universities in the nation would want to spend their spare time beating on each other. To rid themselves of a deep desire for violence and gain pleasure in hurting one another? To compensate for a childhood spent being pushed around by schoolyard bullies? Neither explanation seems likely. Mean streaks and past humiliations rarely push their sufferers through the endless repetition of masochistic exercise that prepares one for the ring. There is another emotional force at work here: ego.

Boxing is the most basic form of self-assertion, the simplest expression of ego. Boxers know they're good at something. No one needs to tell them because the proof sits dejected in the opposite corner. Even the nastiest fighters in history have seemed proud of their victories, marching around the ring with arms held high and posing vainly for photographs with fists cocked at improbable angles.

If the winner of a boxing match knows at the instant of victory that he is better at something than someone else, the loser is forced to face the opposite truth. This is a conclusion most of us would rather avoid, and overcoming that prospect must be a victory in itself. It also must do wonders for the self-confidence.

Cal coach Riksheim, who seems to have done some thinking on the subject, explained, "If you can conquer a feat like this that's very, very real, the fears you make up don't stand a chance. Your opponent is only a sounding board or a mirror."

Riksheim is a puzzle. He neither looks nor acts like a boxing coach. He is a clean-cut, fair-haired skinny man who looks like he stepped out of a pulpit somewhere in the Midwest. A slightly flattened nose is the only mark boxing has left on him. His coaching style is very much low-key. The last time I visited him at the club's gym underneath Edwards Stadium, two of his boxers were engaged in a heated sparring session. The quicker of the two seemed almost disdainful of his opponent, moving in toward him on very straight legs, his hands held low. These must be nagging bad habits because they were corrected as soon as Riksheim called them out.

When the boxers were finished, Riksheim pantomimed the style of each, showing them ways to improve. And always, as I noticed at the invitational, there is Riksheim's concern for safety. When, at another sparring session, one boxer was beginning to get tagged too often, Riksheim was quickly at the rope, admonishing the boxer's opponent to "pull your punches — box defense." Not once was Riksheim the rabid, growling person I expected him to be.

Riksheim's assistant, Floyd Salas, was the first student to ever attend the University of California on a boxing scholarship. He is a small man who moves around the ring in a perplexing manner. As I watched him spar with Chris Morales, I was often surprised at his unorthodox style. Riksheim said that he is very tricky to box, and that "you'll see him move one way and all of a sudden from another direction you'll get hit."

Salas is an easygoing, bantering man who really seems to enjoy working with developing fighters. When he worked the corner with Riksheim at the invitational, he would catch the eye of the Cal boxer in the ring and throw the punch he thought most appropriate for the situation. Floyd was almost a funny figure, a natty man in dress slacks and turtleneck sweater, suddenly breaking out of an attentive sitting position on his stool to uppercut the air before him. But his obvious absorption in what was taking place in the ring, along with his concern, kept me from laughing.

The gym, where the Cal fighters practice, is true to the images of boxing gyms in general. It is cavernous, gray and dingy. There are no pretty carpets, wall coverings, acres of track lighting. There is, however, inadequate ventilation and enough floor space to conduct training. The gym is one large room separated into three areas of activity.

In the middle of it all is the padded canvas ring, enclosed by 12 canvas-covered ropes. One side of the ring is an area dominated by heavy punching bags and lockers. Mirrors that the fighters shadow box in front of line the wall at the end of the room. The wall at the other end is hollowed out and three double-ended bags are suspended between the floor and ceiling. A room housing a series of shower stalls is adjacent to the westernmost side of the ring that isn't near the punching bags.

Between two speed bag platforms near the shower room door, a plastic writing board is hung, bearing a message that is echoed on a chalkboard near the main entrance of the gym: "1. Get off the first and last punches. 2. Work the body. 3. Stay off the ropes: put your man

SEE PAGE 7

The California boxing team

FROM PAGE 6

there." Every time I visited the gym, a well-amplified radio gave us music and a loud buzzer went off at three-minute intervals to let the boxers know when to move and when to rest.

Frank Delzompo, a husky business major whose record is 11-5-1, twisted before me, throwing phantom body hooks and describing his fighting style.

"I'm shorter than most of the guys I fight," Delzompo said. "I either win by knockout or I lose." He went on to explain how important it is to impress the judges and how hard it sometimes is to look good when you're chasing an opponent. Occasionally, he would tap me on the chest for emphasis.

About halfway through our conversation, Delzompo stopped his animated talking and a serious look settled incongruously on his jovial Italian face. "Look," he said, "don't make me out to be a violent guy. It's an art." His face still serious, Delzompo went on to describe the turmoil boxing put him through last year. He is a reborn Christian and had to spend a year away from the sport to see if it was something he really wanted to do. Beating someone for six minutes seems wrong from a Christian viewpoint, but in a skilled contest the wrongness doesn't seem to apply. In the Bible, Jacob receives the blessing of God and the name Israel after wrestling a man for over 12 hours. (Genesis 32:24-32:30.) Delzompo said, "I prayed about it." What helped him to make his decision was the fact that "God gets a certain pleasure when people achieve things."

Kurt Hefferman, the heavyweight who defeated the fighter from Nevada, told me he never thought he'd be boxing. He just came to the gym to "stay in shape." Being proficient in difficult physical skills, however, attracted him.

Other boxers told me they enjoyed the challenge of staying in the ring, even when they had little chance of winning. Just gutting it out offered satisfaction, something a lot of our daily struggles don't offer at all.

1984

1984 National Collegiate Boxing CHAMPIONSHIPS

The nation's top college boxers meet to decide 12 individual titles as well as the team championship

NCBA SEMI-FINALS   Friday, April 6   7pm
NCBA NATIONALS   Saturday, April 7   8pm

Ticket Prices

Friday night   ALL SEATS $3.00

Saturday night   RINGSIDE $8.00
                      GENERAL ADMISSION $5.00
              STUDETS (with valid ID) $3.00

Ticket Information

* Advance tickets are available by mail or at the Strawberry Canyon Recreational Area on the Berkeley campus.

* For further information please call Mike Huff or Bill Treseler at (415) 642-5575.

APRIL 6&7   HARMON GYM
UNIVERSITY OF CALIFORNIA

The Anheuser Busch Brewing Company supports the concept of socially responsible drinking.

1984

From the 1984 Nationals Program

GOLDEN BEAR PROFILES

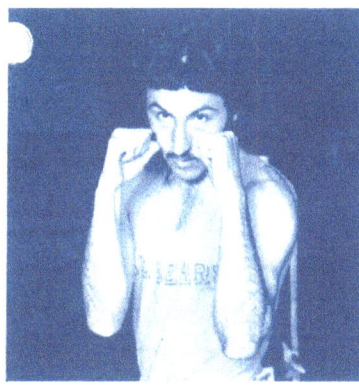

CHRIS MORALES

Chris Morales, one of the smoothest boxers and classiest gentlemen in the recent history of California Boxing, winds up his college boxing career this weekend as he vies for the 125 pound title.

During his two years of fighting for Cal, Morales has won two conference championships and nearly everything else in sight; the only thing which has eluded the senior from San Francisco is a National Title. Chris' loss in the 1982 National Championship bout to Ray Fernandez of West Chester State is the only blemish on his 9-1 record as a collegian.

Morales, like Frank Delzompo, sat out last season. Chris could not ignore "the call" this season because of the boxing in his blood (his father was also a boxer, in addition to being a blackbelt in judo). Chris attended St. Ignatius High School and played on the Wildcat soccer team. He studied at UCLA before transferring to Berkeley, where he will graduate with a degree in Earth Sciences this spring.

In addition to his accomplishments in the ring, the California coaching staff noted Chris' attitude and leadership abilities as being unique qualities which will be missed after his graduation.

KURT HEFFERNON

For the third straight season, Cal heavyweight Kurt Heffernon is the WCBA's Champion and representative in the Nationals. The senior thus joins a select few athletes in the history of Cal Boxing to achieve this feat. His career ends this weekend with the Albany native looking forward to competing before the hometown crowd after traveling to National Championships in Colorado and Pennsylvania the past two years.

The Heffernon name should be somewhat familiar to avid California fans. Kurt's brother Mike pitched for the Golden Bears from 1976-78 and Kurt spent a year on the wrestling team here before turning his attention to the ring. Kurt was also a football standout at Albany High School, and was named the school's Athlete of the Year as a senior.

Kurt will graduate with a degree in Conservation and Resource Studies this spring. He lists birdwatching as his favorite hobby; in turn, he has provided Cal boxing fans with plenty of enjoyable Kurt-watching over the past three years. The hard-hitting heavyweight, who's in the best shape of his career, hopes to provide his father, Andy, and his other supporters with two more nights of excitement this weekend.

FRANK DELZOMPO

Don't run under a doorway if Harmon Gym beings to tremble slightly this evening when Frank Delzompo climbs into the ring. The eruption has nothing to do with the San Andreas Fault, it's merely Frank's enthusiastic following from the Phi Gamma Delta fraternity here on campus.

Delzompo and his Fiji mates have provided excitement here at Harmon Gym three of the past four seasons. The hard-hitting boxer from San Francisco won the WCBA 156 pound title in 1982 and again this season. Frank sat out the '82-'83 season but has shown no apparent rustiness as a result of the lay-off.

Frank attended Riordan High School in The City and won all-league honors as a running back on the Crusader football team. A devout young man, Frank will graduate in the spring with a degree in business administration.

During Frank's freshman year he was one of the few first year fighters to make it to the National Championship final bout. In his sophomore season he again made it to Nationals, losing in the semi-finals. This weekend, with the support of his Greek brothers and the rest of the home folks, Frank is hoping to take the final step and cap his career in style.

CHRIS HADDAWY

Chris Haddawy, a 132 pound junior from Reno, won the WCBA Championship last week in his hometown. This weekend, he will again be looking to take advantage of familiar surroundings in his underdog bid to advance to Saturday night's championship.

The 20 year old Haddawy was actually born in France, but attended Reno High, where he competed in track and cross country. Chris, a Political Economy major, also boxed on the Bears 1982 WCBA championship team.

1984

Kindling the Killer Instinct

By Avram Gimbel

UC-Berkeley played host this last weekend to the national Collegiate Boxing Championship at Harmon Gym. UC won the featherweight and heavyweight national championships. Author/writer Avram Gimbel covered the fights for The Voice and spent the week preceding the bouts with the UC-Berkeley team. Here is his report.

Next Time

The blue wood entrance door tucked beside shrubbery off busy Bancroft Way leads to an inner chamber beneath the concrete tiers of Edwards Stadium. You go down some stairs to another door with a sign: "Enter at Your Own Risk." Open the door and the stench of fresh and stale sweat assaults your nostrils. Step inside and the sight is that of a blue and filthy yellow cavern reaching up to the sharply slanted concrete ceiling.

Here on the underside of the clipped and trimmed UC sports field exists a classical grimy low-rent district boxing gym, the kind of place from which probably every great boxing champion emerged.

There's the RATTA TAT TAT of speed bags, the WHACK WHACK WHACK of power bags that dangle from chains, the smooth easy rock from the stereo. There's a tan carpet through the workout area up to the ring which is enclosed by three padded ropes strung between the concrete building pillars. There's a shower room and locker room to the side, a drinking fountain on the wall. Stereo is on, trash piled in the corners, notes stacked on the bulletin board.

There's a sense that this place is appropriate. The music is good and after a time the atmosphere wears in comfortably, the focus shifts from the place to the men who are working the bags, shadow boxing, sparring.

Working out are Cal's five winners from the West Coast championship boxing tournament in Reno last month: 119-pound Heriberto (Herbie) Fermin, 125-pound Chris Morales, 132-pound Chris Haddawy, 156-pound Frank Delzompo, and 210-pound Kurt Heffernon. Here also are the team's head coach Jim Riksheim and assistant coach and fighter/writer Floyd Salas.

Continued on back page

Berkeley Voice/Debra Jensen

Kurt Heffernon raises his arms in victory after knocking out his opponent for the Heavyweight Championship.

Kindling...

Continued from front page

In 1956 Floyd was Cal's first boxing scholarship recipient. He wrote the novels *What Now*, *Lay My Body on the Line*, and the acclaimed *Tattoo The Witch? Cross*. He stands five-foot-five but has presence three foot higher and nine foot wide. He has a triangular, bony face with high cheeks, a flattened nose, and wary watchful eyes. His frame is trained-lean and hard, his posture slightly forward, a man on the move. His voice crackles and carries above the comfortable soft rock from the stereo.

"My job," says Floyd, "is to develope the killer instinct in these guys."

He talks about Kurt Heffernon, Cal's West Coast champion heavyweight.

"Jim (Riksheim) and I taught him all the punches: jabs, cuts, combinations, and the defenses, to hold his hands up over his face so they could absorb any punishment, the footwork, the stances, and how to weave and react.

"In Santa Cruz last year Kurt had his opponent against the ropes. He was wailing at him with body blows, but he kept coming back. He had him on the ropes and he smashed the guy with an overhead loop, and fup, he was out. Kurt had tasted blood. I taught him how to recognize it and how to find it and how to use it."

Chris Morales is pointy and speaks softly. He's lost only one fight in the three years he's been boxing, and that was against a four-time national champion. Till then Chris had fought only four tournament fights.

Kurt is tall (nicknamed Tiny, of course) with dark curly hair. He's quick on his feet for a big man, his muscles sheathed loosely over shoulders, back, arms, thighs, calves: He has a flat stomach.

For two years he fought successfully until losing in the final championship fights. This time he intends to win.

Kurt jumps into the ring and begins shadow boxing, singing the words to Floyd's poem, *Near Time*, the poem he wrote and read aloud in the team van on the way back after the team's defeat at the 1983 Collegiate Boxing Nationals in Colorado.

He sings Floyd's phrases to the melody of Bruce Springsteen's "Born to Run."

We could have won/We lost it in the dark corners of our hearts/We lost it in the little places of ourselves/where no light shines on the surface/where no mirror shoots back/the picture on the screen.

Kurt's banging around the big punching bag. His muscles and tendons shape his skin as he moves forward, slams his fist into the large bag which dangles from an overhead chain.

"I'm ready," he says. "I've been in shape all year."

It's that once-in-a-lifetime shape of a young athlete when the weight and muscular structure are perfect. Floyd calls it "competitive shape."

When Kurt works the bag there's not the slightest doubt in his face. It's the face of a determined man, the face of a killer.

Floyd's going to spar with Herbie.

He stretches, twists, dances, shadow boxes. "I don't want to hurt him. I don't want him to hurt me. I just want to make him good."

In the ring Floyd and Herbie touch gloves. Floyd snaps to a crouch, his gloves held high toward his forehead. He steps one way then the other and weaves like a street brawler, in and out, side stepping. Herbie can't tell what he's going to do, but he keeps after him. Floyd bounces off the ropes, weaves under Herbie's cuts. Herbie gets in an occasional blow, and so does Floyd, but they're soft. This is sparring.

In the dark corners of our hearts we lost it/But we'll open them to the light/We'll let the sun shine in/Heat will heal the cuts/The bruises will fade/The swelling will go down/These boxers will fight again and win/They're young/They've got the mountain of the world to climb/Next time!/Next time!/Next time!

Preliminaries

In Friday night's tournament at Harmon Gym last Friday evening, the preliminaries, 48 boxers fought 24 matches. The 24 winners would fight in Saturday night's 12 matches, the finals.

Until Friday evening the boxers didn't know who they were fighting. Half an hour before fight time the Cal team sat in a circle in the warmup room. First they said a prayer, then the Buddist thing. They held hands for a moment of silence.

Floyd said, "We got five great fighters, two great coaches, we're going to kick some ass tonight."

Someone told Kurt, (the team's only heavyweight, that they had seen some very big boxer walking around the campus.

Floyd said to Kurt, "Give him body shots and he'll tumble down."

As the team moved toward the main Harmon gym where the ring was set up, Chris Morales said, "Someone told me who I was going to fight and I started sweating, the adrenalin started flowing."

"That's when the fight started for you," Floyd said.

As the tournament progressed, Herbie Ferrrin, Chris Haddawy, and Frank Delzompo lost their fights. Frank's loss was a quirk. After he was knocked down and snapped quickly to his feet, the referee pronounced him technically knocked out. Amidst booing and hissing directed at the referee, Frank stepped down. A loud crack exploded through the gym as Frank went behind the stands and smashed his fist through a wooden door.

"I told you," Floyd said. "You can't tell what's going to happen."

Chris Morales, like the lull before a storm, stood quietly watching the other fights before his own came up. In the ring he attacked his opponent relentlessly, an easy win.

Kurt sat on the stands. In his sweats he looked normal in bodily appearance, slim, even mild of temperment. With his glasses, he looked studious. He sat calmly, his body reposed, while his opponent, Tim Philips of Ohio University, wearing a green satin robe, moved about across the floor flexing, dancing, cutting the air with powerful slams.

Kurt got up and walked around. He was not graceful. He lumbered. His face, finely chiseled, remained undaunted, calm, thoughtful. One of his teammates meandered across the floor to check out the opposing heavyweight fighter.

The teammate came back. "He's six foot three." "Good," coach Jim Rikesheim said. "Kurt's six four."

As his fight neared Kurt took off his sweats, folded his glasses, and put them away with his sweats. He had on his navy blue Cal Bears tanktop and irridescent blue trunks with a gold vertical stripe on each side. He shook out his arms and danced, jabbing the air. His muscles were not bulky, as are weightlifter's, but long and loose, not a muscle wasted in development except for the job at hand. As he warmed up his face became hard, aggressive.

A roar filled the gym as Kurt stepped into the ring. The fighters moved about, circling, light jabs with reaching arms, keeping their distance, each respectful of the other, made possible from a 200 pound fighter. Tim boldly rushed Kurt. Gone was Kurt's awkwardness. He held his gloves high in his defensive posture, gracefully weaved, countered his opponent's attacks with combinations, one two, one two, one two three. Tim connected, not hard, but enough to cause Kurt's composure to slip. But he came back.

Round two. The fighters continued to circle and test one another cautiously, keeping their distance. The referee, unsatisfied, waves his hand vertically between their outstretched gloves, pointing up the distance. "Okay. Box!"

Prodded, they both tore into action. Tim rushed. Kurt warded the onslaught with a highfisted defense. Tim's blows merely hit Kurt's raised gloves or landed on his headgear or his shoulder, the force of the blow already expended in the air. Kurt's responses wore Tim down causing him to collapse exhausted onto the stool in his corner at the end of the round.

In the third round Kurt, with persistent combinations of jabs and cuts to Tim's body, drove him against the ropes, then into the ropes. The referee pushed Kurt back, cupped Tim's head in his hands, peering into his eyes. He let the fight go on. It was Kurt's fight to the roaring end.

Cal now had two contenders for Saturday night's national collegiate championship titles: 125-pound Chris Morales and heavyweight Kurt Heffernon.

Champions

Saturday night, during the preliminaries, Chris and Kurt saw their opponents for the final championship fight in action. Both their opponents are chargers. They attack with brute force. Kurt's opponent moved across the canvas like a buzz saw. His stance exhibited all the style of a pit bull.

"Made to order, man," Floyd says. "Those kind of boxers are made to order for our guys."

Chris' opponent, as expected, comes at him hard. With every rush toward him, every viscious jag at him, Chris has a defense, an instant counterattack. He is superb, but cautious. He refrains from venturing in, choosing rather to remain just beyond his opponent's range.

During the round break Jim gives him punching pointers. Floyd tells him to start fighting. Chris comes out of his corner a different boxer. He savagely attacks his opponent with body jabs and jabs to the face. Blood from the opponent's nose smears both of them. The crowd goes wild. The bell rings, another break, more instructions to fight hard. Another fast paced, hard hitting round. It's Chris' fight all the way.

After the decision in his favor, Chris, the new featherweight national champ, hugs head coach Jim Riksheim, then Floyd. He steps down from the ring and hugs last year's coach Mike Huff.

Kurt's opponent is more cautious than last night, more wary. In seconds, Kurt sends him to the canvas with a left hook that connects with the side of his head. The crowd roars. Up again, the opponent fights on. Kurt hurdles in another left hook and the guy again thumps down on the canvas, this time too dazed to get up. The referee helps him up and leads him to a corner. Kurt's the winner, a first round knockout, a new heavyweight champion.

The crowd bangs the floor and roars. People rush to ringside. Kurt leaps four feet off the canvas, his body arched, his hands reaching for the ceiling.

Floyd (to anyone within earshot): "I told you. He was made to order."

Jim climbs into the ring, Floyd behind him. Floyd, the child in him breaking through its tough shell, dances, slaps Kurt's back. "Right on, Champ. Right on."

The TV cameras are on Kurt who is flanked by Jim and Floyd. Floyd doesn't mind taking credit for the victory. "He did it exactly according to plan," he tells the TV audience. Everyone looks at him for a moment, perplexed.

"Kurt breaks into a grin. "You called the shots, Floyd. Give me a hug."

Kurt signs autographs, savoring his new role as champion.

1984

Oakland Tribune, Sunday, April 8, 1984

Cal's Morales, Heffernon win titles

By Dave LoVecchio
The Tribune

BOXING

BERKELEY — Chris Morales stepped out of the ring last night sporting a bloody nose and several facial cuts. But you should have seen the other guy.

Morales became the University of California's first national boxing champion in six years when the 125-pounder scored a unanimous decision over John Callas of Central Connecticut at Harmon Gym.

Cal's Kurt Heffernon and Pat Penneck of Santa Clara also fought their way to titles. Heffernon took the heavyweight crown with a first-round technical knockout of Mike Regan of Shippensburg. Penneck won the 172-pound title by decisioning Dennis Madden of Xavier.

"I'm glad it's over," said a tired Morales, who finished his college career with an 11-1 record after battering Callas' head with stinging jabs all three rounds. "This is a great way to go out. Go out a champion. That's good."

"He's a brawler, not a boxer," said Morales. "But he was the toughest guy I've faced in a long time."

Callas was very impressive Friday night when he floored his opponent three times before the semifinal was stopped in the second round. Callas was the aggressor for the first minute against Morales. The Cal senior from San Francisco then went to work with his jab.

"I was tentative early in the first round," said Morales, whose only loss was in the 1982 nationals final. "I kept going with the jabs because that's my style. I kept the jabs in his face. They did a lot of damage."

Morales drew blood midway through the second round when he opened a cut on Callas' nose. The cut got nastier as the six minutes of boxing wound down.

"I watched him (Friday) and knew he would be really aggressive," Morales said after the national championship ribbon was placed around his neck. "I wanted to concentrate on counter punching and throw right hand leads when I got him in the corner."

Morales landed three straight jabs and a sharp right to Callas' head near the end of the second round. Callas' counter punches missed wildly as Morales backed out of danger.

Morales said he "wasn't sure" if he had the fight won while awaiting the judges' ruling, but it seemed obvious to the partisan crowd the only hope for Callas was a knockout in the third round.

Callas never came close to the knockout and had to settle for second place.

"His shots were medium hard but not devastating," Morales said. "Having the crowd behind me really helped."

Heffernon knocked Regan to the canvas twice in the first round before the bout was stopped.

Dave Washington of Lock Haven (Penn.) won the 119-pound title after finishing second last year. Washington, who eliminated Cal's Heriberto Fermin Friday, won a close decision over Ohio University's Sander Wolf last night.

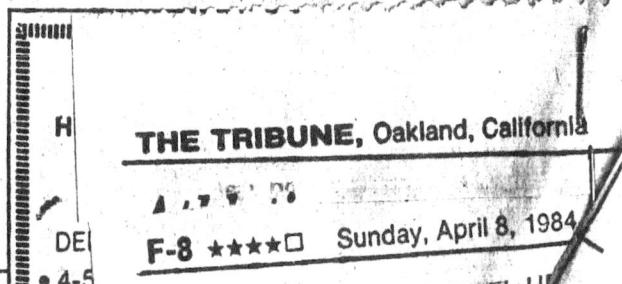

Express April 13, 1984

EAST SIDE STORY

Hometown Hero Tackles Tornado

By David Darlington

One wall of the intramural athletics office in Harmon Gym on the UC campus is a window. The others are all painted yellow. There are three large metal desks, bulletin boards full of schedules, trophies sticking out of boxes on top of a locker, and a framed poster-size photograph of a lion. In the soft fluorescent light, a small man in an orange tank-top is talking to a student in a navy blue "Cal" sweatsuit.

"He's gonna try and overwhelm you," the small man says. "He's gonna use power. Your best weapon: Stop him. Block him." The small man goes into a crouch with his elbows at his sides and his fists alongside his head. Then one of his fists darts out.

"Sharpshoot him," he says. "Boom! Move away. Boom! Move away. Okay—it's working. Then, the next time he charges you: Boom-*boom*!" His left and then his right lash forth. "Now you try it."

The student begins bouncing on the balls of his feet. His head is bowed and his eyes glare at the small man from under an overhanging brow. He steps forward and his left arm shoots straight out toward his teacher; his fist is perfectly parallel with his shoulder.

"*That's* it! Oh boy! That's a killer. When he slugs, you slug too. This guy leads with his face; if he starts throwing hooks, hit him right here"—the small man points to his chin—"and I guarantee you he's gonna fall down. If he's wobbling, stay on him—hit him with the fuckin' hook. *That's* the boy! *That's* the boy! If he gets in close and starts that shit"—the small man looks away and shakes his head disdainfully—"*knock him out*, man."

The student sits down and begins to read a *Time* magazine cover story on Nastassja Kinski.

"Be the greatest boxer that ever walked the earth," says the little guy. "Okay, man? We're lookin' at a national championship." He turns toward the door and grips the knob, but then he turns around again.

"*The greatest boxer that ever walked the earth,*" he repeats.

The small man's name is Floyd Salas. He is an assistant coach of boxing at the University of California, Berkeley. The student's name is Kurt Heffernon; he was about to fight for the heavyweight championship of the National Collegiate Boxing Association (NCBA).

The championships were held at Cal last weekend; I went because I heard that collegiate boxing was enjoying a resurgence. Prior to the 1960s, NCAA boxing had been a wide-open affair in which some schools recruited heavily, offering athletic scholarships to skilled and experienced fighters, while others took a low-key, teach-the-sport-to-novices tack; the result had been a kind of national free-for-all in which mismatches were common and the potential for injury great. When this culminated in the death of a college boxer from a brain aneurysm, it effectively killed the sport. Cal and other schools withdrew from the NCAA boxing competition, maintaining their interest in the sport only through club programs; by 1970, only four colleges in the country still had active boxing teams.

However, in the years following—whether because of Muhammad Ali, Sugar Ray Leonard, or simply the passing of the popular peace-and-love era—boxing surged back. Eastern schools began to compete again in '71; in '75 they merged with the California Collegiate Boxing Conference (including

Kurt Heffernon (left) and Mike Regan (right)

Cal, Chico State, Santa Clara, and the University of Nevada, among others) to form the NCBA. The new emphasis was, avowedly, on safety: All fights consist of only three two-minute rounds, and all boxers must wear protective headgear; the heaviest gloves weigh less than a pound. If a fighter is stunned, he must take a standing eight-count. A knockdown punch is scored the same as any other, so there's no great incentive to beat up one's opponent. Most telling though, are the facts that no athletic scholarships are awarded for boxing, and no boxer who has fought outside of college after his sixteenth birthday is allowed to compete. Therefore college boxers really are novices, while the pro-bound types are funneled into the AAU and Golden Gloves.

"College fighters have as much ability as any

> "All life is a tension between Eros and death. The urge to procreate and the will to survive—you can never get rid of those instincts. But you can steer them into civilized channels."

fighters on earth," insists Floyd Salas, "they just don't pursue it and develop it. All your really great fighters—Ali, Leonard, Sugar Ray Robinson—have high IQs; they just didn't have any education. College fighters have alternatives—they can be a doctor or lawyer and make a hundred G's a year—so they don't develop their boxing skill."

Salas, 5' 5", is an intense guy with olive skin, heavy sideburns, and a receding line of dark curly hair. He does not get paid to coach boxing at Cal (as does the head coach, Jim Ricksheim). Rather, he teaches creative writing at UC Extension, Foothill College, and San Quentin. He has published three novels: *Tattoo the Wicked Cross*, *Lay My Body on the Line*, and *What Now My Love*. (He also refers to himself as "one of the original peaceniks, the Mario Savio of San Francisco State.")

"If boxing were banned, it would one of the worst things that ever happened to violence in America," Salas told me. "It's a safety valve for the killer instinct. The man watching vicariously releases his killer instinct also. Most kids out of the ghetto who get into boxing don't get into trouble; it's the others who wind up in reform school or prison.

"All life is a tension between Eros and death," Salas went on, warming to his subject. "The urge to procreate and the will to survive—you can never get rid of those instincts. But you can steer them into civilized channels so that they're constructive rather than destructive. I always tell our kids that the person with the greatest character wins—the greatest warrior, the *purest* person, morally and spiritually speaking. Our guys, like Kurt and Chris Morales, are really sweet and well-mannered, without any seeming toughness. But boy, they're tough as nails, and very brave."

Heffernon, who grew up in Albany, has the classic look of a boxer: broad shoulders, flat nose, high cheekbones, looming forehead. He only began boxing a couple of years ago, though. Wanting to get in shape, he'd started working out in the Cal boxing room and became excited about the sport. Prior to last weekend, he had been to national championships twice, but hadn't won.

"I don't really have the killer instinct," Heffernon told me. "I don't particularly enjoy the brutal aspect of boxing—I have to force it on myself." Heffernon is a conservation and resource studies major; he says his real interest is in wildlife, and he's *thinking* about a career with the Audubon Society. He has been described as a "pure" boxer, i.e., a scientific rather than an overpowering one. He had had a difficult time in his semifinal bout because his opponent, Tim Phillips of Ohio University, was cut from roughly the same cloth. Indeed, both boxers were so scientific that the referee had to interrupt the match and encourage them to fight. Even after Heffernon seemed to have weakened him, Phillips managed to duck a lot of his punches. Heffernon finally won on points, without looking terribly impressive.

In the final semifinal bout, by contrast, a bellicose character named Mike Regan—the heavyweight contender from Shippensburg State—came roaring out and, in a fearsome display of animosity, pummeled his opponent into unconsciousness in something under a minute. Some moments after the brief fight had ended, the defeated boxer—surrounded by coaches and doctors—was still on his knees, trying to figure out where he was. Regan would be Heffernon's opponent the next evening for the heavyweight title. From where I sat, this was an intimidating prospect. But as Salas was leaving the gym, he came up to Heffernon and said, "That guy's made to order for you." He went into his crouch. "All you gotta do is jab-jab-jab."

Harmon Gym was a riot of primary colors for the championships: red and blue ropes, yellow painted roof rafters, white canvas mat, big red Budweiser banner at one end of the hall. The fighters wore sleeveless jerseys above their trunks in bright school colors: blue and white for Air Force, Penn State, Central Connecticut, and Nevada-Reno; red and white for Santa Clara, Miami of Ohio, Lock Haven, and Dickinson; purple and gold for West Chester (Pennsylvania); and blue and gold, of course, for Cal and Navy. The military academies, which require their students to take boxing, have emerged as the collegiate powerhouses—though an Air Force cadet who gets knocked out is never allowed to fly again.) The atmosphere was, more than anything else, *clean*; Harmon's no-smoking rule kept boxing's major accessory, the cigar, outside the gym, and the crowd was undeniably collegiate. It was also relatively sparse. As the punches flew, you could even hear the boxers' breath being expelled—sharp zinging hisses accompanying each blow like the high-pitched war noises of a video arcade.

continued on page 22

Continuation of previous page

East Side Story

continued from page 6

Regan of Shippensburg was stalking the hardwood like a zombie, his mouth pursed in a frown and his eyes half-closed. Broad shouldered and massive in a silver jacket and red warm-up pants, he looked positively Frankensteinian—lost in some private, malevolent world. During the introductions, when all the fighters assembled in the ring, he walked all the way over to Heffernon's corner to shake his hand in this trance while Heffernon grinned in disbelief.

Cal's Morales won the 125-pound championship in the third bout of the evening. The night before, he had beaten the defending champion, Johnny Owens of Air Force, by fighting defensively, jabbing and punching while moving backwards. He repeated the performance tonight, bloodying his eager opponent's nose in the second round and outscoring him handily in the third. "He's kickin' his ass!" yelled Salas. Head coach Ricksheim had actually had to put his hand over his peace-loving assistant's mouth between rounds. "Do we have a champ? Do we have a champ?" Salas screamed from the corner as Morales punched his way to the title.

Morales's victory whetted the Cal crowd's appetite for the heavyweight bout, the last one of the night. Given their size, Regan and Heffernon were visually the most gladiatorial of all the fighters; an effect heightened in Heffernon by his Everlast headgear, which had leather extensions over the cheekbones. As his match approached, he shadow-boxed patiently in a rear corner of the gym and finally just stood waiting in his dark blue "Cal Bears" shirt, his gloves at his sides and a strange look of distaste on his lips.

When the hometown hero entered the ring, the crowd went crazy. Heffernon bounced and feinted in his corner, then planted his feet, raised his mitts, and fixed on Regan, who now did the grinning, his plastic mouthpiece protruding from his face.

Heffernon maintained this frozen posture until the bell sounded, then met Regan in the middle of the ring, leading with jabs that didn't really fall. Regan hesitated for a moment, then drove the Cal boxer into the ropes, unleashing a predictably furious flurry of uppercuts. Heffernon looked like he might be in trouble. But he bounced off the ropes and the two fighters exchanged a volley of punches which, quite suddenly, sent Regan onto his knees.

The Shippensburg tornado got up right away and took the mandatory eight-count. He looked a little dazed, but came back hooking hard to reassert himself. Heffernon dropped his elbows to his sides as Salas had advised him in the intramural office. Then (boom-*boom*) he punched straight through Regan's wild roundhouses and knocked him out cold. The gym erupted; Heffernon went leaping away across the canvas; and Floyd Salas jumped up and down on the ropes, waving a towel and yelling, "Made to order! Made to order!"

1985

EDDIE NEMIR MEMORIAL AWARD: **CHRIS HADDAWY** won the Eddie Nemir Memorial Award for 1985. A three year competitor for the Bears, Chris lead by example. Chris's aggressive style and superb conditioning were trademarks which served as inspiration to teammates. Many CAL fans will remember Chris from the semi-finals from the 1984 National Championships in Harmon Gym. Chris rallied from behind to take the third round only to lose a close decision to eventual champion Moses Winston of Air Force.

Born in France, Chris grew up in Reno where he competed on the Reno High track and cross country teams. Ironically, Chris grew up on the same street as former Nevada boxing mentor Jim Olivas. Chris received his degree in Political Economics of Industrialized Societies. This year he plans to add his experience and leadership to the CAL coaching staff.

NCBA—LEADER IN SAFETY: College boxing has traditionally served as a leader in developing rules and innovations designed to protect the boxer. The headgear and standing eight count are examples of collegiate safeguards which were later adopted by other amateur programs. In a time when boxing is maligned and criticized, the National Collegiate Boxing Association (NCBA) is the leader in developing and promoting safe boxing. NCBA safety officer Emerson Smith has developed a closed cell thumbless boxing glove and special headgear at his boxing equipment research center at the Naval Academy. The thumbless glove and headgear, which reduce impact by up to 50%, were adopted by the NCBA two years ago. This past summer Smith convinced the USABF to adopt the thumbless glove. California is proud to be a member of an association providing leadership in boxing safety.

LEADER IN COLLEGIATE BOXING

UNIVERSITY OF CALIFORNIA BOXING CLUB
SPORTS CLUB PROGRAM, DEPARTMENT OF RECREATIONAL SPORTS

1985

Golden Bear Challenge to Maintain Quality

GOLDEN BEAR BOXERS FACE A DIFFICULT TASK in rebuilding this year's squad to the high level of performance achieved by the team in '84. Last year the Bears shocked traditional collegiate powerhouses by placing 2nd at the National Collegiate Boxing Association Championships hosted by Cal. Elusive Chris Morales (125) and powerful Kurt Heffernon (HWT) each captured National titles to propel the Bears into a second place tie with Central Connecticutt University. Cal will be without Morales and Heffernon in 1985 as well as Nationals competitors Heriberto Fermin (119) and Frank Delzompo (156), losing all four men to graduation. Spearheading the Golden Bear attack this season will be 132 pound Chris Haddawy. Haddawy, a native of Reno, Nevada, was Western Regional champion last year and lost a tough bout at Nationals to eventual champion Marlow Martin of Air Force. Joining Haddawy on the 1985 California team will be returnees Jack Light (147), Jim Fardeen (165) and impressive newcomer Bob Bankard (156).

1984 National Champions Chris Morales and Kurt Heffernon

The Late Eddie Nemir

THE EDDIE NEMIR BOXING ROOM, which opened in late September, provides the Bears with one of the nation's top collegiate boxing facilities. The new facility, which actually housed Cal boxers for more than twenty years, was dedicated to the late coach at the National Championships last April. The room features three times the square footage of the most recent facility which was located beneath Edwards Track Stadium. Coach Riksheim and his students are "ecstatic" about the new facility and are working hard to renovate it. Current renovation includes installation of heavy bag supports, restoration of the cork flooring and the old corner floor ring. Coach Riksheim believes the "new facility will increase visibility as well as student interest and participation." Boxing is fortunate to be back in Harmon and much of this move is directly attributed to the effort and success of the alumni support group: Cal Boxing Backers.

YOU CAN HELP US STAY AT THE TOP by making a pledge or donation to California Boxing Backers. In 1984, alumni contributions totaled $8755. Monies helped pay team operational costs and helped support the National Collegiate Boxing Association Championships hosted by Cal. California Boxing Backers is seeking $10,000 again in 1984-85. Donations this season will help team operational expenditures and generate funds for capital improvements for the new Eddie Nemir Boxing Room. Surplus monies will be used to establish an endowment fund for the Boxing Club.

Last year, over 90 alumni and friends of Cal Boxing helped the Cal team find its place among the nation's top collegiate boxing programs. Please make a generous donation today and help us keep California Boxing at the top.

Heriberto Fermin punches the heavy bag in the Eddie Nemir Boxing Room

CAL BOXING NEWSLETTER
MARCH '87

CAL OPEN RESULTS

CAL HOSTED THE YEAR'S FIRST BOUT ON FEB. 6 WITH THE BEARS SPLITTING 4-4 IN BOUTS WITH RENO, NAVY AND SANTA CLARA. THE CARD STARTED SLOWLY FOR CAL, WITH BOTH DAVE CASSETTY AT 132 AND BILL DERROUGH AT 139 DROPPING CLOSE DECISIONS THOUGH BOTH SHOWED GREAT HEART AND DETERMINATION. AT 147, MATT SCANLON GOT THE BALL ROLLING WITH AN EXCITING SEE-SAW BATTLE AGAINST A SANTA CLARA FIGHTER, FINALLY GIVING CAL VICTORY NUMBER ONE WHEN THE CONTEST WAS STOPPED IN THE THIRD ROOUND. AFTER BYRON FIGUEROA AT 147 LOST A WAR BY DECISION, ED GORDON OF CAL (165) POUNDED OUT A TWO ROUND VICTORY OVER A GAME BUT EXHAUSED RENO FOE. MATT KAUFMAN WENT THE DISTANCE AT 180 BEFORE LOSING TO NAVY. THE EVENING ENDED WITH TWO MORE CAL VICTORIES. BO SOLIS USED HIS SUPERIOR HAND AND FOOT SPEED TO BAFFLE HIS NAVY OPPONENT AND EARN THE NOD. IN AN APT FINALE TO THE EVENING LEO OCEGUERA OVERCAME RENO VETRAN AND NATIONAL TOURNAMENT COMPETITOR DAVE FREED BY TAKING THE FIGHT TO HIM AND NOT LETTING UP. WHEN THE DUST CLEARED CAL EMERGED ON TOP.

MARE ISLAND

CAL SENT THREE FIGHTERS TO THE MARE ISLAND NAVAL COLLEGIATE INVITITATIONAL: MARK FOWLER (156), BO SOLIS (172) AND LEO OCEGUERA (180). WHILE CAL WENT WINLESS AND THE COLLEGES AS A WHOLE WERE OUTBOXED 10-2, ALL THREE BEAR FIGHTERS FOUGHT CLOSE, EXCITING BATTLES, EACH ONE A TOUGH CALL. THIS WAS ONE INSTANCE IN WHICH THE WIN OR LOSS WAS SECONDARY TO THE INVALUABLE EXPIERIENCE GAINED.

RENO OPEN

ONLY FOUR CAL FIGHTERS WENT TO NEVADA FOR THE 1987 RENO OPEN BUT THE BEARS MADE A DEFINITE IMPACT. CAL WENT 2-2 WITH ED GORDON (165) AND MARTY MEDINA(147) BOTH EARNING KNOCKOUT WINS, MEDINA'S IN THE FIRST ROUND. IN THE OTHER CAL BOUTS BYRON FIGUEROA LOST A TOUGH BATTLE AND DAVE CASSETTY FOUGHT UP A WEIGHT CLASS TO LOSE A CLOSE DECISION.

California - Berkeley

Head Coach: Jim Riksheim
Assistants: Sean Mockler
Floyd Salas

Advisors: Phil Nemir
Mike Huff

California will enter four boxers into the tournament. California's most experienced veteran is 156 lb Mark Fowler. In 1986 Fowler defeated 1985 National Champion Dan Holmes, Nevada. Mark earned a bronze medal at last years championships. Dave Cassetty 132 lbs, Leo Oceguera 172 lbs and Bo Solis 180 lbs will be very competitive in their weight divisions.

The University of California boasts the oldest continuous collegiate boxing program in the United States. Boxing was first contested at California in 1912 and there has been a team on campus since that date.

California was instrumental in the development of the California Collegiate Boxing Association and contributed to the Foundation of the current NCBA guidelines. California's most famous coach was Edgar Nemir, 1933 season through 1968. A graduate of Boh Hall Law School, he earned a silver medal in wrestling, 1932 Olympics. Nemir died on February 1, 1968 of a heart attack, moments after his son, Phil, won a decision in a dual match against Reno in this gymnasium.

California's alumni include: 1984 125 lb National Champion Chris Morales, now attending law school; 1984 Heavyweight Champion Kurt Heffernon, a prison guard in San Quentin, California; Floyd Salas, a published author in the bay area, and current coach Jim Riksheim. Jim captured the 1978 Western Regional Championships. During the bout he had his ribs broke by Nevada's Dave Morgan. Unable to compete in the Nationals, Morgan was named the alternate. Dave upset defending Villanova Champion Juan Montez to win the National Title. Tough break Riksheim!

Nickname: Golden Bears

1988

CAL BOXING BACKERS

NEWSLETTER NO. 1
December 14, 1988

HOLIDAY GREETINGS -- from those of us associated with the Cal Boxing program. We hope yours is a joyous celebration with friends and family.

ED NEMIR -- The ceremonies including the induction of Eddie Nemir into the U.C. Athletic Hall of Fame were well done. On Friday night the Men's Department of Intercollegiate Athletics hosted a banquet and ceremony complete with an excellent video of all the inductees into the Hall of Fame. Cal Boxing was well-represented with those present including Brian Kahn, Dave Weiner, Dave Rodgers, Paul Ward, Earl Stevens, Sam Gold, Dirk Noyes, Don Nemir and Phil Nemir. Other friends included Erna Nemir Curtis, Melanie Weiner, Howard & Claudia Nemir and Thom MacAlone. The event was well-organized. Saturday morning we were able to view the Hall of Fame display which was very professionally done. On Sunday, 30 friends and ex-boxers turned out for the memorial service where most present shared memories and contributed to a very moving occasion. The weather was pleasant for the outdoor barbeque which followed and was a great opportunity to renew old friendships.

BOXING HOTLINE -- Tired of not knowing when the next boxing meet would be held or if there was a cancellation??? Well, now there's a solution. In order to facilitate alumni communication, the Cal Boxing Staff has installed an answering machine in their office. If you would like to leave a message, or have a question for us, or would like to find out the latest practice and bout information, give us a call at 643-9724. Hopefully, we can alleviate some of the problems we've had in getting in touch with each other.

CLASSES -- Cal Boxing has recently completed fall instructional classes, with another large turnout of over 50 students. Interest in boxing on campus is high, perhaps due to the recent Olympics, and we're looking forward to another large team for the 1989 season.

INTERCOLLEGIATES -- This year the Western Region will add three teams; Texas A & M, Iowa, and the University of Nevada - Las Vegas ... bringing the total number of west teams to seven. The schedue of bouts for the upcoming year is being finalized at this moment, and will be available shortly. The first bout will be held near the end of January. NCBA Championships at the Air Force Academy in April. More information later.

BOXING CLOTHING -- We have just received an initial order of Cal Boxing sweat suits in various sizes. They are navy blue with gold lettering, 95% cotton and built to last. If you would like to order a set, please send a check for $50 to:

U.C. Boxing Club
2301 Bancroft Way
Berkeley, CA 94720

Include size (both top and bottom) -- sizes are overlarge to include shrinkage. Don't miss out on this SPECIAL offer! If your sizes are sold out, we will either refund your $ or re-order at your request.

1988

Plannings For Reunions: 1988

On October 16, 1988, a reunion of former Cal Boxers was held in honor of Coach Eddie Nemir, who coached all but 3 years between 1933 and 1969. In attendance at the Strawberry Canyon Clubhouse event were: Mrs. Erna Nemir, Eddie's son, Phil Nemir and nephew Don Nemir, Mr. and Mrs. Gary Evers (who travelled from Idaho to attend), Hall of Fame Referree Jack Downey, Bill Harrison, Bill Corrigan, Floyd Salas and Claire Ortalda, John Grennan, Jim Handle, Gordon Van Kessel, Steve Ricketts (now from Meadow Vista), Coach Jim Riksheim, and Assistant Coach Sean Mockler.

Other alumni who couldn't make it but sent their regards included: Sam Gold (1924-1927, and undefeated), Leslie Kessler (who fought in the 1930s), Dennis Natali, Tom Gioseffi, Bob Hink and Dale Chamblin. (Note: Sam Gold later attended 2004 Reunion, at age of 97.)

At the reunion it was decided to hold Alumni Reunions in the Spring as fundraisers, and the concept of Varsity vs. Alumni exhibition fights, as a fundraiser. Paul Rein agreed to help organize the reunion and get together an "oldie but goodie" team of not-quite "over the hill" alumni to fight the varsity! This exhibition was eventually fought on February 11, 1989.

Sean Mockler(3rd from left), Floyd Salas, Claire Ortalda, Mike Huff (far right).

1988

Sam Moreno at the 1988 Reunion.

1988

Jim Riksheim and Sean Mockler at the 1988 Reunion.

CAL BOXING NEWSLETTER
MARCH 1989

THE CAL OPEN ON SATURDAY MARCH 11 WAS A GREAT TUNE UP FOR THE BEARS AS THEY HEAD TOWARD THE WCBA CHAMPIONSHIP TOURNAMENT WHICH CAL WILL HOST ON MARCH 24&25. CLUB PRESIDENT DALTON CONLEY FACED DEFENDING NCBA 125 LB. SCOTT NELSON OF SANTA CLARA, SON OF BRONCO COACH DAVE NELSON. AFTER THREE ROUNDS OF FAST AND FURIOUS ACTION, NELSON TOOK THE DECISION BUT CONLEY SHOWED GREAT PROMISE AND SHOULD BE A DEFINITE FACTOR AT THE REGIONAL TOURNAMENT. BEAR 165 POUNDER MATT KAUFMAN FOUGHT UP IN WEIGHT AND GAVE UP TEN POUNDS AS HE FACED NEVADA RENO'S CHRIS BETTS. AFTER A CLASSIC BATTLE OF BOXER VS. PUNCHER KAUFMAN LOST AN EXTREMELY CONTROVERSIAL AND CLOSE DECISION. THE CROWD WAS VOCAL IN THEIR DISAGREEMENT. 1988 WCBA HEAVYWEIGHT CHAMPION KARLTON SHAW FOUGHT A SPIRITED AND EXCITING EXHIBITION WITH 1984 NCBA HEAVYWEIGHT CHAMP KURT HEFFERNON. BASED ON HIS PERFORMANCE, SHAW IS PRIMED TO DEFEND HIS TITLE. THE HIGHLIGHT OF THE EVENING FOR CAL WAS WELTERWEIGHT BRIAN BUNCH WHO SCORED A SECOND ROUND KNOCKOUT OVER UNR'S MIKE CARVER. BRIAN IS A FIRST YEAR BOXER AND THE CAL OPEN MARKED HIS SECOND VICTORY IN TWO BOUTS. HIS COMBINATION OF ATHLETIC ABILITY, PUNCHING POWER AND NATURAL RING SAVVY MAKES HIM SOMEONE TO WATCH FOR AT REGIONALS.

THE FOLLOWING PEOPLE HAVE ALREADY DONATED THIS YEAR. THESE DONATIONS ARE THE LIFEBLOOD OF THE PROGRAM. WE CAN'T SURVIVE WITHOUT THEM. MANY THANKS FOR YOUR CONTINUED GENEROSITY.

Gordon Van Kessel	Bob Sakai	Tim Mc Carthy
Richard Carter	Sam Moreno*	Dennis Natali *
Brian Kahn	Dirk Noyes	John Hall
John Grennan	Dale Chamblin	Jack Downey
Ed Roberts	Andy Wallstrum	Andrew Heffernon
Tom Gioseffi	Fred Sheiman	Dale Jeong
William Gimbel	Glenn Takei	Jim Handel
Bill Harrison	Paul Ward	Mike Cusick
E.C. Larson	Jim Mower	Warner Gysin
William Eastin	Jim Martin	Jack Kawamoto
Ken Hansen	Warren Simmons	Gus Filice
Gary Evans	Steve Ricketts	Alan Pryor
Scott Rasmussen		

* Denotes multiple donations

THE COSTS OF HOSTING THE REGIONAL CHAMPIONSHIPS AND SENDING MORE FIGHTERS THAN PLANNED TO NATIONALS IN COLORADO HAS PUT A FINANCIAL STRAIN ON THE PROGRAM. WE HAVE RECIEVED $3200 ALREADY. THIS STILL LEAVES US SHORT OF OUR GOAL OF $5000. IT IS VITAL THAT WE REACH OR EXCEED THIS GOAL. IF YOU HAVE NOT GIVEN YET PLEASE DO SO AS SOON AS POSSIBLE. IF YOU HAVE ALREADY GIVEN AND ARE ABLE TO GIVE AGAIN ANY CONTRIBUTION WOUD BE GREATLY APPRECIATED.

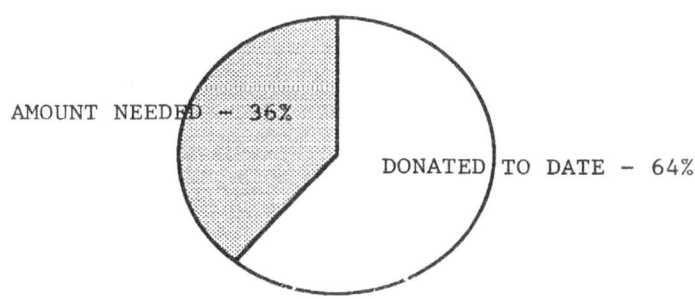

1989 WCBA CHAMPIONSHIP TOURNAMENT

THE FINAL HOME BOUT FOR THE BEARS IN 1989 WILL BE THE REGIONAL CHAMPIONSHIPS ON FRIDAY AND SATURDAY MARCH 24&25. SEMI-FINALS WILL BE FRIDAY NIGHT BEGINNING AT 7PM AND CHAMPIONSHIPS WILL BE SATURDAY NIGHT BEGINNING AT 7:30PM. COMPETING SCHOOLS WILL BE IOWA ST., TEXAS A&M, SANTA CLARA, NEVADA@RENO AND OF COURSE OUR OWN GOLDEN BEARS. ALUMNI RELATIONS COORDINATOR WILL HOST A RECEPTION FOR ALUMNI AND SUPPORTERS IN THE RSF ATRIUM SATURDAY NIGHT BEGINNING AT 7PM. IT SHOUD BE A GREAT OPPURTUNITY TO SEE OLD FRIENDS AND MAKE NEW ONES.

THE REGIONAL TOURNAMENT IS OF COURSE THE BIGGEST EVENT OF THE YEAR FOR THE BEARS. THE ADDITION OF IOWA ST. AND TEXAS A&M TO THE REGION SHOULD MAKE THE 1989 TOURNAMENT THE MOST COMPETITIVE IN YEARS. LET'S SHOW THE BEAR FIGHTERS HOW MUCH WE SUPPORT THEM AND PACK THE HOUSE FOR THIS EVENT. WE WOULD LIKE TO HAVE <u>ALL</u> OF OUR ALUMNI AND SUPPORTERS THERE. SO, TELL YOUR FRIENDS AND BRING THEM ALONG-- IF THAT DOESN'T WORK TELL YOUR ENEMIES AND BRING THEM ALONG AND LET'S ROOT THE BEARS ON TO A REGIONAL CHAMPIONSHIP!

LAW OFFICES OF
PAUL L. REIN
427 GRAND AVENUE
OAKLAND, CA 94610
PHONE 415/832-5001

January 17, 1989

Re: FEBRUARY 11 CAL ALUMNI / VARSITY BOXING MEET
U.C. Boxing Club/Recreational Sports Facility
Bancroft and Dana Streets, Berkeley
Reception at 7:15 PM, Bouts at 8:00 PM

Dear Friends, College Boxing Alumni and Fans:

Coach Jim Riksheim and the U.C. Boxing Club have announced Saturday, February 11, for a major social and athletic function: A series of bouts between the Cal Varsity and a team of top Alumni fighters from past years. A reception for Boxing Alumni, friends, and Cal Boxing supporters will precede the bouts. Place this event on your calendar now, advise us of your interest, and help us update our mailing list. We need your participation for a great start for the 1989 season.

ALUMNI/CAL VARSITY BOXING MATCH - FEBRUARY 11, 1989

We're soliciting all former Cal boxers interested in boxing for the Alumni. Pre-conditions for participation will be medical release and attending training sessions so we can line up appropriately balanced matches. Please contact me or contact **Boxing Coach Jim Riksheim at (415) 643-9724 or home (653-1714)** immediately as fight-time is only a few weeks away. (Even "Rocky" needed time to prepare!) Coach Riksheim is scheduling evening training sessions (Tuesdays and Thursdays, 7 - 9 PM) for boxers who can't make "team" training hours (4 - 6 PM.) Call the Coach for further information.

I hope all of you will come to the Reunion/Reception scheduled before the match at 7:15 PM, say hello to old friends, and share your ideas for supporting the team. Tickets for the match will be $5 in advance or at the door, with student tickets at $3.

Among the top 1989 Intercollegiate fighters for the UC Boxing Club (Cal Varsity) will be Dalton Conley (139 lb.), Brian Columbo (165 lb.), David Plum (180 lb.), and Karlton Shaw, heavyweight. Coach Jim Riksheim believes a number of his fighters have excellent chances to win championships this year. A probable top Alumni bout match-up will be Karlton Shaw, 1988 Western Regional Heavyweight Champion against Kurt Heffernon, 1984 National Intercollegiate Heavyweight Champion. Other "top contenders" will include Tom Gioseffi, three time middleweight champion (1965), his 165 lb.

1989

teammate, Paul Rein (1965), Floyd Salas (1956) and others of the "Over the Hill Gang", meaner than ever.

More recent graduates include Chris Morales, (1984) 125 lb. champion; Chris Haddawy, a top 132 lb. battler from 1985; Dave Cassetty, who narrowly missed a National Championship in 1988; Frank Delzompo, 156 lb. champ in 1984; Assistant Coach Sean Mockler, (172 lb.) from 1985; 147 lb. Matt Scanlon and 180 lb. Leo Oceguerra, two tigers from 1987.

The February 11 pre-fight Reunion/Reception anticipates visits from long time boxing referees Jack Downey, Jack Campbell, and Dale Chamblin, (a 1965 champ), former Cal boxing coaches Phil Nemir, Mike Huff, Brian Kahn and Dick Carter, and former assistant coaches Bill Harrison (1959), and Gordon Van Kessell (1961).

Money raised through tickets and contributions will be used for equipment, operating costs and travel expenses for conference competition and for sending our fighters to the Regional and National Championships. The U.C. Boxing Club receives some support from the University but depends primarily upon <u>contributions and fund raising</u> to keep the boxing program alive. Your contributions to the "U. C. Boxing Club" are appreciated and may be sent directly to Phil Nemir, P.O. Box 1717, Susanville, CA 96137, or with any of your correspondence to me.

ALUMNI ORGANIZATION AND MAILING LIST UPDATE

I'm taking over management of the "alumni and fans" aspects and look forward to hearing from you and seeing you at the fights. Could each of you please call or write, confirming or correcting your current address and phone number so we can update our records? Please also send names, addresses, and phone numbers of any alumni or fans who may wish to be on our mailing list.

Support and publicity have been offered by several prominent "fighters" of the ring and courtroom, Judges Myron "Tony" Martin and Leonard Dieden, attorneys Sam Gold, Wayne Hooper, and Public Defender Jim Jenner.

We're excited about getting together with friends who share our love for intercollegiate boxing and feel that our college boxing experiences were positive factors in our lives. Please share any ideas for the Alumni bout team with myself or Coach Riksheim. "Keep Punching!"

Best personal regards,

PAUL L. REIN
Alumni Coordinator

#38/calbxclb.d2

1989 UNIV. OF CAL. BOXING TEAM
VS.
UNIV. OF CAL. BOXING TEAM ALUMNI

ON SATURDAY, FEBRUARY 11, AT 8PM IN THE RSF FIELD HOUSE ON THE CAL BERKELEY CAMPUS (BANCROFT WAY AT DANA STREET), THE U.C. BOXING TEAM WILL HOST A BOUT BETWEEN THE 1989 SQUAD AND AND CAL FIGHTERS FROM THE PAST. TICKETS ARE AVAILABE AT THE DOOR AND ARE $5 FOR ADULTS AND $3 FOR STUDENTS AND CHILDREN 12 OR UNDER.

FEATURED ALUMNI SPAN THE CLASS OF 1955 TO THE CLASS OF 1988. HIGHLIGHTED AMONG THE OLDER CONTINGENT OF FORMER BEAR FIGHTER IS MIDDLEWEIGHT TOM GIOSEFFI WHO HAS BEEN LABELED BY SOME "THE BEST COLLEGE BOXER EVER." ALSO ON THE CARD ARE GIOSEFFI'S TEAMMATE PAUL REIN, AND COACHES DICK CARTER AND BILL HARRISON.

MORE RECENT ALUMNI COMPETING ARE 1984 NATIONAL COLLEGIATE CHAMPIONS CHRIS MORALES AT 125 LBS. AND KURT HEFFERNON (HWT), 1987 NATIONAL RUNNERS-UP DAVE CASSETTY AND LEO OCEGUERA, AND PRESENT COACHES JIM RIKSHEIM AND SEAN MOCKLER.

MORE INFORMATION IS AVAILABLE BY CALLING:
PAUL REIN   832-5001
CAL BOXING OFFICE 643-9724

1989

BOXING
CAL ALUMNI vs VARSITY
SATURDAY FEB. 11

FEATURING PAST CHAMPIONS
AND
STARS OF THE 1989 CAL TEAM

WELCOME

THE CAL BOXING TEAM WOULD LIKE TO WELCOME YOU TO TONIGHT'S BOUTS AND THANK THE MANY PEOPLE WHO HAVE SHOWN TREMENDOUS SUPPORT TO THE PROGRAM OVER THE YEARS. WE CAN NOT THINK OF A BETTER WAY TO KICK OFF THE 1989 SEASON BOTH IN THE RING AND OUT OF IT. ITS BEEN A GREAT OPPORTUNITY TO SEE SOME OLD FRIENDS AND SOME OLDER FIGHTERS. CAL WILL HOST THREE MORE BOUTS THIS SEASON INCLUDING THE WESTERN COLLEGIATE BOXING CHAMPIONSHIPS ON MARCH 24TH AND 25TH. YOUR SUPPORT AT THESE MATCHES WOULD BE BOTH WELCOMED AND APPRECIATED.

WE WOULD ALSO LIKE TO THANK INDIVIDUALLY SOME OF THE INDIVIDUALS WHO MADE TONIGHT POSSIBLE. PHIL NEMIR WHO HOSTED TONIGHT'S ALUMNI RECEPTION. DIANE ALDEN WHO ALWAYS HAD AN ANSWER TO COACHES RIKSHEIM AND MOCKLER'S MYRIAD OF QUESTIONS AND REQUESTS, AND MOST OF ALL PAUL REIN WHOSE RELENTLESS AND DOGGED STYLE IN THE RING WAS EQUALED IN HIS EFFORTS TO ORGANIZE AND PUBLICIZE TONIGHT'S MATCH.

THANKS ONCE AGAIN FOR YOUR SUPPORT. PLEASE REMEMBER THAT THE CAL BOXING TEAM DEPENDS ON DONATIONS IN ORDER TO EXIST. THERE ARE DONATION BOXES SET UP IN THE ARENA, OR YOU CAN SEND IN YOUR CONTRIBUTION TO:

U.C. BOXING CLUB
2301 BANCROFT WAY
UNIVERSITY OF CALIFORNIA
BERKELEY, CA 94720

OTHER 1989 HOME MATCHES:

FEB. 25 — CAL INVITATIONAL
MAR. 11 — CAL OPEN
MAR. 24 & 25 — WCBA REGIONAL CHAMPIONSHIPS

1989

TONIGHT'S BOUTS

BLUE CORNER	RED CORNER

ROGELIO SANDOVAL — CHRIS MORALES
ROGELIO IS A FIRST YEAR BOXER APPEARING TONIGHT IN HIS FIRST MATCH. MORALES IS A NATIONAL CHAMPION FROM 1984 NOW PURSUING A LAW DEGREE AT SANTA CLARA UNIVERSITY. CHRIS IS A CLASSIC BOXER/PUNCHER WHO WILL TRY TO USE HIS EXPERIENCE TO CONTAIN SANDOVAL'S AGGRESSIVE TACTICS.

DALTON CONLEY — DAVE CASSETTY
A CLASSIC GRUDGE MATCH. THE CLUB PRESIDENT OF 1988 AGAINST THE CLUB PRESIDENT OF 1989. DAVE, A 1988 GRADUATE, WAS A NATIONAL RUNNER-UP IN 1987. CONLEY HAS BEEN MAKING A LOT OF NOISE ABOUT "WANTING CASSETTY" EVER SINCE TONIGHT'S EVENT WAS ANNOUCED. LOOK FOR FURIOUS ACTION WHEN THESE TWO FORMER SPARRING PARTNERS CLIMB IN THE RING.

BRIAN BUNCH — MATT SCANLON
BRIAN IS ANOTHER FIRST YEAR COMPETITOR WHO HAS COMPETED ON THE CAL WATER POLO TEAM. SCANLON WON THE 1988 OUTSTANDING BOXER AWARD. CLASSIC BOXING STYLES AND LOTS OF STRAIGHT PUNCHING WILL BE THE RULE HERE.

JAMES WEISBERG — DICK CARTER
FORMER COACH CARTER WILL BRING CONSIDERABLE EXPERIENCE AND CRAFTINESS TO BEAR ON WEISBERG, A SMOOTH COUNTERPUNCHER. BOTH COMPETITORS PROMISE TO SHOW CLEAN AND ECONOMICAL BOXING STRATEGIES.

MATT KAUFMAN — BILL HARRISON
KAUFMAN WILL NEED ALL OF HIS AGGRESSIVE ENERGIES AGAINST HARRISON, AN ASSISTANT COACH UNDER RECENT HALL OF FAME INDUCTEE EDDIE NEMIR. NOW TEACHING DRAMA AT SANTA ROSA JC, HARRISON WILL TRY TO CLOSE THE CURTAIN ON MATT'S 1989 OPENING.

EGINO PENARANDA — CHRIS HADDAWY
BOOM! CRASH! JOHN MADDEN WOULD LOVE THIS ONE. EGINO CAL'S HARD PUNCHING MARINE CORPS LAWYER FACES ANOTHER SLUGGER IN HADDAWY A NATIONAL RUNNER-UP FROM 1984. THESE TWO PROMISE TO FLOAT LIKE AN ANVIL AND STING LIKE A SLEDGE HAMMER

JASON JULIAN — PAUL REIN
THE SLUGGING CONTINUES IN THIS MATCH UP. 1988 NATIONAL COMPETITOR AT 190 LBS. JASON JULIAN WILL USE HIS HARD PUNCHING, AGGRESSIVE STYLE TO DAMPEN THE ENTHUSIASM OF THE ORGANIZER OF TONIGHT'S EVENT 1965 GRADUATE, PAUL "HARD" REIN. INSIDERS TELL US THAT THE "HARD" COMES NOT FROM PAUL'S CONSIDERABLE PUNCHING POWER BUT FROM THE TEXTURE OF HIS SKULL.

LEO OCEGUERA — TOM GIOSEFFI
THIS SHAPES UP TO BE ONE OF THE BEST BOUTS OF THE NIGHT. GIOSEFFI HAS BEEN HERALDED AS THE "BEST COLLEGIATE BOXER EVER" DURING A SPARKLING CAREER IN THE SIXTIES. LEO "THE PEOPLE'S CHAMP" OCEGUERA IS ONE OF THE CRAFTIEST BOXERS CAL HAS PRODUCED. LOOK FOR EACH FIGHTER TO DIG DOWN DEEP INTO HIS BAG OF TRICKS TONIGHT.

KARLTON SHAW — KURT HEFFERNON
NO ONE WHO HAS WATCHED CAL BOXING IN RECENT YEARS WILL WANT TO BE IN SHAW'S SHOES WHEN HE GETS IN THE RING. HE FACES 1984 NATIONAL HEAVYWEIGHT CHAMPION AND POLICE OLYMPIC CHAMPION, KURT HEFFERNON. KARLTON WILL HAVE TO GET AROUND THE TALLER HEFFERNON'S EXCELLENT STRAIGHT PUNCHES OR HE'S IN FOR A LONG EVENING. IF HE DOES MANAGE TO GET INSIDE HIS CONSIDERABLE INFIGHTING SKILLS SHOULD GIVE KURT PLENTY OF TROUBLE.

1989

Paul Rein (left) v. Jason Julian, Cal Alumni Fight, 1989

CAL BOXING NEWSLETTER
FEBRUARY 16, 1989

ALUMNI BOUT

On Saturday February 11, Cal Boxing hosted a highly successful Alumni vs. varsity bout. The eight bout card featured former Cal greats Chris Morales '84, Dave Cassetty '88, Dick Carter '67, Matt Scanlon '88, Paul Rein '65, Leo Oceguera '87 Tom Gioseffi '65, Bill Harrison '60, Chris Haddawy '85, Egino Penaranda '86 and Jason Julian '88. They faced a Cal team of Dalton Conley, James Weisberg, Brian Bunch, Rogelio Sandoval and Matt Kaufman. All matches were exhibitions, so there were no decisions but no one told the competitors. Each match was hard fought and close with an enthusiastic crowd of over 400 cheering on their favorites. The sportsmanship and ability displayed by all made the card a tremendous success.

Prior to the bouts there was a reception for alumni and supporters in the RSF atrium. It was a great opportunity for old friends to get together and reminisce about the "good old days". Phil Nemir brought pictures, rosters, newspaper clippings, and other memorobilia from his father's years as coach which were appreciatively perused by many. All in all it was a great way to kickoff the 1989 season. We would like to have one of these get-togethers before every match. More info to come.

THANKS

We would like to thank those who have already donated to this year's team:

Gordon Van Kessel	Bob Sakai	Tim Mc Carthy
Richard Carter	Sam Moreno	Dennis Natali
Richard Carter	Brian Kahn	Dirk Noyes
John Grennan	Dale Chamblin	John Hall
Ed Roberts	Andy Wallstrum	Jack Downey
Tom Gioseffi	Fred Sheiman	Jack Kawamoto
William Gimbel	Glenn Takei	Andrew Heffernon
Bill Harrison	Paul Ward	Dale Jeong
E.C. Larson	Jim Mower	Jim Handel
William Eastin	Jim Martin	Mike Cusick
Ken Hansen	Warren Simmons	Warner Gysin
Gary Evans	Steve Ricketts	

Cal Boxing exists because of your continued support. Thanks again, you're the greatest!

If you have not donated yet for 1989, we still need your donation! Send your contribution to:

Cal Boxing Backers
c/o Phil Nemir
P.O. 1717
Susanville, CA. 96130

If you need to get in touch with Phil, his number is: (916) 257-2294

COMING UP

THE NEXT CAL HOME BOUTS ARE THE CAL INVITATIONAL ON FEB. 25 AND THE CAL OPEN ON MARCH 11 IN THE RSF FIELD HOUSE. BOUTS WILL BEGIN AT 7:30. HOPE TO SEE YOU THERE.

IF YOU NEED ANY OTHER BOUT OR TEAM INFO, YOU CAN CALL THE CAL BOXING OFFICE AT (415) 643-9724.

1989

SANTA CLARA BRONCOS

IOWA ST CYCLONES

1989 WESTERN COLLEGIATE BOXING ASSOCIATION CHAMPIONSHIP TOURNAMENT

TEXAS A&M AGGIES

NEVADA-RENO WOLFPACK

CALIFORNIA GOLDEN BEARS

MANY THANKS

THE UNIVERSITY OF CALIFORNIA BOXING CLUB WOULD LIKE TO THANK JUST A FEW OF THE PEOPLE WHO MADE THIS TOURNAMENT POSSIBLE.

OFFICIALS:
- DICK RALL
- VIC DRACULICH
- JACK CAMPBELL
- STU BARTELL
- JOE TINNEY
- DALE CHAMBLIN

RING ANNOUNCER: BILL TRESLER

RINGSIDE PHYSICIAN: DR. ROBERT SHIURBA

WE WOULD ALSO LIKE TO THANK PAUL RIEN FOR HIS HELP ALL SEASON WITH ALUMNI RELATIONS AND HIS ORGANIZATION OF LAST MONTH'S HIGHLY SUCCESSFUL ALUMNI BOUT AND TO HIS BROTHER STEVE FOR ALL HIS ADMINISTRATIVE HELP. SPECIAL THANKS GO TO THE DEPARTMENT OF RECREATIONAL SPORTS STAFF FOR ALL THEIR SUPPORT, DIRECTOR BILL MANNING, SPORTS CLUB COORDINATOR KATHY RITTER ANDREWS, FORMER CAL COACH AND NCBA PRESIDENT MIKE HUFF AND MOST OF ALL TO ASSISTANT SPORTS CLUB COORDINATOR DIANE ALDEN WITHOUT WHOM THIS TOURNAMENT WOULD NEVER HAVE HAPPENED AND WHOSE RELATIVELY CHEERY OUTLOOK KEPT COACHES RIKSHEIM AND MOCKLER SANE THROUGH THE ENTIRE ORDEAL. FURTHER THANKS GO TO THE BERKELEY BOOSTERS POLICE ATHLETIC LEAGUE BOXING CLUB WHO PROVIDED FIGHTERS WILL ARAGON, JUAN MANUEL GONZALEZ, LUIS BAPTISTA, AND JOSE TAMAYO FOR THE EXHIBITIONS ON SATURDAY NIGHT AND TO THE BERKELEY BOOSTERS PAL DIRECTOR OVE WITTSTOCK, AND THEIR COACHES NORM LETCHER, ALEC BOGA AND BRIAN GOOD.

THE MOST IMPORTANT THANKS GO TO ALL THE CAL BOXING SUPPORTERS AND CONTRIBUTORS. THEY ARE THE PRIMARY SUPPORT FOR THE PROGRAM. THANKS! YOU'RE THE GREATEST! YOUR DONATIONS ARE STILL NEEDED TO SEND THE BEARS TO NATIONALS. CONTRIBUTIONS CAN BE SENT TO:

CALIFORNIA BOXING
2301 BANCROFT
BERK. CA. 94720

1989

ABOUT THE NCBA

THE NATIONAL COLLEGIATE BOXING ASSOCIATION (NCBA) IS COMPOSED OF FOUR REGIONS NATIONWIDE. EVERY YEAR EACH REGION CONDUCTS A TOURNAMENT FOR THE RIGHT TO COMPETE AT THE NATIONAL CHAMPIONSHIPS. WINNERS OF THIS WEEKEND'S TOURNAMENT WILL MOVE ON TO THE 1989 NATIONAL CHAMPIONSHIPS AT THE UNITED STATES AIR FORCE ACADEMY IN COLORADO SPRINGS. THERE ARE CURRENTLY 28 SCHOOLS IN THE NCBA AND WE ARE LOOKING FORWARD TO GROWTH IN THE NEAR FUTURE DUE TO THE INCREASED POPULARITY OF AMATEUR BOXING AND THE LEAGUE'S NEW ASSOCIATION WITH THE UNITED STATES AMATEUR BOXING FEDERATION (USA/ABF).

THE NCBA HAS ALWAYS BEEN IN THE FOREFRONT OF BOXER SAFETY. THE MANDATORY USE OF PROTECTIVE HEADGEAR AND THE USE OF THUMBLESS GLOVES ARE TWO SAFEGUARDS THAT WERE FIRST ADOPTED BY THE NCBA AND LATER PICKED UP BY THE OLYMPICS, GOLDEN GLOVES, AND OTHER AMATEUR BOXING ORGANIZATIONS. THE USE OF 12 AND 14 OUNCE GLOVES (AS OPPOSED TO 10 AND 12 OUNCE) AND TWO MINUTE ROUNDS ARE SAFETY PRECAUTIONS THAT ARE UNIQUE TO THE NCBA. IN ADDITION COLLEGIATE BOXING HAS A "16 OR OLDER" RULE THAT PROHIBITS COMPETITION ON THE COLLEGIATE LEVEL FOR ANYONE WHO HAS HAD A BOXING MATCH AFTER THEIR SIXTEENTH BIRTHDAY. THIS IS DONE IN THE INTEREST OF PREVENTING MISMATCHES BETWEEN INEXPERIENCED AND VETERAN COMPETITORS.

CALIFORNIA GOLDEN BEARS

THE UNIVERSITY OF CALIFORNIA AT BERKELEY HAS THE OLDEST CONTINUOUS COLLEGIATE BOXING PROGRAM IN THE UNITED STATES. FROM 1919 TO THE PRESENT CAL HAS ALWAYS MAINTAINED A TRADITION OF EXCELLENCE. THIS YEAR'S SQUAD CONTINUES THAT TRADITION. THE 1989 BEARS ARE COACHED BY JIM RIKSHEIM IN HIS EIGHTH YEAR. HE IS ASSISTED BY FORMER BEAR FIGHTERS SEAN MOCKLER AND FLOYD SALAS.

112 LBS. ERIC MIMS
JUST A FRESHMAN, THIS COMPTON, CALIFORNIA NATIVE SHOWS A SLICK BOXING STYLE AND RING SAVVY THAT BELIE HIS YEARS.

119 LBS. ROGELIO SANDOVAL
ROGELIO IS A POWERFUL PUNCHER AT 119, WHO'S CONSTANT ATTACK WILL SURELY CAUSE TROUBLE FOR HIS OPPONENTS. A SOPHOMORE, HE IS SOON TO BE A POLI-SCI MAJOR.

132 LBS. DALTON CONLEY
ORIGINALLY FROM NEW YORK CITY, DALTON IS THIS YEAR'S CLUB PRESIDENT. HIS HALLMARK IS HIS CONDITIONING, AND ABILITY TO PRESSURE HIS MAN AT ALL TIMES.

139 LBS. BRIAN BUNCH
BRIAN IS AN EX-CAL WATERPOLO PLAYER WHO TRADED HIS SWIMSUIT FOR HANDWRAPS. THIS ORINDA NATIVE POSSESSES A CLEAN, POWERFUL, AND ECONOMIC STYLE THAT IS A JOY TO WATCH.

147 LBS. NORMAN SANCHEZ
NEW THIS YEAR TO CAL BOXING, NORMAN HAILS FROM MEXICO AND IS AN ARCHITECTURE MAJOR. HE IS A TENACIOUS AND DETERMINED BOXER.

165 LBS. MATT KAUFMAN
THIRD-YEAR BOXER, KAUFMAN ALWAYS COMES TO FIGHT. SHOWING NEW FOUND CONTROL AND POISE THIS SEASON MATT PROMISES AN ACTION-PACKED CONTEST

HEAVYWEIGHT KARLTON SHAW
TEAM CAPTAIN SHAW COMES TO BERKELEY VIA CHICAGO AND WILL GRADUATE IN LEGAL STUDIES THIS YEAR. KARLTON IS A BOXER-PUNCHER WHO CARRIES A LOAD IN BOTH HANDS.

1990

Jim Riksheim, Rogelio Sandoval and Sean Mockler.

1990

1990

Jim Riksheim and Cal Boxer Rogelio Sandoval, in Reno, 1990

1977-1991

"Cal Boxing" By Floyd Salas

I come from a boxing family. My brother, Al Salas, was a Golden Gloves lightweight champion of California (1942), Texas (1943) and Michigan (1944) and, after the war, pursued a pro career in Oakland, where he was known as a knock-out puncher. I, along with Sam Moreno, was awarded the first UC Boxing Scholarship when I was 25 in September, 1956, fall semester. Both Sam Moreno and I were picked for having outstanding boxing skills though we were the same weight, featherweight, 126 pounds. (Coach Ed Nemir said I had the skills of a professional). Ed Nemir said, "You guys fight it out. Whoever loses goes down in weight." I never actually fought for the Cal team, as I left Cal as a student after the fall term but I did return in 1977 as a Creative Writing instructor and also in 2003 as Regent's Lecturer. I became a writer, often about boxing themes. My manuscripts and letters are archived in the Floyd Salas collection in the Bancroft Library.

My coaching career at Cal followed my effort in 1976, to get my boxing license, which I was denied because of my age. I worked out under the guidance of my friend, trainer Art Garcia at the New Oakland Boxing Gym. The next year, 1977, I started assisting the Cal boxing team. Phil Nemir was coach that year, then Mike Huff took over. I was an assistant boxing coach from 1977 to 1991, also with Jim Riksheim.

Floyd Salas with Cal Boxing regalia, Oakland Museum exhibit, 1991

In training my boxers, I would often compare the preparation for boxing with the preparation of the Samurai warrior. David Darlington wrote of my boxing philosophy in an April 11, 1984 East Bay Express article entitled "Hometown Hero," quoting me: "If boxing were banned, it would be one of the worst things that ever happened to violence in America. It's a safety valve for the killer instinct. The man watching vicariously releases his killer instinct also. Most kids out of the ghetto who get into boxing don't get into trouble. It's the others who wind up in reform school or prison.

"Sigmund Freud said, 'All life is a tension between Eros and death. The urge to procreate and the will to survive' – you can never get rid of those instincts. But you can steer them into civilized channels so that they're constructive rather than destructive. I always tell our kids that the person with the greatest character wins – the greatest warrior, the purest person, morally and spiritually, speaking."

El Observador

-Largest weekly Hispanic circulation in the nation-

Vol. 14, No. 02

Serving Santa Clara, San Mateo, Alameda, Monterey & San Benito Counties

October 12 - 19, 1994

Ring gives unique view of life to boxer-turned-novelist

BY JUDY ERKANAT

Floyd Salas, author of four critically acclaimed books, started out pounding opponents instead of a computer keyboard.

Salas' first novel, *Tattoo the Wicked Cross* (Grove Press, 1967) was followed by *What Now My Love* (Grove Press, 1970; Arte Publico Press, 1994), *Lay My Body on the Line* (Y' Bird Press, 1978), and *Buffalo Nickel* (Arte Publico Press, 1992), a non-fiction memoir, which was chosen to be in *Masterpieces of Latino Literature*.

Family bloodlines

Salas traces his bloodline back to Spain.

Born in Colorado, in 1931, his paternal roots go back to 17th century Spanish immigrants to Florida, then on to Colorado via the Santa Fe Trail in the mid-1800s.

His mother's ancestors immigrated to New Mexico from Spain in the 16th century.

Mix a little Navaho and Basque blood into the family tree and the result is Salas.

His family moved to California when Salas was eight and he did his growing up in the Bay Area with his two brothers and sisters.

FLOYD SALAS

Tragedy struck when Salas' mother died when he was 12. "I went blind when I saw her coffin," he said.

Actually due to an ulcer in his eye, the blindness was cured. But every June for the next five years, Salas would again temporarily loose his sight on the anniversary of his mother's death.

After this irreplaceable loss, the Salas family was still strong, but no longer whole.

"She held the family together," the author recalled with affection. "A broad-minded woman with only

See NOVELIST, Page 2

a convent education, she still thought and read. It was a watershed time. Before my mother's death there was joy, after, sadness."

His sadness led to trouble and, by the time he was in the 9th grade, Salas had been arrested three times for misdemeanors.

Writing career

In reaction to his mother's death and perhaps because he attended six high schools in four years, Salas became a scrappy youngster, developing a natural talent for boxing.

This was enhanced by his older brother, Alberto, a professional boxer. Although Salas never boxed professionally, the sport did help him pursue higher education.

After graduating from Alameda High School, in Alameda, Salas went to work. "I had a series of good jobs, but I was frustrated," he recalled. "Writing changed all that."

Boxer-turned-novelist

♦ NOVELIST *from page 1*

By age 24, Salas decided to become a writer.

But it was his boxing prowess that, in 1956, impressed the coach at the University of California, Berkeley, enough to give Salas the first boxing scholarship ever given there.

Two years later, he garnered another scholarship, this time for writing, from the Rockefeller Foundation, which enabled Salas to attend *El Centro Mexicano de Escritores*, a writing school in Mexico City.

From there he went on to graduate from San Jose State University with a bachelor's and master's in creative writing.

Writer's accomplishments

Salas writes every day, for three to four hours. "At this pace, before I know it, the book's done," he laughed.

He has been teaching fiction at Foothill Junior College in Los Altos Hills since 1979 and has taught at other Bay Area universities, as well as Folsom, Vacaville, and San Quentin prisons.

Although he no longer boxes in the ring, Salas is now a boxing instructor at UC Berkeley and president of the Oakland chapter of PEN, the international society of poets, essayists and novelists.

He advises would-be writers "to try to understand the truth in the stories around you. This is what is meant by write what you know."

1992

1992 Alumni v. Varsity Exhibition

In Spring, 1992, an Alumni v. Varsity match was set as a fundraiser for the U.C. Boxing Club. Fights were all "exhibitions," without scoring, as had been the case in the 1989 Alumni v. Varsity Match - The fights were as follows:

Alumni		Varsity
Bill Harrison	v.	Eric French
Ed Szacky	v.	Bo Solis
Tom Pedamonte	v.	Steve Zembsch
Paul Rein	v.	James Walker
Bob Winter	v.	Jeff "Sonny" Banks

(Several of the Varsity may also have been Alumni!) Back in 1972, several "old timers," including Jim Handel and Floyd Salas, easily handled varsity fighters 20 and 30 years their junior. In the 1989 Alumni Matches, 22 year old Jason Julian, CCBC 190 lb Champ, had a rousing fight against 44 year-old '65 Alumni Paul Rein. Rein said he had "a 2 to 1 advantage."

1992

Tonight's Boxers

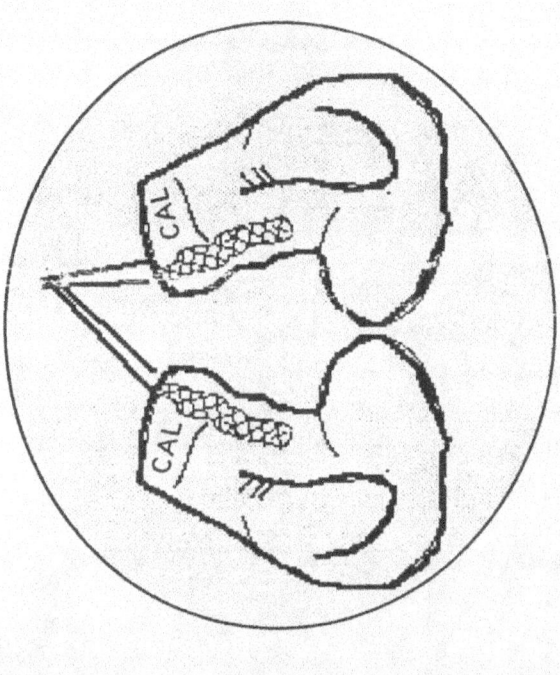

Bo Solis: The self-proclaimed "Party King of the Boxing Ring" Bo competed in the 180 lb. division in the 1987 National Collegiate Boxing Association championship tournament. He is currently a practicing attorney in San Diego.

Bill Harrison: The "old man" in an event where that really means something. A former Cal coach as well as boxer, Harrison will once again show that experience and guile can overcome youth and speed—he hopes.

Bob Winter: The giant of our alumni contingent. Bob will use his excellent straight punches to keep his opponent at bay. If that doesn't work, he'll use his size to scare the daylights out of him.

Tom Pedamonte: Possibly the only alum more feared now than during his days on the team. Tom trained for tonight by taking on all comers at team practices the last few months.

John Williams: An excellent athlete, John starred on the gridiron as well as in the ring for the Golden Bears. Tonight we should see some of the form that made him one of Cal's best heavyweights.

Paul Rein: "Punching Paul" signed on for tonight because he was hoping to cap his career with a win after his loss to his wife Brenda at their much publicized October wedding. Look for Brenda to jump to Paul's aid if things get too tough.

Ed Szacky: Ed has been a constant figure in the gym in preparation for tonight. We'll see if all that training is enough to sustain his aggressive, stalking style for three rounds.

James Walker: In his first boxing experience outside of the gym, James, a 190 pound sophomore will try to use his speed and athletic ability. Look for the southpaw to try to dominate with his right jab.

Jeff Banks: A promising heavyweight, Jeff has shown exceptional progress in a very short amount of time. The Cal coaches hold very high hopes for him in the future.

Eric French: Tall and rangy with exceptional reach; Eric is a tenacious competitor who only moves in one direction, forward.

CAL BOXING NEWSLETTER

'91-92 SEASON LOOKS BRIGHT FOR BEARS

Cal Boxing is alive and well and looking forward to the 1991-92 season. This year's team will be coached by Jim Riksheim and assisted by Sean Mockler. We are still looking for looking for coaching replacements for Riksheim and Mockler who are entering their twelfth and eighth years of service respectively. At present, the club continues to offer instructional and competitive opportunities to interested students.

The new season looks promising for the Bear Boxers. Fall instructional classes are exceptionally large. The 1992 team will also feature a number of returning veterans. Coaches Riksheim and Mockler are excited about the outlook for the 1992 team. " The level of enthusiasm and commitment from the kids is incredible." said Riksheim. Returning campaigners include welterweight Norman Sanchez who looks strong as ever after missing most of last season with a rib injury; Javier Tirado, a regional finalist at 125 last year and Lou Zeidberg, a tough middleweight. Combined with a large group of talented newcomers, these veterans will form the core of a squad that faces the formidable task of challenging 1991 national champion University of Nevada, Reno.

Practices officially start November 4 and lots of exciting events are planned for the 1992 season. An alumni bout is tentatively scheduled for early 1992, and a "Cal vs. lawyers" bout, organized by recent member of the bar, Chris Morales (Chris won a 125 lb. championship for the Bears in 1984). More information on these events will be coming in future newsletters. The team and the coaches are looking forward to a great year, and we hope to involve our alumni and supporters as much as possible.

CARTER NEW FACULTY ADVISOR

Cal Boxing is pleased to welcome Dick Carter as the new faculty advisor for the boxing team. Many Bear alums will remember Dick for taking over the coaching duties after the death of legendary Cal coach, Eddie Nemir. At present, Dick runs his own marketing firm in San Francisco and teaches an undergraduate class in marketing for the Business Administration department at Cal. He lives in Piedmont with his wife and three children.

Dick is very enthusiastic about working with the boxers and strengthening links between the team and the alumni. "I hope the team can provide the support needed for its members to reach their academic and athletic goals."

The Bears are thrilled to have Dick involved in the program and look forward to working with him this season.

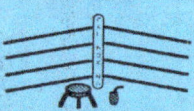

ALUMNI CORNER

A baby boom of sorts has taken place among former Cal Boxing coaches. Congratulations to Mike Huff and his wife Linda on the birth of their daughter, Marisa. Not to be outdone, new faculty advisor Dick Carter and his wife Mary are the new parents of twin boys, Mike and Bill. Further congratulations go out to Bert Sandell and his wife Ginny on the birth of their daughter Kelly.

We would love to hear what's going on with any of our alums or supporters. Send any news to:
Cal Boxing
2301 Bancroft
Berkeley, CA 94720

BOXING NEWSLETTER
FALL 1992

BEARS LOOK FORWARD TO BUSY SEASON

Nearly thirty boxers are in the gym readying themselves to represent Cal in the ring this season. Popular summer and fall classes have provided a large group of novices who, combined with twelve returning lettermen, make up the largest Bear squad in recent years. Open gym times have had to be nearly doubled to accomodate all the enthusiasm and interest.

Iowa State University will be the starting point of the '92-'93 campaign as Cal travels to Ames, Iowa on November 13 to take on the always talented Cyclones. Following the Iowa trip will be Western Collegiate Boxing Association competition. The Bears will host bouts on February 6, February 20 and March 6 and will travel to Santa Clara, Nevada, and Arizona. This tough schedule should have the Blue and Gold in top form for the western and national championship tournaments.

NEW BOOK BY SALAS GAINS RAVES

Cal Boxing's own Floyd Salas has written a new novel that is the toast of literary critics. The autobiographical piece entitled *Buffalo Nickel* has been praised by Kirkus Reviews as, "Beautifully written, gritty and deeply human..."

Buffalo Nickel is due in bookstores very soon. Congratulations to Salas and best wishes for the future success of *Buffalo Nickel*.

For those of you in the Bay Area, Floyd will have two readings that you may be interested in.
- Monday November 9, Modern Times 888 Valencia, San Francisco 7:30pm
- Tuesday November 24 Walden Pond Books 3316 Grand, Oakland 7:30pm

I WONDER WHATEVER HAPPENED TO...

If anyone is interested in finding a teammate with whom he has lost touch, we would be happy to try to put you in contact. Simply send us a note or give us a call(510-643-9724) with the name of the individual you are looking for with your phone number and if we have a current address we let that person know that you are interested in getting in touch with him.

YOUR DONATIONS NEEDED !!

Due to the the costs involved with our early season trip to Iowa State, we are counting on your support now more than ever. Please send your generous contributions as soon as possible to:

Cal Boxing
2301 Bancroft
Berkeley, CA 94610

Cal BOXING NEWSLETTER
January 1993

Bears gain experience at Iowa Bout

On November 13-17 the University of California sent seven boxers to Iowa State University for the season's first dual bout. Although the judges scored the match 5-2 for the host Cyclones, Cal coach Jim Riksheim believed a more accurate tally would read 4-3 Cal. " We knew we weren't going to get any gifts. The experience we gained was a lot more important that the judging, although you're always disappointed when your boxers aren't rewarded for their performances." Ath 132 lbs., Javier Tirado punished his more experienced opponent and showed promise for this year's competition. Newcomer Borquaye Thomas used constant motion to baffle his man and earn the decision in a 139 pound bout, while at 156 lbs. first year man Hugh Pedy used a textbook 1-2 to score continuously and neutrallize his foe. The most disappointing bout of the evening was in the 165 lb. division. The Bear's Chris Carmona put together his best effort yet, totally controlling his man, but coming up on the short end of the decision. In summing up the trip Riksheim stated, "They might have been a little stronger but we were definitely in better shape and more skilled. I'm optimistic that we can build on the experience we gained and make '93 a big success."

The Cal team and coaches would like to express deep and heartfelt thanks to Iowa State coach Terry Dowd and the entire Cyclone team. They were excellent hosts and went out of their way to make us feel at home.

Thanks for Your Help !!

Many thanks to all thoses alumni and supporters who have already donated to the 1993 team. We couldn't make it without you. Donations are still needed. Send contributions to:
U.C. Boxing Club
2301 Bancroft
Berkeley, CA 94720

1993 Donors

The following supporters have already contributed to the 1993 Cal Boxing team.

Ken Hansen	Warner Gysin
Paul Ward	Lyon Rathbun
Doug Keith	James Mower
Andy Heffernon	Chris Morales
Dick Carter	Jack Kawamoto
Phil Nemir	Glenn Takei
Mark Fowler	Mike Cusick
Mike Valli	Don Flaherty

1993 Bouts

Cal will host three bouts this year. 1993 home dates are February 6 and 20 and March 6. All bouts begin at 7:30 pm and will be held in the Recreational Sports Facility (Bancroft Way just west of Dana) Come out and support the Bears!!

1996

Two students, heavily protected by their equiptment, practice their boxing moves.

1997

> "I still have an Olympic dream."
> —Tom Clayton

GreekProfile

For most people, the next Olympics games is three long years away. But that's not how Acacia member, Tom Clayton, sees it. A winning season can possibly bring him an Olympic experience in boxing. "It's forty fights I have to win to get to Sydney," he said. "I'll do my best. It's a dream, but I want to take things one step at a time." Tom has come a long way in the two years he has been boxing for Cal. As a sophomore, he is team captain and the gold medalist in the 1996 Western Regional Boxing Championships. Also that year, he won the bronze medal at nationals. Currently, Tom is the Interfraternity Council vice-president and Acacia's social chair. He intends to major in business.

Acacia member Tom Clayton dreams in bronze, silver and gold.

Champion in the ring

lambda chi alpha ΛΧΑ

GREEK FACTS

FRONT ROW: Jared Lash, Scott Matthews, Eric Taylor, Aaron Dutra, James Mocci. **BACK ROW:** Ryan Hayashida, Glen Fornasier, Clifor Gudiel, Louis Perez, Kris Tendall, Rod Omite. **NOT SHOWN:** Larry Aagensen, Monroe Burch, Sudipta Chatteugee, Chad Dutvor, Jay Florian, German Jimmenez, Joe Little, Mougo Nikol, Spenser Obryan, Mike Piken, Charles Price, Eric Rodriguez, Steve Sharatz

Nickname: Lambda Chi
Founded: 1913 at Cal
Colors: Purple, green and gold
Flower: White rose
Motto: Not without labor
Philanthropies: Daffodil Festival, Raiders Canned Food Drive

lambda phi epsilon ΛΦΕ

FRONT ROW: Raymond Kim, Jason B. Lee, Glenn Kim, Kevin Wong, Chris Hayashi, Desi Tom, Kelvin Lin, Albert Yang, Victon Tham. **SECOND ROW:** Russell Low, David Cho, Mark Kano, Micah Fleming, Damien Tashiro, Kenneth Lo, Don Jhung, Mark Young, Eric Tam, Chris Yeung, Ernest Louie, Sang Ho Lee

GREEK FACTS

Nickname: Lambdas
Founded: 1988 at Cal
Colors: Royal blue and white
Motto: To be leaders among men
Philanthropies: Asian American Donor Program

"1998"

FALL 1997 CAL BOXING NEWSLETTER

NEW HOME FOR BEARS (AT LAST)! The off season has been a trying one for the Cal Boxing staff, with trying to finalize arrangements for our new practice facility. After losing our long-time home in 185 Harmon Gym to the new Haas Pavilion reconstruction project, we were fortunate enough to be promised the use of courts #16 and #17 in the downstairs racquetball area for our boxing program. While the new area has disadvantages as well as advantages when compared to our old facility, we are committed to developing this space into a top flight gym, capable of supporting the several facets of Cal Boxing: instruction, fitness, recreation, and most importantly, the Cal Boxing Team. Unfortunately, our new are is located exactly on the perimeter of the construction zone for the new basketball arena. With the vagaries of building projects this size, our functional status has changed several times this fall from complete shutdown to all systems go. So, with a gym half-completed, and over thirty old and new boxers working out to the best of our capabilities, the FINAL word has been received just in time for the holidays-- we WILL be able to stay open in our new home for the 97-98 season! Thanks also go to ex-Coach Mike Huff, Kathy Andrews, and Tamara Tripp of the DIARS staff, for keeping us on track (and somewhat sane).

1998 BOUTS Cal will host two home bouts in the new year, a season abbreviated by an early date for Nationals back east. The dates will be:

February 7   Saturday   7:30pm   RSF

February 28   Saturday   7:30pm   RSF

Cal will also participate in several shows at other schools. Our complete schedule will be available in January.

THANKS, SEAN After twelve long years of coaching service to Cal Boxing, our own Sean Mockler is "retiring" from everyday duty, to concentrate on career and family. It was my privilege to coach Sean as well as coach with him, and I can honestly say that Sean successfully embodies those qualities our program strives to instill-- courage, perseverance, and the pursuit of honor. Sean worked countless hours for no pay and not enough acclaim, only to share his enthusiasm and love of boxing at Cal. If there was a difficult or unrewarding job to be done(including the dreaded morning runs), Sean was always there. He was an invaluable source of ideas for promoting the Team and training the fighters. Sean once said that while cornerwork was his favorite part of coaching," you sure get spit on a lot." As my best friend and co-conspirator these many years, I can't think of too many messes we *haven't* gotten into when it comes to Cal Boxing. Thanks Sean, you're the best.-- Jim Riksheim

SEASON OUTLOOK Cal's strength looks to be in the lighter weights this season, with several veteran fighters in the sub-middleweight classes. Cal returns 1996 silver medalist Tom Clayton from injury at 132, 1997 regional team members Cedric Lee at 125, Rafael Hernandez at 139, Javier Hernandez (no relation) at 147, and Neil Rao at 135. Box-offs for coveted weight classes look to be intense this year. Other names to watch are William Kim at 156, Clayton Schupp at 172, and newcomers Scott Bambacigno at 172 and Colby Barrett at 190.

CAL BOXING NEWS

JANUARY 1999

WE'RE BACK !

Finally. Thanks to all of you for your patience in awaiting news of this year's California Golden Bear Boxing Team. The summer and fall of 1998 have been eventful not only for our current squad, but also for the future of boxing at Cal. At long last, we received permission to finish construction of our gymnasium in the downstairs racquetball area of the RSF. We've built an elevated practice ring and are in the process of hanging the rest of our bags-- when complete, we'll have six heavy bags, two double end bags, and a speed bag (plus, as many mirrors as we can get our hands on). Since this will be our home for a while, we're going to spare no effort in making it a top-flight facility. Attendance has been steady with over 45 students taking part in fall instruction, and over 20 (men *and* women) signed up for competition. Also this fall, team members took part in scrimmages at the Air Force Academy in Colorado Springs, and at an invitational in Reno, Nevada. The gym has seen extended use from this summer on by team members drilling and training for this year's campaign. Now is the time to see the results of their dedication and hard work.

OUTLOOK

At press time, Cal has filled weight classes from 125 labs. through heavyweight. Most positions are filled with veteran fighters, but several newcomers look to make an impression as well. Notable returnees include Sanjay Shah and Cedric Lee at 135 (both National competitors), Manuel Varela at 139, Ben Larman at 147, Walt Jang at 165, and

Scott Bambacigno at 180. Cal will face a stiff challenge from the other West schools, though- Reno will be looking for a good showing as host of this year's Nationals, Air Force always fields a strong team, Santa Clara returns several talented boxers, and first-year member UNLV will be adding to the action as well. The West Regional Championships, held at Cal on March 13 and 14 (Saturday and Sunday, time TBA), promise to be tremendous bouts with some of the nation's best college boxers in attendance.

NEW COACH

Cal is pleased to announce the addition of Yvonne Caples to our coaching staff. Yvonne will be in charge of developing a women's boxing program to augment our men's team— nationwide, about half of the member schools have women in training, and it our hope two have women competing in both regular season and championship bouts this year. Yvonne, a Cal grad in English, has been boxing for five years and has compiled a 6-3 record (including a Golden gloves title). In February, Yvonne will compete in her first professional bout in Atlanta, and is currently juggling her duties as a junior high school teacher, her work with the Cal team, and her own rigorous training regimen, as well. Yvonne is technically very sound and has excellent work habits and communication skills— we are lucky to have her with us and are looking forward to future successes.

ALUMNI TOPS

Once again, we would like to express our gratitude to our loyal alums for their patience with our unsettled state in recent months. This past season and preseason have not been easy for the staff and student leaders of Cal Boxing. Uncertainty about the future of our training facility have resulted in delays in programming, fundraising, and recruitment, while ongoing construction of the new Haas Pavilion has pushed many intercollegiate programs into the RSF resulting in reduced access to the facility for special events. Luckily, it seems as if we have turned the corner at last, and our patience has been rewarded. We would like to extend our special thanks to long-time benefactors **DALE JEONG, PHIL NEMIR,** and **PAUL REIN**, who donated before we could even ask! It is with your interest and care and generosity that the spirit of Cal Boxing endures, and will prevail in the years to come. Go Bears!

Please send donations (and inquiries) to:

U.C. BOXING CLUB
2301 BANCROFT WAY
BERKELEY, CA 94720

Our voice mail number is:
(510) 643-9724

And, no, we do not have e-mail yet, but hope to by the end of the season!

2000s

One of the best boxers of the 21st Century has been Todd Gaylord, who continued helping the Boxing Team as an Assistant Coach after he graduated. Todd won four Western Regional Championships, Two National Championships, and was twice runner-up to the National Championships. In 2007, he won both the 147 lb National Championship and the lower weight category's Outstanding Boxer Award.

Todd Gaylord

Cal Boxing News

January 2000

Bears Attack in 2000

"At the sound of the bell, come out fighting!" The bell has just rung for the new-millennium Bears with a busy schedule of bouts before this years' championship series in March and April. Cal will travel to both Reno and Las Vegas twice before coming home to Berkeley for two home shows, highlighting the best boxers in the west from member schools Cal, Nevada-Reno, Nevada-Las Vegas, Santa Clara, and Air Force. Cal will be led by coaches Jim Riksheim, Tom Pedemonte, and Yvonne Caples, assisted by former Cal standouts Borquaye Thomas, William Kim, Mark Fowler, and David Ralston. Cal's strength looks to be in the middle weights this year-- names to look for include Team Captain Walt Jang(165), Gene Kim(147), Nick Byrd(165), Manuel Varela(139), Luis Alarcon(132), Kash Afshar(175), John Murphy(hwt) and female Bears Mary Wang(106), and Crystal Silva(125). The Cal Boxing facility underneath the RSF has been bursting at the seams with old and new boxers getting prepared for an exciting season in 2000. Gym hours are 4-7pm M-F with morning and weekend times

by arrangement. Please come and visit us, or phone at (510)643-9724.

Bears in Vegas?

For the first time ever this fall, Cal visited Las Vegas in the inaugural home show for the second-year UNLV boxing team, joining fighters from Nevada-Reno, Santa Clara, Michigan, and Kentucky. The bout, held in a local health club just off the Strip, treated 700 boxing fans to a full 17 bout card.

The best in college boxing since 1918

The hosts came out strong behind the coaching of former Olympian Skipper Kelp and captured the majority of the contests using an aggressive "go for broke" style that was enthusiastically received by the partisan crowd. Cal's performance at 3-4 was the strongest visitor showing, and each Bear bout was hotly contested and closely scored. Captain Walt Jang lost a heartbreaking 3-2 decision at 165lbs. but showed great promise in almost stopping his man. Other Bear highlights include the powerful performance of Nick Byrd(also at 165) winner by medical retirement in the third, and newcomer Kash Afshar at 175 dominating his Reno opponent and forcing an early ending. Other Bear stalwarts were: John Murphy(hwt), winner by disqualification, Gene Kim(139), losing a close one at 139, and Cal favorite Mary Wang, giving a gutsy performance at 106 lbs. All in all, this was a solid performance for the 2000 squad and bodes well for continued success this season.

Keep in Touch!

Please join our ever expanding digital world – email us at **info@ucboxingclub.org** so we can add your name to our bout notification list – receive all the late breaking information on bout schedule changes & upcoming fights…

We'd also be happy to simply add others to our snail mail list too! And let us know if your old boxing pals aren't getting the latest word from Cal Boxing!

Dear Alumni and Friends of Cal Boxing,

Salutations from the squared circle entrenched deep in the guts of Berkeley's RSF! We hope this newsletter finds you well as we check in with a Cal Boxing update. We're staying busy as always, managing to keep up a steady practice and scrimmage schedule in the midst of exam and term paper season. Here's some of our news:

Bears Finish 2001-2002 Ranked 8th in Nation

We have great results to report from this spring's National Collegiate Boxing Association Championships: the Bears finished the competition ranked 8th in the country. Four Cal boxers qualified for the national tournament by finishing 1st or 2nd in their weight classes at regionals: Abu Ramin at 147 pounds, Mike Schuck at 175, Bill Wheeler at 195, and Derrick Zahler at 201. Schuck and Wheeler each earned All-America honors by advancing to the semifinals at Nationals.

Cal Women Charge Ahead

The upstart Cal women's boxing squad has leapt into training with alacrity this fall, guided by Javier Hernandez, a former Cal boxer and competitor at Nationals who will be coaching them this season. Several women return who saw action last year, including Kim Hope and Bahija Hamraj. Their jabs are looking crisp and we've seen them drop some devastating hooks in sparring rounds. Watch out for this group in the spring!

Novice Boxing Class a Success

This semester was another successful one for the novice boxing class offered by Cal Boxing to Cal students and staff as a way to raise money for the team. This fall we had more than 60 students in the class, and as many as 8 different boxing team members volunteered their time (in addition to their regular training schedules) to help with instruction. Several students from the class are promising candidates to join the team in the spring.

2002-2003 Men Led by Corps of Veterans

The Cal men fighters should be coming into a strong season, with a good chance of improving upon last year's results. Mike Schuck returns at 175 pounds, already looking just a little meaner and quicker than he did in advancing to the national semis last spring. Bobby Humphrey is back at 165 pounds, along with Hwasung Lee at 156, Abu Ramin at 147, and Jon Zaul 139. The guys are keeping the close quarters of our gym plenty crowded during evening practice sessions, and they're already going toe-to-toe at each other in some intense sparing sessions.

Cal's Oldest Sports Club More Competitive Than Ever
By Ian M. Fein
Contributing Writer, The Daily Californian
March 20, 2002

Down in the basement of the RSF, at the end of the corridor, tucked away in the far corner, you will find the stale smell of sweaty equipment, mouth guards crusted with spit and blood, along with the regular sounds of fists smacking leather.

There you will also find some of Cal's often overlooked athletes dedicatedly training for one of the most physically demanding sports.

Modern day gladiators of sorts, sacrificing and punishing their bodies and those of others for the sake of competition and pride, and, in a sometimes twisted way, because they like it.

There you will find the ancient sport of boxing at its heart, its most pure.

You won't find the stink of corruption that exists in its professional manifestation.

You won't find Don King's hair.

The Cal boxing team is one of the 24 sports clubs offered to students by the university through the Department of Intercollegiate Athletics and Recreational Sports.

The students who participate in such clubs receive none of the benefits afforded to athletes who participate in Cal's 27 Division I sports. No early Tele-Bears appointments, no extra units for participating and no scholarships. They do it for the pleasure of the sport-they do it for fun.

The Cal Boxing Club, in its 85th year, was the first club formed at Cal and is the oldest collegiate boxing program in country. Its continuous existence dates back as early as 1917-though records weren't kept any earlier than 1916, so its origins may extend even further.

The team is a member of both the National Collegiate Boxing Association and USA Boxing. Cal competes in a Western region that includes UNLV, Nevada, Air Force, Arizona State, Santa Clara and San Jose State.

This weekend, Cal will send six or seven boxers to the El Dorado Hotel in Reno, Nev., to compete in the Western Regional Collegiate Boxing Championships.

The winners and runner-ups of each weight category will then go to the National Collegiate Boxing Championships held the first weekend of April at the Naval Academy in Annapolis, Md.

"We stand a good chance of sending at least two or three guys (to Nationals), but probably more like four or five," predicts Cal coach Jim Ricksheim. "We've got some good guys out there. I think we're looking pretty strong."

The strength of the program owes much to the dedication of Ricksheim. He has more than 20 years experience in amateur boxing, dating back to his own boxing days as a student at Cal in the late 1970s.

After he finished boxing, Ricksheim learned what he calls a "zen lesson of humility."

"I realized I'm a much better coach than I was a boxer," says Ricksheim.

He's been training students at Cal ever since-first teaching recreational classes before taking over as coach of the team.

To pay his bills, Ricksheim works full-time as a painter and carpenter for campus sports facilities. All the time he spends with the team is unpaid and voluntary.

"It's a lot of time," he admits. "But it's something I choose to do."

Ricksheim notes that the boxing team benefits from strong alumni support. He talked briefly about the changes he's seen in the program since his days as a fighter in the 1970s.

"We didn't take training very seriously then," he confesses. "(The team) has just really gotten better and better over the years."

The veteran coach attributes this to a more serious approach in training.

"We've got a lot more guys coming out now who train a lot harder," says Ricksheim. "And the competition is getting tougher too."

Another development in the program has been the addition of women's boxing.

About seven females participate, in addition to the 15 men.

Senior Hope Feldman is in her second year of boxing at Cal, though she says she's only become "serious" about it this semester.

"You come in here in a bad mood," she says of the gym. "And you leave in a good one."

The women are coached by Crystal Silva, who just finished a rather successful boxing career of her own at Cal.

Last year Silva was the 'unofficial' women's national champion in her weight class. Her title is unofficial because there is no official women's championship yet.

This year Cal will send three or four women to the Regional Championships to fight in novice bouts.

"For people who are interested in boxing, this is the probably the best venue for learning because it's safe." says Ricksheim. "We really take very good care of our students."

The primary importance of safety differentiates collegiate boxing from amateur fights.

Collegiate boxers fight shorter rounds (two minutes instead of three) and use oversized gear (gloves are 12-14 ounces instead of 10-12).

Also, you must be a novice when you enter collegiate boxing. Rules stipulate no fighting experience past the age of 16.

Cal senior Hwasung Lee is the boxing club's president and he teaches introductory boxing classes for beginners at the RSF. Those who excel, and choose to continue, then "graduate" to compete on the team.

Within the team you'll find varying levels of dedication or intensity.

"We've got some guys who are pretty serious about it, training all the time," says Ricksheim. "And then we've got a lot of guys who aren't taking it seriously, guys with school concerns or whatever. So you try to fit the bill equally for different team members who aren't necessarily on the same track."

Cal sophomore Mike Shuck is one of the more dedicated boxers on the team. Shuck will fight in the 175-pound weight class at the Regional Championships this weekend.

He acknowledges the pressures one faces in fighting at such a big tournament in front of so many people-and especially in Reno, of all places.

He says that everything is televised in their stadium. So the inexperienced boxers have to worry not only about their opponents, but also the large number of cameras in their faces.

Though, with a smile on his face, Shuck admits, "It's just a good time."

Wearing the Belt Proudly

By Barry Kelly
Contributing Writer, The Daily Californian
April 7, 2004

Walk down Bancroft. Walk away from the azure skies and golden rays that flicker off the Campanile, away from the familiarity of a spring afternoon.

Walk further.

Step inside the Recreational Sports Facility. Go down the stairs, past the juice bar and the stationary cyclists. Keep going down, past the middle-aged men reverberating racquetballs off the walls.

Go down the other flight of stairs at the end of the corridor, down into the furthest depths of the RSF.

There, beneath the grey lighting of small fixtures, surrounded by the muffled roar of the gym, next to the dilapidated pair of rusty water fountains that are stained reddish-brown from a murky puddle of dirt, sweat and blood-the aesthetic leftovers of too many gory spitting sessions-is Cal's Todd Gaylord, recently crowned National College Boxing Association champion in the 132-pound weight class.

"I brought my belt with me," he says with a sly half-smile. "Wanna see it?"

He ducks inside one of the two racquetball courts that have been converted into training space for the boxing club team and returns with a hulking black leather belt. It feels like it weighs as much as a full backpack and clearly identifies its 5-foot-5, 132-pound owner as the national title-holder.

"I told my team if I won I would go to every class with my belt," Gaylord says. "I've done that for the last two days now, but that will be the extent of my bragging."

Indeed it is.

The junior math major who became the best fighter in the country at his level Saturday in front of a sold-out crowd at the El Dorado in Reno, Nev., never utters another word that has even the slightest egotistical connotations.

"I happened to get lucky," Gaylord says, shockingly. "One of the guys in my bracket came down with pneumonia, so I had a bye (in Thursday's opening round of the tournament). That made it a little easier, because three-straight days of fighting takes its toll."

Gaylord completed his undefeated season by pounding his semifinal opponent-a cadet from West Point-in a unanimous decision and triumphing over the Naval Academy's Jeremey Biggs 4-1.

"The ref said it was pretty one-sided," says longtime Cal boxing coach Jim Riksheim, who seemed perturbed by the judges' lack of a consensus verdict.

Gaylord, an Oroville, Calif., native, approached Riksheim last year about joining the team. Following a prestigious high school athletic career in northern California-during which he played cornerback for the football team, ran sprints and distance races in track and field and wrestled-Gaylord was frustrated by Cal's lack of a wrestling program.

"My freshman year, I tried to start a wrestling club, but that required too much money," Gaylord says. "I figured I could at least fair decently in boxing."

Riksheim, with his 22 years of coaching experience, quickly saw in Gaylord the potential to gain Cal's third-ever national title and first since 1984.

"We've had a long dry spell," says Riksheim. "Todd is a tremendous athlete-he came a long way in a hurry."

Five fights into his career last year, Gaylord found himself in the national championship picture ring for the first time, battling a man with seven times as much experience. He lost-one of only three career losses-and earned the No. 2 distinction.

By utilizing his wrestling skills, Gaylord arrived in Reno determined to become the champ.

"Wrestling has a lot to do with hip control," he explains. "With boxing, all your strength comes from your legs and that's a lot about hip control. The really good boxers are the ones who can punch from the legs."

Gaylord also benefits from supportive parents-they were in attendance for their son's title run-but his mother worries about her child's well-being.

Gaylord pauses to grip his left wrist and stares at his hand, lamenting on a ligament injury he suffered last fall.

"The doctor basically said I wasn't supposed to use (that hand) for six weeks," he recalls. "That bothered my mom because she knew I'm not big on listening to doctors."

Gaylord fought through the pain during autumn, occasionally resorting to fighting one-handed while continuing to train. Riksheim noticed and insisted Gaylord allow the wound to heal.

By early February, he resumed boxing with two full functioning appendages.

"Coach told me, 'It's wonderful you can fight with one hand, but come nationals, you're going to want both hands,'" Gaylord says. "I'm more inclined to listen to my coach instead of the doctor, because he understands what my goals are and how hard I am willing to work for them."

After reaching his goal, Gaylord needed his two healthy hands as he hoisted his belt above his head and soaked in the sensation of being a national champion.

2005

NCBA – WESTERN REGIONAL CHAMPIONSHIP

FRIDAY – MARCH 18TH, 2005

	BLUE		RED
#1	EZEKIEL IGNACO (USAF)	-125-	ARTURO ALVAREZ (SANTA CLARA)
#2	MATT JOHNSON (NEVADA)	-175-	JASON CROCCO (UNLV)
#3	LUIS PENA (USAF)	-139-	MARIANO ESPARZA (CAL BERKELEY)
#4	SABESTAN WONG (SAN JOSE STATE)	-139-	DANIEL REESE (UNLV)
#5	BLAKE BALDI (USAF)	-147-	TODD GAYLORD (CAL BERKELEY)
#6	THOMAS GENNARO (NEVADA)	-147-	PATRICK MEYERS (SAN JOSE STATE)
#7	ADAM VANCE (USAF)	-156-	JEFF WATKINS (UNLV)
#8	JEREMY WALTEMEYER (CAL BERKELEY)	-156-	YUTAKA HOSOAI (SAN JOSE STATE)
#9	DAVE SCHACTER (NEVADA)	-132-	BRIAN NAVIN (USAF)
#10	MIKE SACKENHEIM (USAF)	-165-	ZACK WHITE (CAL BERKELEY)
#11	RYAN HEALY (NEVADA)	-165-	GREG MURRELL (UNLV)
#12	BOB BULGER (CAL BERKELEY)	-175-	ERIC ROY (UNLV)

JIMMY OLIVAS
ATHLETIC FOUNDATION
3724 Lakeside Drive, Suite 100
Reno, NV 89509

2005

Nine fighters from the 2005 Cal Boxing Team

Lord of the Ring

By Nima Wedlake
October 11, 2006

Beneath the treadmills and stationary bikes of the Recreational Sports Facility, just below the yoga class and weight room, senior Todd Gaylord works tirelessly in the Cal boxing club's basement training facility. Above him, tacked on the wall of an aged and molding racquetball court-turned-boxing ring, a sign reads, "You Train. You Win. Enough Said."

Gaylord has learned to live by these words.

"I train so much that I can bypass my thought process," says Gaylord. "During a fight, it becomes instinctual."

He's done plenty of training, and plenty of winning too, amassing a 28-3 record in his career for the Bears.

In his first year on the team, with no prior boxing experience, Gaylord earned second-place honors in the National Collegiate Boxing Association championships, competing in the lightweight division (130-135 pounds).

Gaylord attributes his immediate success to his lifelong passion for sports. In high school, he played cornerback for his varsity football team, ran track and captained his wrestling squad. His athletic experience, especially in wrestling, facilitated his transition into boxing.

"Wrestlers get their control from their hips," explains Gaylord. "Good boxers do the same, using their legs when punching."

Under the mentorship of longtime coach Jim Riksheim, Gaylord adapted to the techniques and strategies of boxing necessary to compete at a national level. Riksheim's expertise has proven invaluable in Gaylord's development as a boxer.

"Jim is like an endless well of information," says Gaylord. "He's been around Cal boxing longer than I've been alive."

With the assistance of Riksheim and one year of boxing under his belt, Gaylord went on to win the national championship as a sophomore, becoming the third Cal boxer to win a national title and first since 1984.

He finished his season undefeated, beating Jeremey Briggs of Navy, 4-1, to secure the championship.

However, as more boxers around the country began to take notice of Gaylord's promising talent, he found that few were willing to challenge him.

"When my coach would line up a fight for me, I would usually get a call a few days later saying that my opponent had backed out," says Gaylord.

The senior saw the lack of competition as an opportunity to set new goals as a boxer.

The following year, he put on fifteen pounds, moving up to the more physically-demanding welterweight division, which includes fighters between 140 and 147 pounds.

"I thought I could get more of a challenge as a welterweight," says Gaylord. "And besides, my natural body weight is around 160 pounds. Maintaining a weight of 132 pounds was having a negative effect on my energy and academics."

Despite competing in the new division, Gaylord had little trouble achieving the same results he had come to expect of himself as a lightweight. At the national tournament in 2004, he placed second, earning All-American honors for the third straight year.

"Todd is a tremendous athlete," said Riksheim after Gaylord's impressive showing at nationals. "He came a long way in a hurry."

After taking a year off from both school and boxing, Gaylord has entered his final year at Cal and resumed his normal training regimen, working tirelessly to regain a national title.

He is currently preparing for the Hilltop Cup, to be held this weekend at San Francisco's War Memorial Gym. The tournament features boxers from Stanford, Notre Dame, Air Force, Santa Clara and Saint Mary's and tradionally draws more than five thousand spectators.

Since its inception in 2004, the tournament has grown into one of the nation's premier intercollegiate boxing events.

Gaylord is scheduled to face off with the Dons' Santos Soto, a highly-touted northern California boxer, in the tournament's main event. Soto is favored to win the tournament as a potential 2008 Olympic qualifier.

None of this, however, fazes Gaylord. Facing a formidable opponent does not concern him.

"There's no one else to blame—I like that," says Gaylord. "As soon as you get into the ring, it's all on you."

Coach Jim Riksheim and Todd Gaylord

2007

Todd Gaylord in Fall 2006 (2007 Season)

2009

Jim Riksheim and the 2009 Cal Boxing Team.

March Madness: College Boxers Seek Tournament Glory of Their Own
by Ryan Maquiñana

The University of California is an academic institution unlike any other. Located in Berkeley, it is the birthplace of both the free speech movement and the atomic bomb. No other college in America has produced more PhD students or places more academic departments in the top ten of the rankings today. A couple years ago, I strolled through campus and fortuitously ran into NFL star DeSean Jackson and 2009 Nobel Prize co-winner Oliver Williamson on the same day. This Friday, fans clad in blue and gold will support their Pac-10 champion Golden Bears in the first round of the NCAA Men's Basketball Tournament.

So why are a political science/history double major, a graduate student, and a university facilities painter meeting in the dingy dungeon of a basement in the school's Recreational Sports Facility instead of filling out their brackets? Each of them is an integral member of the Cal Boxing team, which is, incidentally enough, the oldest competitive amateur sport on campus. This weekend, the team will take a 25-minute drive across the Bay Bridge to San Francisco for the Western Regional Finals of the National Collegiate Boxing Association's version of the "Big Dance." And scratching beneath the surface, I found that their stories could be just as compelling as the professionals whom they seek to emulate.

THE COACH...
Jim Riksheim has seen it all. A former fighter himself at Cal, with 27 subsequent years of coaching experience at his alma mater, he's been around long enough to regale anyone with tales of the days when collegiate boxing thrived with popularity.

"We have a tradition here that goes back to 1916, and we're the oldest continuous boxing program in the country," Riksheim informed me. "My first coach, Phil Nemir, was the son of Cal's longest standing coach, Ed Nemir, who boxed and wrestled at Cal. He actually won a wrestling silver medal in the [1932] Olympics. Early on, I got a sense of how big the legacy was and how important it was."

Back then, college boxing was held in high standing at a level comparable to amateur sports that have stood the test of time today, such as baseball, basketball, or football. In 1932, responding to the rise in the establishment of boxing as a club sport on campuses across America, the NCAA made it an official sport and started awarding both team and individual national championships. It was at this juncture, sadly, when the ugly side of amateur sports emerged.

"In the bygone days, you had a lot of recruiting violations, kind of like football. Ringers pretending to be students. Guys coming in with disguised records. Coaches were doing anything they could to get a win because it was their livelihood. Now coaches aren't paid like that anymore, and it's a whole different atmosphere now because the level of skill isn't that far apart. I really don't think I could condone what was going on back then."

The NCAA, unfortunately, did not foresee the amount of mismatches that would occur in the ring between well-trained fighters from powerhouse programs and relative novices from other schools. Contrary to a sport like basketball, where a blowout loss inflicted on an outgunned team solely led to bruised egos, such a result in boxing could be literally fatal. As the amount of casualties in the ring gradually multiplied, a movement to abolish the sport from the NCAA became increasingly powerful. It was not until Charlie Mohr, a middleweight from the University of Wisconsin, died as a result of head injuries sustained in the 1960 national championship, when the NCAA ultimately discontinued the sport.

The coach chimed in on the Mohr tragedy. "You hope it never gets that late," he lamented, shaking his head. "I'd rather have [a referee stoppage] a second too early than a second too late. I'm pretty aware of what college boxing used to be, but it's a lot safer now. But that danger's always there, and you'll see that danger in an even fight, too."

In response to athletic departments cutting the funding of programs from coast to coast, the status of boxing soon reverted from varsity sport back to club level. As a result, the National Collegiate Boxing Association (NCBA) was founded in 1976 under the umbrella of USA Boxing. Cal joined the Far West subdivision of the NCBA, which included such schools as neighboring UC Davis, UCLA, the Air Force Academy, and Nevada-Reno, which at one time featured current referee Jay Nady and veteran boxing writer Michael Marley on the same team.

While collegiate boxing never returned to the heights it attained in the earlier part of the century, keepers of the flame like Riksheim were undeterred from continuing to breathe life into the sport. Necessity is the mother of invention, and one way to simultaneously harvest recruits and raise funds came through in the form of holding a boxing class for students.

But first, Riksheim had to cast his line and find an audience. "When I started coaching in 1983, I had to crank out hundreds of stinky copies of fliers by hand. It's made our job attracting students a lot easier. What's really interesting now with the speed of communication, whether it's Facebook or e-mail, we can reach 500 people online overnight."

However, while the means of marketing have evolved, some things never change. "For all of that, the game is pretty much the same because, for all of the 200 kids we go through in the class, there may be 10% of them that would be interested in fighting, and then maybe half of those that end up on the team. And that's the way it's always been, even in my day where a lot of kids would go through the program and only a few would stick," continued Riksheim.

Only a handful of pugilists are left after the scores of students are pared down to the team that competes in the NCBA, but those who earn the right to wear the blue and gold uniform are often successful. Five fighters have earned national championships and over 50 have earned All-America recognition under Riksheim's watch. Nonetheless, don't ask him to single any of them out for special mention, especially since he's kept in contact with so many former students for almost three decades.

"If I think of one fighter, then I think of another and another and another," declared the coach, sporting an ear-to-ear grin at the thought of his former pupils. "It's like family. The great thing about the internet is that it's easy to find each other. I get calls from old fighters wanting to touch base and see how things are, and it's a good feeling."

Riksheim's dedication to his fighters is evident, and while he would like nothing more than to paint a masterpiece with each blank canvas that dares to step in his dungeon, he understands the amateur nature of a club sport where student-athletes resemble more of the former than the latter.

"My hope is that [my fighters] have the time and the drive to go as far as they can. There's a lot of limiting factors, and the first thing I tell my guys is that the only time you'll ever be 100% is the first day you walk into the gym, because you're going to be dinged up, sore, or recuperating from an injury. Maybe you'll have school, you might be sick, or you might miss practice because of work. You might have a hundred things that could happen."

Regardless, he remains steadfast in requiring his fighters to refrain from making excuses. "What it comes down to is that when the fight is upon you, you still have to fight. If you have 70%, you want to use that 70%. But don't let those shortcomings hold you back. You have to give all you got at any given time and you'll have nothing to be ashamed of or feel sorry for. That's all I want to see out of my kids. That's probably the biggest lesson."

Coaching is Riksheim's passion, but due to the budget cuts, the main portion of his salary is derived from another source. The university employs him full-time as a painter in the facilities department.

"I have a family to support now. I just got married two years ago and have a two-year-old son, Everett, so I've had a lot happen in my life in a short amount of time. Also, it turns out that my boss is Mike Huff, who was actually my second boxing coach when I was at Cal, which is great when I need time for coaching or when the team travels." Such is the case this Thursday.

This season, the team is going through a quasi-rebuilding mode. I use this term because while the roster is filled with inexperience, the final chapter has yet to be written about the 2010 Golden Bears as they prepare for the postseason. Six male and three female boxers will make the trip to "The City." Those who advance from this weekend's tournament will fight in the national championships at the United States Military Academy on April 8-10 in West Point, New York.

"There's a punching chance that two or three of them could make it back east," opines Riksheim, taking a breath to make his next point. "And then, it's really the luck of the draw. Maybe you could pull a great fight out or someone gets injured. This is boxing. You just don't know what's going to happen."

Sounds a lot like the upcoming mayhem on the hardwood.

THE CAPTAIN...

David Rosenfield disobeyed a golden rule of boxing, and he dearly paid the price.

"I had lowered my hands. He got on my inside and hit me with a right cross. Then it happened."

The 132-pounder was competing in his third-ever fight last season against a fellow lightweight from the University of San Francisco. The result of that sequence was the graphic image you see above, the explosion of Rosenfield's nose and the consequent splash of red hue decorating the golden "California" printed on his chest.

"My opponent was from USF and he counter-punched me," David continued, seemingly enjoying every moment of this anecdote. "I didn't bring my hands back quick enough and my defense slipped a little bit. Hey, if I wanted to look good, I would've picked a different sport."

It's clear that the outgoing senior has a zest for combat, and he decided to prepare himself for his upcoming four-year commitment in the Marine Corps' Quantico, Virginia-based Officer Candidate School by learning the ways of the square ring.

"I'm a pressure fighter who likes to throw a lot of straight punches. I like to get you in the corner or against the ropes and throw as hard as I can. I like to slip. I'd rather slip and hit than block the punches."

With four years of Krav Maga (the Israeli hand-to-hand combat system) under his belt, the Cal boxing club immediately appealed to Rosenfield when he arrived on the Berkeley campus last year as a junior college transfer. "Just like in Krav Maga, it's just you and your opponent, and somehow you have to overcome him. There's something basic in boxing that I love about it," said Rosenfield.

However, before any beaks were bloodied or uniforms soiled, David had to first take the class and earn his spot on the team just like everyone else. From learning how to wrap his hands to keeping his poise when sparring in the pocket, he grasped concepts so quickly that by the beginning of the next season, he not only had made the team, he was made team captain.

Rosenfield reflected on his new assignment. "Jim saw something in me. I was extremely hungry as a boxer. Jim knew I was going to Officer Candidate School so he thought I had leadership potential and ability."

While a team captain is arguably an extension of the head coach in the ring, David has found himself performing that same role outside of it as well. "It's a student-based club sport, so I've taken on a lot of administrative duties. We really don't get any support from the university except our little dungeon of a gym because it constantly floods. We get a little bit of money from USA Boxing, but it's hardly enough."

So where does the money come from? Rosenfield explains. "I'm in charge of finances. We teach [an] eight-to-ten hour class, four days a week, at the beginning of the semester, which is basically a team tryout. We also raised money by painting six sections of the Cal football stadium. It took us four days."

The Tustin, California, product wasn't done describing the extent of his tasks. "I have to set up schedules for practices and classes. I myself teach classes and even hire assistant coaches. We have to raise money for travel and equipment. This year, we bought all new bags and purchased the uniforms."

One would be hard-pressed to find too many student-athletes with those responsibilities, much less one who also finds the time to double major in political science and history. Not bad for someone who has gone through life with two learning disabilities.

"I'm dyslexic and dysgraphic, so I'm in the DSP (Disabled Students Program) at Cal. I'm not a very good reader or writer, but I enjoy political science and history so much I'm able to get through it. It's very difficult. But while boxing has been a "time-suck" on my study time, it brings a relief."

After running through Rosenfield's transcript, he's "getting through it" a little more successfully than his words would suggest; he's currently on track to graduate with a 3.5 GPA.

His coach chimed in with an evaluation of his designated team captain. "He's very strong, he's a southpaw, and he's smart. He's a long-arm standup fighter who likes to brawl, and if I could just get him to sit back and box a little bit more, I think he can be more effective," noted Riksheim. "But he really just likes to stick his head down and start swinging away, so if I could just take that aggression and polish it up a little, he could go farther [in the tournament] than he did last year."

After taking into account Rosenfield's experience at the 2009 Western Regional Finals, it's clear that he wants to make amends in San Francisco.

"I needed to win my last fight to get to nationals," Rosenfield sighed. By now his jaw tightened up, almost bracing himself for the end of a story he knew far too well. "After the second round, I had nothing left in my tank, I was in bad shape because I couldn't breathe through my nose, I was coughing up nasty yellow-brown sh*t, and I had a weird pressure in my head. Even if I had won, I would not have been able to fight at nationals, because I had to get nose surgery immediately. When I came home, I got my infected hematoma drained and my two fractures and separation in my nose fixed."

If David Rosenfield is unable to make the trip to West Point, it won't be for a lack of motivation.

THE "CHAMPION"...

Having a conversation with Lauren Pettis in an academic setting is like talking to any vibrant member of the Berkeley student body, one that is historically renowned for social activism.

"My ideal job one day would be as a program evaluator for a substance abuse prevention program," says the 25-year-old graduate student. "That's why I'm here."

So did Rosenfield tell me it's essential that I to talk to her?

"She's the defending national champion at welterweight," replied the captain.

Pettis is currently pursuing her master's degree in the School of Social Welfare, but she has decided to pack her schedule with a daily dose of boxing. Even she gets tired reciting it. "At 6:30 AM, I'll wake up. From 7:00 until about 8:30, I'm at Edwards Track Stadium doing roadwork. Then I'm on campus taking classes until 5:00. Training with the team goes from 5:00 to 7:30. Maybe I'll lift weights and then do an ab workout for an hour after that. After that, I head home to do whatever homework I've been assigned."

So when is sleep? "Midnight," Pettis laughs. "And then I'll do it all over again tomorrow."

Having roots in the Bay Area, L.A., and Phoenix, boxing became more than an outlet for Lauren. "It's a great sport. I've played basketball, soccer, and tennis, but boxing isn't necessarily a team sport because you have no team to rely on in the ring. It's the heart that makes it great."

It was in the Valley of the Sun (the Metropolitan Phoenix area) when she learned her craft at the Rodriguez Boxing Club. However, Lauren's initial days in the gym weren't exactly ideal. "As a girl learning to box, it's tough because on one end, I had relatives telling me things like, they didn't want me to lose brain cells, and, on the other hand, I had people telling me I was too pretty to fight."

Pettis decided to break through those stereotypes by letting her actions speak volumes about her character. "I had to prove my commitment before I could get the training I needed, and I did just that."

After overcoming the obstacles that she faced just trying to pick up the sport, carrying over the knowledge and skills she developed to the college scene afterward seemed easy by comparison.

"She's one of the best boxers on the team, if not the best," her coach stated. "She's very intimidating to get in the ring with because she's taller than most of her opponents, at 5'11"; she's faster, and she's also stronger. The funny thing about her is that she doesn't believe how good she is, and we have to keep telling her that. She just gets so nervous before her fights. In fact, she wraps herself up to the point where we're constantly calming her down and cheering her up before her fights. And then, invariably, she just crushes her opponents."

Pettis' nervous spells are well-documented within her team and, most of all, by the fighter herself.

"Getting in there is nerve-wracking. I'm nervous the whole day leading up to a fight. For one, I have to eat my pre-fight meal of pot stickers and shrimp cocktail. Write that down." My hand is shaking just putting the pen to paper after listening to her tell me about her routine that day.

On the other hand, once she's in the ring, Pettis' meek demeanor instantly dissolves in the aroma of sweat and worn leather. Instead, it's replaced with unbroken focus and a killer instinct, as evidenced by her triumphant run to the de facto national championship at the University of Maryland's campus last season.

Pettis remembers few details from the bout. "They sang the national anthem. I listened for the bell. In the ring, I couldn't hear anything. In reality, I forgot everything else except the objective, which was beating this girl up for the next nine minutes."

Having a limited number of female collegiate boxers at her weight class works both as a gift and a curse for Lauren. While she only had to fight twice to reach the final bout of a virtual national championship- a 5-0 shutout of USF's Renae Santa Cruz- the easy road didn't get her the extensive ring competition and experience any fighter would like to acquire.

"There aren't a lot of female fighters at the heavier end of the spectrum [being at 147 pounds]." Pettis admits. "It definitely limits your exposure."

Even though she's on the brink of receiving her diploma in the near future, the defending "national champion" isn't quite ready to hang up her gloves.

"I'd love to turn pro some day, if I can get the chance," added Pettis, "but right now, I'd just like to return to nationals."

If Lauren Pettis and her teammates have their way, the University of California will have another reason to keep dancing until April.

From March 18-20, the National Collegiate Boxing Association will hold its Western Regional Tournament at the Koret Boxing Room on the University of San Francisco campus (222 Stanyan Street).Tickets are $20 for general admission, $10 for any student with ID, and $5 for USF students with an ID. Tickets can be purchased at the door. For more information, call (415) 422-2773.

Ryan can be reached at rMaquinana@gmail.com

A member of the Boxing writer's Association of America and Ring Magazine's Ratings Panel. Ryan Maquiñana also wrote an article on the Cal Boxing Team of 2011 and its coach, Jim Riksheim.

2011 Cal Boxing Team
By Ryan Maquiñana

It's been a rebuilding year for the Golden Bears, and head coach Jim Riksheim pulls no punches regarding that feeling.

"With the tournament coming up, I feel like I'm going into a tiger hut with a pea shooter," he said. "We're all brand new, and as far as bout experience, our most veteran guy heading into this season only had three bouts under his belt."

One bright spot has been Andrei Vasilj, a 156-pound junior with a penchant for combat, having past experience in Muay Thai. For an international development studies major with designs on joining the Peace Corps after graduation, the 22-year-old junior from North Hollywood is quite the walking dichotomy when the gloves are on.

"We practice twice a day, so I've been able to learn faster than usual," Vasilj said. "I love boxing because I love to be active, and it helps me get through my studies."

"He's got a unique style," said team captain Mike Hastings. "He comes out hard and fast in every fight, which is surprising for being one of the new guys on the team."

Styles make fights, and such a maxim has carried Vasilj to the regionals in only his first year of competition.

"I'm aggressive when I need to be," Vasilj said. "I have a really long jab, and I use it to set up my opponents for the left hook and straight right."

"Andrei's a very unusual fighter in that he'll catch you off-balance with his footwork or uppercuts at unpredictable times," said Riksheim. "You can never figure out what he's going to drop on you."

Nonetheless, due to his lack of experience, Vasilj acknowledges that he will be a bit of an underdog to make it to West Point.

"I trust the coaches, and we've worked on a couple techniques these last few weeks," he said. "I'd say I'm the underdog, but I've got a lot of heart."

--From article by boxing writer Ryan Maquiñana.

2010

Dave Rosenfield

_2010_

Phil Bremner and David Rosenfield, 2010

2010

Dave Rosenfield

2011

Cal boxing alums share much more than war stories at 95th reunion

By Ryan Maquiñana (Originally published on the Intercollegiate Boxing Blog)

BERKELEY, CA – The other day, I talked to a guy who once had Big George Foreman down for the count.

Really, I did!

"We fought in the finals of the 1967 Golden Gloves junior division," recalled the towering Bob Winter '63, my hand vanishing inside his upon greeting me. "I told my brother that Foreman was going to stick that cornball left jab because he would leave it out there. At the beginning of the fight, he jabbed once, jabbed the second time, and just like I planned, I hit him with a counter straight right hand. It actually lifted him off his feet and put him straight on his back."

So did Bob pull off the upset?

"He got up and they gave him a split decision," Winter replied, shaking his head while he grinned. "But he was a tough kid, and I ended up with this story."

That conversation in the Haas Pavilion Club Room marked the beginning of my day as a guest of the University of California boxing program for their 95th Reunion, and it wouldn't be the last to raise an eyebrow or two.

Where else but Berkeley would you find an eclectic mix of judges and oncologists, authors and bright-eyed current collegians, discussing their jolly exploits bashing in their opponents' skulls as *well *as sharing their professional accomplishments? Sifting through the myriad albums and scrapbooks felt like immersing myself in a time machine.

"I think it's great that I can be a graduate student in computer science and yet, have so much in common with everyone else after hearing their war stories," said Bonnie Kirkpatrick '11.

In all, the head count administered by Master of Ceremonies Phil Nemir '69 tallied close to 90, an attendance figure that ranged from the class of 2011 all the way back to the 1940s. He emphasized the importance of renewing the bonds between the boxers.

"Since I moved out of Berkeley, I'm not there as much as I used to be," said Nemir, who followed in his legendary father's footsteps as head coach in 1977. "The camaraderie among fighters is something that we had when I was there, and some of my closest friends are former Cal boxers."

After a hearty lunch where the participants ate their fill, fighters from a diverse range of eras took the blue and gold robe from Nemir and spoke their respective pieces at the podium, regaling us with nostalgia that elicited both laughs and longing sighs from the crowd.

"Personally it's been great to see all the old boxers meet the new kids and for us to share stories," opined the spirited Floyd Salas '56, whose life outside the ring has led him from juvenile hall in his early years to several accolades as an author and teacher at Cal.

Besides drinking water out of the toilets at the infamous old training facility near the track stadium, or recalling the measures taken to boil every last pound off their bodies to make weight, an underlying theme in many memories encircled the impact Phil Nemir's father Ed, a Cal Hall of Famer and coach for 35 years, had on their lives.

"Ed Nemir was my lifesaver and (Ed's) Mother Nemir adopted me," said Ed Farris '49, the former welterweight spry as ever in his classic blue and gold knitted sweater. "Fighting in the Navy in World War II, he was tough as nails and led by example. I remember some hoodlums in Berkeley challenged him on the corner of University and Shattuck [Avenues] and he ended up beating all of them up!"

"Being on the Cal boxing team under the guidance of Ed Nemir taught me that hard work and perseverance pay off in the long run," added Herb Davis '58, whose taste for the pugilistic tangle long after college had him trading friendly blows in the ring with longtime friend Art Twain on the former's 50 th birthday. "The experience also gave me wonderful memories and great friendships."

Paul Rein '65, who has plied his trade in Oakland as a pioneer in the field of disability law, emphasized the punching pride that comes with fighting for California.

"When people ask me what I did in college, I rarely say I was a political science major or that I was Phi Betta Kappa or pre-law," said Rein, a gregarious national titlist at middleweight who was a teammate of three-time collegiate champ and Cal Hall of Fame inductee Tom Gioseffi. "I say that I was a Cal boxer."

Another man who earned national championship honors almost two decades later spoke fondly of his time as a ringside warrior and the tinge of bravado it entailed.

"I remember fighting this guy from USC who had more experience than me and wanted to take my head off," stated Chris Morales '84, who incidentally enough continues to do combat in the courtroom today as a defense attorney. "When I went to my corner after a tough first round, I was looking to sit down, but my coach Mike Huff told me, 'You're a Cal fighter. We don't use stools.' "

Sure enough, Morales heeded Huff's words of wisdom and ended up victorious, unequivocally learning about the value of testing one's limits in the process.

Speaking of alums with juris doctorate degrees, Terence and Patrick "Butch" Hallinan, a pair of Bay Area legends in law, were in attendance as well. The brotherly tandem fought valiantly for the Bears and will be remembered for their actions in 1959 regarding African-American teammate Bill Holliman, the target of racial discrimination at a Reno hotel.

"As the story goes, after Bill was told he wasn't welcome, the Hallinan brothers made phone calls to the governors of Nevada and California, and then to Earl Warren, the Chief Justice of the Supreme Court, and within an hour the hotel retracted from its racist policy *with* apologies!" exclaimed Rein.

Terence, the former district attorney of San Francisco who proudly embraced his nickname of "Kayo," drew parallels between lacing up the gloves in the squared circle and verbally duking it out before a judge.

"Being a Cal boxer was perfect for a job as a D.A. because you were coming from a public school and you had to be tough to stand up to anything," he said, steadfast to the art of the scrap even at the tender age of 74.

Of course, while remembering the past is one of the key functions of a reunion, what transpired in the Club Room also served to build a bridge to both the present and future. In the midst of statewide budget cuts, Cal Boxing has stayed afloat as a club sport due to the ingenuity of the student-athletes and generosity of the alumni.

"For years, we had an intercollegiate model that was me doing all the work top-down," said current head coach Jim Riksheim '80, whose tireless efforts on behalf of the program as both a fighter and cornerman have spanned 34 years. "Now our students have taken an interest and ownership in the program to give their time and input. It's all one team and I'm just one person in a long line of people, and it's great to be part of something that special."

Last year's team captain, David Rosenfield '10, implemented the first steps for an endowment, a task he passed along to Mike Hastings '11 this season. Unfortunately, the 2010 All-American lightweight was unable to attend the reunion but felt compelled to chime in via telephone.

"During my time, I helped triple the team budget, doubled the club size, and led the team to nationals under Jim," said Rosenfield, who is currently entrenched in the Marine Corps Infantry Officer Course in Quantico, Va. "But really, what I will remember above all is that Cal boxing was here before me, and I feel honored that I was able to keep it going during my time here."

Fiduciary duties aside, there's a more compelling, intangible reason why the program has survived after almost a century in existence, and the reunion was a testament to the men and women in the room who have kept the fiery soul of the program ablaze beyond the wins and losses throughout the decades.

"When you get in the ring, you have to face your fears," said Nemir, "and so in life, sometimes you experience times where you have to keep a clear head. You can't let your fears take control of you. You just develop a certain sense of confidence that helps you accomplish anything. The thing is I've had boxers come up to me that didn't have the best record but they all say how valuable the experience has been to them."

The day concluded with a rousing speech from next year's team captain, lightweight Jean Carlo Oviedo '12, who later reflected on the day's events with an anecdote of his own.

"When I told my dad I joined the boxing team, he didn't like it because he thought that boxing was going to mess up my brain. He gave me the ultimatum of quitting or he was going to cut me off," said the bioengineering major from Peru who made it all the way to the national quarterfinals this past spring.

With the prospect of burning a bridge with his own father, Oviedo made his choice.

"I knew what made me happy," he declared. "I told him I'm not quitting. I hang out with my teammates so much they're like my brothers and sisters, and when we bleed or get injured, we're always going through it together. Eventually, my dad started to support me. He respected me in a different way. At first, he thought I was just doing it for the moment, but I wake up at five in the morning everyday just to train. It's not a thrill. He learned that it's my passion."

Nemir best summed up the festivities.

"It was impressive to listen to [Jean Carlo's] story and all the other ones," he said, beaming. "My dad coached for 35 years, the alums stepped in during difficult times, and Jim Riksheim's been keeping it going today. I just know how valuable it's been personally for me, and I'm glad other young people have the opportunity to experience that. I hope it continues for another 95 years."

March Madness begins for college boxers

March 21, 2012, 10:11 am

 RYAN MAQUINANA
CSNBAYAREA.COM

Basketball isn't the only college sport caught up in the midst of March Madness.

From Thursday through Saturday, local boxers will assemble in Reno to compete in the National Collegiate Boxing Association (NCBA) Western Regionals. The two finalists in each weight class will secure berths in the National Championships, which take place April 5-7 at the Air Force Academy.

Unlike their counterparts on the hardwood, however, these young men and women's journeys are far from glamorized, away from the television cameras and devoid of office pool bracket banter.

It's a club sport; none of the fighters are on scholarship. A few programs are student-run, a time commitment which can become extremely demanding when taking care of everything from the equipment to the travel arrangements. College boxing is arguably an amateur sport at its purest level.

CSNBayArea.com profiles four fighters who hope to make a deep run in the tournament and leave their mark on their respective schools' history books.

JOSE JIMENEZ, JUNIOR MIDDLEWEIGHT, CAL

Before Aaron Rodgers set the football world on fire, he was a relatively under-the-radar recruit who came to Berkeley via the junior college route.

Head coach Jim Riksheim and the boxing Bears may have found their version of lightning in a bottle in Jose "Jay" Jimenez, a junior transfer from Pierce Community College in Los Angeles.

"Jose's an amazing athlete, and he can box and move, but man, he hits hard," assistant coach David Keegan said, pausing before reiterating his utterance for emphasis. "He really hits hard."

Jose Jimenez is 3-0 since joining Cal. (Jose Jimenez)

LOCAL BOXERS AT NCBA REGIONALS

CAL
Jewell Fix (Sr.) – Women's Bantamweight (119 lbs.)
Jose Avila (Sr.) – Men's Jr. Welterweight (139 lbs.)
Jose Jimenez (Jr.) – Men's Jr. Middleweight (156 lbs.)
Juan Ramos (Sr.) – Men's Middleweight (165 lbs.)
Mike Cordoba (Jr.) – Men's Cruiserweight (185 lbs.)

SAN JOSE STATE
Oscar Gomez (Sr.) – Men's Welterweight (147 lbs.)
Gabriel Sanchez (Sr.) – Men's Jr. Middleweight (156 lbs.)
Andrew Cabatic (Jr.) – Men's Middleweight (165 lbs.)
Daulton Osuka (Sr.) – Men's Heavyweight (195 lbs.)

SANTA CLARA
No Entrants

UC DAVIS
Colin Schmitt (Jr.) – Men's Jr. Middleweight (156 lbs.)
Fabian Rivera (Grad.) – Men's Middleweight (165 lbs.)

USF
Carmen Fernandez (Sr.) – Women's Bantamweight (119 lbs.)
Jaren Hayashi (Jr.) – Men's Bantamweight (119 lbs.)
Nargis Shaghasi (Sr.) – Women's Jr. Welterweight (139 lbs.)
Sebastian Doerner (Jr.) – Men's Middleweight (165 lbs.)
Carlos Green (Sr.) – Men's Cruiserweight (195 lbs.)
Andrew Caceres (Jr.) – Men's Super Heavyweight (195+ lbs.)

SJSU captain Oscar Gomez is 8-6 overall. (Oscar Gomez)

Colin Schmitt has a 3-1 record. (Colin Schmitt)

Continued on following page

2012

Continued from previous page:

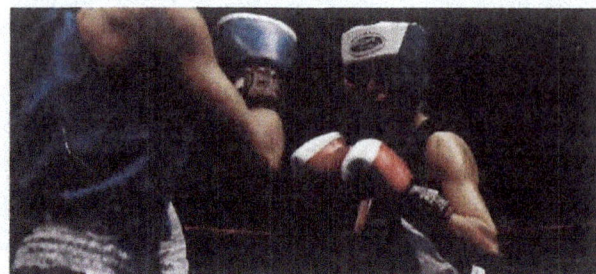

Nargis Shaghasi heads into Regionals with a 4-1 mark. (USF Boxing)

Since joining the team, the heavy-handed Jimenez has instantly become a national title contender by going 3-0 with two stoppages, scoring wins over two perennial powerhouses in Air Force and Nevada.

"I'm more of a slugger," Jimenez said. "I put some snap into my punches, and one of the opposing coaches once asked me if I had lead in my handwraps. I do think I could use more work with my combinations."

Originally from South Central Los Angeles, an adolescent Jimenez first learned the craft at some of Southern California's most renowned clubs like the Oscar De La Hoya Youth Boxing Center in Boyle Heights and Hollywood's Fortune Gym.

"It just seemed like a lot of fun at the time," Jimenez said, "but then I started playing other sports and stopped boxing until I decided to give it another shot when I came to Cal."

Given Jimenez' instant success in the 165-pound middleweight division, the only thing seemingly capable of stopping him is the scale. When senior teammate Juan Ramos wanted to campaign at middleweight for Regionals, Jimenez accommodated him by moving nine pounds south to junior middleweight—a laborious task much easier said than done.

"It's been challenging mentally. I've been eating nothing but salads, boiled chicken breast, tuna, fruit, and vitamins, while increasing my cardio work at the same time," Jimenez said. "I thought I would feel weak, but I'm at 158 right now, and so far so good. We'll see on Thursday."

A sociology major and pre-law student, Jimenez once dabbled in joining the police academy. Now he aims to regulate the west's best junior middleweights this weekend.

"I've done really well at 165, so if I can just make weight, I'm confident I'll give the people a good show and give them what they want to see," he said.

2012

Cal's Jose Jimenez with Coach Jim Riksheim.

On March 25, 2012, columnist/boxing writer Ryan Maquinina wrote about the CCBC (NCBA Regional) Finals, with the headline *Cal's Ramos Best Middleweight in West:*

"At the NCBA Western Regionals, held in Reno at the El Dorado Hotel, Cal 165-pounder Juan Ramos took home the middleweight title, edging Air Force's Casey Habluetzel in a close 3-2 decision. In the 156 lb final, Ramos' Junior middleweight teammate, Jose "Jay" Jiminez, dropped his first bout of the year, a points loss to Air Force's Tyrus Korecki. A third golden bear fighter, 175 lb Mike Cordova, was forced into an early corner retirement minutes into the light heavyweight final, after injuring his knee, against Air Force's Mike McClair."

2013

University of California Boxing Team

2013 NCBA Western Regional Championships
March 22-23, 2013
El Dorado Hotel Casino

Blue Corner	Weight Class	Red Corner
Evan Kamei • CAL	125	Jay Doh • UNLV
Jarred Santos • NEVADA	132	Kenneth Tadeo • SAN JOSE ST.
Gabriel Sanchez • SAN JOSE ST.	139	Will Perterson • AFA
Caleb Trotter • NEVADA	147	Andre Lu • CAL
Oscar Gomez • SAN JOSE ST.	147	Glenn Miltenberg • WASHINGTON
Colin Schmidt • CAL DAVIS	156	Fabian Ramos • SAN JOSE ST.
Sam Frankel • WASHINGTON	156	James Monk • AFA
Zach Barbara • NEVADA	165	Albert Tau Washington • WA.
Richard Vansiclen • WASHINGTON	175	Logan Brandt • AFA
Mac McDonald • WASHINGTON	185	Philip Mayes • AFA
Josue Gaytan • NEVADA	185	Lee Jensen • CAL
Mac Pham • CAL DAVIS	125	Roy Taylor • AFA
Steven Le • Cal DAVIS	132	Jacob Berggren • AFA

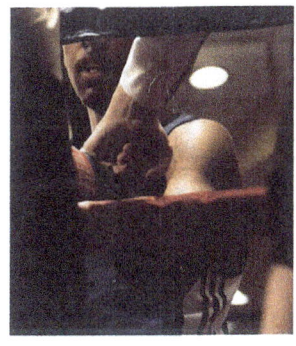

2014

2014 U.C. Boxing Club

2015 "UC Berkeley Invitational"

February 28, 2015 was Cal Boxing's only 2015 home meet, the "UC Berkeley Invitational."

Cal winners were Claire Glowniak, and Ryan Wen. Claire, at 137 lbs. defeated Elizabeth Pratt of UCLA in an exciting fight. Similarly, Ryan won another bout this year, defeating at 167 lbs. a tough Washington fighter, Gurkirat Sidhu. Kenny Dang of Cal lost a close match at 152 to Eden Bradford of Nevada. Kenny showed a tough chin, but got hit more than he should have, showing courage but keeping his head and chin too high! Cal's Patrick Avila fell and was counted out for a TKO loss to Johnny Aguilar of Nevada (156 lbs.). At 150 lbs. Britt Brown of Nevada outpointed Ron Desmond of Cal.

All of these Cal fighters are relatively new, and the ones experienced from last year showed notable improvement. Sophomore Claire Glowniak, one of the stars of the night, showed increasing boxing skills, and has two more years of eligibility. The Women's Boxing matches, as usual, showed great skills and courageous fights that matched those of the men.

Two in the audience attending were Phil Nemir, a two time CCBC Champion (1969, 1970), and second in 1967, and later Coach on Cal teams in the early 70s, and Phil's daughter, Nessa Nemir, a wonderful combination of skill, toughness and beauty, who trained for the "Perfect 10" boxing program. Nessa led the Women's Boxing coaching staff for several years. She and Phil are granddaughter and son, respectively, of Cal coaching legend Eddie Nemir, who coached the Cal team from 1933 to 1969, after winning an Olympic silver medal in wrestling at the 1932 Olympic Games.

2015

Nessa Nemir and father Phil Nemir.

Nessa Nemir and cousin Don Nemir, who boxed 1956-1958.
Don was Ed Nemir's nephew. Photo from 2011

2015

Coach Dave Keegan, Gerald Santos, Claire Glowniak, Coach Jon Zaul

CALIFORNIA BOXING FIGHT NIGHT

This Saturday Feb. 28 6:00 PM

RSF Fieldhouse
2301 Bancroft Way
Berkeley, CA 94704

Facebook.com/CalBoxing | calboxing.weebly.com

Treasurer, Ryan Wen, in his victory over Reno, NV

Doors open at 5 pm, Fights start at 6:00 pm

Represent Cal and support your Cal Boxing Club's fighters against schools from our Western Region -- UCLA, USD, UC Davis, San Jose State, Santa Clara, Reno, USF and others!

Tickets available at the Door 5-7 pm

Students (w/ ID): $8 | Alumni and General Public: $15

Pre-Sale Tickets and Cal Boxing gear available at
https://myrecreation.berkeley.edu/store
Search Boxing under Sport Club Management

2015 NCBA WESTERN REGIONAL CHAMPIONSHIP
El Dorado Hotel Casino • Reno, Nevada • March 13 -14 2015

2015 Cal Boxing Team

Cal has the longest continuous boxing program in the nation at 99 years. After boxing stopped being a NCAA sport due to the death of a collegiate athlete and most colleges dropped their boxing programs. Cal Boxing Coach Ed Nemir co-founded the California Collegiate Boxing Conference with Chico State, Nevada and Stanford. In the mid-eighties Jim Riksheim took over as head coach and carried the program for over 30 years, training multiple National Champions and All-Americans. Currently, the team is lead by coaches David Keegan and Jon Zaul, alumni of Cal Boxing. This year over 100 students tried out for 40 spots in the club.

2015 Western Regional Championships,
March 13 and 14th, 2015, at the El Dorado Hotel and Convention Center, Reno Nevada

Representing Cal at the semifinals were Gerald Santos (Team Captain) at 139 lbs, and Ryan Wen, at 156 lbs, sophmore Claire Glowniak, representing Cal in the women's divisional finals at 139 lbs. (This was the first time, to my knowledge, that the WCBA had four women's finals (at 119, 125, 132 and 139 lbs) in addition to the men's 11 weight divisions.

Both Gerald Santos and Ryan Wen lost close fights in the semi-finals Friday night. Gerald boxed well, <u>clearly</u> won the first round against a more experienced fighter, and lost on a close decision that "could have gone either way." Ryan also lost to a more experienced fighter, then came back on Saturday only to lose in a fight for third to try for a berth in the National Championships.

But the star of the finals was Cal's Claire Glowniak, who fought an excellent and courageous bout against a very strong and resilient opponent, Lorin Lee of Washington. Claire showed skill and toughness against an opponent with a chin apparently made concrete, who refused to be knocked out despite dozens of excellent punches by Claire. This was one of the best fights of the night.

2015

CAL BOXING CLUB RECEIVES RECOGNITION

During the 1960s, after the CCBC (California Collegiate Boxing Conference) broke away from the NCAA in 1959, and the NCAA dropped boxing as a sponsored sport after an unfortunate death of one figher in the National Championship, boxing was a "Big C" sport: Boxers could earn a "Big C Letter," just as in football, basketball, track and baseball, as a major sport.

After legendary coach Ed Nemir's death in 1969, after he had coached from 1933 to 1969, the University Administration withdrew its support, and the Cal Boxing Team was forced to continue as a privately sponsored "Club Sport," a status it holds to this day.

Current Cal Boxing Coach Jon Zaul reports that the team received significant recognition at the Spring 2015, 27th Annual Cal Sports Club Banquet. (There are currently 34 Cal Sports Clubs with a total of 1800 members.) At the 2015 Banquet, the Cal Boxing Club received major recognition in four categories.

Club President Gerald Santos won the "Officer of the Year" Award; Claire Glowniak earned an Honorable Mention for the "Athlete of the Year" Award; Cal Boxing earned an Honorable Mention for the "Most Improved Club" Award;" and Coach Jon Zaul received an Honorable Mention for the "Coach of the Year" Award.

Left to Right: Ron Desmond, Gerald Santos, Claire Glowniak, Ryan Wen

2015-2016

September 26, 2015 - Reno, Nevada Tournament with Nevada and Army

Starting in the 2015-2016 season early this year, two Cal boxers fought well in a tournament in Reno, featuring University of Nevada "Wolfpack" fighters and seven experienced boxers from "Army" (The United States Military Academy at West Point.

Cal boxer Patrick Avila lost a close and controversial decision at 145 lbs against a much more experienced Army fighter, Mike Garrett. Patrick fought a great and courageous fight and many in the crowd thought he should have been given the decision. Patrick Avila is much improved over last year, and should have a good season ahead this year.

Another very close match saw returning veteran Gerald Santos outpointed by one of the best fighters in the country, J.J. Mariano, of Nevada, at 145 lbs, last year's NCBA National Champion. Although the decision was popular among the Nevada fans, it could have gone either way, and Gerald Santos was also a much improved fighter since last season. (At the Spring, 2015 Annual Cal Sports Club Banquet, Gerald, the Cal Boxing Club President, won the "Officer of the Year" award.)

2015

2015 Cal Boxing Team

2015

2015 Cal Boxing Team - Photo by Juan Reyes.

2015

2015 Cal Boxing Team

2016

2016 Cal Boxing Club

2016

2016 Cal Boxing Team

THE DAILY CALIFORNIAN
Sunday, March 6, 2016

SPORTS

News | Sports | Arts | Opinion | Blogs | Multimedia | Weekender | Featured | PRESS PASS

FOOTBALL | M. HOOPS | W. HOOPS | BASEBALL | SOFTBALL | RUGBY | W. WATER POLO | W. SWIM | M. SWIM | M. TENNIS | W. TENNIS | BEACH

BOXING   SATURDAY, FEBRUARY 27, 2016

UC Berkeley Boxing Club celebrates 100-year anniversary with 6 wins

BY ALEX QUINTANA | STAFF   LAST UPDATED FEBRUARY 27, 2016

By Alex Quintana for the Daily Cal - February 27, 2016

On Saturday night, the boxers of the UC Berkeley Boxing Club, or Cal Boxing, celebrated their 100-year anniversary the only way they knew how — by fighting. They tested their skills against fighters from several West Coast Region universities, including the University of Washington, the University of San Francisco, UC Davis and Santa Clara Univeristy.

In the end, Cal Boxing's members won in six out of their seven total fights at Haas Pavilion, and fans got to experience firsthand why this organization is still going strong even after a full century.

2016

Cal's Vivian Chuang got things headed in the right direction to begin the night, beating UW's Renada Walcome in a 123-pound bout. Chuang quickly exploited a weakness in her opponent's defense, and established the jab early on in the first round. Walcome sent a flurry of jabs herself, but Chaung was able to keep her composure, utilizing the jab to keep her opponent at bay. This strategy allowed Chuang to pick up a unanimous decision victory, foreshadowing the great night Cal Boxing would have.

Cal's 132-pounder Eric Pan followed the success of Chuang and won unanimously in his bout against USF's Anthony Nguyen.

But the first really exciting fight of the night came in Cal Boxing's third bout, when 132-pounder Sunny Bae stepped in the ring against a much taller opponent in USF's Luke Haley. Bae reacted to the height of Haley by adopting a brilliant strategy: attacking the body, weakening his opponent and getting open head shots.

The hard body shots from Bae flustered Haley, which only allowed Bae to land hook shots on his opponent's head. It all worked out for Bae in the end, as he was able to continue the team's streak by picking up another unanimous decision victory.

"I felt like going to the body definitely worked, once I saw him getting tired I saw him lowering his gloves so I kept working that," Bae said. "I think I could have pushed harder, but overall I stuck to the plan and listened to what the coach told me, and I got a 'W' so it turned out for the best."

The fight of the night, however, came when Cal's 175-pounder Benjamin Kaveladze stepped into the ring against UC Davis' Anthony Mayberry.

The crowd was able to see early on in the fight that Kaveladze packed plenty of power behind his punches, most notably when it came to his hooks. And every single one of his punches flustered Mayberry.

Despite this, Mayberry showed no quit, responding with counterpunches that more times than not found their target, leading to the end of a close first round. Mayberry took the opportunity to be the aggressor in the second round, and instantly started with a series of punches that landed.

But in the end all of it served no purpose, and Kaveladze's power was just too much for Mayberry to handle.

All it took to end the fight was a single left hook by Kaveladze to Mayberry's jaw, dropping him to the canvas and forcing the knockout after he was unable to fully recover before a 10-second countdown.

After the fight Kaveladze was at a loss for words.

"It was completely ridiculous because I was totally resigned to losing that fight," Kaveladze said. "I couldn't ask for anything more dramatic than that."

This was the most memorable victory for Cal Boxing on Saturday night, but it was far from being the club's last. Cal's Brent Scheidemantle (165 pounds) and Jarred Mendoza (183 pounds) were also able to taste victory Saturday night, making the historic night for Cal Boxing even sweeter.

The strong night only proves that Cal Boxing's title as the longest continuously established collegiate boxing program in the nation is something it'll keep for a long time.

Many believe that the sport of boxing has been on the decline, and is close to being dead if it's not already. But at Cal, boxing is far from dead, and it won't be anytime soon.

"It's a good community to be a part of, the coaches try to push you to be the best you can be," Bae said. "I'm proud and honored to represent Cal; I never thought I would get to say that but here I am."

Contact Alex Quintana at aquintana@dailycal.org

Women Fighters Remember Cal Boxing

In 1999, women started boxing for Cal. Yvonne Capels was the first women's coach, in 1999.

Nessa Nemir (Ed Nemir's granddaughter and Phil Nemir's daughter) continued her family's tradition by Co-coaching the women's U.C. Boxing Club fighters from 2006-2011.
Nessa took a few moments to tell us about a few of the fighters she remembers training.

Nessa Nemir remembers Christine Aiken:

"Christine Aiken was the first woman I trained consistently. She was delightful to work with and a fantastic athlete.and a great sparring partner. She fought at 112 and went on to have several fights in Australia.

She always dedicated hours in the gym to training. We would often spend all Sunday evenings and other evenings in the gym training."

Christina Aiken winning in Reno, Nevada 2009

Nessa Nemir remembers Gymmel Garcia:

"Another great fighter I remember is Gymmel Garcia. Gymmel and I are about an inch apart and maybe 10 lbs apart in weight. She's the smallest sparring partner I've ever had and also the toughest.(Usually everyone outweighs me by at least 20 lbs, as my fighting weight was 101 and my resting weight is 108.)

Both being shorter fighters we had a similar "inside fighting" technique and quickly learned that although we are both tough enough to stand toe to toe and duke it out, that it was much wiser to work on moving in and out!

Nessa Nemir

Gymmel also managed to give me a black eye in one of our sparring sessions (gotta work on keeping my left up!) and apparently I split her lip. Our skill level was similar and we were very evenly matched as sparring partners. I was very proud of her for giving her coach a shiner! (Although pop gave me grief about my *lack of* defense.)"

Gymmel Garcia looks back on Boxing at Cal:

"I can't thank Nessa Nemir enough for challenging me in the ring. Boxing is more than a sport to me. This was a time in my life where a lot felt outside of my control. I was an undocumented first generation college student working over 50 hours per week. Boxing was the only place I felt I could be in control of the outcome. When I told Nessa my status and why I could not fight, she did not judge me, nor tell me what I could not do. Instead, she encouraged me to keep training and do better. Her coaching went beyond the ring and I am so thankful to have met her.

As a Deferred Action recipient, I now work for 10,000 Degrees (http://www.10000degrees.org/), a non-profit organization committed to educational equity; it has allowed me to challenge societal barriers that directly impact the ability for marginalized communities to ascend socio-economically, and to encourage students with backgrounds similar to my own to pursue a college education. I am now transitioning to a new career where I can further my commitment to social justice. I will be attending UC Davis School of Law, King Hall this fall and am very excited for the new opportunities ahead."

Gymmel Garcia - UC Boxing Club Alumni & UC Davis King Hall Law Student

Vivian Chuang at Cal Invitational, February 20, 2016

Vivian Chuang remembers winning that day:

February 20, 2016 is a date I will remember forever. Thanks to Coach Jon and my teammates, it was the night I won my first fight. The rush of joy from hearing my name at the end of those three rounds was honestly indescribable. It was one of those times where I felt completely happy and utterly supported by the people around me. By the first half of the night, my voice was throughly gone from cheering on our fighters alongside teammates without any drop of regret. In those moments, all of the hours spent training in the basement gym and all the blood, sweat, and tears, in a very literal sense, that we put into the sport seemed to pay off. We won six decisions that night, but the victories felt like much more than simple fights won. In those moments, I looked around at the people who made up my team, and realized they became people who made up my family.

Inga Lamvik (Left) and Lauren Pettis

Jewell Fix (in blue and gold) and Nevada fighter

Jewell Fix, Jim Riksheim and Jay Jimenez

Conclusion

For 100 years, Cal Students, despite their academic demands, have enjoyed learning the skills of Boxing and competing as amateurs, carrying on the traditions of those who came before. At a 2004 Alumni Reunion, about 50 former boxers testified on camera to the very positive effect that being on the Boxing Team had on their lives.

Most of those attending the reunion -- and I've been to most of the formal and informal reunions of Cal Boxers over the last 50 years, including those involving Varsity v. Alumni sparring -- have considered Boxing one of the most positive forces in their lives. Most have gone into professions, some became doctors, many became lawyers and judges. Almost none of these College Boxers have gone on to "fight professional," although Joey Gilbert, a 3 time National Champion from UNR and now an attorney in Reno, Nevada, and a local favorite, boxed on "The Contender" and fought a number of professional fights. (A broken nose helped to convince him that boxing was not a "long term" profession.) He's become a successful Reno trial lawyer; sometimes teaming up with attorney Vic Drakulich, who is also a top professional referee.

Examples were set by legendary boxers such as Walter Gordon, Sam Gold, and Ed Nemir -- all of who coincidentally went to Boalt Hall to get their law degrees. Other more contemporary lawyers include: Chris Morales (1984 National 125 lb Champ), Paul Rein (1965 CCBC 165 lb Champ), Bill MacAdam (1960-1962), now a San Diego Superior Court Judge, and Frank Roesch (1990) now an Alameda County Superior Court Judge.

Even more than a continuance of principled and challenging competition, boxing was an intense test of personal courage, fortitude, challenges that were heavily affected by how hard each man or woman <u>wanted</u> to train, and every former boxer has told me, a proving ground for sportsmanship and fair play, because it involved testing yourself against other trained athletes. I've rarely heard of a successful boxer who turned into a bully outside of the ring. The appreciative hugs boxers often give their opponents at the end of a fight are a genuine show of respect and often genuine affection for the person who has had the fortitude to absorb their punches over three rounds.

For all of the concern over the years with potential brain trauma, with proper protective equipment there have been few injuries in intercollegiate boxing; boxers have always been among the top sportsmen in academic grades; and the number of boxers who became successful lawyers and doctors argues against the brain damage concept. (Or, as 49er quarterback Steve Young showed when he left football because of multiple concussions, and became a lawyer instead, you can be too "braindamaged" for football or boxing, and still have enough brains to succeed as a lawyer!)

Anyone who finds the courage to enter the ring and go toe to toe with another athlete whose goal is to knock you out, comes out of the experience - win or lose the fight according to the judges - with an increase in <u>their</u> confidence and self-respect. The more recent advent of women boxers has opened these opportunities to women as well, and, as anyone who has seen two skilled women boxers battle it out, has helped to dispose of another negative stereotype of a woman's supposed limitations. The last few years, female gladiators have often put on some of the most spirited and skilled fights in the tournament.

As we go through this 100 year anniversary of the 1916 Cal v. Stanford match, which began Cal's record as the longest continuous intercollegiate boxing program in the United States, we can appreciate those who taught us skills and-always-high ethical standards, coaches such as Ed Nemir (for 37 years) and Jim Riksheim (for 30 years) -- and enjoy helping to maintain the program which has done so much for so many young athletes over the past century. Each of us can say "I was a Cal Boxer" and be both proud and grateful for the opportunities this brought to us.

— Paul Rein, Cal Boxing 1963-1965.

Coaches Jon Zaul and David Keegan

2004 Reunion

Augie Ong and Jim Handel

Joe Tinney, Mike Huff and Paul O'Neil

Bill Harrison, Sam Gold, Phil Nemir and Bill McAdam

Kurt Heffernon and Chris Morales (1984 Champions at Heavyweight and 125 lbs)

Jim Martin and Jim Handel (Both fought in the 1950s)

Steve Rickets and Dale Chamblin.

Floyd Salas and Lisa Rein (Paul Rein's daughter, co-editor of this book)

Paul Rein and Lisa Rein made a documentary film about the 2004 Cal Boxing Reunion. Paul is a Civil Rights Lawyer in Oakland, California, representing disabled persons. Copies are available from Paul Rein in DVD format, upon request.

INDEX: BOXERS BY YEAR

1916
Coach: Frank Kleeberger

Walter Gordon
Donald Lawton

1917
Jimmy Doolittle (WWII General; as Lt. Colonel, he led "Bombs Over Tokyo" Raid in April 1942.
Walter Gordon - Also All-American Football Selection, Cal's First and one of Nation's First African American "All American" Selections (See text about Walter Gordon.) (At approximately same time, Paul Robeson played football for Rutgers College, and was also named to the "All American" Football Team.) Walt Gordon later became a lawyer, Judge, and Governor of the Virgin Islands. He was named "Cal Alumnus of the Year" in 1955.)

1918
Hiram R. Baker (135 lbs)
Calvin C. Chapman
Joseph E. Covington (145 lbs)
Jimmy Doolittle
Walter A. Gordon
Fred W. Huntington (158 lbs)
Harry A. Mazzara
Al Picetti (115 lbs)
Samuel M. Shapero
Harold C. Whittlesey (125 lbs)

1919
Milton Aftergut
Hiram Baker (145 lbs)
Joseph Covington (135 lbs)
Jimmy Doolittle - Led WWII "30 Seconds Over Tokyo" 1942 Raid on Japanese Main Islands
Fred W. Huntington (158 lbs)
Harry A. Mazzera (Lost close and "doubtful" decision to Stanford opponent.)
A.L. Picetti (115 lbs) Knocked out his Stanford opponent.
Harold C. Whittlesey (125 lbs) Knocked out his Stanford opponent.

1920
Jimmy Doolittle - Colonel James Doolittle, Led the B-25 WWII described in "30 Seconds Over Tokyo" Bombing (April 18, 1942). Later awarded Congressional Medal of honor.
Sol Silverman - Supported "Cal Boxing" for more than 50 years.

1921
Milton Aftergut (Heavyweight)
Abe Rubin
Sol Silverman
James "Crip" Toomey

1922
Milton Aftergut
R.T. Crowley
Ben Einzig
O.J. Long
W.K. Robinson
Abe Rubin
Sol Silverman, Team Captain
Forrest Theiss
James "Crip" Toomey

1923
Coach Stanley Jones "Former phenomenal Favorite of the Middleweight Ring" Team 4-0, "captured the California Intercollegiate Championship"
R. Bowers
R. Caldwell
F. Garner
Kenneth Gow
Errol Jones - Cal Team unanimously resisted and overcame Stanford's attempt to ban "Negro" fighter from Tournament.

J. Moran
J. O'Donnell
S. Quackenbush
G. Reed
Abe Rubin
Sol Silverman, Captain
Irving Stone (Famous author of Biographical Novels, including "Lust for Life," "Clarence Darrow for the Defense" and "The Agony and the Ecstacy."
Forrest Theiss
T. Thompson

1924
Coach Stanley Jones
Sam Gold - 20-0 record at Cal, 1924-1927 undefeated. Attended many Cal fights over the years. Lawyer in Oakland for 64 years. (See "Sam Gold" story.) Attended 2004 reunion 80 years after he'd boxed for CAL.
Kenneth Gow
Errol Jones
J. Moran
J. O'Donnell

1925
Coach Stanley Jones
Raymond Bowers
Glen Cherry
Sam Gold (175 lbs)
Lewis Lecara
William Meadows
Lestor Rapheld
Bob Toby\

1926
Coach Stanley Jones
Glen Cherry
Sam Gold
Captain Bob Tobey - "Knocked out all 4 opponents," Champion

1927
Coach, Stanley Jones
Glen Cherry - Intercollegiate Champion
Germino
Sam Gold - Team captain 1927, undefeated in 20 fights
Grossman
George Iserquin (119 lbs)
Norman Kobayashi (112 lbs)
Lew Lecara (Became Alameda County Superior Court Judge)
Parish
Frank Ribbel (192 lbs) (Later became Coach) (Team won Pacific Intercollegiate Meet)
Rodriguez

1928
Coach Stanley Jones
Frank Ribbel, (147 lbs) Captain, "Pacific Coast Champion"
George Iserquin (119 lbs)
Norman Kobayashi (112 lbs)
Francis Kearney (129 lbs)
Varnum Paul (134 lbs)
Harry Ruby (134 lbs)
George Sherwood (160 lbs)
Lynwood Spier (160 lbs)

1929
Coach Stanley Jones
Merle Ansberry (119 lbs) 2nd Place, Pacific Coast Conference
Ted Beckett (Hvy) 2nd Place, Pacific Coast Conference
Leslie Bryant (164 lbs)
Enrico Dell'Osso (139 lbs)
Al Dubecker
George Garner (175 lbs) Pacific Coast Conference champion
Dwight Gribben (160 lbs) Pacific Coast Conference champion
Wilbur Kindig (139 lbs)
Andy Miller (middleweight)
Ed Nemir (126 lb, 2nd Place, Pacific Coast Conference)
Nystrum
Frank Ribbel (149 lb, Captain)
George Sherwood (160 lbs)

1930
Coach Stanley Jones
Merle Ansberry (119 lbs) Pacific Coast Conference champion
Al Cahn (175 lbs)
Dadigian
Davis
Gerald Easterbrooks
George Garner (175 lbs)
Garrity
Dwight Gribben (160 lbs) Captain
Ken Hargrove – practiced family medicine in Berkeley
Hilton
Hotopp
John Jan
Jones
Wilbur Kindig (139 lbs)
James McDonald
MacMillan
Magid
Milo Mallory
McGrath
Ed Nemir (Champion Pacific Coast Conference) (Also intercollegiate wrestling champion, won silver medal at 134 lbs in 1932 Olympics)
Nystrom
Charle Pacagnella
Ben Robinson (Hvy, Pacific Coast Conference Champion)
Searle
George Sherwood (149 lbs)
Earl Stevens
Walters
Valentine

1931
Coach Stone
Dadigian
Davis
Easterbrooks
Garrity
Hilton
Hotopp
Jones (Coach)
MacMillan
Magid
Milo Mallory
McGrath
Nystrum
Ben Robinson
Searle
Earl Stevens (Captain)
Walter Stone (Coach)
(Ed Nemir was also Assistant Coach of the Wrestling Team)
Valentine
Walters

1932
Ed Nemir in photo of Boxing Team - went on to win Silver Olympic Medal in wrestling, 1932.
John Jan
Don Smith (Captain)
Earl Stevens

1933
Nemir (Coach)
Boucher
Dagdigian
DeRisi
Marshall Elvin (Father of Ken Elvin)
Stanley Gouland
Hogle
John Jan (Captain)(Conference Champion)
Louie
Mandels
Mazetta
Mierback
Earl Mitchell
Moon
Shigeo Nitta
Mario Pozzo (Conference Champion)
Pyles (Manager)
Don Smith (Conference Champion)
George Thurston
Townsley

1934
Coach Ed Nemir
Ken Butler
James Castle (Lost one fight)
William Frances
Shigeo Nitta (Lost one fight)
Stan Shell (Undefeated in dual meets)
Charles Tatum
George Henry Thurston (Undefeated in Season)
Andy Wallstrum (Knockout year)

1927-1934 (others listed by Ed Nemir)
Joe Hillman
Sanborn Kearney
Sanford Kearney
Eugene Lamb
Mario Pozzo
Walter Stone
Marc Swinney
Robert Thorpe
Glen Cherry
Earl Stevens
Lin Speier

1935
Coach Ed Nemir
Rudolph Henry Bode
Ernest Boucher
Ken Butler
Robert B. Carlton
James Castle
Haig Dagdigian
Earl Dakan
Stanley E. Goulard
William Raymond L'Hommidieu
Mandle Mierbach
Earl Brewster Mitchell
Al Moody
Shigeo Nitta
Fred H. Offerman
Stanley C. Ruopp
Don Smith
Charles E. Tatum
George Henry Thurston
Richard F. Westdahl

1936
Coach Ed Nemir
Gene Auburn (155 lbs)
Neil Armstrong (165 lbs)
Beryl Boyce (147 lbs)
Buck Brancis (175 lbs)
Paul Cho (120 lbs) Pacific Coast Champion
Elwood "Dick" Derr (135 lbs) Worked for Shell Oil Company as a chemical engineer. Lived in Pleasant Hill and Texas.
Joseph DeRisi (165, 175 lbs)
Phil Duggan (147 lbs)
Ben Fisher (126 lbs)
William "Buck" Frances (175 lbs)
Dick Glendinning (135 lbs)
Don Heron (147 lbs)
Ed Luker (155 lbs)
Stan Massie (147 lbs)
Jim McDowell (Hvy) Worked as a dentist in San Francisco
Art Morimitsu (118 lbs) (Second in National Finals)
Dick Smith (155 lbs)
John Sprague (147 lbs)
John Storch (126 lbs)
Vin Stratton (135 lbs)
Jack Schweizer (135 lbs)
Perry Thomas (Hvy)
Andy Wallstrum (147, 156 lbs) (Captain) (Was principal at Santa Rosa High School and close friend of Eddie Nemir.)

1937
Coach Ed Nemir
Gene Auburn (155 lbs)
Dick Derr (129) (PCC champion, Semi-Finalist in Nationals)
Tom Folsom (145 lbs)
Dick Glendenning (125, 139 lbs) Worked for CALTRANS and designed the parkway south of San Francisco
Don Heron (135 lbs)
Kai Kim (115 lbs)
Homer Mead (165 lbs) (Semi-finalist in Nationals)
Ralph Milleron (155 lbs)

Pease
Jack Schweizer (139 lbs)
Stan Shell (175 lbs) (Semi-finalist in Nationals)
Dick Smith (155 lbs)
Jesse Swan
Perry Thomas (Hvy)
Andy Wallstrum (145 lbs) (Captain) (Runner up Pacific Coast Collegiate Champion)
(Note: Derr, Mead and Shell were semi-finalists in National Championship.)

1938
Coach Ed Nemir
Gene Auburn (145 lbs)
Paul Cho (115 lbs) 2nd in PCC
Joel Droubay (145 lbs)
Forrest Dubois (Hvy)
Bob Feist (135 lbs)
Dick Glendenning (125 lbs)
Rolfe Hagan (165 lbs)
Jim Henderson (125 lbs)
Don Herron (135 lbs)
Herb Kalman (145 lbs)
Wilson Lord (145 lbs)
James McDowell (175 lbs)
Homer Mead (Captain) (165 lbs) 2nd in PCC
Jesse Swan (Undefeated) (155 lbs)

1939
Coach Ed Nemir
Tye Barre (165 lbs)
Paul Cho (120, 129 lbs) 1st P.C.C.
Milt Cunha (170 lb – Exh)
John Drachnik (135 lbs)
Joel Droubay (145 lbs)
Forest Dubois (Hvy)
Frank Goble (135 lb – Exh)
John Hennessy (145 lbf – Exh)
Wilson Lord (155 lbs)
James McDowell (175, Hvy)
Ron Mathews (Hvy)
Homer Mead (165 lbs) 2nd in PCC
Earl Mittler (135 lbs)
John Nielsen (145 lbs)

George Sakanari (127 lbs)
George Shipley
Jesse Swan (155 lbs)

1940
Coach Ed Nemir
Tye Barre (165 lbs)
Milton Cunha (165 lbs)
Joel Droubay (145 lbs)
Bill Ehmcke (127 lbs)
Don Flaherty (127 lbs)
William Bob Foster (127 lbs)
Abe Fuji (135 lbs)
Ray Greenwood (175 lbs)
Yoshio Handa (120 lbs)
Ewald Larson
Bob McEvilly (155 lbs)
Everett Ben Mitchell (155 lbs)
Eddie Roberts (135 lbs)
Jack Rogers (120 lbs)
George Warton (Hvy)
Len Woolams

1941
Coach Ed Nemir
Herb Bagley (145 lbs)
Milt Cunha (165 lbs) 1st PCC
Vic Cain (155 lbs)
Bill Ehmcke (127 lbs)
Don Flaherty (127 lbs)
Chris Fox (155 lbs)
Ray Greenwood (175 lbs)
Ewald Larson (135 lbs)
Bob McEvilly (145 lbs)
Dave Rodgers (165 lbs)
Jack Rogers 2nd PCC
Eddie Roberts (135 lbs) 2nd PCC
Robert Shimoff (120 lbs)
Ron Slater (127 lbs)
Gene Smith (155 lbs)
Jack Thorburn (Hvy) 2nd PCC

1942
Coach Ed Nemir
Robert Adams (135 lbs)
Milt Cunha (165 lbs) (Twice Pacific Coast Champion. Killed in WWII. The UC Boxing Club set up the Cunha Trophy Award for best intramural fighter.)
Bill Eastin (145 lbs)
Bill Gimbel (135 lbs)
Ray Greenwood (175 lbs)
Jack Kenney (175 lbs)
Ewald Larson (127 lbs)
Seymour Lewis (155 lbs)
Bob McEvilly (145 lbs)
Roy Shaw (135 lbs)
Bob Shimoff (120 lbs)
Merrick Taylor (175 lbs)
Shiro Tokuno (135 lbs)
Bob Torney (155 lbs)
Robert Shimoff (120 lbs)
Jack Thorburn (Hvy)

1943
Coach: Tom Cureton
Donald Bell
Gordon Brittle
Bob Broxholme
Ray Cerles
Brunel Christensen (Hvy)
Gus Clarke (127 lbs)
Jim Cuthbertson
Bill Fothergill
Kong Go
Paul Hillinger
Andy McKelvy (145 lbs)
Clifford Misener
Donald Quinn
Dick Shoenig
Bob Torney
Paul Ward
Jim Wigton

1944
Coach: Tom Cureton
Asst Coach: Tony Pia
Manager: Donald Bell
Gus Clark
Brunel
Mansfield Clinnick
Myron Close
Robert Cole
Hugh Curtis
Walt Fiedler
Richard Grouix
Donald Love
Elias Long
Harry Martens
Bill Nourse
Floyd Pettit
Haden Reinecker
Walter Reinholdt
Thomas Stuelpnagel
Harold Walt
Louis Weldman
John Wise
William Young

1945
Coach: Tom Cureton
Homer Anderson (127 lbs)
Bill Bartley (165 lbs)
Jack Bishop (135 lbs)
Eldon Crump
Joe Grothus (Heavyweight)
Thomas Greathouse (155 lbs)
Bob Howard (145 lbs)
Harold Kelton
John Laughlin (145 lbs)
Dick Lovette
Bill Nash (175 lbs)
Al Nies (145 lbs)
Thomas Stuelpnagel
Charles Welby
Bob Whited

1946
Coach Tom Cureton (till March 1, when Ed Nemir, the "prewar" coach, returned after WWII.)
Del Bartley
Chew
William Fray

Harle
Bob Howard (Co-Captain)
Moore
Bill Nash (Co-Captain)
Shafer
Bill Shaw
Symonds
Walkotte
Walsh
Paul Ward
Charles Welby

1947 (See Team Photo page 19)
Coach Ed Nemir
Del Bartley (165 lbs)
Glen Buell (175 lbs)
Phil Booth (135 lbs)
Matt Brady (145 lbs)
Herb Bruce
Rod Doerr
Gordon Doke (175 lbs)
George Domaz
Jim Doss (155 lbs)
James Enemark (155 lbs)
Ed Farris - Close friend of Ed Nemir's; 2 Nemir letters to Ed in this book.
William Fray (155 lbs)
Harry Galloway (155 lbs)
John Grennan - Continued to attend Cal boxing matches even after disabled and used wheelchair.
Bill Hight (165 lbs)
James Johns
John Keliiaa
Howard Koch (165 lbs)
Don Koors (135 lbs)
Jack Lamke (175 lbs)
Charles Laswell (Hvy)
Bob Lustig (135 lbs)
Alex Markoff (175 lbs)
Jim Martin – (165 lbs) Supported Cal boxing long after graduating; successful lawyer.
Pete Miller (145 lbs)
Leland Sapiro (130 lbs)
Harry Schultze (Hvy)
Warren Simmons (145 lbs) 2nd PCC

(Outstanding boxer, who later developed "Pier 39" in San Francisco, was founder of the Chevy's Mexican restaurant chain, a commercial airline pilot for 20 years. He attended the 2004 Cal Boxer Reunion at the age of 77.)
Bud Smith
Irv Tucker
Hal Walt (165 lbs)
Paul Ward (125 lbs)
Scrap Zalba (135 lbs)

1948
Coach Ed Nemir
Herb Bruce (Hvy)
Rod Doerr (135 lbs)
Jim Doss (155 lbs)
Ed Farris (145 lbs)
John Grennan (135 lbs)
Henry Harvey (155 lbs)
Jim Johnston (170, 175 lbs)
John Keliiaa
Jack Lamke (165 lbs)
Jim Martin (175 lbs)
Pat Mower (126 lbs)
Arnold Pagano
Leland Sapiro (125 lbs)
Harry Schultze (Hvy)
Bill Shaw (155 lbs)
Warren Simmons (145 lbs)
Walt Smith (135 lbs)
Irv Tucker
John Wallace (175 lbs)
Harold "Hal" Walt
Paul Ward (Manager)
Scrap Zalba (135 lbs)

1949
Coach Ed Nemir
Del Bartley (175 lbs)
Rod Doerr (135 lbs)
John Emerson (175 lbs)
Ed Farris (145 lbs) (Close friend of Ed Nemir, see his 1965 letters from Ed Nemir, later in this book.)
Harry Galloway (165 lbs)
Ed Griffin (135 lbs)
John Groff (Hvy)
Jim Handel (125 lbs)
Henry Harvey (155 lbs)
Doug Keith (145 lbs)
Dick Knesevitch (155 lbs)
Jack Lamke (175 lbs)
Bob Lustig (140 lbs)
Pat Mower (130 lbs)
Augie Ong (120 lbs)
John Parham (125 lbs)
Leland Sapiro (130 lbs)
Bill Sapsis (145 lbs)
Irv Tucker (165 lbs)
Dick Tullsen (Hvy)
Manley Wu

1950
Coach Ed Nemir
Del Bartley (175 lbs)
Paxton Beale (Hvy)
Vic Corbett (175 lbs) won Cunha intramurals award in fall
Fore
Emmett Forrester
Ed Griffin (135 lbs)
John Groff (Hvy)
Jim Handel (125 lbs) (Fought in 1972 Alumni Bout; Outboxed Cal Varsity fighter 20 years younger.)
Henry Harvey (155 lbs)
Bruce Jahnke (165 lbs)
Doug Keith (145 lbs) (Came to Cal Boxing meets many years after he graduated.)
Bill Kitchin (175 lbs)
Dick Knezovich (155 lbs)
Pat McNulty
John Parham (130 lbs)
Bob Rouse (135 lbs)
Leland Sapiro (135 lbs)
Bill Sapsis (145 lbs)
Randy Stoke (165 lbs)
Cap Thompsen (145 lbs)
Bruno Torreano (145 lbs)
Dick Tullsen (Hvy)
Williams
Witter
Scrap Zalba (135 lbs)

1951
Coach Ed Nemir
Pax Beale (Heavyweight) 2nd PCI (Only loss to Ed Sanders, 1952 Olympic Gold Medal Champion; Famed athlete)(Also played football; body building champion in his 60s. Author of "Body For The Ages." Still going strong in 2015, 65 years after he fought for Cal and played football.)
Canady
Don Clausen (178 lbs)
Emmett Forester (126, 135 lbs)
Ed Griffin
Jim Handel (125 lbs)
Myron Hansen (155 lbs)
Ken Hansen (130, 132 lbs) 2nd PCI
Henry Harvey (165 lbs)
Art Hillman (156 lbs)
Bill Kitchen
Carl Koenig (178 lbs)
McBeath
Jim McCann (155 lbs)
McCrady
Paul Petruzelli (165 lbs)
George Pelonis (175) 2nd PCI, went to NCAA, won Cunha intramurals award
Dick Quarente (155 lbs)
Bill Sapsis (145 lbs) Went to NCAA
Ed Sato (125 lbs)
Fred Sheiman (165 lbs)
Jay Slaybough (147 lbs)
Bruno Torreano (135, 145 lbs)
Dick Tullsen (Heavyweight)
Witter

1952
Coach Ed Nemir
Don Clawson (178 lbs)
Al Dutra (148 lbs)
Emmett Forrester (132 lbs)
Max Gutierrez (139 lbs)
Ken Hansen (132 lbs)
Myron Hansen (139 lbs)
Art Hillman (165 lbs)
Karl Koenig (178 lbs)
Bill Lamont
Ray Lyon
Jim McCann (156 lbs)
Floyd McFarland (178 lbs)
McKalip
Ed Sato (119, 125 lbs)
Fred Shieman (165 lbs)
Jay Slaybaugh (147 lbs) winner of Cunha intramural award in fall of 1951
Dick Tullsen (Hvy)
Vin Young (156 lbs)

1953
Coach Ed Nemir
Cain (132 lbs)
Clarence Champlin (147 lbs)
Al Dutra
Don Gercich- winner of Cunha intramural award in December 1952
Max Guiterrez
Ken Hansen (132 lbs) 2nd PCI
Myron Hansen (139 lbs)
Nelson "Skip" Hansen (132 lbs)
Phil Ishimaru (125 lbs)
Dick King (Hvy) 2nd PCI
Dick Londahl (139 lbs) 2nd PCI
Gene Markley (147, 155 lbs)
Jim McCann (156 lbs)
Floyd McFarland (175 lbs)
Klavs Mortimer (139 lbs)
Fred Shieman (165, 175 lbs) 2nd NCAA
Jay Slaybaugh (147 lbs)
Don Wilson (Hvy)
Vin Young (165 lbs)

1954
Coach Ed Nemir
Dave Ackerman (Hvy)
Jerry Ambinder (Hvy)
Gary Fulbright (147 lbs)
Alan Galbreath (132 lbs)
Leo Gaspardone (132 lbs)
James Green (125 lbs) 2nd in PCI
Len Isabelle (178 lbs)
Phil Ishimaru (125 lbs)
Dick King (Hvy) (2nd in PCI)
Dick Londahl (139 lbs)
Gene Markley (155 lbs)
Bob Nelson (125 lbs)
Andy Paisal (139 lbs)
James Smith
Gary Smook (139 lbs)
Henry Van Galen (156 lbs)
Vin Young (165 lbs)

1955
Coach Ed Nemir
Gaston de Prat Gay (139 lbs)
Steve Dimeff (Hvy)
Ed Fong (125 lbs)
Gary Fulbright (147 lbs)
Leo Gaspardone (132 lbs)
Phil Ishimaru (125 lbs)
Don Jones (139 lbs)
Jim Lackery (178 lbs)
Don Morton (155 lbs)
Bill Neufeld (165 lbs)
George Pelonis (178 lbs) (2nd NCAA Finalist)
Ivan Polk (147 lbs)
Al Torres (125 lbs)
Don Wilson (165 lbs)

1956
Coach Ed Nemir
Bill Anderson (147 lbs)
Pat Bromfeld
Herb Davis (156 lb, Cunha Trophy as "Best Boxer in Intramurals")(Described by Ed Nemir as "one of the cleverest boys on the squad.")
Gaston de Prat Gay (139 lbs)

George Eshoo
Bob Ettinger (167 lbs)
Gary Fulbright (147 lbs)
Leo Gaspardone (132 lbs) (Team Captain)
Terrance "Kayo" Hallinan (Heavyweight, 178 lbs) Two term District Attorney (elected) of San Francisco; son of legendary lawyer and Progressive Party politician Vincent Hallinan; brother of Cal fighter and later criminal defense lawyer Patrick "Butch" Hallinan.
Patrick "Butch" Hallinan (165 lbs)- Excellent criminal defense lawyer framed on bogus drug charges by Federal Authorities in Nevada, but found "not guilty" by a jury.
Dick Homuth (156 lbs)
Bill Hotchkiss (178 lbs)
Clarke Ide (132 lbs)
Del Krause
Mike McPherson (Heavyweight)
Sam Moreno (126 lbs)
Gordon Morrow (160 lbs)
Don Nemir (Hvy)
George Pelonis (178 lbs) First PCI, Lost controversial NCAA semifinals fight. Reputed to be one of Ed Nemir's best boxers. Marty Sammon (still a referee and judge of boxing, Fought Pelonis in a 1956: "Before the fight, both Pelonis and I were undefeated; after the fight, Pelonis was still undefeated."
Jerry Pimentel
Don Ricci (147 lbs)
Floyd Salas (165, 178 lbs) (Helped as an assistant Cal Coach for next 40 years! Also noted novelist and poet. A self-proclaimed "figher-writer."
Gary Smook (139 lbs)
Eddy Tanaka (126 lbs)
Paul Tilden (Hvy)
Charles Turner (125 lbs) ("Chuck" also helped with 60s teams.)
Don Wilson (165 lbs)

1957
Coach Ed Nemir
Al Adams (147 lbs)
Klaus Arons (132 lbs)
Bill Anderson (147 lbs)
Pat Brownfield (147 lbs)
John William Buckman (147 lbs)
Herb Davis (165lbs, Team Captain) (See his story in 1956-1957 pages.) (Has kept "boxing blog" for many years. Still active Alumni, team supporter in 2016.)
Charles Duncan (Hvy)
Bob Ettinger (165, 178 lbs)
Leo Gaspardone (132 lbs)
Patrick "Butch" Hallinan (156 lbs)
Terrance "Kayo" Hallinan (Heavyweight and 178 lbs)
Dick Homuth (156 lbs)
Clark Ide (139 lbs)
Mike McPherson (Hvy)
Sam Moreno (125 lbs) (Had boxed at UCLA previously.)(Took over as coach during Ed Nemir's serious illness) (See photo from 1988 reunion page 269.)
Don Nemir (Heavyweight)
Carl Charles (Jim) Vogt (156 lbs)

1958
Coach Sam Moreno (Coached team during Ed Nemir's illness.)
Al Adams (147 lbs)
Klaus Arons (132 lbs)
Patrick Brownfield (139 lbs)
John Buckman
Bob Ettinger (165 lbs)
Patrick "Butch" Hallinan - Excellent criminal defense lawyer, framed on bogus drug charges by Federal Authorities in Nevada, but found "not guilty" by a jury.

Terrance "Kayo" Hallinan (Heavyweight, 178 lbs) Two term District Attorney (elected) of San Francisco; son of legendary lawyer and Progressive Party politician Vincent Hallinan; brother of Cal fighter and later criminal defense lawyer Patrick "Butch" Hallinan.
Bill Holliman (139 lbs)
Richard Homuth (156, 165 lbs)
Don Kennady
Ken Kofman (125 lbs)
Andy Lockwood (178, Hvy lbs) (Charles A. Lockwood)
Donald "Pat" Newell
Bill Neufeld (178 lbs) (Captain)
Jack Oakie
Andy Paisal
Forrest Price
Don Ricci
Dick Sikora
Ernie Solomon
Doug Tavmann
Fred Weaver (175 lbs)
Ron Westburg (178, Hvy lbs)

1959
Coach Ed Nemir
Al Adams
Bill Anderson (139 lbs)
Henry Lewis Augustine (125 lbs)
Bob Bechtel (165 lbs)
John "Jack" Domich (Hvy) went to Nationals
Chuck Eastman
Kenneth Duane Geil (156, 165 lbs)
Patrick "Butch" Hallinan - Excellent criminal defense lawyer, framed on bogus drug charges by Federal Authorities in Nevada, but found "not guilty" by a jury.
Terrance "Kayo" Hallinan (178 lbs) went to Nationals
(Both Hallinans contacted state officials to force Reno Hotel to rent a room to the only black fighter on the 1959 team.)
Bill Harrison (Was drafted into army in 1960, later terrific Asst. Coach 1963-1966)
Bill Holliman (132 lbs)

Don Kennady
Jim Moody (178 lbs)
Don Ricci (156 lbs) (Went to Nationals in 1959)
Shiori Sakamoto (119 lbs)
Jim Sontag
Gordon Van Kessel (Two time CCBC Champion) (147 lbs) (Became Hastings law professor.) Winner of Cunha intramurals award.
Fred Weaver (165 lbs)
Warren Widener (139, 147 lbs)
John Wylie (165 lbs)

1960
Coach Ed Nemir
Al Adams (156 lbs)
Robert Brosamer
Tobey Cornsweet
Larry Costa
John "Jack" Domich (Hvy)
Chuck Eastman (156 lbs)
Jim Hagedorn (147 lbs) winner of Cunha intramurals award
Mike Huffman (132 lbs)
Joe Kapp
Jack Kawamoto (125, 132 lbs)
Don Kennady (156 lbs) (Later a referee and boxing judge)
Roger Kent
Kerry Kiltbride (132 lbs)
Bill MacAdam (Worked Paul Rein's corner in Fall 1961 Intramural Championship. Became a Superior Court Judge in San Diego.)
Dave McCollough
Dennis Natali (CCBC Champ)(Top San Francisco criminal defense lawyer and close friends with District Attorney Terrence "Kayo" Hallinan.)
Pat Newell (Hvy)
Ed O'Dea (139 lbs)
Don Ricci (156 lbs) 1st CCBC, went to Nationals
Michael Roback
Shiori Sakamoto
Jim Sontag (Hvy)

Archie Sweeney (147 lbs)
Kent Thompson (178 lbs)
Dennis Treadway
Gordon Van Kessel (147 lbs) went to Nationals
Fred Weaver (178 lbs) went to Nationals
John Wylie (165 lbs) 2nd CCBC

1961
Toby Cornsweet
Larry Costa (147 lbs)
Clark Dooley (Heavyweight - CCBC Champion)
Jack Kawamoto (125, 132 lbs)
Don Kennady (156, 165 lbs)
Roger Kent (160 lbs)
Bill MacAdam (147, 156 lbs) (Worked Paul Rein's corner in Fall 1961 Intramural Championship)
(Became a Superior Court Judge in San Diego.)
Dennis McCullough (156 lbs)
Dennis Natali (139, 147 lbs) (CCBC Champion) (4 year Letterman) (Top San Francisco criminal defense lawyer and close friends with District Attorney Terrence "Kayo" Hallinan.)
Stew Nyholm (125 lbs)
Don Ricci (156 lbs CCBC Champion) 4 year letterman
Shiori Sakamoto (125 lbs)
Dennis Treadway (139 lbs) winner of Cunha intramurals award
Gordon Van Kessel (147 lbs) (1961 CCBC Champion
Fred Weaver (178 lbs)
John Wylie (165 lbs)

1962
Coach Ed Nemir
Roger Baker (147)
Don Bell (178 lbs)
Tom Bulgin (125 lbs)
Larry Costa (147 lbs)
James Digrazia 132 lbs)
Mike Huffman (132 lbs)
Willie Kelley (156 lbs)
Roger Kent (165 lbs)

Bill MacAdam (156 lbs)
Dennis Natali (139 lbs) 1st CCBC
Cliff Surko (125 lbs)
Dennis Treadway (139, 147 lbs)
Gordon Van Kessel (147 lbs)(Became Hastings Law Professor)
Dave Weiner (147 lbs)
John Phelan (Cunha intramurals award winner 1961, Fall)

1963
Coach Ed Nemir
Paul Alpert (132 lbs)
Bob Arevalo (132 lbs)
Bill Corrigan
Tom Drewek (Heavyweight) (Also Heavyweight wrestler.)
Tom Gioseffi (147 lbs Conference Champion and Outstanding Boxer Award)
Max Levine (Heavyweight)
Dave Licata
Brian Loveman (125 lbs)
Rod Marraccini (178 lbs)
Jim Moore (165, 178 lbs) (co-winner of Cunha intramurals award)
Dennis Natali (139 lbs)
John Parks (165 lbs)
Paul Rein (156 lbs)
Steve Ricketts (139, 147 lbs) (co-winner of Cunha intramurals award)
Terry Timmons (156, 165 lbs)
Josh Tofield (125 lbs)
Dennis Treadway (139, 147 lbs) (Undefeated and CCBC Champion)
Frank Welsh (Heavyweight, also top heavyweight on wrestling team)
Dave Weiner (147 lbs)

1964
Coach Ed Nemir
John Barnard (139 lbs)
Paul "Chip" Bell (132 lbs)
Bill Corrigan(139 lbs)
Tommy Gioseffi (Went from 147 lbs up to 156 lbs, undefeated, 3 time CCBC Champion. Twice CCBC Outstanding Boxer. Eventual

college record was 22-1-1.)
Kunia Inoue (125 lbs)
Jerry Knapp (178 lbs)
Larry Lusardi (156 lbs)
Rod Marraccini (178 lbs) (Courageous fighter who stayed on team despite multiple broken noses; wore catchers mask when sparring in practice for this reason.)
Jim Moore (165 lbs)
Dave Newhouse (172, 178 lbs)
Lee Phillips (139 lbs)
Paul Rein (165 lbs) (4 wins, 2 draws in dual meets 1964, 165 lbs "dual meet" Champion; Fought out of weight division (172 lbs) in 1964CCBC Tournament, Lost split decision in Reno to Nevada's Joe Curry. Beat Nevada's champion and football hero, John McSweeny, at 165 lbs, in Reno, on points. A great, bloody fight. Undefeated Champion in 1965 (7-0). Disability rights lawyer.)
Dave Weiner (147 lbs) (Gutty fighter and all around athlete. Sons and daughters became All-American athletes.
Bob Winter (Hvy) (Excellent heavyweight fighter who dropped out of Cal after 1964 Free Speech Movement demonstrations, etc., so didn't box for 1965 team. Kept fighting in Golden Gloves, Knocked down George Foreman in 1967, but lost decision. (Foreman won 1968 Olympic Heavyweight Gold Medal. Winter was the only fighter to knock down Foreman until Mohammad Ali did so in Zaire, 1974.)
Don Worden (147 lbs)

1965
(Team won 6 of 9 CCBC Championships. Three fighters were undefeated.)
Coach: Ed Nemir
Asst Coach: Bill Harrison
Asst Coach: Gordon Van Kessel
Paul "Chip" Bell (132 lbs) (CCBC Champ)
Dale Chamblin (125 lbs) (Supported college boxing long after he graduated, became judge and referee.)
Pete Cowan (139 lbs) (CCBC Champ)

Walt Cunningham (Heavyweight)
Tom Gioseffi (156 lbs) (Undefeated 1965, CCBC Champion and Outstanding Boxer in tournament. CCBC Outstanding Boxer Award twice, in 1963 and 1965, 3 time CCBC Champion, 22-1-1 record over 3 years, only loss and draw to Skip Houk of Nevada, but came back to beat Houk in Championship finals (1963). In 1964, Houk won outstanding Boxer Award, fighting at 147 lbs, while Gioseffi won at 156 lbs, in 1964 and 1965. In 2008, Tom Gioseffi became first boxer to be inducted into Cal Athletics Hall of Fame.)
Terry Holberton (165 lbs) (Outstanding boxer in Intramurals.)
Jerry Knapp (180 lbs) (Undefeated 1965, CCBC Champion at 178 lbs)
Ray Kropp (178 lbs)
Dave Newhouse (172 lbs)
Jerry Olson (147 lbs)
Lee Phillips (139 lbs)
Paul Rein (165 lbs) (7-0 record in 1965 Senior Year) Knocked out Tony Schuler of Nevada (Schuler became 1966 CCBC Champ) and knocked out Mike Jones of Chico, who had, in a previous bout, knocked out Cal's Terry Holberton) (In CCBC Finals at Cal, decisioned Riley Becket of Nevada and Mike Jones of Chico, to win CCBC Championship.)
Tim Rodgers (139 lbs)
John Sobczyk
Phil Walson (125 lbs) (CCBC Champ) (Also on Cal wrestling team.)
Don Worden (147 lbs)

1966
Coach: Ed Nemir
Asst. Coach: Bill Harrison
Dave Archibald (172 lbs) (A strong fighter, after being a top national track star at 400 and 800 meters; Admitted to Cal Athletic Hall of Fame as track runner in 2008, at same ceremony as Tom Gioseffi - see page 131)
Paul Bell (132 lbs)

Dale Chamblin (125 lbs) 1st CCBC
Pete Cowan (139 lbs) 1st CCBC
Walt Cunningham (Hvy)
John Harder (156 lbs) (Also a wrestler)
Freeman Harris (139 lbs)
Rich Hill (172 lbs)
Ray Kropp (180 lbs) 1st CCBC
Mike Jay (125 lbs) (Won Fall, 1965 Intramural Championship, on decision over Steve Rein.)
Greg Monahan (156 lbs) (2nd in CCBC)
Jim Moore (165 lbs)
Dave Newhouse (172 lbs) (CCBC Champion)
Tim Rodgers (147 lbs)
Bob Sakai (132 lbs)
Steve Spreiter (Hvy)
Bruce Tichinin (165 lbs)
Dick Weinbrandt (156 lbs) (Remained loyal supporter and contributor to Cal Boxing Team and Cal Boxing Club for many years.)

1967
Coach: Ed Nemir
Dick Carter
Dale Chamblin (125 lbs) (2nd in CCBC)
John Chappell
John Cowart
Troy Cox (180 lbs) (1st in CCBC)
Walt Cunningham (Asst. Coach)
Ron Dell'Immagine (Hvy)
Freeman Harris (139 lbs)
Bob Hink (Heavyweight)
Fred Hite (156 lbs)
Jim Hoobler (147 lbs) (1st in CCBC)
Mike Jay (125 lbs)
Webb Lloyd (180 lbs)
Paul McNally
Greg Monahan (165 lbs) (Won the December 1965 Milton T. Cunha Award as "Outstanding Boxer in the Intramural Championships") (Fought Varsity 1966-1969) (Was also Team Captain, 1967, undefeated in dual meets.) (2nd in CCBC)
Phil Nemir (139 lbs) (2nd in CCBC, Outstanding Sportsman, undefeated in dual meets) (Later Champion in 1969 and 1970.) (Later became Cal Boxing Coach and co-organizer of May 2016 reunion.)
Bill Neyland (172 lbs)
Dirk Noyes (147 lbs)
Tim Rodgers (139 lbs) (Became medical doctor.)
Bob Sakai (132 lbs) (2nd in CCBC)
Steve Spreiter (Heavyweight)
Terry Stewart (156 lbs)
Bruce Tichinin
Dick Weinbrandt (147 lbs)

1968
Coach: Ed Nemir
Ron Dell'Immagine, Asst. Coach
Rick Aftergut
John Bedri (147 lbs)
Dan Burnstein (132 lbs) (CCBC Champion)
Dick Carter (125 lbs)
Dave Clement (139 lbs)
John Chappel
James Cowart (125 lbs)
Troy Cox (172 lbs) (CCBC Champion) (Scored 5 Knockouts)
Gary Evers (139 lbs) (CCBC Champion) (Later traveled from Idaho for 2004 Boxing Reunion)
Steve Fallai (156 lbs)
John Gianaras (172 lbs)
Mike Hogan (139 lbs)
Bill Holmes (156 lbs)
Ray Koch (165 lbs)
Webb Lloyd (180 lbs) (CCBC Champion)
Paul McNally (Later coached team in 1970.)
Greg Monahan
Dirk Noyes (147 lbs)
Rod Ott (Hvy)
Sol Quintero
Mike Ramsey
John Samuelson (112 lbs)
Jeff Stewart

1969
Coach Ron Dell'Immagine after Ed Nemir's death midseason, Feb 1, 1969)
Frank Boyd Alexander (172 lbs)

Dick Carter (132 lbs)
Dave Clement (147 lbs)
James Cowart
Gary Evers (147 lbs) (CCBC Runner up)
Steve Fallai (156 lbs)
Genero "Gus" Felice (156 lbs)
John Incerti (125 lbs)
Brian Kahn (165 lbs) undefeated dual meet season
Webb Loyd (180 lbs) (Second in CCBC)
Paul McNally (172 lbs)
Greg Monahan
Phil Nemir (139 lbs CCBC Champion) (1969 & 1970; 2nd CCBC in 1967; Coach in 1977, undefeated season; co-organizer of May 2016 "100 Years of Cal Boxing Reunion."
Dirk Noyes
Rod Ott (Hvy)
Glen Takei (125 lbs)
James Walsh (156 lbs)
Kirk John Wilson (Hvy)
Dan Yamamoto (147 lbs)

1970
Coach Paul McNally
Asst Coach Dick Carter (See his article page 56)
Ted Blankenburg
Jim Cavin (160 lbs)
John Cosley (172 lbs)
Gary Evers (147 lbs) (CCBC Conference Champion)
"Gus" Felice (165 lbs)
Orb Greenwald (Hvy)
Dick Hanlon (182 lbs)
John Incerti (132 lbs)
Dale Jeong (139 lbs)
Ray Koch (165 lbs)
Dan London (156 lbs)
Tom Meriweather (156 lbs)
Phil Nemir (139 lbs) (CCBC Conference Champion, Outstanding Boxer) undefeated season, career record 15-1
Frank Roesch (125 lbs) (Later an Alameda County Superior Court Judge)
Gerald Rogers (180 lbs)
Glenn Takei (125 lbs)

Jim Walsh (156 lbs)
Dan Yamamoto (147 lbs)

1971
Coach Dick Carter (See his article in this book: "Cal Boxing's Tradition After Coach Ed Nemir.")
Asst. Coach Brian Kahn (See his article in this book: "Cal Boxing; 1968-1975")
Sam Bort
Hank Davalos
Gus Felice
Paul Giroday
Fred Gusman
John Incerti
Jeff Karp
Mike Ramsey
Scott Roberts
Sid Strickland
Stan Stanek
Glenn Takei
Rick Taylor
Jim Walsh

1972
Coach Dick Carter (See his article in this book: "Cal Boxing's Tradition After Coach Ed Nemir.")
Asst. Coach Brian
Paul Rein and Sonny Mills (Volunteer Assistant Coaches) Paul Rein (1965 Graduate at 180 lbs) fought exhibition match against 235 lb Navy District Champ)
Ray Gatchalian
Paul Giroday (Heavyweight) (Lost CCBC Championship to Nevada "Ringer," a Georgia Golden Gloves Champion.) Later played pro football. 1972 spirited exhibition v. 1965 alumni Tom Gioseffi.)
Bob Guirmarin (132 lbs)
Pat Kostiz (156 lbs)
Roy Solis (132 lbs)
Stan Stanek (Heavyweight)
Scott Stringer (Light Heavyweight)
Glenn Takai

1973
Coach Brian Kahn
Asst coach: Ken Bigham
Roger Chaverin
Ron Frazier
John Hammarley
Mel Menda
Myles O'Dwyer
Jim Russell
Scott Stringer
Chuck Walsh
John Williams (Heavyweight CCBC Champion)
    (Star Football Halfback)
Steve Zembsch

1974
Cal won CCBC Team Championship
Coach Brian Kahn
Assistant Coach: Ken Bingham
Tom Bottorf (132 lbs)
Creighton Chan (139 lbs)
Joe Lehman (145 lbs)
John McCann (180 lbs)
Ken Porto (Heavyweight)
Randy Rogers (156 lbs)
Pete Shields (165 lbs)
Ed Szacky (172 lbs)
Steve Zembsch

1975
Coach Brian Kahn
Asst Coach Ken Bigham
Tom Bottorf
Tom Bradfield (119 lbs) (CCBC Champion)
Mike Huff
Steve Zembsh

1976
Coach Ken Bigham
Asst Coach Phil Nemir
Antonio Aguirre (132 lbs)
Bob Black (Heavyweight)
Tom Bradfield (119 lbs) CCBC Champion, won
    1st NCBA East-West fight
Joe Chairez (125 lbs)
Warner Guysin (125 lbs) (Won East v. West
    Championship)
Mike Huff
Pete Lindstrom (180 lbs)
Ed Mitchell (139 lbs)
Jose Ortega (132 lbs) (Won East v. West
    Championship)
Tom Pedamonte (172 lbs)
Lyon Rathbun (156 lbs)
Bill Sandoval (139 lbs) CCBC Champion
Dave Scruggs (165 lbs)
Steve Zembsch

1977
Coach Phil Nemir
Assistant Coach Mike Huff
Mike Anast (112 lbs) CCBC Champion
Tony Aguirre (132 lbs)
Dave Bartick (139 lbs)
Sal Benevidez (156, 165 lbs)
Eric Bogin (165 lbs)
Tom Bradfield (119, 125 lbs) CCBC Champion
Larry Cheng (139 lbs)
Steve Cummins (Hvy)
Peter Howes (172 lbs)
Jay Kubakawa (125)
Dick Lee (156, 165)
Greg McIntosh (160 lbs)
Dusty Mahoney (156 lbs)
Carolos Matta (165 lbs)
Junior Matta (156 lbs)
Paul (Ambrosio) O'Neil (169 lbs)
Alan Pryor (135 lbs)
George Reyes (135 lbs)
Jim Riksheim (125 lbs)
Bill Sandoval (139 lbs)
Bruce Simon (125)
Jim Thompson (156)
John Williams (Hvy) CCBC Champion,
    undefeated regular season
Steve Zembsch (147 lbs) CCBC Champion,
    NCBA East-West fight

1978
Coach Mike Huff
Ed Arboleda (156 lbs)
Dave Bartick (139 lbs)
Sal Benevidez (156, 165 lbs)
Larry Cheng (139 lbs)

George Choulos (147 lbs) Won the Milton T. Cunha Award as the Intramural Tournament's Most Outstanding Boxer; became outstanding San Francisco trial lawyer.
Mark Copeland (132, 139 lbs)
Ben Jarvis (172 lbs)
Beau Mitchum (125 lbs) (CCBC Champ, Bronze Medal at Nationals)
Paul (Ambrosio) O'Neil (156 lbs) (See his 1977-1978 story "LA Road Trip")
Tom Pedemonte (172 lbs)
Alan Pryor (132, 139 lbs) - Conference Champion
Charlie Price (156, 165 lbs) - Conference Champion, 2nd in Nationals
Jim Riksheim - (Conference Champion, Western Regional Champion. Kept from Nationals by a broken rib. Later Cal Coach 1982-2011 - 30 years!)
Dave Scruggs (172 lbs)
Joe Tombari (156 lbs) winner of Cunha intramurals award
John Williams (Heavyweight) (and football half back) – CCBC champion and second in Nationals)

1979
Coach Mike Huff
Ed Arboleta (156 lbs)
John Davies
Beau Mitchum (125 lbs)(CCBC Champ)
Dave Oster (112 lbs)(Qualified for Nationals Tournament in Chicago)
Tom Pedamonte (175 lbs)
Charlie Price (165 lbs)
Alan Pryor (139 lbs)
Jim Riksheim (Qualified for Nationals)
John Williams (Heavyweight)(CCBC Champion)

1980
Coach Mike Huff
Assistant Coach, Jim Riksheim
Alex Choulos (In fall, 1980 Intramural Championships, Alex won the Milton T. Cunha Award as "Outstanding Boxer.")
Pat Madden (156 lbs)
Beau Mitchum - (CCBC 125 lbs Champ) Bronze Medal at Nationals
David Oster - (112 lbs) (Conference 112 lbs Champ, 2nd in Nationals in Chicago) (Won CCBC Championship)
Tom Pedamonte (175 lbs)
Tim Potter (190 lbs)
Charlie Price (165 lbs)
Alan Pryor (139 lbs)
Jim Riksheim (Ed Nemir Award Winner)
Jeff Rubin (139 lbs, Fought in Nationals, Won Bronze Medal)

1981
Frank Delzompo (156 lbs) (CAL's "Italian Stallion") (2nd in CCBC, 2nd in Nationals NCBA (Team Captain)
Kurt Heffernon, Conference Heavyweight Champion
Dan Krishock (156 lbs)
Chris Morales (125 lbs)
Alan Pagle (139 lbs)
Raul Pardo (139 lbs)
Tim Potter (190 lbs)
Nick Radetsky (147 lbs)
Albert Sandell (180 lbs) (CCBC Champion) (and winner of the Tournament's "Most Outstanding Boxer" Award, Also won 1981 Edgar Nemir Outstanding Boxer Award
Paul Templin (190 lbs) (2nd in CCBC)
Michael Valli - (147 lbs) (Won award as "Outstanding Collegiate Boxer in the Annual Mare Island Invitational. Nicknamed "the Missle.")

1982
Co-Coach Jim Riksheim
Co-Coach Mike Huff
Assistant Coach: Floyd Salas - Novelist and Poet. (His 9th year assisting with team.)
Assistant Coach: Al Sandell
Wolfe Birkie (156 lbs)
Frank Del Zampo (156 lbs) (CCBC Champ and Team Captain)

Jim Fardeen (Team was 13-0 in individualized bouts at Harmon Gym)
Kurt Heffernon (Heavyweight) (CCBC Champ)
John Holbrook (139 lbs) (Winner of 1982 Edgar Nemir Memorial Scholarship Award)
Adlai Jourdin (180 lbs)
Craig Jordon (165 lbs)
Dennis Kehoe (147 lbs)
Chan Kim (139 lbs)
Garrell Kirtley (132 lbs) (CCBC Champ) (Regional Champ)
Norris Moore (147) (Regional Champ)
Chris Morales (125 lbs) (CCBC Champ, 2nd in Nationals)
Raul Pardo (139 lbs)
Stan Pierchoski (165 lbs)
Tim Potter (190 lbs)
Scott Rasmussen (180 lbs) (CCBC Champ; 2nd in Nationals)
John Shimmick (139 lbs)
Paul Templin (180 lbs)
Mike Valli (139 lbs) ("The Missile")

1983

Coach Jim Riksheim, Assisted by Floyd Salas, Albert Sandell, Mike Huff
Jim Riksheim started as coach (boxed 1976-1980) Novelist/Poet Floyd Salas begins his 10th year with Cal Squad as Assistant Coach. Author of "Tattoo the Wicked Cross" and "Buffalo Nickel."
Wolfe Birkie (156 lbs)
Dan Carr (172 lbs)
Jim Dedelow (137 lbs)
Jim Fardeen (165 lbs)
Heriberto Fermin (125 lbs)
Adlai Jourdin (172 lbs)
Kurt Heffernon (Heavyweight) (CCBC Champ)
Dennis Kehoe (147 lbs)
Chan Kim (119 lbs) (CCBC Champ)
Garrell Kirtley (132 lbs) (CCBC Champ, 2nd in Nationals)
Sean Mockler (156 lbs)
Norris Moore (147 lbs) (CCBC Champ)
Chris Morales (125 lbs)
Kevin Octavio (125 lbs)
Carl Orsi (165 lbs)
Raul Pardo (139 lbs)

Tim Potter
Steve Pugh (132 lbs)
Alphonso Quintor
Scott Rasmussen (190 lbs)
John Shimmick (139 lbs)
George Straggas (190 lbs)
Paul Templin (180 lbs)

1984

Coach: Jim Riksheim
National Championship Bouts held April 6-7 in Harmon Gymnasium
Dan Carr (172)
Frank Delzompo (156 lbs) Conference Champ
Jim Fardeen (165 lbs)
Heriberto Fermin (119 lbs) Conference Champ
Kurt Heffernon (National Heavyweight Champion) (Regional Champion) (WCBA Three Year Champ) (Knocked out huge opponent in first round of finals.) (Pictured on front cover after winning National Championship by knockout.)
Chris Haddawy (132 lbs) Conference Champ
Chan Kim (119 lbs)
Jack Light (147 lbs)
Chris Morales (125 lb National Champion) (Conference Champ, Outstanding Boxer Award, Became outstanding San Francisco Criminal Defense Lawyer, co-organizer of May 2016 "100 years of Cal Boxing" Reunion.)
Team took 2nd in Nationals when NCBC included more than 30 schools.

1985

Coach: Jim Riksheim
Bob Bankard (156 lbs)
Wolfe Birkie (165 lbs)
Cort Day (125 lbs)
Heriberto Fermin
Jim Fardeen (172 lbs)
Mark Fowler (156 lbs) (Outstanding Boxer Award) (CCBC Champion)
Chris Haddawy (132 lbs) Won the Eddie Nemir Memorial Award, Won WCBA Champion
Jack Light (147 lbs)
Sean Mockler (172 lbs)
Egino Penaranda (139 lbs)

Gavin Polone (156 lbs)
John Rosenthal (156 lbs)
Steve Schwartz (165 lbs)

1986
Coach Jim Riksheim, Assistant Coaches: Chris Haddawy, Floyd Salas, Sean Mockler, Tom Pedamonte, Kurt Heffernan, Jim Fardeen
Dave Cassety (132 lbs) (Winner, Ed Nemir Memorial Award)
Louie Cervantes (119)
Cort Day (125 lbs)
Bill Derrough (139 lbs)
Byron Figeroa (147 lbs)
Mark Fowler (156 lbs) (Outstanding Boxer Award at Mare Island Invitational)
Leo Oceguera (180 lbs)
Egino Peneranda (147 lbs)
Scott Robertson (139 lbs)
Matt Scanlon (147 lbs)
Bo Solis (172 lbs, 180 lbs)
John Serna (165)
Jimmy Yakota (132 lbs)

1987
Coach: Jim Riksheim; Asst Coach Sean Mockler
Dave Cassety (132 lbs, WCBA Champ, Won Ed Nemir Award, Fought in Nationals)
Bill Derraugh (139 lbs)
Byron Figeroa (147 lbs)
Mark Fowler (156 lbs, Fought in Nationals)
Ed Gordon (165 lbs, Several Knockouts)
Matt Kaufman (165 lbs)
Marty Medina (147 lbs) (K.O. win at Reno open)
Leo Ocequera (172 lbs, Nationals) (Fought Tom Gioseffi in 1989 Alumni Bouts)
Matt Scanlon (147 lbs)
Scott Robertson (139 lbs)
Bo Solis (180 lbs - Nationals)

1988
Coach: Jim Riksheim
Reunion for Ex-boxers of Ed Nemir held 10/16/88
Ed Nemir inducted into Cal Athletic Hall of Fame as Boxer, Wrestler, and Boxing Coach (1988)
Brian Bunch (139 lbs)
Dalton Conley (132 lbs)
Jason Julian (190 lbs, Fought in Nationals, WCBA Champ)(Fought Exhibition v. Paul Rein,'65, in 1989)
Matt Kaufman (156 lbs)
Eric Mims (112 lbs)
Leo Ocequera (172 lbs)
Norman Sanchez (147 lbs)
Rogelio Sandoval (119 lbs)
Karlton Shaw (Heavyweight, WCBA Champ, Fought in Nationals)

1989 Varsity V. Alumni Exhibition
Alumni v. Varsity Fundraiser, February 11, 1989
Names of Exhibitions Fighters:
Regulio Sandoval v. Chris Morales (1984 National Champ, 125 lbs)
Dalton Conley v. Dave Cassetty
Brian Bunch v. Matt Scanlon (1988 "Outstanding Boxer" Award)
James Weisberg v. Dick Carter
Matt Kaufman v. Bill Harrison
Egino Peneranda (1986 alumni) (Marine Corps Lawyer) v. Chris Haddawy (1984 National Runner up)
Jason Julian (1988 Nationals Competitor) v. Paul Rein (1965 CCBC 165 lb Champ)
Leo Ocequera v. Tom Gioseffi (1963-65 CCBC Champ, 156 lbs)

1989
Coach: Jim Riksheim
Eric Bergen (156 lbs)
Brian Bunch (139 lbs, 147 lbs)
Dalton Conley (132 lbs)
Egisto Francheschi (156 lbs)
Karim Hayath (132 lbs)
Matt Kaufman (172 lbs)
Eric Mims (112 lbs)
Norman Sanchez (147 lbs, 156 lbs)

Rogelio Sandoval (119 lbs)
Karlton Shaw (Heavyweight)
Erik French

1990
Coach: Jim Riksheim
Brian Bunch (139 lbs)
Charles Faulkner (156 lbs, 165 lbs)
Rogelio Sandoval (119 lbs)
Karlton Shaw (Heavyweight)
James Weisberg

1991
Coach: Jim Riksheim
Ray Joshua (132 lbs)
Alonzo Levington (147 lbs)
Norman Sanchez (147 lbs)
Javier Tirado (125 lbs)
Pavel Wolfbeyn (156 lbs)
Lou Zeidberg (156 lbs)

1992
Coach Jim Riksheim
Jeff Beoca (147 lbs)
George Cresson (156 lbs)
Cedric Lee (135 lbs)
Norman Sanchez ("Stormin Norman") (147 lbs)
Sanjay Shah (135 lbs)
Javier Tirado (125 lbs)
James Walker (190 lbs) (In middle of 1992 season fought exhibition bout against 1963-1965 Alumnus
Paul Rein (During 1992 Season, fought in CCBC Championships.)

1993
Coach: Jim Riksheim
Start of Women's Coach Yvonne Caples
Women's Boxing fight on same card as men, some scored, some exhibition, depending on agreement of coaches.
Chris Carmona (165 lbs)
John Fitzpatrick (125 lbs Western Conference Champ)
Albert Garcia
Nick Heredia

Walt Jang (165 lbs)
Ben Larman (147 lbs)
Cedric Lee (135 lbs)
Greg Macias (165 lbs) Western Conference Champ
Efren Olivas (180 lbs)
Hugh Pedy (156 lbs)
Sanjay Shah (135 lbs)
Rich Tang (165 lbs)
Barquay Thomas (132 lbs) (Nationals Competitor)
Javier Tirado (132 lbs)
Daniel Trinidad (139 lbs)
Manuel Varela (139 lbs)

1994
Coach: Jim Riksheim
Dan Beck (165 lbs)
Chris Carmona (180 lbs)
Roger Cheny (147 lbs)
John Fitzpatrick (125 lbs) (Conference Champ) (To Nationals)
Andrew Frank (147 lbs)
Porfirio Garcia (119 lbs) (Conference Champ) (To Nationals)
Willie Grief (139 lbs)
Shan Johnson (190 lbs)
Justin Messenheimer (156 lbs)
David Ralston (172 lbs)
Dan Sakaguchi (165 lbs)
Greg Simon (180 lbs) (Conference Champ) (To Nationals)
Borquaye Thomas (132 lbs) (Conference Champ) (To Nationals)
Lou Zeidberg (165 lbs) (To Nationals)

1995
Coach: Jim Riksheim
Jeremy Conner (156 lbs)
Josh Conner (147 lbs)
Daniel Edington (112 lbs)
Albert Garcia
Russ Hammons (156 lbs)
Nick Heredia
Alex Gotlieb (147 lbs)
Brian Kung (139 lbs)

Greg Macias (165 lbs)
Hugh Metzger (172 lbs)
Peter Wong (139 lbs)

1996
Coaches: Jim Riksheim, Sean Mockler, Tom Pedamonte
Nationals held in Reno, 1996.
Ross Berbeco (132 lbs)
John Bermudez (147 lbs)
Tom Clayton (125 lbs) (Champion) (WCBA Conference) (Fought in Nationals, lost to Fighter Awarded "Outstanding Boxer," won Bronze Medal)
Josh Conner (139 lbs) (Lost to "Joey Gilbert" of Nevada, A three time National Champ and Four Time WCBA Champ who became a professional boxer while in Law School.)
Daniel Edington (112 lbs)
Hutch Meltzer (172 lbs)
Naresh Rajan (147 lbs)
Sanjah Shah (119 lbs) (Champion, WCBA)
Mike Williamson (132 lbs)
Pete Wong (132 lbs)

1997
Coach: Jim Riksheim
Sean Mockler - Assistant Coach for 12 years.
Scott Bambacigno (172 lbs)
Colby Bryant (190 lbs)
Tom Clayton (132 lbs)
Eric Fogel (147 lbs)
Javier Hernandez (147 lbs)
Rafael Hernandez (139 lbs)
Kamal Hood (139 lbs)
William Kim (147 lbs, 156 lbs)
Cedric Lee (125 lbs) [also listed in 1993]
Chris Lee (139 lbs)
Daniel Murphy (147 lbs)
Manolo Perate (190 lbs)
Neil Rao (135 lbs)
Ahmed Abdul Rahman (139 lbs)
Clayton Schapp (172 lbs)

1998
Coach Jim Riksheim
Assistant Coach Tom Pedamonte
Scott Bambacigno (175 lbs)
Colby Barret (190 lbs)
Tom Clayton (132 lbs)
Jim Dunn (147 lbs)
Javier Hernandez (147 lbs)
Raphael Hernandez (139 lbs)
William Kim (147 lbs)
Ben Larman (156 lbs)
Cedric Lee (132 lbs)
Clayton Schapp (172 lbs)
Sanjay Shah (135 lbs)

1999
Coach: Jim Riksheim
Luis Alarcon (139 lbs)
Scott Bambacigno (180 lbs)
Javier Hernandez (147 lbs)
Walt Jang (165 lbs)
William Kim (147 lbs)
Ben Larman (147 lbs, 156 lbs)
Cedric Lee (132 lbs)
Sanjay Shah (135 lbs)
Manuel Varela (139 lbs)

Women:
Coach: Yvonne Capels (Worked to develop women's boxing team.)
Emily Abbott (132 lbs)
Aimee Kelley (132 lbs)
Mary Wang (112 lbs)

2000
Coach: Jim Riksheim,
Asst Coaches: Tom Pedamonte, Greg Pedamonte, Mark Fowler, Borquae ThomasWomen's Coach: Yvonne Capels
Kash Afshari (175 lbs)
Luis Alarcon (132 lbs)
Nick Byrd (165 lbs)
Stephen Di Grejorio (165 lbs)
Chris Draper (Heavyweight)
Walt Jang (156 lbs) (Team Captain)
Gene Kim (147 lbs)
William Kim (156 lbs)
John Murphy (Heavyweight)
David Ralston (Asst. Coach)
Manual Varela (139 lbs)

Women:
Crystal Silva (125 lbs)
Mary Wang (106 lbs)

2001
Coach: Jim Riksheim
Jamal Cherry (Heavyweight) (Also played Cal football. Later played pro football in Canada.)
Walt Jang (156 lbs)
Gene Kim (147 lbs)
Dan Lee (147 lbs)
Hwasung Lee (156 lbs)
Lee Plantmason (Heavyweight)
Abu Ramin (147 lbs)
Jake Wildberger (147 lbs)

2002
Coaches: Jim Riksheim, Tom Pedamonte, Greg Pedamonte, Jamal Valdez-Allen
Kash Afshari (172 lbs)
Nick Byrd (170 lbs)
Adam Chen (156 lbs)
Gaidi Faraj (190 lbs)
Bob Humphrey (165 lbs)
Hwasung Lee (156 lbs)
Lee Plantmason (Heavyweight)
Marc Rahlves (139 lbs)
Abu Ramin (156 lbs) (To Nationals)
Eduardo Rocha (156 lbs)
Mike Schuck (175 lbs) (To Nationals)
Stanley Shen (147 lbs)
Bill Wheeler (195 lbs) (To Nationals, Semi-Finals)
Derrick Zahler (Heavyweight) (To Nationals, Semi-Finals. Cal football player)
Jon Zaul (147 lbs) (Later Assistant Coach 2005-2006, Co-Coach 2011-2015, Coach 2015-2016)

Women:
Coach: Crystal Silva
Naseem Ehsan
Bahija Hamraz
Kimberly Hope

2003
Coaches: Jim Riksheim, Mark Lucia, Jamal Valdez-Allen
Justin Barad (Heavyweight)
Adam Chen (156 lbs)
Ricky Cheung (139 lbs)
Brandon Copeland (CCBC Champion 139 lbs) (147 lbs) (To Nationals)
Todd Gaylord (132 lbs) (2nd at Nationals) (CCBC Champion) (2003 Western Regional Champion)
Bobby Humphrey (165 lbs) (To Nationals)
Russell Kummer (132 lbs)
Hwasung Lee (156 lbs)
Chasen Queen (175 lbs)
Abu Ramin (147 lbs) (To Nationals)
Mike Schuck (175 lbs) (To Nationals)
Dikran Sevlian (205 lbs)
Bill Wheeler (195 lbs)
Jon Zaul (139 lbs) (Later Assistant Coach 2005-2006, Co-Coach 2011-2015, Coach 2015-2016)

Women:
Coach: Javier Hernandez
Naseem Ehsan
Bahija Hamraz
Kimberly Hope (156 lbs)

2004
Coaches: Jim Riksheim, Mark Lucia, Jamal Valdez-Allen
Justin Barad (195 lbs)
Bobby Bolger (185 lbs)
Gaidi Faraj (200 lbs)
Todd Gaylord (132 lbs) (2004 National Champion) (Western Regional Champion)
Mu Huang (175 lbs)
Andrew Kosel (156 lbs) Russell Kummer (135 lbs)
Josh Kuns (175 lbs)
Kevin Lee (125 lbs) Nathan Morton (165 lbs)
Abu Ramin (147 lbs)
Dikran Sevlian (195 lbs)
Andre Vasil, 156 lbs, with past Muay Thai experience "Vasil comes out, hard and fast,

in every fight." Vasil: "I have a really long left jab and I use it to set up my opponents for the left hook and straight right." Jon Zaul (139 lbs) (Later Assistant Coach 2005-2006, Co-Coach 2011-2015, Coach 2015-2016)

Women:
Leona Lanza (140 lbs)

2005
Coach: Jim Riksheim
Asst Coach: Mark Lucia
Asst Coach: Jon Zaul (Later Co-Coach 2011-2015, Coach 2016)
Eric Ari (147 lbs)
Bobby Bolger (175 lbs)
Mariano Esparza (147 lbs, 139 lbs)
Phillip Chang (135 lbs) Todd Gaylord (147 lbs) (Western Regionals Champ, beat Nevado hero Tom Gennaro) (Second at the Nationals) Joey Le (147 lbs)
Luis Martinez (135 lbs)
David Springer (125 lbs)
John Stead (195 lbs)
Jermain Waltemeyer (165 lbs, 156 lbs)
Zack White (165 lbs)
RavimWhitington (175 lbs) Adam Xu (135 lbs)

Women:
Kersten Keber (112 lbs)

2006
Coach: Jim Riksheim
Asst Coach: Mark Lucia
Asst Coach: Jon Zaul (Later Co-Coach 2011-2015, Coach 2016)
Bobby Bolger (175 lbs)
Garrick Bjur (190 lbs)
Matt Denny (132 lbs, 125 lbs)
Triniece Durst Siamac Ehsan (147 lbs)
Emmett Forester
Carlos Fuentes (185 lbs)
Henry Jones (170 lbs)
David Springer (125 lbs)
Brandon Walker (165 lbs)
Ifan Wei

2007
Coach: Jim Riksheim
Asst Coach: Mark Lucia
Reid Albano (178 lbs)
Matt Batacalan (128 lbs)
Karl Berta (Heavyweight)
Kyle Brady (147, 152 lbs)
David Bui (135 lbs)
Siamac Ehsan (156 lbs)
Todd Gaylord (147 lb Western Regionals Champ, National Champ, Beat Nevada's favorite, Thomas Genero, in Reno. Selected as the "Outstanding Boxer.")
David Keegan (139 lbs)
Scheide (147 lbs)
Zack White (165 lbs)
Finley Wise (125 lbs)

Women:
Christine Aiken (116 lbs)

2008
Coach: Jim Riksheim
Eric Allen (185 lbs) (Advanced to Nationals) Karl Berta (195 lbs) (2nd in West) (Gutty fight against Airforce Champion)
Matt Betalcan (130 lbs)
Kyle Brady (147 lbs)
Siamoe Ehsan (156 lbs) Aaron Fung (125 lbs)
David Keegan (139 lbs) (2nd in NCBA West Regionals, Always gutty fighter and later Cal Boxing Coach)
Daniel Keggan (185 lbs)
Fiorello Klein (145 lbs)
Kevin Lomeli (156 lbs)
Don Poole (185 lbs)
Daniel Reggan (185 lbs)
Hisashi Tanaka (156 lbs)
Ifan Wei (140 lbs)

Women:
Christine Aiken: 116 lb

2009
Coach: Jim Riksheim
Art Avetisyan (195 lbs) (Western Champion)
Matt Battaclan (135 lbs)
John D. Fitzpatrick (Co-Captain)
Mike Hastings (195 lbs)
David Keegan (147 lbs)
Mauricio Rangel (Heavyweight)
Dave Rosenfield (132 lbs)
Amos Song (175 lbs)
Andrew Tan (156 lbs)
Ifan Wei (139 lb) (Western Champ)

Women:
Inga Lamvick (132 lb)
Lauren Pettis (150 lbs) - Won Women's Championship with good left jab and right cross

2010
Coach: Jim Riksheim
Kyle Brady (147 lbs)
Phil Bremner (132 lbs)
Vince Ferretti (132 lbs)
John D. Fitzpatrick (Co-Captain)
Dan Keegan (185 lbs)
Keri Murphy (132 lbs)
Thuy Le (195 lbs)
David Rosenfield (132 lbs) (Team Captain) (Took 4th in Nationals)
Russell Smith (156 lbs)
Arman Syed (195 lbs)
Andrew Vasilj (156 lbs)

Women:
Kathleen Jaeger
Keri Murphy (132 lbs)
Lauren Pettis (132 lbs) (Won WCBA and National Championship) (See her interview in an article by Ryan Macquiñana on page 318.)

2011
Coaches: Jim Riksheim
Mike Hastings (185 lbs) (Team Captain)
Jose "Jay" Jimenez (156 lbs)
Ethan Mire J.C. Oveido (125 lbs)
Juan Ramos (165 lbs)
Arman Sayed Andre Vasilj (156 lbs)

Women:
Nessa Nemir, Asst. Coach
Jewell Fix

2012
Coaches: Jim Riksheim, Jon Zaul, and David Keegan
Mike Brennan
Jose Avila (139 lbs) (Boxed in NCBA West Regionals)
Michael Cardona (175 lbs) (Boxed in NCBA Regionals)
Jose Jimenez (156 lbs) (Boxed in NCBA West Regionals and earned All-American Honors at NCBA Nationals; Won Quarterfinal bout against a Penn State fighter)
Juan Ramos (165 lbs) (NCBA West Regional Champ, earned Second Place in NCBA Nationals and All-American Honors)

Women:
Jewell Fix (119 lbs) (Boxed in NCBA West Regionals) (Club Officer)

2013
Coaches: David Keegan and Jon Zaul
Patrick Arthur Avila (147 lbs)
Vince Dang (139)
Lee Jensen (185 lbs) (Boxed in NCBA West Regionals and fought a courageously against prior year's National Champion, Club Treasurer)
Andrew Luu (147 lbs) (Boxed in NCBA West Regionals. Club President for Fall 2012-Spring 2013)
Evan Kamei (125 lbs) (Boxed in NCBA West Regionals and NCBA Nationals, Club Vice President)
Enzo Nabiev (132)
Samuel Oh
Abelardo Lora Reyes (139 lbs)
Tristan Tao
Albert van Schmeller (195 lbs)

2014
Coaches: David Keegan and Jon Zaul
Patrick Arthur Avila (147 lbs)
Brian Cheng
Kenny Pham Dang (152 lbs)
Ronald Harrington Desmond (147 lbs)
Rodrigo Corona Flores (175 lbs)
Gordon Gottsegen (125 lbs)
Lee Jensen (185 lbs) (fought previous year's National Champion at NCBA West Regionals. Courageous Fighter.)
Evan Kamei (125 lbs) (Club President Fall 2013-Spring 2014)
Gerald Greg Santos (139 lbs) (3rd Place, NCBA West Regionals) (Fought National Champ at NCBA Nationals)
Ryan Wen (156 lbs)

Women:
Therese Bjoernaas
Claire Glowniak (125 lbs) (2nd at NCBA Nationals earning All-American Honors.) (Won against national champion at NCBA West Regionals, but lost a controversial decision to her at NCBA Nationals.)

2015
Coaches: Jon Zaul (Cal Sport Clubs Honorable Mention for Coach of the Year Award) and David Keegan
Patrick Avila (147 lbs)
Brian Cheng Kenny Dang (152 lbs) Ron Desmond (147 lbs)
Jeffery Hirschey
Daejin Lee
Toni Lee Patrick Martins
Brian Naston (156 lbs)
Eric Pan (132 lbs)
Gerald Santos (139 lbs) (Fought at NCBA Nationals twice) (Club President and Captain Fall 2014-Spring 2015) (Won Cal Sport Clubs Officer of the Year Award) (3rd Place in NCBA Regionals) (Fought best fighters in his weight class from UN Reno (2-time National Champion), West Point (team Captain and 2nd at Nationals), Air Force (National Champion), and Navy)
Ryan Wen (156 lbs) won the most fights on the team in 2015 and 4th Place in NCBA Regionals, Club Treasurer)

Women:
Therese Bjoernaas
Claire Glowniak (139 lbs) (second place at 2014 NCBA Nationals, 2015 NCBA West Regional Champion) (All-American Honors in 2014 and 2015, Cal Sport Clubs Honorable Mention for Women's Athlete of the Year Award) (Won against 4 different female NCBA national champions from 3 separate weight divisions) (Club Vice President).

2016
Coach: Jon Zaul
Assistant Coaches: Evan Kamei and Gerald Santos
Patrick Avila (147 lbs) (Represented Cal at NCBA Western Regionals)
Sunny Bae (139 lbs) (Won at February 20, 2016 at Cal 100 Years Invitational)
Joseph Harrison (139 lbs)
Benjamin Kaveladze (185 lbs) (Won by knockout at February 20, 2016 at Cal 100 Years Invitational)
Jarred Mendoza (175 lbs) (Won against strong fighter with MMA fighting experience at Feburary 20, 2016 Cal 100 Years Invitational and finished second place in March 26, 2016 NCBA Western Regionals)
Eric Pan (132 lbs) (Won at February 20, 2016 at Cal 100 Years Invitational)
Gerald Santos (139 lbs and 147 lbs)

Brent Scheidemantle (165 lbs) (Defeated strong opponent, best fight of night at February 20, 2016 Cal 100 Years Invitational) (Club President and Co-Captain)

Women:

Vivian Chuang (119 lbs) (Won at February 20, 2016 Cal 100 Years Invitational) (Club Vice President and Co-Captain) (Semi-Finalist in NCBA Western Regionals) (represented Cal at 2016 NCBA Nationals).

CAL COACHES AND ASSISTANT COACHES

Donald Bell (Manager) (1949)

Ken Bigham (1976) (Assistant Coach 1973-1975, to Head Coach Brian Kahn. Helped set up the East-West Championship in 1976. Reportedly still boxing in 2016 in USAA Masters Division. Won the Lightweight Championship in the World Masters in 2014.

Dick Carter (1971, 1972) Asst. Coach 1970

Yvonne Caples (Female coach starting 1993) (First female coach) (1999, 2000)

Tom Cureton (1943, 1944, 1945 and 1946 Coach, while Ed Nemir in military) (WWII, Part of 1946 till March 1951, when Ed Nemir returned.)

Ron Dell'Immagine (1969) Ron, an assistant coach, took over as coach after Ed Nemir's death, midseason.

Jim Fardeen (Asst Coach to Jim Riksheim)

Javier Hernandez (Womens Team Coach 2002, 2003)

Mark Fowler (Asst. Coach) (2000)

Todd Gaylord (Asst Coach 2008-2015)

Bill Harrison (Asst. Coach 1963-1966)(Then, for 30 years, coached Drama Department at Santa Rosa College)

Kurt Heffernan (Asst. Coach to Jim Riksheim) (Also 1984 National Heavyweight Champion)

Bob Hink (Asst. Coach 1966)

Mike Huff (1978 -1982)

Stanley Jones (1923, 1924, 1925, 1926, 1927, 1928)

Brian Kahn (Coach 1973-1975) (Assistant Coach 1971) (See his article in this book.)

Evan Kamei (Assistant Coach 2016)

Dave Keegan (Coach 2011-2015) (Co-coaching with Jon Zaul)

William Kim (2000)

Frank Kleeberger (1916)

Mark Lucia (Asst. Coach, 2003-2006)

Tony Manzi

Rod Maracini (Asst Coach, 1965)

Paul McNally (1970)

Sean Mockler (Asst. Coach for 12 years, with Jim Riksheim)

Sam Moreno (1958 Coach when Ed Nemir became ill during 1957 season) (Boxed on 1956, 1957 teams)

Ed Nemir (37 years - 1933-1969) (Former Intercollegiate Champ as boxer and as wrestler. Silver Medal winner at 1932 Olympics as wrestler; Cal Athletic Hall of Fame as wrestler and Boxing Coach.

Nessa Nemir [Women's Coach in 2011 and other years] (Daughter of Phil Nemir, Granddaughter of Ed Nemir.)

Phil Nemir (1975 and 1976 - Head Coach) (Major team supporter to the present (2016)

Greg Pedemonte (Asst. Coach)
Tom Pedamonte (Asst. Coach) (1996-2000)

Tom Pendleton (Asst. Coach 1982)

David Ralston (Asst. Coach) (2000)

Jim Riksheim (1982-2012) (30 year's Cal Head Coach and still assisting!)

Floyd Salas (Assistant Coach) - Forever! 1956-2004 (Still going strong at 84, as of 2016) Respected novelist (including "Tattoo the Wicked Cross") and Poet, he assisted with Cal Boxing, either officially as an assistant coach, and "unofficially" for more than 50 years. A popular semi-autobiographical book on growing up in Oakland was "Buffalo Nickel." (See articles by and about Floyd in this book.)

Al Sandell (Assistant Coach, 1982)

Walter Stone (1927-1930)

Bourquaye Thomas (1997-2000) Asst. Coach

Jamal Valdez-Allen

Gordon Van Kessel (Asst. Coach) (1965) (Former Conference Champion welterweight.) (Boalt Hall Law School Graduate and Hastings Law Professor.)

Jon Zaul (Asst Coach 2007-2010, Co-Coach with Dave Keegan 2011-2015, Head Coach 2016)

COACHES FROM UNIVERSITY OF NEVADA, RENO (THE 2015 NCBA NATIONAL CHAMPIONS)

The late Jimmy Olivas

Riley Becket - UNR Boxing 1965, 1966, 1967

Joey Gilbert - 3 time National NCBA Champion, Pro fighter and attorney.

Dan Holmes - Former National Champion and Coach Since 2012

Pat "Paddy" Jefferson (2012-Present) (World Ranked Champion and Professional Boxing S. Dakota Hall of Fame

Mike Martino (Former Champion Boxer and President of NCBA/Coach and Leader for UNR for many years. 2016 Executive Director USA Boxing, which oversees all US amateur boxing, including Olympic team selection.

Mike Mentaberry - UNR Boxer, Rodeo Association President and Major UNR Supporter

Mike Schellin (Alumni Coordinator past 30 years; 1966-68 CCBC Champion)

Pat Schellin (1976-Present) UNR Boxer and UNR Coach

Tony Scheuller - 1966 CCBC Champ and Major Fan, UNR 1965, 1966 and 1967)

REFEREES AND JUDGES

Stu Bartell - Won the 165 lb NCAA championship in 1960 and went on to coach for many years at San Jose State.

Jack Campbell (Refereed many years of Cal fights)

Frankie Carter (referee on many Cal bouts, including 1972 Cal v. Navy.)

Dale Chamblin - Also a Cal Boxer, 1964, 1965, 1966

Jack Downey - One of the top referees in the world and associated with Cal Boxing for many years. Professional Referee for 58 years for many world championship fights.

Vic Drakulich - For many years and to the present, a top professional referee and noted Reno attorney, has refereed intercollegiate fights for many years. Nevada State Athletic Commission Referee.

Mike Huff - Cal Coach 1978-1982

Don Kennedy

Mills Lane (At Nevada) - Until felled by a stroke in 2002, Mills was considered by many to be the top referee in the world, refereeing many world championship fights. The NCAA Welterweight National Champ in 1960 for Nevada (Reno), (the last year of NCAA Boxing) he continued to referee both college and professional fights from 1963 on, while also being elected Washoe County (Reno) District Attorney for years and Superior Court Judge for more than 10 years. He refereed all Cal v. U of Nevada Reno fights in Reno for 30 years. Inducted into the International Boxing Hall of Fame in 2013.

Jay Nady - UNR Football star and undefeated heavyweight. CCBC Boxing Champion 1968, 1969. UNR Hall of Fame. Professional referee since 1972 for World Championship fights.

Dave Nelson (former Santa Clara Coach) (Referee pictured on book cover.)

Dick Rall

Marty Sammon - For many years, up to the present (2016), worked as a referee and Judge of California College Fights and Professional Fights. An excellent Santa Clara University fighter in the 1950's, he would joke about his fight with Cal star George Pelonis: "When we fought, both Pelonis and I were undefeated! After we fought, Pelonis was undefeated." Now a stockbroker, Marty was also one of the paratroopers sent by President Eisenhower to Little Rock, Arkansas, in 1957, to safely escort the "Little Rock 9" black teenagers to integrate Central High School, to enforce a court order despite the threats of hundreds of vicious segregationists encouraged by notorius Arkansas Governor Orville Faubus.

Jack Scheberies

Joe Tinney - Former Santa Clara Boxing Champion, referreed or judged many intercollegiate fights at Cal.

Snort Winstead – Timekeeper for many years, known to occasionally time a long round.

INDEX: BOXERS ALPHABETICALLY

We have tried to collect as much information as possible in a relatively short time. Apologies to anyone left out or if this list contains any inaccurate information about anyone.

Dave Ackerman (1954) (Heavyweight)

Al Adams (1957, 1958, 1959) (147 lbs, 156 lbs)

Bob Adams (1941, 1942) (135 lbs)

Kash Afshari (2000, 2002) (172 lbs)

Milton Aftergut (1919-1922) (Heavyweight)

Rick Aftergut (1968)

Antonio "Tony" Aguire (1976-1978) (132 lbs)

Luis Alarcon (1999, 2000) (132 lbs, 139 lbs)

Reid Albano (2006, 2007) (172 lbs)

Paul Albert (1963) (132 lbs)

Boyd Alexander (1968, 1969) (172 lbs)

Eric Allen (2008) (185 lbs) (Advanced to Nationals)

Jerry Ambinder (1954) (Heavyweight)

Mike Anast (1977) (112 lbs) (CCBC Champion)

Bill Anderson (1956, 1957, 1959) (147 lbs)

Homer Anderson (1945) (127 lbs)

Merle Ansberry (1929) (119 lbs) (2nd Place Pacific Coast Conference)

Ed Arboleda (1978) (156 lbs) (179 lbs)

Dave Archibald (1966) (172 lbs) (Strong fighter, a national track star at 440 and 880 yds. Inducted into Cal Athletic Hall of Fame in 2008, as runner, same night as Tom Gioseffi (see article in this book).

Bob Arevalo (1963) (132 lbs)

Eric Ari (2005) (147 lbs)

Neil Armstrong (1936)

Klaus Arons (1957, 1958) (132 lbs)

Kash Ashfari (2002) (172 lbs)

Gene Auburn (1936, 1937, 1938) (145 lbs) (156 lbs)

Henry Lewis Augustine (1959) (125 lbs)

Art Avetisyan (2009) (195 lbs) (Western Regional Champion)

Jose Avila (2012) (139 lbs) (Boxed in Regionals, WCBA)

Patrick Arthur Avila (156 lbs) (2013, 2014, 2015, 2016)

Sunny Bae (2016) (140 lbs) (Won at 2016 100 Year Anniversary Cal Invitational)

Herb Bagley (1941) (145 lbs)

Hiram Baker (1918, 1919) (145 lbs)

Roger Baker (1962) (147 lbs)

Scott Bambacigno (1997, 1998, 1999) (172 lbs) (180 lbs)

Bob Bankard (1985) (156 lbs)

Jeff Banks (1992)

Justin Barad (Heavyweight) (2003, 2004)

Ross Barbeco (1996) (132 lbs)

John Barnard (1964) (139 lbs)

Tye Barre (1939, 1940) (165 lbs)

Colby Barret (1998) (190 lbs)

Dave Bartick (1977, 1978) (139 lb)

Del Bartley (1945, 1946, 1947, 1949, 1950) (165 lbs, 175 lbs)

Matt Bataclan (2007, 2008, 2009) (135 lbs)

Paxton Beale (1950, 1951) (Heavyweight) Pax Beale is still an active team supporter in 2016; Champion Athlete and Bodybuilder; Author of "Body for the Ages." (Cal Football 1950.)

Bob Bechtel (1959) (165 lbs)

Dan Beck (1994) (165 lbs)

Ted Beckett (1929) (Heavyweight) (Second Place, Pacific Coast Conference)

John Bedri (1968) (147 lbs)

Sal Benevidez (1977, 1978) (156 lbs) (165 lbs)

Don Bell (1943) (Manager, 1944)

Don Bell (1962) (178 lbs)

Paul Bell (1964, 1965, 1966) ("Chip" Bell) (132 lbs) (1965 CCBC Champ)

Jeff Beoca (1992) (147 lbs)

Eric Bergen (156 lbs) (1989)

John Bermudez (1996)

John Bernard (1964)

Karl Berta (2007, 2008) (195 lbs) (2nd in West, Gutty finals fight against experienced Air Force Champion.)

Wolfe Birkie (156 lbs, 165 lbs) (1982, 1983, 1985)

Jack Bishop (1945) (135 lbs)

Garrick Bjur (2006) (190 lbs)

Bob Black (1976) (Heavyweight)

Ted Blankenburg (1970)

Randolf Henry Bode (1935)

Eric Bogin (1977) (165 lbs)

Bobby Bolger (2004, 2005, 2006) (175 lbs, 185 lbs)

David Bom (2006)

Phil Booth (1947) (135 lbs)

Sam Bort (1971)

Tom Bottorff (1974, 1975, 1976) (132 lbs)

Ernest Boucher (1933, 1934)

Beryl Boyce (1936) (147 lbs)

R. Bowers (1923)

Tom Bradfield (1975, 1976) (119 lbs) (1976 Intercollegiate Champion) (CCBC Champion. Won 1st NCBA East v. West Fight)

Kyle Brady (2007, 2008, 2010) (147 lbs, 152 lbs)

Matt Brady (1947) (145 lbs)

Buck Brancis (1936) (175 lbs)

Mike Brennan (2012)

Philip Bremner (2010) (147 lbs)

Gordon Brittle (1943)

Pat Bromfeld (1956)

Robert Brosamer (1960) (139 lbs)

Patrick Brownfield (1958) (147 lbs)

Bob Broxholme (1943)

Herb Bruce (1947, 1948) (Heavyweight)

Colby Bryant (1997) (190 lbs)

Don John Buck (1957)

John William Buckman (1957, 1958) (147 lbs)

Glen Buell (1947) (175 lbs)

David Bui (2007) (135 lbs)

Tom Bulgin (1962) (125 lbs)

Brian Bunch (1988, 1989, 1990) (139 lbs)

Dan Burnstein (1968) (132 lbs) (CCBC Champion)

Ken Butler (1934, 1935)

Nick Byrd (2000, 2002) (165 lbs) (170 lbs)

Al Cahn (1930) (175 lbs)

Vic Cain (1941) (155 lbs)

Cain (1953)

R. Caldwell (1923, 1924)

Canady (1951)

Yvonne Caples (1993) (Began as women's coach.)

Michael Cardova (2012) (175 lbs) (Fought in Regionals, WCBA)

Robert Carlton (1934, 1935)

Chris Carmona (165 lbs) (1993, 1994)

Dan Carr (172 lbs) (1983, 1984)

Dick Carter (1966, 1967, 1968, 1969) (125 lbs) (Later coach 1971, 1972) (See his article in this book.)

Dave Cassety (132 lbs) (1986, 1987) (Winner Eddie Nemir Memorial Award, WCBA Champ, fought in Nationals)

James Castle (1934) (Lost one fight) (1935)

Jim Cavin (1970) (160 lbs)

Ray Cerles (1943)

John Cerma (1986)

Louis Cervantes (1986) (191 lbs)

Joe Chairez (1976) (125 lbs)

Dale Chamblin (1964, 1965, 1966, 1967) (1st in CCBC, 1966, 2nd in 1967) (Later served as referee and fight judge; became banker.)

Clarence Champlin (1953) (147 lbs)

Paul Chang (135 lbs) (2005)

Creighton Chan (1974) (139 lbs)

Calvin C. Chapman (1918)

John Chappell (1967, 1968)

Roger Chaverin (1973)

Adam Chen (2003) (156 lbs)

Brian Cheng (2014, 2015)

Larry Cheng (1977, 1978) (139 lbs)

Roger Cheny (1994) (147 lbs)

Glen Cherry (1925, 1926, 1927)

Jamal Cherry (2001) (Heavyweight) (Defensive End, Cal Football Team) (Later played Pro Football in Canada.)

Ricky Cheung (2003) (139 lbs)

Chew (1946)

Paul Cho (1936, 1938, 1939) (120 lbs) (Pacific Coast Champion 1939, 2nd in 1938)

Alex Choulos (1980) (Cunha Award - Most Outstanding Intramural Boxing Champion)

George Choulos (1978) (Claude Wyle's law partner) (1978 Intramural 147 lb Champion and winner of Milton T. Cunha Award as outstanding Boxer in Tournament) (Brother of Alex Choulos, Son of Vasilous Choulos) (Became outstanding San Francisco Trial Lawyer.)

Vasilous Choulos (A great trial lawyer in San Francisco, partner with Melvin Belli, the "King of Torts," and father of Intramural Champions Alex Choulos and George

Choulos, each of whom won the "Cunha" Award.)

Mansfield Clinnick (1944)

Brunel Christianson (1943, 1944) (Heavyweight)

Gus Clarke (1943, 1944) (127 lbs)

Don Clausen (178 lbs) (1951, 1952)

Tom Clayton (125 lbs) (1996) (WCBA Champion, 1997, 1998) (Fought in Nationals at Reno, lost to Fighter who won Nationals and was Nationals' "Outstanding Boxer")

Dave Clement (1968) (139 lbs)

Mansfield Clinnick (1944)

Myron Close (1944)

Robert Cole (1944)

Dalton Conley (1988, 1989) (132 lbs)

Jeremy Conner (1995) (156 lbs)

Josh Conner (1995, 1996) (147 lbs) (Josh lost to 4 time CCBC Champ, and three time National Champ from Nevada, Joey Gilbert. Gilbert became a professional fighter and Reno crowd favorite, while simultaneously earning a law degree, and is now a Nevada trial lawyer.)

Josh Coons (2004)

Brandon Copeland - 2003 (CCBC 139 lb Champion, went to Nationals)

Mark Copeland (1978) (132 lbs, 139 lbs)
Vic Corbett (1950) (175 lbs) (Winner of Cunha Intramural Award)

Mike Cordova (2012) (175 lbs) (Boxed in WCBA Regionals, qualified for Nationals)

Tobey Cornsweet (1960, 1961)

Bill Corrigan (1963, 1964) (139 lbs)

John Cosley (1970) (172 lbs)

Larry Costa (1960, 1961, 1962) (147 lbs)

Joseph Covington (1918, 1919) (145 lbs)

Pete Cowan (1965, 1966) (1st in CCBC both years.) (139 lbs)

John Cowart (1967, 1968, 1969) (125 lbs)

Troy Cox (1967) (1st in CCBC) (1968) (178 lbs) (Had five knockouts en route to CCBC Championship)

Don Crane

George Cresson (1992) (156 lbs)

R.T. Crowley (1922)

Eldon Cruz (1945)

Steve Cummins (1977) (Heavyweight)

Milt Cunha (1940, 1941, 1942) (Twice Pacific Coast 165 lb Champion, in 1941 and 1942. After his death in combat during World War II, his family set up the Milton Cunha Award to be given to each year's outstanding Intramural Boxer, in Milton Cunha's honor.)

Walt Cunningham (1965, 1966) (Heavyweight) (Asst. Coach 1967)

Hugh Curtis (1944)

Jim Cuthbertson (1943)Haig Dadigian (1930, 1931, 1935)

Haig Dadigian (1930, 1931, 1935)

Earl Dakan (1934) (1935)

Jack Damich

Kenny Dang (152 lbs) (2014) (2015)

Vince Dang (2013)

Hand Davalos (1971)

Davis (1930, 1931)

John Davies (1979)

Herb Davis (1956,156 lbs, won Cunha trophy in Intramurals) (1957, 165 lbs, Team Captain.) Ed Nemir, in an Oakland Tribune article is quoted describing Herb as "one of the cleverest boys on the squad." (See his story in this book.)

Cort Day (125 lbs) (1985, 1986)

Jim Dedelow (1983) (137 lbs)

James DeGrazia (1962) (132 lbs)

Enrico Del Osso (1929) (139 lbs)

Ron Dell'Immagine (1966, 1967, 1968)(1969 - Ron filled in as coach after Ed Nemir died, Feb 1, 1969, Assistant Coach before that.) (Heavyweight) (Became High School Principal) (Came to Cal on a Football Scholarship.)

Frank Delzompo (1981, 1982, 1984) (156 lbs) (1981 2nd in Nationals) (1982 CCBC Champ) (1984 CCBC Conference Champ) ("The Italian Stallion") (Team Captain 1982) ("Fury in the Ring") (Twice second in Nationals.)

John Demergasso (Boxer or team supporter; Alameda Co. Asst. Public Defender)

Matt Denny (125 lbs, 135 lbs) (2006)

Gaston de Pratgay (1955) (139 lbs)

Joseph Derisi (1936) (165 lbs)

Elwood "Dick" Derr (1936) (1937) (135 lbs) (Semi-Finalist in Nationals) (Became chemical engineer for Shell Oil Co.)

Bill Derrough (1985, 1986, 1987) (139 lbs)

Ron Desmond (2014)(2015) (150 lbs)

Stephen Di Grejorio (2000) (165 lbs)

Steve Dimeff (1955) (Heavyweight)

Geo Domaz (1947)

Rod Doerr (1947, 1948, 1949) (135 lbs)

Gordon Doke (1947) (175 lbs)

George Domaz (1947)

John Thomas Domich (1959, 1960) (Heavyweight) (Went to Nationals)

Clark Dooley (1961) (Heavyweight CCBC Champion 1961)

Jimmy Doolittle (1917-1920) (WWII General, Led 1942 "Bombs Over Tokyo" Raid

Jim Doss (1948) (155 lbs)

Jack Downey - Referee for 58 years, elected to World Wide Boxing Hall of Fame; refereed Cal Fights for many years.

John Drachnick (1939) (135 lbs)

Chris Draper (2000) (Heavyweight)

Tom Drewek (1963) (Heavyweight) (Also Heavyweight wrestler.)

Joel Droubay (1938, 1939, 1940) (145 lbs)

Al Dubecker (1929)

Forest Dubois (1938, 1939) (Heavyweight)

Phil Duggan (1936) (147 lbs)

Charles Duncan (1957) (Heavyweight)

Jim Dunn (1998) (147 lbs)

Al Dutra (1952, 1953) (148 lbs)

Triniece Durst (2006)

Easterbrooks (1930, 1931)

Chuck Eastman (1959, 1960) (156 lbs)

Bill Easton (1942) (145 lbs)

Daniel Edington (1995) (112 lbs, 125 lbs)

Bill Ehmcke (1940, 1941) (127 lbs)

Siamac Ehsan (147 lbs) (2006, 2007, 2008)

Ben Einzig (1922)

Joseph Eisner (2006)

Marshall Elvin (1933) (Fought under Ed Nemir as a light heavyweight) (Father of Cal Boxing Fan Ken Elvin)

John Emerson (1949) (175 lbs)

James Enemark (1947) (155 lbs)

George Eshoo (1956)

Mariano Esparza (2005) (139 lbs, 147 lbs)

Bob Ettinger (1956, 1957, 1958, 1959) (167 lbs) (178 lbs)

Gary Evers (1968, 1969, 1970) (139 lbs, 147 lbs) (1969 CCBC Runner up, then 1970 CCBC Champion) (Traveled 1500 miles to attend 2004 Reunion)

Steve Fallai (1968, 1969) (156 lbs)

Gadai Faraj (2002, 2004) (190 lbs, Heavyweight)

Jim Fardeen (165 lbs) (1982, 1983, 1984, 1985)

Ed Farris (1947, 1948, 1949) (145 lbs) (Became close friend of Ed Nemir and supported Cal Boxing for many years, spoke at 2011 Reunion. Claimed he acted as "baby sitter" for young Phil Nemir.)

Charles Faulkner (165 lbs) (1990)

"Gus" (Genero) Felice (1969) (156 lbs) (1970) (165 lbs) (1971)

Hariberto "Herbie" Fermin (1983, 1984, 1985) (119 lbs) (1984 Conference Champ) (1985 Second in Nationals)

Joey Fermin (1976)

Vince Ferretti (132 lbs) (2010)

Walt Fiedler (1944)

Byron Figeroa (1986, 1987) (142 lbs, 147 lbs)

Ben Fisher (1936) (126 lbs)

John Fitzpatrick (125 lbs) (Western Conference Champ) (1993, 1994) (Fought in Nationals)

John D. Fitzpatrick (2009, 2010)

Don Flaherty (1940, 1941) (127 lbs)

Rodrigo Flores (2014) (175 lbs)

Eric Fogel (1997) (147 lbs)

Tom Folsom (1937) (145 lbs)

Ed Fong (1955) (125 lbs)

Fore (1950)

Emmett Forester (1950, 1951, 1952) (126 lbs, 135 lbs)

Emmett Forester (2006)

William Bob Foster (1940) (127 lbs)

Bill Fothergill (1943)

Mark Fowler (156 lbs) (1985, 1986, 1987; CCBC Champ 1985, Outstanding Boxer Award, 1986 at Mare Island Invitational, 156 lbs) (Asst. Coach 2000)

Chris Fox (1941) (1955)

William "Buck" Frances (1934, 1935, 1936) (175 lbs)

Esisto Francheschi (1989) (156 lbs)

Andrew Frank (147 lbs) (1994)

Andrew Frankl (142 lbs)

William Fray (1946, 1947) (155 lbs)

Ron Frazier (1973)

Eric French (1989, 1992)

Carlos Fuentes (185 lbs)(2006)

Gary Fulbright (1954, 1955, 1956) (147 lbs)

Aaron Fung (125 lbs) (2006, 2007, 2008)

Abe Fuji (1940) (135 lbs)

Alan Galbreath (1954) (132 lbs)

Harry Galloway (1949) (155 lbs)

Albert Garcia (1993, 1995)

Porfirio Garcia (119 lbs) (1994) (Conference Champ, Fought in Nationals)

F. Garner (1923)

George Garner (1929) (175 lbs) (Pacific Coast Conference Champion)

Garrity (1930, 1931)

Leo Gaspardone (1954, 1955, 1956, 1957) (132 lbs) (Team Captain) (Attended 2004 Alumni Reunion)

Ray Gatchalian (1972) (Became noted Oakland Fire Fighter)

Todd Gaylord (2003, 2004, 2005, 2007) (Twice National Champion, 2004, 2007, and twice runner up in 2003 and 2005.) (Three Times Regional Champ), 139 lbs, 147 lbs. Boxed for four years at weights from 132 - 147. He fought from 2003 to 2007, and was honored in 2007 as Cal's Sport Club Athlete of the year. His excellent overall bout record was 32-4. After graduating in May 2007, he continued to assist Cal Boxing as an excellent Assistant Coach. In 2007, he won the National Champtionship by beating Nevada's favorite fighter, Thomas Genero, in Reno, and was selected as Outstanding Boxer in lower half of weight divisions, at 147 lbs.)

Denneth Duane Geil (1959) (156 lbs, 165 lbs)

Don Gercich (1953) (Winner Fall 1952 Cunha Intramural Award)

Germino (1927, 1930)

John Gianaras (1968) (172 lbs)

Tom Gioseffi (1963, 1964, 1965) (First boxer admitted to Cal Athetics Hall of Fame, 2010, 45 years after he fought.) (Ed Nemir admitted as coach and wrestler) (3 Time CCBC Champion) (Collegiate Record: 22-1-1) (Also Team Captain, 1965) (1963 and 1965 CCBC Outstanding Boxer in Tournement)

Bill Gimbel (1942) (135 lbs)

Paul Giroday (1971, 1972) (Heavyweight) (Fought Alumni exhibition against Tom Gioseffi, 1963-65 Middleweight Champion, in 1972. Played 5 years in Canadian Football League.)

Richard (Dick) Glendinning (1936, 1937, 1938) (135 lbs)

Claire Glowniack (Women's) 2nd place WCBA, 125 lbs, 2014; 1st place WCBC Champion, 137 lbs (2015)

Kong Go (1943)

Frank Goble (1939) (135 lbs)

Sam Gold (1924, 1925, 1926, 1927) (175 lbs) (Captain 1927 team, attended Cal Matches till 2005) (Undefeated during entire boxing career.) (Practiced law in Oakland for 64 years.) (Boalt Hall 1927-1930) (Attended 2004 Reunion at age of 98.)

Ed Gordon (1965 lbs) (1987) (Several Knock Outs)

Walter Gordon (1916, 1917, 1918) (Cal All-American Football player and Heavyweight Boxer) (Inducted into Cal Athletic Hall of Fame in 1986, later lawyer, Governor of Virgin Islands, Federal Judge. See article in text.)

Alex Gotlieb (147 lbs) (1995)

Gordon Gottsegen (2014) (125 lbs)

Stanley Goulard (1934, 1935)

Kenneth Gow (1923, 1924)

Thomas Greathouse (1945) (155 lbs)

James Green (1954) (125 lbs) (2nd in P.C.I)

Ray Greenwood (1940, 1941, 1942) (175 lbs)

John Grennan (1947, 1948) (135 lbs) (Attended Cal Boxing matches for many years.)

Orb Greenwald (1970) (Heavyweight)

Dwight Gribben (1929) (160 lbs) (Pacific Coast Conference Champ)

Willie Grief (139 lbs) (1994)

Ed Griffin (1949, 1950, 1951) (135 lbs)

John Groff (1949, 1950) (Heavyweight)

Grossman (1927)

Joe Grothus (1945) (Heavyweight)

Richard Grouix (1944, 1949)

Bob Guirmarin (1972) (132 lbs)

Max Guiterrez (1952, 1953) (139 lbs)

Warner Guysin (1976) (125 lbs) (Won East v. West Championship)

Chris Haddawy (1984, 1985) (132 lbs) (1985 won Eddie Nemir Award) (WCBA Champion, 3rd in Nationals)

Rolfe Hagan (1938) (165 lbs)

Jim Hagedorn (1959, 1960) (147 lbs) (Winner of Cunha Intramural Award)

John Halbrook (1982)

Patrick "Butch" Hallinan (1956, 165 lbs)(1957, 156 lbs) (Became a respected criminal defense attorney in San Francisco.) "Kayo" Hallinan is his brother. Father Vincent Hallinan noted Trial Attorney and Progressive Party Candidate for President in 1952.)

Terrence "Kayo" Hallinan (1956, 178 lbs) (1957, Heavyweight) (1958, 1959) (Criminal defense attorney, elected two terms San Francisco District Attorney.) (Son of lawyer Vincent Hallinan.) (Went to Nationals.) ("Kayo" and "Butch" came to 2011 Reunion.)

John Hammarley (1973)

Ross Hammonds (156 lbs) (1995)

Jim Handel (1949, 1950, 1951) (125 lbs) (In 1972 Alumni fight easily defeated Cal Varsity letterman, 20 years younger.)

Yoshio Handa (1940) (120 lbs)

Ken Hansen (1951, 1952, 1953) (132 lbs) (2nd Place, P.C.I.)

Myron Hansen (1951, 1952, 1953) (139 lbs)

Nelson "Skip" Hansen (1953)

John Harder (1966) (156 lbs) (also on Wrestling Team)

Freeman Harris (1966, 1967) (139 lbs)

G. Ken Hargrove (circa 1927-1934)

Harle (1946)

Bill Harrison (1959) (156 lbs) (Assistant Coach-1963, 1965, 1966) (1965 was CCBC Championship Team, which won 6 of 9 weight divisions); later Drama Coach at Santa Rosa College for 30 years, excellent amateur actor and director; Fought in 1992 Alumni Fight 33 years after he fought for Cal.) In 1960 was drafted into Army, so couldn't fight on team, but boxed in Army.

Joseph Harrison (2016) (138 lbs)

Henry Harvey (1949, 1950, 1951) (155 lbs) (165 lbs)

Mike Hastings (2009) (2011) (185lbs) (195 lbs) (Team Captain 2011)

Karim Hayath (132 lbs) (1989)

Andy Heffernan (Kurt Heffernan's Father)

Kurt Heffernan (1981, 1982, 1983, 1984) (Heavyweight) (1981 Conference Champ, 1982-CCBC Conference Champ, 2nd in Nationals (and again in 1983); CCBC Champ, 1984) (1984 National Heavyweight Champion; At tournament at Cal for National Championship, Kurt knocked out heavily favored finals opponent in 1st Round.) (See 1984 Stories.)

Jim Henderson (1938) (125 lbs)

John Hennessy (1939) (145 lbs)

Nick Heredia (1993, 1995) (125 lbs)

Javier Hernandez (147 lbs) (1997, 1998, 1999)

Raphael Herandez (139 lbs) (1997, 1998)

Don Herron (1936, 1937, 1938) (147 lbs)

Bill Hight (1947) (165 lbs)

Paul Hillinger (1943)

Art Hillman (1951, 1952) (156 lbs, 165 lbs)

Joe Hillsman (circa 1927-1934)

Hilton (1930, 1931)

Bob Hink (1967) (Heavyweight) (Later, Assistant Coach and Cal supporter for many years.) (A "Heavy Hitter.")

Fred Hite (1967) (156 lbs)

Jeffery Hirschey (2015)

Mike Hogan (1968) (139 lbs)

Hogle (1938)

Terry Holberton (1965, 1966) (Also won Cunha Award, Fall 1964) (Outstanding Intramural Champ)

John Holbrook (139 lbs) (1982) Winner of Edgar Nemir Award

Bill Holliman (1957, 1958, 1959) (132, 139 lbs)

Bill Holmes (1968) (156 lbs)

Dick Homuth (1956, 1957, 1958) (156 lbs, 165 lbs)

Jim Hoobler (1967) (147 lbs) (1st in CCBC)

Kamal Hood (1997) (139 lbs)

Bill Hotchkiss (1956) (178 lbs)

Hotopp (1930, 1931)

Bob Howard (1945, 1946) Co-captain (145 lbs)

Peter Howes (1974-1977) (172 lbs)

Mike Huff (1976) Boxer and later Coach (1977-1982)

Mike Huffman (1959, 1961, 1962) (132 lbs)

Mu Huang (2004) (175 lbs)

Bobby Humphrey (2002, 2003) (165 lbs) (175 lbs) (Went to Nationals)

Fred W. Huntington (1918, 1919) (158 lbs)

Clarke Ide (1956, 1957) (132 lbs) (139 lbs)

John Incerti (1969, 1970, 1971) (132 lbs)

Kunia Inoue (1964) (125 lbs)

Len Isabelle (1954) (178 lbs)

George Iserquin (1927, 1928) (119 lbs)

Phil Ishimaru (1953, 1954, 1955) (125 lbs)

Bruce Jahnke (1950) (165 lbs)

John Jan (1932, 1933) (Team Captain)

Walt Jang (156 lbs, 165 lbs) (1993, 1999, 2000, 2001) (Team Captain, 2000)

Ben Jarvis (1978) (172 lbs)

Mike Jay (125 lbs) (1966, 1967)

Lee Jensen (2013, 2014) (185 lbs) (Courageous fighter who fought experienced National Champion at WCBA Regionals.)

Jose "Jay" Jiminez (2011, 2012) (156 lbs) (Took second place in his weight division at the NCBA Regional finals, and he, plus 175 lb Mike Cardova, qualified for the Nationals.) (Cordova awarded second place in the Regionals, when a knee injury forced him to retire in his Finals bout 2012) (Earned All-American honors at NCBA.)

Dale Jeong (1969, 1970) (139 lbs)

James Johns (1947)

Shan Johnson (1994) (190 lbs)

Jim Johnston (1948) (170 lbs, 175 lbs)

Donald Jones (1953, 1955, 1957) (139 lbs)

Errol Jones (1923, 1924)

Henry Jones (2006) (170 lbs)

Stanley Jones "Middleweight Champ" (prior to 1923, when he was Coach)

Jones (1931)

Ray Joshua (1991) (132 lbs)

Craig Jordan (1982) (165 lbs)

Robert Jost (2006)

Adlai Jourdin (1982, 1983) (172 lbs, 180 lbs)

Jason Julian (1988) Conference Champ at 190 lbs, Fought in Nationals; Fought Paul Rein (1963-1965, Class of 1965) in March 1989 Alumni v. Varsity Fight Exhibition

Brian Kahn (1969) (CCBC Dual Meet Champion, later Coach of Team.) (See his article in this book "Cal Boxing: 1968-1975"; Author of "Real Common Sense" and advocate for the public interest.)

Herb Kalman (1938) (145 lbs) (Boxed in WCBA Regionals) (U.C. Boxing Club President, 2013-2014 Season)

Evan Kamei (2013, 2014) (125 lbs) (Boxed in NCBA Regionals and NCBA Nationals; U.C. Boxing Club Vice President.)

Joe Kapp (1960) (Quarterbacked the Golden Bears to the Rose Bowl in 1959 and later was a Cal Football Coach.)

Jeff Karp (1971)

Benjamin Kaveladze (2016) (175 lbs) (Won by knock out at 2016 "Cal Invitational")

Matt Kaufman (1987, 1988, 1989) (156 lbs, 172 lbs)

Jack Kawamoto (1959, 1960, 1961) (125 lbs, 132 lbs)

Frances Kearney (1928) (129 lbs)

Sanford Kearney (circa 1927-1934)

Dave Keegan (2007, 2008, 2009, 2010) (140 lbs, 147 lbs) (Coach 2011-2015) (Learned to box well and teach boxing as Coach. Fought mainly at 140 lbs and admired for his personal courage and ability to take a punch. As coach, he tried to teach how to avoid taking too many punches. In 2008, he was 2nd in Western Regional Conference.)

Daniel Kegan (2008) (2010) (185 lbs)

Dennie Kehoe (1982, 1983) (147 lbs)

Doug Keith (1949, 1950) (145 lbs) (Long time supporter of Cal Boxing.)

John Keliiaa (1947, 1948)

Harold Kelton (1945)

Wilbur Kendig (1929) (139 lbs)

Don Kennady (1958, 1959, 1960, 1961) (Later Referee and Boxing Judge) (156 lbs) (165 lbs)

Jack Kenney (1942) (175 lbs)

Roger Kent (1960, 1961, 1962) (165 lbs)

Leslie Kessler

Ken Kofman (1957, 1958, 1959, 1960)

Ed Killbride (1959)

Kerry Killbride (1960)

Chan Kim (1982, 1983, 1984) (119 lbs) (CCBC Champ, 1984, 139 lbs)

Gene Kim (2000, 2001) (147 lbs)

Kai Kim (1937) (115 lbs)

William Kim (1997, 1998, 1999, 2000) (147 lbs, 156 lbs)

Willbur Kindig (1929)

Dick King (1953, 1954) (Heavyweight) (2nd in P.C.I.)

Garrell Kirtley (152 lbs) (1982, 1983) (1982 CCBC Champ) (1983 CCBC Champ, 2nd in Nationals)

Bill Kitchin (1950, 1951) (175 lbs)

Fiorello Klein (2008) (145 lbs)

Jerry Knapp (1964, 1965) (178 lbs) (Undefeated CCBC Champ in 1965.)

Doug Knesevich (1949) (1950) (155 lbs)

Norman Kobayashi (1927, 1928) (112 lbs)

Howard Koch (1947) (165 lbs)

Ray Koch (1968, 1970) (165 lbs)

Carl Koenig (1951, 1952) (165 lbs, 178 lbs)

Pat Kostiz (1972) (156 lbs)

Ken Kofman (1957, 1958) (125 lbs)

Don Koors (1947) (135 lbs)

Andrew Kosel (2004) (156 lbs)

Del Krause (1956)

Ray Kropp (1965, 1966) (178 lbs) (1st Place, CCBC Champion)

Dan Krischock (1981) (156 lbs)

Jay Kubakawa (1977) (125 lbs)

Russell Kummer (2003, 2004) (132 lbs)

Brian Kung (1995) (139 lbs)

Josh Kuns (2004) (175 lbs)

Jim Lackery (1955) (178 lbs)

Jack Lamke (1947, 1948, 1949) (175 lbs)

Bill Lamont (1952)

Ben Larman (1993, 1998, 1999) (156 lbs)

Wm. Raymond L'Hommidieu (circa 1934, 1935)

Eugene Lamb (circa 1927-34)

Ewald Larson (1940, 1941, 1942) (135 lbs)

John Laughlin (1945, 1946) (145 lbs)

Donald Lawton (1916) (170 lbs) (Fought as Heavyweight.) (Wrote about 1916 fight against Stanford, when Stanford wouldn't allow Walter Gordon to box due to racial discrimination. See article in this book.)

Joey Le (2004, 2005) (147 lbs)

Kevin Le (2004) (125 lbs)

Thuy Le (2010) (195 lbs)

Andrew Lee (1974) (125 lbs)

Cedric Lee (1992, 1993, 1997, 1998, 1999) (139 lbs)

Chris Lee (1997) (139 lbs)

Daejin Lee (2015)

Dan Lee (2001) (147 lbs)

Dick Lee (1977) (156 lbs, 165 lbs)

Hwasung Lee (2001, 2002, 2003) (156 lbs)

John Lee (2006)

Kevin Lee (2004) (125 lbs)

Toni Lee (2015)

Joe Lehman (1974) (145 lbs)

Lewis Lercara (1927) (Became an Alameda County Superior Court Judge in the 60s.) (Team mate of Sam Gold in 1927)

Seymour Lewis (1942) (155 lbs)

Max Levine (1963) (Heavyweight)

Alonzo Levington (1990) (147 lbs)

Dave Licata (1963)

Jack Light (1984, 1985) (147 lbs)

Pete Lindstrom (1976) (180 lbs)

Webb Lloyd (1967, 1968, 1969) (180 lbs) (CCBC Champion, 1968) (2nd in CCBC, 1969)

Charles "Andy" Lockwood (1957, 1958) (178 lbs)

Kevin Lomeli (2008)

Dick Londahl (1953, 1954) (139 lbs) (2nd, P.C.I.)

Dan London (1970) (156 lbs)

Elias Long (1944)

O.J. Long (1922)

Wilson Lord (1938, 1939) (155 lbs)

Donald Love (1944)

Brian Loveman (1963) (125 lbs)

Dick Lovette (1946)

Jim Louie (1938)

Andrew Luu (2013) (147 lbs) (Boxed in WCBA Regionals) (Cal Boxing Club President for 2012-2013 Season)

Mark Lucia (Boxer and later, Assistant Coach, 2003, 2004, 2005, 2006, 2007)

Ed Luker (1936) (155 lbs)

Larry Lusardi (1964) (156 lbs)

Bob Lustig (1947, 1949) (135 lbs)

Ray Lyon (1952)

Bill MacAdam (1960, 1961, 1962) (147 lbs, 156 lbs) (Became Superior Court Judge, San Diego)

Greg Macias (165 lbs) (1993, 1994) (Western Conference Champ, 165 lbs)

Macmillan (1930, 1931)

Pat Madden (1980) (156 lbs)

Madidle

Magid (1930, 1931)

John McCann (1974) (180 lbs)

Greg McIntosh (1977) (160 lbs)

McGrath (1930, 1931)

Paul McNally (1968) (Later Boxing Coach, 1970)

Milo Mallory (1930, 1931)

Dusty Mahoney (1977) 156 lbs

Rod Maracini (1963, 1964, 1965) (178 lbs) (Also Assistant Manager) As a light heavyweight fighter, 1963 to 1965, Rod was a courageous fighter but broke his nose so many times he was allowed to wear a catchers mask in team sparring sessions (originally broken playing rugby). He became a trial lawyer for Civil Defendants.

Alex Markoff (1947) (175 lbs)

Harry Martens (1944)

Jim Martin (1942) (165 lbs) (1947, 1948) (175 lbs) (Started Cal 1942, joined military WWII service, back to Cal 1947, 1948; became excellent Attorney. Supporter of Cal Boxing.)

Patrick Martins (2015)

Gene Markley (1953, 1954) (147, 156 lbs)

Lee Plantmason (Heavyweight) (2001, 2002)

Luis Martinez (135 lbs) (2005)

Stan Massie (1936) (147 lbs)

Tony Manzi

Ron Mathews (1939) (Heavyweight)

Carlos Matta (1977) (165 lbs)

Junior Matta (1977) (156 lbs)

Harry A. Mazzera (1918, 1919)

Bill McAdam (1960, 1961, 1962) (Later a Superior Court Judge in San Diego)

Jim McCann (1951, 1952, 1953) (156 lbs)

John McCann (1974) (180 lbs)

McKalip (1952)

John McClay

Dave McCollough (1960) (156 lbs)

Dennis McCullough (1961) (156 lbs)

McCrady

Bob McEvilly (1940, 1941, 1942) (145 lbs)

James McDonald (1930)

James McDowell (1938, 1939) (175 lbs)

Floyd McFarland (1952, 1953) (178 lbs)

McGrath (1930, 1931)

Andy McKelvy (1943) (145 lbs)

Paul McNally (1967, 1968) (Coached team in 1970.)

Pat McNulty (1950)

Mike McPherson (1956,1957) (Heavyweight)

Homer Mead (1937, 1938, 1939) (165 lbs) (1937 Semi-finalist in Nationals.) (Captain in 1938.) (1939 Second in Pacific Coast Conference)

Marty Medina (147 lbs) (1987)

Mel Menda (1973)

Hutch Meltzer (172 lbs) (1996)

Meiver (1949)

Jarred Mendoza (2016) (183 lbs) (Won 2nd place in 2016 Western Regionals; At 2016 Cal Invitational, won against strong fighter with MMA fighting experience.)

Justin Messenheimer (156 lbs) (1994)

Hutch Meltzer (1996) (172 lbs)

Hugh Metzger (1994, 1995) (172 lbs)

Mandle Mierbach (1933, 1935)

Andy Miller (1929) (Middleweight)

Pete Miller (1947) (145 lbs)

Ralph Milliron (1937) (155 lbs)

Eric Mims (112 lbs) (1988, 1989)

Ethan Mire (2011)

Clifford Misener (1943)

Earl Mitchell (1935)

Ed Mitchell (1976) (139 lbs)

Ferguson Mitchell (1942)

Everett Ben Mitchell (1940) (155 lbs)

Beau Mitchum (1978, 1979, 1980) (CCBC 125 lbs Champ; Bronze Medal at Nationals)

Earl Mittler (1939) (135 lbs)

Sean Mockler (156 lbs) (1983) (Later assistant coach to Jim Riksheim for 12 years.)

Greg Monahan (1966, 1967, 1968, 1969) (Team Captain 1967) (1966 2nd in CCBC) (Won 1965 Cunha Intramural Award)

Al Moody (circa 1934, 1935)

Jim Moody (1959) (178 lbs)

Moon (1933)

Jim Moore (1963, 1964, 1966) (165 lbs) (178 lbs) (Co-winner Fall 1962 Cunha Intramural Award)

Norris Moore (1982, 1983) (Regional Champ at 147 lbs both years)

Moore (1946)

Chris Morales (1981, 1982, 1983, 1984) (125 lbs National Champion in 1984 and won Conference Outstanding Boxer Award; later outstanding criminal defense trial lawyer with office in San Francisco, and helped organize Alumni Reunions and was an Alumni Fighter.) (Second in Nationals in 1982.)

J. Moran (1923, 1924)

Art Morimitsu (1936) (118 lbs) (2nd in National Finals)

Sam Moreno (1956, 1957) (126 lbs) (Coached when Ed Nemir was ill, 1958)

Pete Morris (1968)

Gordon Morrow (1956) (160 lbs)

Klaus Mortimer (1953) (139 lbs)

Don Morton (1953, 1955) (155 lbs)

Nathan Morton (2004) (165 lbs)

Pat Mower (1948, 1949) (126 lbs)

Daniel Murphy (1997) (147 lbs)

John Murphy (Heavyweight) (2000)

Enzo Nabiev (2013) (132 lbs)

Bill Nash (1945, 1946) (175 lbs) (Co-captain)

Brian Naston (2015) (156 lbs)

Dennis Natali (1960, 1961, 1962, 1963) (1961 and 1962 CCBC Champion at 139 lbs) (Criminal Defense Attorney in San Francisco for 30 years, affectionately called "Birdlegs" by his team mates. Lifelong friend of District Attorney Terrence "Kayo" Hallinan.)

Al Neis (1945) (145 lbs)

Bob Nelson (1954) (125 lbs)

John Nelson (1934)

Don Nemir (1956, 1957, 1958) (Heavyweight) (Ed Nemir's Nephew)

Ed Nemir (Boxer - 1928, 1929 [126 lbs] Second place, Pacific Conference, 1930, won Pacific Coast Conference Championship and Boxing Team Captain; also a Wrestler, 1932 Olympic Silver Medal) (Boxing Coach 1933-1969, with "interruption" by Military service during World War II, and 1 year illness (1958) when Sam Moreno coached. Inducted into Cal Athletic Hall of Fame in 1988 as coach.

Nessa Nemir (Women's Assistant Coach) (Daughter of Phil Nemir, granddaughter of Ed Nemir, and an excellent amateur boxer.) (Has assisted Cal Boxers, especially women, since 2006.)

Phil Nemir (1967, 1969, 1970) (Coach 1974 and 1975) (2nd in 1967) (1st in 1969, 1970 CCBC) (Career Boxing Alumni leader for many years, helped save Cal Boxing program after Phil's father, the legendary Ed Nemir, died suddenly on February 11, 1969, at ringside, in Reno, after coaching Phil to a win. Leader in organizing several Boxers' Reunions, including 2004, 2011 and 2016.)

Joseph Nepomuceno (2006)

Dave Newhouse (1964, 1965, 1966) (172 lb CCBC Champion, 1966)

Bill Neufeld (1955, 1957, 1958) (165 lbs) (178 lbs) (Co-Captain) (Conference Champion)

Donald "Pat" Newell (1958, 1959, 1960) (Heavyweight)

Bill Neyland (1967) (172 lbs)

Ron Nichols

John Nielson (1939) (145 lbs)

Shigeo Nitta (1933, 1934, 1935) (Lost only one fight.)

Enzo Nobier (2013)

Bill Nourse (1944)

Dirk Noyes (1967, 1968, 1969) (147 lbs)

Stewart Nyholm (1960, 1961) (125 lbs)

Nystrum (1929, 1930, 1931)

Jack Oakie (1958)

Leo Oceguerra (180 lbs) (1986, 1987) (Fought in Nationals.)

Kevin Octavio (125 lbs) (1983)

Ed O'Dea (1959, 1960) (139 lbs)

J. O'Donnell (1923, 1924)

Miles O'Dwyer (1973)

Fred Offerman (1934, 1935)

Samuel Oh (2013)

Efren Olivas (180 lbs) (1993)

Jerry Olson (1964, 1965) (147 lbs) (Jerry and Craig Morton opened Berkeley book store; Craig played quarterback for Cal, then for Denver Broncos. Came to our fights.)

Paul O'Neil (1977, 1978) (156 lbs) (169 lbs) ("Paul Ambrosio") (See his story re: 1977-1978)

Augie Ong (1947, 1948, 1949) (120 lbs)

Carl Orsi (1983) (165 lbs)

Jose Ortega (1976) (132 lbs) (Won East v. West Championship Fight)

David Oster (112 lbs) (1980) (Conference Champion, 2nd in Nationals)

Rod Ott (1968, 1969) (Heavyweight)

Samuel Ott (2013)

J.C. Oveido (125 lbs) (2011)

Charles Pacagnella (circa 1927-34)

Arnold Pagano (1948)

Alan Pagle (139 lbs) (1981)

Andy Paisal (1954, 1958) (139 lbs)

Eric Pan (2016) (132 lbs) (Won at 2016 Cal Invitational.)

Raul Pardo (139 lbs) (1981, 1982, 1983)

John Parks (1963) (165 lbs)

John Parham (1949, 1950) (125 lbs)

Parish (1927)

Varnam Paul (circa 1927-34)

Pease (1937)

Greg Pedamonte (Asst. Coach) (2002)

Tom Pedamonte (1976, 1978, 1979, 1980) (175 lbs) (Later, Assistant Coach to Jim Riksheim, 2002, 2003.)

Hugh Pedy (156 lbs) (1993)

George Pelonis (1951, 1955, 1956, 1957) (178 lbs) (Ed Nemir once stated, "George Pelonis was the best boy I ever had as far as boxing and cleverness go." (WCBA Champ, 2nd in Nationals) (Won Cunha Award in Intramurals, 1951) (Lost controversial NCAA Semi-finals Fight.)

Egino Penaranda (1985, 1986) (139 lbs)

Tom Pendleton

Manolo Perate (190 lbs) (1997)

Paul Petruzelli (1951) (165 lbs)

Lauren Pettis (2009, 2010) (Womens' welterweight National Champion - See "March Madness: College Boxers Seek Tournament Glory of Their Own" by Ryan Maquinana, at page 318.)

Floyd Pettit (1944)

Lee Phillips (1964, 1965) (139 lbs)

Al Picetti (1918, 1919) (115 lbs)

Tony Pia (Asst coach - 1944)

Stan Pierchoski (1982) (165 lbs)

Jerry Pimental (1956)

Lee Plantmason (Heavyweight) (2001, 2002)

Ivan Polk (1956, 1957) (147 lbs)

Gavin Polone (1985) (156 lbs)

Ken Porto (Heavyweight) (1974)

Don Poole (2008) (185 lbs)

Tim Potter (1980, 1981, 1982, 1983) (190 lbs)

Mario Pozzo (1933) (Conference Champion)

Charlie Price (1978) (1980) (156 lbs) (165 lbs) (Conference Champion) (2nd in Nationals)

Forest Price (1958)

Alan Pryor (1977, 1978, 1980) (135 lbs, 139 lbs) (Conference Champion)

Steve Pugh (1983) (132 lbs)

Pyles (1933) (Manager)

S. Quackenbush (1923)

Dick Quarente (1951) (155 lbs)

Chasen Queen (2003) (175 lbs)

Donald Quinn (1943)

Alphonso Quintor (1983)

Sol Quintero (1968)

Nick Radetsky (1981) (147 lbs)

Ahmed Abdul Rahman (1997) (139 lbs)

Naresh Rajan (1996) (147 lbs)

David Ralston (1994, 2000) (172 lbs)

Marc Rahives (2002) (139 lbs)

Abu Ramin (2001, 2002, 2003, 2004) (147 lbs) (2004, Went to Nationals Twice)

Juan Ramos (2011, 2012) (165 lbs) (Won 2012 Western Regional Boxing Championship) (Defeated Casey Habluetzel (Air Force) (Second Place in Nationals, won "All American" honors.)

Mike Ramsey (1968) (1971)

Maurico Rangel (Heavyweight) (2009)

Neil Rao (135 lbs) (1997)

Roger Rasmussen (1983)

Scott Rasmussen (1982, 1983) (180 lbs) (190 lbs)(CCBC Champ) (1983, Second in Nationals)

Lyon Rathbun (1976) (156 lbs)

G. Reed (1924)

Daniel Reggan (2008) (185 lbs)

Paul Rein (156 lbs) (165 lbs) (1963, 1964, 1965) (In 1964 was Dual Meet 165 lbs Champion but lost in split decision to Nevada's Joe Curry in 172 lbs finals in Reno.) (1965 Middleweight Conference Champion and undefeated in 1965.) (Became Oakland Disability Rights Attorney and book author.)

Haden Reinecker (1944)

Walter Reinholdt (1944)

Abelardo Lora Reyes (2013) (139 lbs)

George Reyes (1977) (135 lbs)

Frank Ribbel (1927, 1928, 1929) (Heavyweight) (Team Captain and Conference Champion)

Don Ricci (1956, 1957, 1958, 1959, 1960, 1961) (CCBC Champion at 156 lbs, 1960, 1961) (Fought in 1959 Nationals.)

Steve Rickets (1963) (139 lbs, 147 lbs) (Co-winner Fall 1962 Cunha Invitational Award)

Jim Riksheim (1976-1980) (125 lbs, 132 lbs) - Excellent Boxer and later Coach for 30 years, from 1981-2011) (1978 Regional Champion, kept from Nationals by Broken Rib, Ed Nemir Award Winner.)

Michael Roback (1960) (Doctor Roback became orthopedic surgeon.)

Eddie Roberts (1940, 1941) (135 lbs) 2nd Place, Pacific Coast Conference

Scott Roberts (1971)

Scott Robertson (1986, 1987) (139 lbs)

Ben Robinson (1930, 1931)

W.K. Robinson (1922)

Dave Rodgers (1941) (165 lbs)

Dr. Tim Rodgers (1965, 1966, 1967) (139 lbs, 147 lbs) (Became doctor.)

Edwardo Rocha (2002) (156 lbs)

Rodriguez (1927)

Frank Roesch (1970) (125 lbs) (Alameda County Superior Court Judge since 2001)

Jack Rogers (1940, 1941) (120 lbs) (2nd Place, Pacific Coast Conference)

Gerald Rogers (1970) (180 lbs)

Randy Rogers (1974) (156 lbs)

Dave Rosenfield (2009) (132 lbs) (2nd in Western Regionals) (2010 Team Captain, Took 4th in Nationals)

John Rosenthal (1985) (156 lbs)

Bob Rouse (1950) (135 lbs)

Abe Rubin (1921, 1922, 1923)

Jeff Rubin (1980) (139 lbs) (Won Bronze Medal at Nationals.)

Harry Ruby (1928) (134 lbs)

Stanley Resopp (circa 1934-1935)

Jim Russell (1973)

Bob Sakai (1966, 1967) (132 bls) (2nd in CCBC)

George Sakanara (1939) (127 lbs)

Shiori Sakamoto (1959, 1960, 1961) (119 lbs) (125 lbs)

Floyd Salas (1956) (125 lbs) (Popular novelist and poet, President of Bay Area Chapter of PEN (a writer's association) and assistant coach for many years (40 or so) of multiple Cal Boxing Teams. Author of "Tattoo the Wicked Cross" and "Buffalo Nickel" about growing up in Oakland. Still attending bouts in 2016.)

Dan Sakaguchi (1994) (165 lbs)

John Samuelson (1968) (112 lbs)

Norman Sanchez (147 lbs) (1988, 1989, 1991, 1992) ("Stormin Norman")

Albert Sandel (1981) CCBC 180 lb Champion and winner of "Ed Nemir Outstanding Tournament Boxer" Award. (Assistant Coach, 1982)

Bill Sandoval (1974, 1976, 1977) (147 lbs) (1976 CCBC Champion at 139 lbs)

Rogelio Sandoval (119 lbs) (1988, 1989, 1990)

Gerald Santos (139 lbs) (2014, 2015) (2014 - 3rd Place Western Regionals) (2015- Advanced to Nationals, lost to National Champ) (Team Captain and Club President) (Won the Cal Sports Club Award as "Officer of the Year.")

Leland Sapiro (1947, 1948, 1949, 1950) (125 lbs) (135 lbs)

Bill Sapsis (1949, 1950, 1951) (145 lbs)

Ed Sato (1951, 1952) (119, 125 lbs)

Matt Scanlon (1986, 1987, 1988) (147 lbs)

Clayton Schapp (1997, 1998) (172 lbs)

Scheide (2007) (147 lbs)

Brent Scheidemantle (2016) (165 lbs) (2016 President, U.C. Boxing Club) (Defeated strong opponent at February 20, 2016 "Cal 100 Year Anniversary Invitational." Best fight of the night.

Mike Schuck (2002, 2003) (175 lbs) (2002 to Nationals, 2003 to Nationals)

Harry "Buzzy" Schultze (1947, 1948, 1949) (Heavyweight)

Jack Schweizer (1936, 1937) (139 lbs)

Steve Schwartz (1985) (165 lbs)

Dave Scruggs (1976, 1978) (165 lbs) (172 lbs)

Searle (1930, 1931)

John Serna (165 lbs) (1986)

Dikran Sevlian (195 lbs) (2003, 2004)

Shafer (1946)

Sanjay Shah (135 lbs) (1992, 1993, 1996, 1998, 1999) (Champion WCBA,1996)

Samuel M. Shapero (1918)

Karlton Shaw (1988, 1989, 1990) (Heavyweight) (WCBA Champion) (Fought in Nationals.)

Bill Shaw (1946, 1948) (155 lbs)

Roy Shaw (1942) (135 lbs)

Fred Sheiman (1951, 1952, 1953) (165 lbs) (2nd NCAA in Nationals)

Stan Shell (1934, 1937) (175 lbs) (Undefeated 1934 in Dual Meets, 1937 Semi-finalist in Nationals)

Stan Shen (2002) (139 lbs)

George Sherwood (1929) (160 lbs)

Pete Shields (1974) (165 lbs)

John Shimmick (1982, 1983) (139 lbs)

Robert Shimoff (1941, 1942) (120 lbs)

Dick Shoenig (1943)

Dick Sikora (1958)

Sol Silverman (1920, 1921, 1922, 1923) (1922 Team Captain) (A supporter of Cal Boxing for six decades!)

Warren Simmons (1947, 1948) (145 lbs) (2nd in Pacific Coast Conference) (Attended 2004 Reunion, longtime supporter of Cal Boxing. Developer of Pier 39, San Francisco)

Bruce Simon (1977) (125 lbs) (Excellent Trial Lawyer, San Francisco Bay Area)

Greg Simon (1994) (180 lbs) (Conference Champion, Went to Nationals)

Matt Skrivanich (1957)

Ron Slater (1941) (127 lbs)

Jay Slaybough (1951, 1952, 1953) (147 lbs) (Winner of 1951 Cunha Intramural Award)

Dick Smith (1936, 1937) (155 lbs)

Don Smith (1932, 1933, 1935) (Captain, 1932)

Bud Smith (1947)

Gene Smith (1941) (155 lbs)

Russell Smith (2010) (156 lbs)

Walt Smith (1948) (135 lbs)

Gary Smook (1954, 1956) (139 lbs)

John Sobczyk (1965)

Bo Solis (1986, 1987) (172 lbs) (Fought in 1987 Nationals)

Ruy Solis (1972) (132 lbs)

Ernie Solomon (1958)

Amos Song (2009) (175 lbs)

Jim Sontag (1959, 1960) (Heavyweight)

Lin Speler (circa 1927-34)

Lynwood Spier (1928) (160 lbs)

John Sprague (1936) (147 lbs)

Steve Spreiter (1966, 1967) (Heavyweight)

David Springer (125 lbs) (2005, 2006)

Stan Stanek (1971, 1972, 1973) Heavyweight (CCBC Champion) (Also played Cal Football.)

William Stanley (1974-1976) (125 lbs) (1974 CCBC 125 lb Champ)

John Stead (195 lbs) (2005, 2006)

Thomas Steulphagel (1944, 1945)

Earl Stevens (1930, 1931, 1932) (Captain, 1931)

Jeff Stewart (1968)

Terry Stewart (1967) (156 lbs)

Irving Stone (Class of 1923) (Famous Author of Biographical Novels including: "Lust for Life" (about Vincent Van Gough), "Clarence Darrow for the Defense," "The Agony and the Ecstacy" (about Michaelangelo) ,"Sailor On Horseback" (about Jack London), and Editor of "There was Light: Autobiography of a University, Berkeley, 1888-1968."

Walter Stone (circa 1927-1932, Coach)

John Storch (1936) (126 lbs)

George Straggas (190 lbs) (1983)

Vin Stratton (1936) (175 lbs)

Sid Strickland (1971)

Randy Stroke (1950) (145 lbs, 165 lbs)

Scott Stringer (1969-1972) (175 lbs) (Cal Football Player, later played Pro Football)

Cliff Surko (1962) (125 lbs)

Jessee Swan (1937, 1938, 1939) (Undefeated in 1938) (155 lbs)

Archie Sweeney (1960) (147 lbs)

Marc Swinney (circa 1927-1934)

Arman Syed (195 lbs) (2010, 2011)

Symonds (1946)

Ed Szaky (1974) (172 lbs)

Glen Takei (1969, 1970, 1971, 1972) (125 lbs)

Andrew Tan (2009) (156 lbs)

Eddy Tanaka (1956) (126 lbs)

Hisashi Tanaka (2008) (156 lbs)

Rich Tang (165 lbs) (1993)

Tristan Tao (2013)

Doug Tarmann (1958)

Charles Tatum (1934, 1935)

Doug Tavmann (1958)

Merrick Taylor (1942) (175 lbs)

Rick Taylor (1971)

Paul Templin (1981, 1982, 1983) (1981 - 2nd in CCBC)

Forrest Theiss (1922, 1923)

Kent Thompson (1960) (178 lbs)

T. Thompson (1923)

Jack Thorburn (1941, 1942) (Heavyweight) (2nd Place in Pacific Coast Conference)

Robert Thorpe (circa 1927-1934)

Bruce Tichinin (1966, 1967) (165 lbs)

Paul Tilden (1956) (Heavyweight)

Terry Timmons (1963) (156 lbs)

Forrest Theiss (1922, 1923)

Bourquay Thomas (139 lbs) (1993) (Nationals Competitor) (1994 Conference Champion, to Nationals)

Perry Thomas (1936, 1937) (Heavyweight)

Cap Thompsen (145 lbs) (1950)

Jim Thompson (1977) (156 lbs)

T. Thompson (1924)

Jack Thorburn (1941, 1942)

Robert Thorpe (circa 1927-1934)

George Henry Thurston (1933, 1934) (1934 Season Undefeated)

Paul Tilden (1956)

Javier Tirado (125 lbs, 132 lbs) (1991, 1992, 1993)

Bob Tobey (1926) (Team Captain) (Knocked out all 4 opponents.)

Josh Tofield (1963) (125 lbs)

Shiro Tokuno (1942) (135 lbs)

Joe Tombari, (1978) (156 lbs) (Winner of Cunha Intramural Award)

James "Crip" Toomey - (1920's) Football and boxing.

Bob Torney (1942, 1943) (156 lbs)

Bruno Torreano (1950, 1951) (145 lbs)

Al Torres (1955, 1956) (125 lbs)

Townsley (1933)

Dennis Treadway (1960, 1961, 1962, 1963) (139 lbs) (147 lbs) (Won Cunha Intramural Award, CCBC Champion 1963, Undefeated.)

Daniel Trinidad (1993) (139 lbs)

Irv Tucker (1947, 1948, 1949) (165 lbs)

Dick Tullsen (1949, 1950, 1951, 1952) (Heavyweight)

Charles "Chuck" Turner (1956, 1958, 1959) (125 lbs) (Later an Asst. Coach during the 1960s.)

Jamal Valdez-Allen (Asst Coach 2002, 2003, 2004)

Michael Valli (139 lbs) (1981, 1982) (Nicknamed "The Missile") (Won "Outstanding Boxer Award" in Mare Island Tournament.)

Valentine (1930, 1931)

Henry Van Galen (1954) (156 lbs)

Gordon Van Kessel (1959, 1960, 1961, 1962) (1959 and 1962 two-time 147 lbs. Conference Champion, went to Nationals.) (Winner of Cunha Award in Intramurals.) (Assistant Coach, 1960s.) (Later, Hastings Law professor.)

Albert Van Schmeller (2013) (195 lbs)

Paul Varnum (1928) (134 lbs)

Andre Vasil (2004) (156 lbs)

Andre Vasilj (2010, 2011, 2012) (156 lbs)

Manuel Verela (1993, 1999, 2000) (139 lbs)

"Jim" Vogt (1957) (Also listed as "Carl Charles Vogt") (156 lbs)

Walkotte (1946)

Brian Walsh (1992)

James Walsh (1969, 1970)

Walsh (1946)

Phil Walson (1965) (Also an excellent wrestler.)

Brandon Walker (2006) (165 lbs)

James Walker (1992) (190 lbs) (Fought Paul Rein (1963- 1965) in 1992 Alumni Bout) (Fought in CCBC Championships)

Wallkotte (1946)

Andy Wallstrum (1934, 1936 Captain, 1937) (147 lbs) (156 lbs) (Became Pricipal, Santa Rosa High School, Stayed a close friend of Ed Nemir and a strong supporter of Cal Boxing.)

Walsh (1946)

Brandon Walker (2006) (165 lbs)

John Wallace (1948) (175 lbs)

James Walsh (1969, 1971) (156 lbs)

Phil Walson (1965) (125 lbs) (CCBC Champ; also on wrestling team.)

Harold Walt (1944, 1947) (165 lbs)

Jermain Waltemeyer (2005) (156 lbs) (165 lbs)

Chuck Walsh (1973)

Jim Walsh (1970, 1971)

Walters (1930, 1931)

Paul Ward (1946, 1947) (Manager in 1948) (125 lbs)

Don Warden (1964, 1965, 1966) (147 lbs)

Fred Weaver (1958, 1959, 1960, 1961) (178 lbs) (Fought in Nationals, 1959) (165 lbs) (175 lbs) (1959 was last time Cal participated in NCAA; NCAA dropped boxing after 1960 Tournament.)

Ifan Wei (2006,2007, 2008) (140 lbs) (Western Champion)

Richard Weinbrandt (1966, 1967) (147 lbs) (Longtime supporter of Cal Boxing)

Dave Weiner (1962, 1963, 1964) (Longtime Cal Boxing Supporter, raised family of All-American athletes. Attended 2016 match with entire family.)

James Weisburg (1990)

Charles Welby (1945, 1946)

Louis Weldman (1944)

Frank Welsh (1963) (Also Heavyweight wrestler)

Ryan Wen (2014, 2015) (156 lbs) (165 lbs) (4th Place WCBA, Went to Nationals, Cal Boxing Treasurer) (In 2015 won the most fights of anyone on team.)

Ron Westburg (1958) (178 lbs) (Heavyweight)

Richard F. Westdahl (1934, 1935)

Bill Wheeler (2001, 2002, 2003) (Semi-finalist in Nationals, 2003) (195 lbs)

Zack White (165 lbs) (2005, 2006, 2007)

Bob Whited (1945)

Ravim Whitington (175 lbs) (2005)

Harold C. Whittlesey (1918, 1919) (125 lbs)

Warren Widener (1959) (139 lbs) (147 lbs) (Later became attorney, Berkeley City Councilman, and two term Mayor of Berkeley.)

Jim Wigton (1943)

Jake Wildberger (147 lbs) (2001)

Williams (1950)

John Williams (1973, 1977, 1978, 1979) (CCBC Conference Heavyweight Champion) (1978 CCBC Champ and 2nd in Nationals.) (Also star Football Halfback.)

Don Wilson (1953, 1955, 1956) (165 lbs)

Mike Williamson (1996) (132 lbs)

Kirk John Wilson (1969) (Heavyweight)

Bob Winter (1964) (Heavyweight) (Dropped out of school December 1964 after "Free Speech Movement." Opened a bar in Berkeley called "The Drought Board" during the Vietnam war.) (Bob Winter knocked down George Foreman in the 1967 Golden Gloves Heavyweight Bout, but lost a controversial split decision. Foreman went on to win the 1968 Olympic Gold Medal, and eventually knocked out Joe Frazier to win the professional Heavyweight Championship, only to lose later to Mohammed Ali, in the 1975 "Rumble in the Jungle," in Zaire.) [See photo as Alumni 40 years later and story about his fight with George Foreman in 1967 in this book.]

Finley Wise (2007) (125 lbs)

John Wise (1944)

Witter (1950)

Pavel Wolfbeyn (1991) (156 lbs)

Rob Wolfe (1979)

Pete Wong (1995, 1996) (139 lbs) (147 lbs)

Len Woolams (1940)

Manley Wu (1949)

Claude Wyle (1978) Intramural champ; later law partner in S.F. with George Choulous - both fine trial lawyers.

John Wylie (1959, 1960, 1961) (165 lbs) (2nd CCBC)

Adam Xu (135 lbs) (2005)

Jimmy Yokota (132 lbs) (1986)

Dan Yamamoto (1969, 1970) (147 lbs)

Vin Young (1952, 1953, 1954) (156 lbs) (165 lbs)

William Young (1944)

Derrick Zahler (201 lbs) (2001, 2002) (In semifinals at Nationals)

Scrap Zalba (1948, 1950) (135 lbs)

Jonathan Zaul (147 lbs) (2001-2004) (<u>Coach</u> for 2016. Co-coach 2011-2015. Assistant Coach 2005-2006.)

Lou Zeidberg (1990, 1994) (165 lbs) (1994 to Nationals)

Steve Zembsch (1973-1977) (Fought in 1992 Alumni v. Varsity Exhibition Bout) (1977 CCBC Champion)

WOMEN BOXERS BY NAME

Emily Abbott (132 lbs) (1999)

Christine Aiken (116 lbs) (2007) (2008)

Therese Bjoernas (2014, 2015)

Yvonne Caples - Women's coach (1999, 2000)

Vivian Chuang (2016) (123 lbs) (Won at February 20, 2016 Cal 100 Years Invitational) (Club Vice President and Co-Captain) (Semi-Finalist in NCBA Western Regionals) (Boxed in 2016 NCBA Nationals).

Triniece Durst (2006)

Naseem Ehsan (2002, 2003)

Gymmel Garcia (2011, 2012)

Jewell Fix (2011, 2012) (119 lbs) (Boxed in 2012 WCBA Regionals) (Officer in U.C. Boxing Club)

Claire Glowniack (2014, 2015) (139 lbs) (Second place at 2014 NCBA Nationals, 2015 NCBA West Regional Champion) (All-American Honors in 2014 and 2015, Cal Sport Clubs Honorable Mention for Women's Athlete of the Year Award) (Won against 4 different female NCBA national champions from 3 separate weight divisions) (Club Vice President).

Bahija Hamraz (2002, 2003)

Javier Hernandez (Coach 2002-2003)

Kimberly Hope (156 lbs) (2002, 2003)

Kathleen Jaeger (2010)

Kirsten Keber (112 lbs) (2005)

Aimee Kelley (132 lbs) (1999)

Inga Lamvick (2009) (132 lb) (Beat Stacy Miller of Nevada in Reno, February, 2009.)

Leonora Lanza (140 lbs) (2004)

Keri Murphy (132 lbs) (2010)

Nessa Nemir, Women's Assistant Coach 2006-2011; Granddaughter of Ed Nemir, daughter of Phil Nemir (See photos of Nessa, Phil, and Don Nemir in this book.)

Lauren Pettis (2009, 2010) (132 lbs) (150 lbs) (2009 National welterweight Champion) (Good Left Jab and Right cross) (2010 WCBA Champion and National NCBA Champion. (See Interview by Ryan Macquiñana on page 318.)

Caitlin Plahn

Crystal Silva (2000) (125 lbs) (Became Women's Coach in 2002)

Mary Wang (1999, 2000) (106 lbs, 112 lbs)

www.ingramcontent.com/pod-product-compliance
Lightning Source LLC
Chambersburg PA
CBHW060417300426
44111CB00018B/2882